Trading and Money Management in a Student-Managed Portfolio

Trading and Money Management in a Student-Managed Portfolio

Brian Bruce
Jason Greene

AMSTERDAM • BOSTON • HEIDELBERG • LONDON
NEW YORK • OXFORD • PARIS • SAN DIEGO
SAN FRANCISCO • SINGAPORE • SYDNEY • TOKYO

Academic Press is an imprint of Elsevier

Academic Press is an imprint of Elsevier
The Boulevard, Langford Lane, Kidlington, Oxford OX5 1GB, UK
525 B Street, Suite 1800, San Diego, CA 92101-4495, USA

First published 2014

British Library Cataloguing in Publication Data
A catalogue record for this book is available from the British Library

Library of Congress Cataloging-in-Publication Data
A catalog record for this book is available from the Library of Congress

ISBN: 978-0-12-374755-6

For information on all Academic Press publications
visit our website at **store.elsevier.com**

Typeset by MPS Limited, Chennai, India
www.adi-mps.com

Transferred to Digital Printing in 2014

Contents

Introduction

This book is about the practice of portfolio management. The book's target audience is advanced undergraduate and graduate students who participate in a student-managed portfolio. We hope that this book successfully fills the gap between the traditional academic textbooks on investments and portfolio management and practice-oriented books on specific investment strategies. As such, we do not attempt to provide a comprehensive guide to investments or portfolios, nor do we focus on a particular investment strategy. Rather, we cover important aspects of the framework within which the practice of portfolio management occurs, regardless of the chosen investment strategy. We assume a basic understanding of investment and portfolio theory, securities markets, and financial analysis — topics that are covered in nearly all undergraduate finance course sequences. We then apply the concepts from these topics to the problem of portfolio management on behalf of a client.

Each of us is a faculty advisor to student-managed investment funds (SMIF) and is a professional in the money management industry. As such, our guiding principle is to provide a professional perspective on the practice of portfolio management in student-managed investment funds toward the goal of further professionalizing the activities of such funds. Like professional money managers, student-managed investment funds generally manage someone else's money. We use professional investment managers, in general, and institutional investment managers, in particular, as a standard toward which student-managed investment funds should strive. Toward this end, we review many of the challenges that professional investment managers face and the various practical approaches to address those challenges.

Within each chapter, we discuss the chapter's topic in conceptual terms before moving on to more concrete examples and applications. For example, we begin the book with a discussion of investment philosophy and process — a topic that pervades the entire book. Rather than jump into specific examples of investment philosophies or processes, we first review the key elements of each to clarify their role and importance as a framework and method for generating investment ideas and building portfolios. We include specific examples of investment philosophies and processes from well-established institutional investment management firms at the end of the chapter.

Nearly all chapters conclude with bulleted summary points and several exercises. The end-of-chapter exercises can be used in a course context as assignments by instructors. However, we hope that every reader will use them as a means to actively explore the subject matter. Nearly all end-of-chapter exercises are open-ended and have no uniquely correct answers.

Finally, we emphasize throughout the book that investing is part science and part art. Most conventional courses in business and finance curricula treat the science quite heavily and have limited opportunities to explore the art. We offer this book as one tool, among many, that can help the student investment manager apply science to the service of the art and thereby have a deeper understanding of both.

Acknowledgments

We could not have included as much information about existing practices in student-managed investment funds and the profession without the meaningful contributions of others. We thank the following individuals and their institutions for their generous help in writing this book. This book would not have been possible without their work in their respective programs and their willingness to contribute to this effort.

Leah Bennet, CFA Institute
Stanley Block, Texas Christian University
Jonathan Boersma, CFA Institute
Genna Brown, Georgia State University
Dan Chung, Fred Alger Management, Inc.
Philip Cooley, Trinity University
Sharon Criswell, ALM First
Eric Davis, Tennessee Valley Authority
Steven Dolvin, Butler University
Jill Foote, Rice University
Chinmoy Ghosh, University of Connecticut
Aimee Harmelink, Smith Breeden Associates
Robert Kissell, JP Morgan
Edward Lawrence, University of Missouri St. Louis
Hal Liebes, Fred Alger Management, Inc.
Anna Marie Lopez, Hotchkis & Wiley
David Louton, Bryant University
Terry Maness, Baylor University
John Minnehan, NEPC, LLC
Timothy Nantell, University of Minnesota
David Nawrocki, Villanova University
Max Palmer, FlexTrade
Amanda Quinn, CFA Institute
Steve Ramsey, Austin College
Marc Reinganum, State Street Global Advisors

William Reichenstein, Baylor University
Peter Ricchiuti, Tulane University
Patrick Rice, Baylor University
Adam Schwartz, Washington and Lee University
Carl Schwinn, Bates College
Ronald Singer, University of Houston
Paul Stewart, University of Houston
Brian Stype, CFA Institute
Kristy D. Tarr, FactSet
Todd Williams, Austin College
John Winegender, Creighton University
Faith Yando, Dimensional Fund Advisors LP

We also thank the following institutions and, in the cases of many of these colleges and universities, the participants in their student-managed investment funds, for graciously providing material for this textbook.

Advent Software
Austin College
Bates College
Baylor University
Bentley University
Bloomberg
Bryant University
Butler University
CFA Institute
Connecticut College
Cornell University
Creighton University
FactSet
Fairfield College
FlexTrade
JP Morgan
LSV Asset Management
Northfield Information Services, Inc
Oberlin College
Rice University
Southern Illinois University Carbondale
Southern Methodist University
State Street Global Advisors
Stetson University

Texas Christian University
Thomson Reuters
Trinity University
Tulane University
UBS
University of California – San Diego
University of Connecticut
University of Minnesota
University of Missouri – St. Louis
University of Toledo
University of Tulsa
Villanova University
Washington and Lee University

We also thank the editors and project managers at Elsevier, especially Scott Bentley and Melissa Murray, for their help and persistence in getting this project off the ground and to completion. Finally, we thank our assistants, Melinda Estelle, Stephen Putbrese, and Bryan Welge for their work in collecting and reviewing material for the book.

About the Authors

Brian is the CEO and Chief Investment Officer of Hillcrest Asset Management LLC, an institutional investment manager. Under Brian, Hillcrest has won 19 awards for outstanding investment performance. Before founding Hillcrest, Brian was Chief Investment Officer at PanAgora Asset Management, a $24 billion AUM subsidiary of Putnam Investments. Previously, Brian held senior investment roles at State Street Global Advisors and the Northern Trust Company.

Brian has taught the $5 million student-managed investment fund at the Hankamer School of Business at Baylor University since 2001. He also taught the student-managed portfolio class at the Cox School of Business at Southern Methodist University where he was Director of the Alternative Asset Management Center.

Brian R. Bruce
CEO & Chief Investment Officer
Hillcrest Asset Management
Adjunct Professor
Baylor University

Brian received his MBA from the University of Chicago, MS in Computer Science from DePaul University, and a BS in Business Administration from Illinois State University. He is a member of the Illinois State University College of Business Hall of Fame, is a recipient of the University of Chicago Graduate School of Business CEO Award, and was awarded the SMU Cox Media Expert of the Year Award. Brian has published numerous scholarly articles and books including *Analysts, Lies, and Statistics* which he co-authored with former Harvard Business School Professor Mark Bradshaw. He is also the Editor of *Journal of Investing* and the *Journal of Behavioral Finance*.

Jason is a Professor of Finance in the College of Business at Southern Illinois University. He is also the faculty advisor to the undergraduate Saluki Student Investment Fund and the Graduate Student Investment Fund student-managed investment funds at SIU, which manage a combined $1.8 million. Jason joined SIU following several years as an executive and Senior Investment Officer at INTECH Investment Management, LLC, a subsidiary of Janus Capital Group. At the time, INTECH managed approximately $60 billion in large cap equities on behalf of its institutional clients, such as public and corporate pension plans and university endowment funds.

Jason T. Greene
Professor of Finance
College of Business
Southern Illinois University
Carbondale

While at INTECH, Jason collaborated closely with the firm's research and investment team of PhD mathematicians and physicists in Princeton, New Jersey, and he headed the firm's research and trading team in its West Palm Beach, Florida, headquarters. Among other things, Jason was responsible for leading the development of a platform for customizing INTECH's products, analyzing portfolio performance, and training investment and client service personnel. He was also called on to work with clients and consultants to help them better understand INTECH's mathematical investment process.

Prior to joining INTECH, Jason was a finance professor at Georgia State University, where he was also a regular presenter at GSU's Center for Economic Forecasting Quarterly Economic Forecasting conferences and lectured for the National Association of Securities Dealers educational programs. Jason has served as an expert consultant and witness in cases involving security valuation, insider trading, and trading of mutual funds. He has consulted in some of the largest civil cases involving market timing of mutual funds and his research, co-authored with Conrad Ciccotello, was used as a basis for the calculation of compensation of more than $1.3 billion to mutual fund shareholders.

Jason's research has been published in leading journals, such as *Journal of Banking and Finance, Journal of Finance, Journal of Financial Economics, Journal of Financial Markets, Journal of Investment Management, Journal of Portfolio Management,* and *Review of Financial Studies*. He has appeared on CNBC's PowerLunch and his research has been cited in numerous newspapers and financial magazines, including *Barrons, Boston Globe, Business Week Online, Dow Jones Newswires,* London's *Financial Times, New York Times, Reuters, Securities Week, USA Today, Wall Street Journal,* and *Washington Post,* and SEC rule-making documents.

CHAPTER 1

Investment Philosophy and Process

Chapter Contents

A student-managed investment fund is a pool of real money that is managed by undergraduate or graduate students. Students have the responsibility for deciding how the money is invested. In some cases, this responsibility covers all aspects of the investment process, including asset allocation, security selection, execution and trading, and monitoring and reporting. In other funds, students are responsible for a subset of these activities, perhaps because they are given a mandate to invest in a specific asset class by a board of advisors or the beneficiary of the fund's assets. In all cases, the common element is that students are entrusted with the responsibility and granted the authority to invest real

Trading and Money Management in a Student-Managed Portfolio.
DOI: http://dx.doi.org/10.1016/B978-0-12-374755-6.00001-7

money. As such, a student-managed investment fund is not a game. It is not a simulation. Risks are taken. Profits can be made. Money can be lost.

Given what is at stake, there are some who might question the wisdom in trusting students with real money. After all, students are not professionals. Yet in a student-managed investment fund, students are being trusted with responsibilities that are typically bestowed only on professionals with years of experience. With the help of professional and academic advisors, educational resources, such as this book, and, most importantly, a high level of diligence, students can achieve results on par with those of true professionals. In so doing, students gain valuable experience and insights that apply to business, in general, and investing, specifically – as well as a broad spectrum of other activities.

The real world experience provides the primary motivation for most colleges and universities in offering a student-managed investment fund. Likewise, it attracts motivated students who seek this experience and a more practical understanding of business and investments. The student-managed investment fund provides a hands-on learning environment in much the same way as laboratory experiments or exercises would enhance learning physics, chemistry, or biology. As with science labs, the theory that is taught in textbooks and classroom lectures becomes tangible and its relevance clearer. This book serves as a sort of "lab book" in helping to present traditional classroom material in an applied setting. As such, the emphasis is on the practice of investing. The relevant theories are not developed in as much detail as they might be in some texts. Rather, we take the approach of providing more discussion of the issues that arise in the application of such theories and offer a framework for the practice of investing. In doing so, we attempt to highlight the diversity of approaches to investing in practice by including numerous examples from student-managed investment funds and professional investment firms alike.

The Student-Managed Investment Fund as an Investment Management Firm

A student-managed investment fund (SMIF) is an investment organization. In many ways, it will resemble a real investment firm as it often serves nearly the same purpose. For an SMIF that manages a mandate from its university's endowment fund, the student-managed investment fund serves the same role as any of the endowment fund's other investment managers. As such, the endowment fund is the SMIF's client, to whom the SMIF must answer. The student-managed investment fund has a challenge to conduct its business with the same standards in mind as the other investment firms that the endowment fund has hired. These investment firms are usually considered to be institutional investment managers, in that they cater to the institutional, as opposed to the retail, marketplace. Institutional investors include public pension plans, such as the California Public Employees' Retirement System (aka CalPERS); corporate pension plans, such as the

Boeing Company Employee Retirement Plan; Taft-Hartley (i.e., labor union) retirement plans, such as the UMWA Health & Retirement Funds; foundations, such as the Andrew W. Mellon Foundation; endowment funds, such as Harvard's Harvard Management Company; and family offices, such as the family offices of Paul Allen or Michel Dell or group family offices like Rockefeller and Tolleson. These types of investors have many common traits, including a large size (from the hundreds of millions of dollars to tens of billions of dollars), long (often infinite) investment horizons, and professional investment staffs. It is with this clientele in mind that we model this book.

As indicated above, one reason we chose the institutional investment approach is that many SMIFs literally have their universities' endowment funds as clients. More importantly, by catering to the professional investors in the marketplace, institutional investors are often more discerning and reliant on sound principles of finance and investing. As a result, the best practices of investing are often found among those who provide investment services to institutional clients. In addition, many students in student-managed investment fund programs seek careers in the institutional money management industry and our goal is to provide a training and educational resource that will allow student-managed investment fund members to excel as professional investors.

Key steps in meeting the standards of an institutional investor are to provide clear expectations regarding the investment approach, and to have a rational organizational and operational structure that can consistently deliver on those expectations. While this chapter addresses the former and the next chapter addresses the latter, it is important to note that these two aspects of a student-managed investment fund and, indeed, any investment firm, are not mutually exclusive. The investment approach must contemplate specific organizational and operational realities. Likewise, the organizational and operational structure must reflect the investment approach. For example, a quantitative investment approach that relies on a specific economic or financial model and requires little qualitative or subjective input would need significant technology, data, and operations to support such systems. In contrast, a fundamental investment approach that requires research by numerous individual analysts must have the depth of knowledge and headcount to provide adequate coverage of the market.

With this institutional investment framework in mind, we begin by discussing the investment approach. In short, we will be discussing *investing*. As indicated above, we discuss investing from the institutional or professional viewpoint and not necessarily as what is portrayed in the popular media or in commercial advertisements for trading services that are targeted at the retail (i.e., individual) investor. Indeed, investing is not something that babies with smart phones can or should do (as portrayed in a recent series of advertisements from E*trade)! Investing is appropriately a professional pursuit. Like other professions, such as medicine, law, and engineering, investments requires a base of knowledge acquired through a coherent program of study, and training on how it is practiced professionally. In short, investing should not be pursued in some *ad hoc* fashion or without an understanding of the field. To do so is irresponsible and unlikely to yield the desired outcomes. Investing that is practiced on behalf of a client or for one's own personal benefit, should be done diligently and in a manner consistent with established knowledge and practices in the field. The thoughtful reader might be tempted to pause to wonder how a group of students, who are, by definition, investing novices and in the process of gaining investing knowledge, might appropriately be expected to build an institutional-quality investment approach. This book takes the view that every investor is a student of investing. Most advanced undergraduates and graduate students have learned the key fundamental material upon which to build an investment approach. Moreover, students are as capable of being diligent and building a thoughtful approach as many professionals. With the help of resources, such as advisors, mentors, and this and other books, students can leverage their own insights to build a compelling and successful fund. Our experience as professors of student-managed investment fund programs has shown us first-hand how even undergraduates can do analysis that rivals that of professional investors.

The key to initiating a program of investing resides in the development of the investment philosophy and process. Together, the investment philosophy and process represent the definition of an individual's or organization's approach to investing. As such, they reflect the purpose and methods that generate the investment results.

Investment Philosophy and Process

The investment philosophy and process combine to define the investor or the investment organization. The investment philosophy and the investment process provide a framework in which to understand markets and select investments. Without these, the entire endeavor is *ad hoc*. In short, the investment philosophy provides the *why* and the investment process provides the *how*.

To illustrate the importance of philosophy and process for an organization, such as an investment management firm or a student-managed investment fund, consider a sports analogy regarding a game of basketball. Without an investment philosophy and investment process, the investment decisions are like a pickup game in which 10 players meet at the court and are divided into two teams in a random, *ad hoc* manner. Each player in the game follows her own approach to the game, without the benefit of knowing her teammate's approach. Each player on a team is working for the common goal of her team scoring more points, but without a common playbook, a coherent game strategy, or a shared understanding of the opposition. The game evolves without forethought, with offense being improvised and defense being decided on-the-spot. The individual talents of certain players might be revealed. It is more likely, however, that whatever talents each player possesses will not be fully realized in such an *ad hoc* approach to the game.

In contrast, having an investment philosophy and process is like having a coherent team and game plan. A true team approach begins by first defining the goal of the team. It progresses by building a team and understanding the team's strengths and weaknesses. Plays are drawn up, based on this understanding. Each player on the team knows the playbook, which might even be customized for the particular strengths or weaknesses of a particular game's opposition. Each player has a role in the execution of the offense and defense. The plays are practiced until they become second nature. There is a *shared* understanding of purpose and execution for how the game will be played. The same idea applies to investing.

The investment philosophy represents a sense of purpose for an individual, and more importantly a *shared* sense of purpose for an organization. It explains what the group believes about markets and *why* it believes it can create or add value. The investment process articulates *how* the philosophy is implemented. In takes the philosophy regarding what opportunities are believed to exist and expresses the methods by which those opportunities are realized. Having the investment philosophy and process memorialized for the group defines the organization and assures its continuity and consistency of approach through time. As indicated in Exhibit 1.1, Creighton University's student-managed investment fund properly begins with a specific exercise to make sure that new students understand the philosophy of the previous students in the fund. In this way, the continuity and consistency through time are facilitated in an environment in which consistency and continuity are a unique challenge due to the structure of a student-managed investment fund that experiences significant turnover of personnel every semester or every year.

While the philosophy and process are important internally to an investor and investment organization, they are equally important in articulating an investment approach externally. The statement of the philosophy allows prospective clients to judge whether there is a match between their own outlook and philosophy and that of the candidate investment manager. Likewise, an investment process defines the general approach that prospective clients can expect the candidate manager to follow. In this way, there should be a logical link between the philosophy and process that can be judged as reasonable.

Exhibit 1.1 Creighton University

The Creighton Student Management equity fund is continuous. Different schools do their transition from class to class, from semester to semester, and from year to year differently. Creighton keeps the selected stocks in the portfolio from the previous year's class. The first requirement of a new class is to understand the philosophy of the past portfolio managers and their management style. This system is similar to students' starting work at a professional mutual fund with their current holdings, their recommended list, and their watch list.

Finally, for an aspiring investment professional who is embarking on a career in investment management, the investment philosophy and process shows that the person approaches investing as a professional. Indeed, a common question in institutional RFPs (Request for Proposal) and in employee interviews at investment management firms is to ask the firm or the individual what their investment philosophy or investment process is. The investment philosophy shows thoughtfulness with respect to purpose and an understanding of the problem. The investment process reveals an understanding of a solution through planning, purposeful execution, and diligence in the act of investing.

Investment Philosophy

According to Merriam-Webster, the definitions of the word "philosophy" include:

1. *"The most basic beliefs, concepts, and attitudes of an individual or group."*
2. *"A theory underlying or regarding a sphere of activity or thought."*

An investment philosophy defines the common set of beliefs for an investment organization. This gives every member of the group a common reference from which to begin doing analysis and contributing ideas to the organization. While individual members need not subscribe to the exact set of beliefs embodied in the group's philosophy, members should use the philosophy as the set of beliefs that define their efforts and activities on behalf of the organization.

Scope of an Investment Philosophy

When developing an investment organization's investment philosophy, the scope should be limited to the realm of investment-related activities. It should not wander off into irrelevant reflections on the state of the world or the state of the economy. Rather, the philosophy should be focused on what will be most relevant in shaping and guiding the investment approach for the group. Many student-managed investment funds might engage in a number of other educational, career-enhancing, or social activities besides undertaking investment activities. The investment philosophy should be limited to the investment activities. Likewise, many investment firms include statements about their own client service outlook (e.g., "we put the client first") in their investment philosophies. This might be fine for an overall firm philosophy, but it is unlikely to have any bearing on investment activities. To say that each client's needs are unique begins to suggest that there is no coherent philosophy that the organization has to offer. Any organization might (or should) have an overall philosophy or mission statement, but this is not a substitute for a cogent investment philosophy. In short, do not confuse a "business philosophy" or "mission statement" with an investment philosophy. Too many investment companies make this mistake by giving potential clients an understanding of their approach to business and client service or their economic outlook. However, they leave the client wondering what their basic principles are when it comes to investing.

Key Elements of an Investment Philosophy

1. Statement of beliefs about the markets.
2. Statement of beliefs about the opportunities to create value.
3. Statement of beliefs about the group's abilities.
4. Statement of beliefs about the group's abilities to exploit the opportunities to create value.

Statement of Beliefs

The investment philosophy should include a statement of beliefs about the state of the market. Ideally, this is one or two sentences that provide a clear and concrete statement of the fund's view of how the world is and perhaps why it is the way it is. This statement should be assailable. By definition, any statement of a belief, as opposed to a fact, is open to agreement or disagreement. Those who agree usually have evidence to support such a position, while the same can be true of those who disagree. Thus, while these are statements of belief, they are not without evidence and therefore are not pure statements of faith. By stating the starting point, potential clients are free to agree or disagree with the statement. The client who hires the manager is implicitly agreeing with the belief or at least admitting the possibility that there is truth in the belief.

For example, consider two funds, E.M. Hutton and Hi-Mark, Ltd., who each pursue very different strategies. E.M. Hutton (or EMH for short), believes that the markets are efficient in the semi-strong form sense. EMH's philosophy might begin with the statement, "We believe the stock prices reflect publicly available information." In contrast, Hi-Mark, Ltd. (or HML for short) might pursue a fundamental equity strategy and begin their philosophy statement with, "We believe that the prices deviate over short horizons from their fundamental values due to investors' overreaction to short-term information." Note that these statements set the foundation for subsequent statements of how each fund will provide valuable services in such a market.

Statement of Opportunities

Given the statement of beliefs, the next element of the investment philosophy should articulate the nature and scope of opportunities available in the marketplace to add value. This statement should be closely connected to the statement of beliefs. That is, this statement should follow directly from the statement of beliefs. While the statement of beliefs is quite general, this statement of opportunities should be quite specific and limited to those opportunities that the individual or organization is focused on exploiting.

Continuing with the EMH and HML examples, EMH might continue to say, "We believe that the market rewards risk in well-diversified portfolios over the long-term. Therefore, we believe that since markets are efficient and cannot be outperformed, the best an investor can do is to implement a well-diversified portfolio with low turnover and trading costs." Likewise, HML might continue their philosophy to say, "Opportunities exist to find undervalued firms that have recently released negative information, resulting in depressed market prices relative to intrinsic values." Clearly, these two investment managers should have very different investment approaches. The statements of beliefs and opportunities allow the organizations to convey their starting points and their purpose in offering investment services.

Statement of Ability

The statements of belief and opportunity establish the potential for any individual or organization to add value through their investment services. However, the philosophy must also establish the specific abilities of the individual or organization to exploit these opportunities. In other words, an opportunity for added value is necessary, but not sufficient for an investment approach to add value. The beliefs and opportunities say what is available in the market. The statement of ability articulates the capability of the individual or organization to realize those opportunities. In this sense, the statement of ability is a statement of competitive advantage. The statements of beliefs and opportunities are externally focused on the markets. The statement of ability should be internally focused beliefs about the individual or organization.

The statement of ability must also be relevant within the context of the statement of beliefs and opportunities. That is, it must relate to those opportunities. In our EMH-HML example, each manager must state an ability that relates to the opportunities he or she has articulated. In doing so, EMH might point out its own particular expertise in targeting risk and efficient implementation by saying, "EMH has the capability to build well-diversified portfolios with low turnover and low trading costs that are able to realize the risks and returns to passive benchmarks in a real portfolio." In essence, EMH is saying that it can achieve exposure to an index or benchmark and achieve the returns from those passive indexes in practice. Similarly, HML might describe their capabilities in identifying undervalued securities. However, in doing so, HML must be careful to articulate how it does not fall prey to the same overreactions that give rise to the opportunities it seeks to exploit. One way that HML might communicate this ability is to say that, "HML employs a quantitative system that is designed to identify stocks that have experienced negative market sentiment, but that have strong long-term fundamentals."

Note that these statements are specific, yet not too detailed. Statements of philosophy should be only as specific and detailed as necessary, and no more. To provide too much detail would be to put the philosophy at risk of being unnecessarily narrow and rigid. In this sense, there exists a balance. Notice that the HML statement does not describe its quantitative model in detail or provide an itemized list of aspects of a company's fundamentals that classify a company as "strong." Rather, it narrows the scope of analysis to being quantitative and the inputs to the model as being both fundamental (as it relates to intrinsic value) and, perhaps, behavioral (as it relates to market sentiment). This leaves plenty of room for detail to be added in the investment process that describes how such a model works. But, it makes clear that the philosophy relies on the belief in such a model's capability.

Statement of Value

The statement of value may be a separate statement within the philosophy or it may be incorporated into the statement of ability. Regardless, the philosophy must make clear the expected benefit from pursuing the individual's or organization's investment approach. There must be a positive statement of the value added from the investment approach. This statement might implicitly or explicitly compare its approach to other (competing) approaches. However, it must not be simply a negative statement of the perils from other approaches. Just as in considering one's own life philosophy, the final statement of value should be one of identity and purpose. It should help summarize the intended virtue of adherence to the philosophy.

The EMH philosophy might conclude, "By building a well-diversified portfolio with efficient execution and low turnover, the EMH strategy seeks to realize returns that compensate for risks taken, without losing returns to unnecessary and unrewarded costs." Likewise, HML might conclude, "With a disciplined implementation of its model, the HML strategy has the potential to reap rewards beyond those of passive benchmarks or indexes, without incurring more risk."

With these statements, the individual or organization has defined the scope of its investment approach and its purpose for investing. The individual or organization has bared its soul in hopes of finding a soul mate. That last statement might sound a little over-the-top, but there is more truth in it than there is hype. The key idea behind an investment philosophy is to provide a "soul" that guides the individual or organization in its investment endeavors. The soul keeps the approach on track, especially during times when the environment becomes particularly challenging. It provides something to return to when the path seems unclear. And it is something that should be questioned at times (as in "soul searching"), especially in light of evidence or experience to cast doubt on it. But, if the philosophy is founded on solid reasoning, insight, and knowledge, it is very likely to survive challenge and provide an important source of stability and strength to an individual or organization as it invests.

Examples of Investment Philosophy

Institutional investment management firms provide excellent examples for student-managed investment funds with respect to investment philosophy and process. While not all investment management firms publicly provide clear statements of their investment philosophy and process, those that do are often found on the companies' websites and in their materials provided to current and prospective clients. As discussed in the overview of investment strategy classifications in Appendix A, investment strategies are often classified into "quantitative" or "fundamental" strategies. This distinction is particularly appropriate when considering the investment philosophy and process of an investment manager. Therefore, we provide examples of investment philosophies of quantitative managers in Exhibit 1.2 and fundamental managers in Exhibit 1.3.

Exhibit 1.2 Investment Philosophies from Investment Firms with Quantitative Strategies

LSV Asset Management
Investment Philosophy
The fundamental premise on which our investment philosophy is based is that superior long-term results can be achieved by systematically exploiting the judgmental biases and behavioral weaknesses that influence the decisions of many investors. These include: the tendency to extrapolate the past too far into the future, to wrongly equate a good company with a good investment irrespective of price, to ignore statistical evidence, and to develop a "mindset" about a company.

LSV uses a quantitative investment model to choose out-of-favor (undervalued) stocks in the marketplace at the time of purchase and have potential for near-term appreciation. LSV believes that these out-of-favor securities will produce superior future returns if their future growth exceeds the market's low expectations.

LSV portfolios typically have a deep value orientation relative to the indices. Market timing is not part of the process and portfolios are fully invested (cash levels usually below 2%).

Source: www.lsvasset.com (March 2013)

Dimensional Fund Advisors
Philosophy/Diversification
Diversification is an essential tool available to investors. It enables them to capture broad market forces while reducing the uncompensated risk associated with individual securities. We have constructed strategies that seek to draw heavily upon this philosophy.

We believe successful investing means not only capturing reliable sources of expected return but managing diversifiable risks and other risks that do not increase expected returns. Avoidable risks include holding too few securities, betting on countries or industries, following market predictions, speculating in areas like interest rate movements, and relying solely on information from third-party analysts or rating services. To all these, diversification is an essential tool available to investors. While it does not eliminate the risk of market loss, diversification does help eliminate the random fortunes of individual securities and positions your portfolio to capture the returns of broad economic forces.

Source: www.dfaus.com (March 2013)

Exhibit 1.3 Investment Philosophies from Investment Firms with Fundamental Strategies

Fred Alger Management, Inc.
Investment Philosophy
Since our founding, we have stayed true to our philosophy of investing in companies undergoing Positive Dynamic Change, which we believe offer the best investment opportunities for our clients. By Positive Dynamic Change, we mean those companies experiencing:

- High Unit Volume Growth
- These companies are experiencing growing demand, have a strong business model, enjoy market dominance, and generate free cash flow. We track the company's growth phases closely, aiming to own its shares during the highest growth period.
- Positive Life Cycle Change
- These companies are benefitting from a positive catalyst in their business, allowing them to enter an accelerated growth phase. Positive catalysts for change could include new management, product innovation, acquisition, or new regulations.

Research
Since our founding in 1964, Alger has remained steadfast to our proprietary, bottom-up, fundamental research process, which we believe is the blueprint for our long-standing success.

We believe that true insight comes from sector specialization. As such, our Analyst team is comprised of experienced sector specialists who cover companies across all market capitalizations. Our Analysts do not rely on external research. Instead, they conduct thorough, original, research, taking into account both quantitative and qualitative data.

What Differentiates Our Research?
Deep Commitment
- Cornerstone of our analyst-driven investment process.
- Focus on building the best research team possible — more investment talent per dollars under management compared to other organizations many times our size.

Sector Specialization
- Deep knowledge across all market capitalizations, sectors, and regions.
- Strong analytical capability to uncover key growth drivers and compelling opportunities within each industry.

Industry Expertise
- Extensive industry and practitioner experience before becoming analysts.
- Valuable insight and contacts acquired over many years.

Differentiated Perspective
- Targeted "outside-the-box" surveys to gain 360-degree understanding of company and its market position. Examples include:
  - Calling chain restaurants for dinner wait times to assess dining trends.
  - Asking physicians how many prescriptions they have written for a new drug to gauge demand and efficacy.
- In-depth analysis of primary information from suppliers, competitors, partners, and customers as well as regulators and legislators instead of relying solely on public information.
- Global presence and intensive due diligence through in-person meetings with management, on-site visits to observe operations, and close interaction with local contacts.

Source: www.alger.com (March 2013)

Hotchkis & Wiley
Philosophy
H&W employs a research-driven, fundamental value investing approach. We invest in companies where, in our opinion, the present value of its future cash flows exceeds the market price. These opportunities often emerge because the market extrapolates current trends into the future, which leads to favoring popular investments and shunning others — regardless of valuation. Empirical evidence suggests that companies generating above average returns on capital attract competition that leads to lower levels of profitability. Conversely, capital leaves depressed areas, often allowing profitability to revert back to normal levels. The difference between a company's price based on an extrapolation of current trends and a more likely reversion to mean creates the value investment opportunity.

To uncover these opportunities, we employ a disciplined, bottom-up investment process emphasizing rigorous, internally generated fundamental research. We believe the consistent application and depth of our independent research can maximize the trade-off between value and risk providing superior returns to a static benchmark over the long term.

Source: www.hwcm.com (March 2013)

The two companies in Exhibit 1.2, LSV Asset Management (LSV) and Dimensional Fund Advisors (DFA), implement quantitative equity strategies. LSV provides a relatively concise statement encompassing the key elements of an investment philosophy. They indicate that they believe that investors in the market suffer from judgmental biases leading to "out-of-favor" securities that are undervalued in the market. We infer that they believe that undervalued securities give rise to an opportunity to outperform the overall market or a passive index. LSV's philosophy statement indicates that its ability resides in its quantitative process to identify these undervalued securities, with their value being the potential for superior long-term returns. LSV supports their investment philosophy with numerous academic research articles, available on the firm's website. Similarly, DFA's investment philosophy is rooted in research and summarized in several pages on the firm's website. A short excerpt from one of those pages is provided in Exhibit 1.2. Readers are encouraged to visit DFA's website for the complete discussion of the firm's investment philosophy.

The investment philosophies of fundamental managers in Exhibit 1.3 range from quite brief to rather lengthy. The common element among these philosophies is that they all emphasize the value of fundamental research in determining the true value of the firms that they hold and the implicit belief that each firm possesses the ability to conduct this research better than others.

Exhibit 1.4 shows the investment philosophy of Baylor University's student-managed investment fund. As indicated in its philosophy, the fund uses a hybrid approach in building

Exhibit 1.4 Baylor University's Student Investment Fund Investment Philosophy

The fund seeks long-term capital appreciation with returns in excess of the S&P 500 market index. The fund is invested primarily in stocks from the various sectors within the S&P 500 index, with a nominal amount of cash maintained to facilitate day-to-day operations and expenses. To achieve superior returns, the fund relies on superior stock selection. Portfolio allocation is not a primary strategy of the fund; our target is to emulate the sector weights of the S&P 500 index as closely as possible and within the guidelines set forth in the Investment Policy Statement. Furthermore, analysts give careful consideration and require consensus to be reached before any sector is significantly over- or under-weighted. The primary objective remains the selection of securities that will provide a superior return using qualitative and quantitative fundamental analysis.

As part of the quantitative analysis, the fund follows a multi-factor model involving three components: value, growth, and hybrid measures. The priority assigned to each of these factors is at the analyst's discretion, but the general methodology is consistent throughout the Practicum course. The overall selection philosophy is a balanced approach combining both value and growth factors. Typical metrics utilized by analysts are the following:

Growth	Value	Hybrid
Quarterly earnings surprise	Price/earnings ratio	Price-to-earnings growth (PEG)
Earnings revisions	Price/book ratio	
Return on equity		
Long-term (5-year) consensus growth rate		

We believe these three components are the best fundamental indicators of a stock's value and long-term return potential. Additionally, the fund seeks to substantiate quantitative stock analysis with the underlying investment "story." The story of a stock includes the company's strategic vision, core competencies, short- and long-term plans of action; the quality of the management team; an analysis of the industry and competitors; and an understanding of macroeconomic factors affecting the business.

its portfolio, with a statement that this blend of quantitative and fundamental research reveals the true "story" behind a company and its value.

Investment Process

While the investment philosophy establishes the rationale for the opportunity for a particular investment approach, the investment process produces the actual results. As noted in the Cayuga Fund's report of its performance in Exhibit 1.5, the returns from a strategy are the result of the application of an investment process. According to Merriam-Webster, the definitions of the word "process" include:

1. *"Something going on"*
2. *"A series of actions or operations conducing to an end; especially: a continuous operation or treatment especially in manufacture."*

We include the first definition because it so eloquently points out the obvious. Any investment approach must have *something going on*! If there is no investment process, a fund risks raising a question as to what, if anything, is going on. As indicated in the second definition, the statement of the investment process explains what is going on by

Exhibit 1.5 The Cayuga Fund at Cornell University's Johnson College of Business

Performance

The fund began as an index-tilt product, with the objective of generating returns above the S&P 500. Since October 2002, the fund has followed a market-neutral strategy. Annual returns since 2003 (the first full year of operation as a market-neutral hedge fund) are shown below. The fund's management believes that its performance over time is the result of a combination of its disciplined investment process, which consists of fundamental analysis layered on the output of a proprietary quantitative model, and careful attention to risk management.

Year	Performance	AUM
2003:	19.20%	2.8 m
2004:	18.60%	6.8 m
2005:	10.40%	10.2 m
2006:	14.20%	13.5 m
2007:	5.95%	14.4 m
2008:	0.42%	14.4 m
2009:	−0.39%	11.5 m

describing the actions. The second definition also alludes to the manufacturing context of the word "process." In manufacturing, the process is what converts raw materials to a final product or output. Indeed, the manufacturing process describes how the raw materials are combined and treated to create the final product. Likewise, in investing, the investment process describes how an investor builds a portfolio from its raw materials. More specifically, the investment process describes the steps that an investor or investment organization follows to arrive at a set of portfolio weights.

A manufacturing process is subject to the laws of physics. For example, a saw blade cannot be made out of cotton, but a comfortable shirt can be. Likewise, a portfolio must be made up of inputs that logically and theoretically contribute to the choice of portfolio weights according to economic and financial theory and principles. An investment process must articulate what the inputs are, how they are used, and what steps are taken to transform the inputs into a useable set of portfolio weights. This process must be motivated by and consistent with the investment philosophy. Like the investment philosophy, the investment process should be informed by the field of knowledge that is relevant. Depending on the investment philosophy and the particular strategy, the field of knowledge might be drawn from the fields of economics, finance, mathematics, and/or psychology, among others.

The philosophy and process are complimentary to one another. In initially conceiving an investment philosophy and process, it is helpful to establish the philosophy first, since the philosophy sets the foundation with a set of beliefs, opportunities, and goals for the process. However, it is often useful to revisit or revise the philosophy after considering the investment process. The creation of the investment process can help clarify both the potential for certain opportunities to be realized and the constraints that make some goals difficult to achieve. Through time, the process is more likely to be adapted to changing market conditions, capabilities, or technology. In making enhancements to the investment process, the investment philosophy provides the framework from which potential changes are conceived. Changes in the process that help more fully realize the opportunities articulated in the philosophy should be sought. In all cases, the investment process and philosophy should be consistent with one another.

An investment process must have a clear beginning, middle, and end. The investment process's beginning or initialization establishes the starting point from which all other decisions and analysis will proceed. The middle of the investment process describes the meat of the process where most of the action takes place through the application of the methods. The end of the investment process implements the strategy and declares the resulting product or output. As the definition above alludes to, the investment process is continuous. As such, there is no specific beginning or end in time. Thus, most investment processes can be thought of as loops, in which the beginning is returned to as soon as one

Exhibit 1.6 Baylor University's Student Investment Fund Investment Process

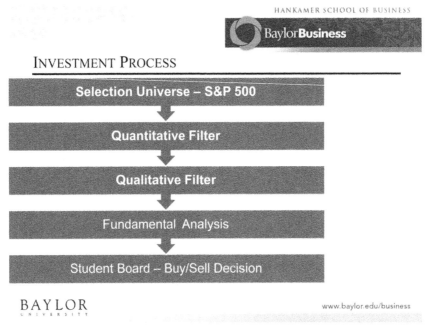

reaches the end. As such, the investment process is typically shown in presentations by institutional investment firms as a flow chart as seen in the example from Baylor University's student-managed investment fund in Exhibit 1.6.

Key Elements of an Investment Process

1. Initialization.
2. Methods.
3. Implementation.

Initialization

The beginning of an investment process can take many different forms. In all forms, the process must be initiated by defining the starting point. Fortunately, the investment philosophy provides the motivation for what form the initialization takes. The form typically depends on whether the investment approach embodied in the philosophy is considered "top-down" or "bottom-up." A top-down approach typically starts with a global or macroeconomic idea that we will identify as a theme. This theme provides the foundation on which the remainder of the process will build. For example, consider an investment philosophy that identifies the forecast of macroeconomic trends as a source of value. This approach's investment process might begin with a measurement or analysis of various economic factors to establish a forecast or a theme. For example, the process might say, "Leading economic indicators are evaluated to forecast which sectors of the economy are expected to experience the most relative growth over the next 12 to 24 months." A more detailed statement might add, "Leading indicators include Corporate Profitability, Inflation, Inventories, Industrial Production, New Manufacturing Orders for Consumer Goods, New Manufacturing Orders for Capital Goods, Building Permits, Housing Starts, Employment, Money Supply, Interest Rates, Consumer Borrowing, and Consumer Confidence." Later steps in the process can further refine this forecast or theme and explain how the ideas are expressed through stock holdings.

For a bottom-up approach, the process begins with the identification of which securities will be the subject of the bottom-up analysis. This step is critical because it often is not feasible for a bottom-up approach to begin with literally every possible security. The identified securities are often referred to as the "eligible universe" or simply the "list of eligible securities." In many cases, the eligible universe is dictated by the specific investment product, mandate, or benchmark. For example, a student-managed investment fund that manages a U.S. large cap core mandate for its university's endowment fund might begin its investment process by saying, "The eligible universe consists of large cap stocks that trade on U.S. exchanges. A stock is considered large cap if it is a constituent of the S&P 500 Index or if its market capitalization is larger than that of the 10th percentile ranking stock in the S&P 500 Index." This example highlights an important contrast to the investment philosophy: the investment process should be quite specific.

Exhibit 1.7 shows an example of the Texas Christian University's student-managed investment fund, the Educational Investment Fund (TCU-EIF). After stating the portfolio's overall strategic asset allocation, the entire first paragraph is concerned with the initialization of the TCU-EIF top-down investment process. This stage of the process clearly indicates not only the key inputs of the macroeconomic variables, but notes that these fall under the responsibility of the Chief Economist for the fund.

Methods

The heart of the investment process is the set of methods used to construct the portfolio. This section is where the value that is identified in the investment philosophy is realized. It describes how the initial inputs are refined, analyzed, or treated to come up with investment ideas. An apt analogy of the investment process is that of a recipe for baking a cake. The recipe usually begins with a list of ingredients, such as eggs, flour, water, sugar, butter,

Exhibit 1.7 Texas Christian University Educational Investment Fund

Top-down Balanced Portfolio Management Approach (TCU)

The TCU-EIF is a well-diversified balanced fund, investing across multiple asset classes. The fund's long-term strategic asset allocation is 70/25/5 percentage allocations to stocks, bonds, and cash, respectively. Exposure to real estate and international assets is also encouraged. Tactical asset deviations from the strategic allocations are exercised within limits. For instance, equity allocations can range between 60 and 80% depending on shorter term capital market forecasts of the fund members. At the beginning of the semester, the Fund's Chief Economist provides a state of the global economy address. Key macroeconomic variables discussed include gross domestic product, industrial production, capacity utilization, inflation, unemployment rates, default risk spreads, maturity risk spreads, intermediate Treasury bond rates, federal debt as a percentage of GDP, U.S. dollar strength relative to key foreign currencies, retail sales, fiscal and monetary policy, housing prices, and foreclosure rates. We use these and other leading indicators to proactively move assets to favorable sectors, evaluate businesses within those sectors using appropriate valuation techniques, and finally, make investment decisions on individual companies.

After the economist's presentation, the class spends one week examining individual sectors. Class members are assigned to examine specific sectors and then to make formal presentations to the class, after which sector allocation targets are established for the semester. Targets are established by majority vote of fund members. Active sector allocations for equities are made relative to the S&P 500 equity industry sector allocations. Allocations can deviate up to 25% relative to the S&P 500 weightings. For instance, if 20% of the S&P 500 is allocated to the information technology sector, the EIF target weight to the sector can be range anywhere from 15% to 25%, depending on the funds expectations for the sector.

Tactical decisions also are made to equities segmented by capital appreciation (dividend yields less than 2%), income and capital appreciation (dividend yields between 2% and 4%) and income (dividend yields over 4%) stocks. The fixed income portion of the portfolio is invested primarily in fixed income mutual funds, which are monitored by the fund's fixed income analysts. Fixed income deliberations focus on maturity and quality sector weightings. Key factors include interest rate movements, business cycle projections, duration, and convexity.

and seasonings. The heart of the recipe starts by discussing the ratios of the ingredients and how they are mixed together. The ratios are important in determining whether you get a cake or a loaf of bread from the same ingredients. The recipe goes on to describe the methods for mixing the ingredients together. In some cases, certain ingredients, such as the dry ingredients, are separated out and mixed together before being added to the other ingredients. The methods used in mixing are often important to how the cake turns out. If the batter is mixed too slow or too fast, for too short or too long a time, the batter can have the wrong consistency, affecting the texture or characteristics of the cake when it is baked. Likewise, the methods used to analyze the inputs to the investment process can affect the quality of the output. Therefore, it is important to memorialize the methods so that they, like a good recipe, can be passed down to future generations.

The specific importance of certain inputs to an investment process is akin to the ratios of the ingredients in a recipe. In the top-down example above, the percentage weight on each economic indicator might be discussed in the methods section of the investment process. Like a recipe's description of how to mix the ingredients, a key element of the investment process is the discussion of methods that are employed. In doing so, it provides the individual or investment organization a clear understanding of the methods so that they can be applied consistently through time. This is especially important for student-managed investment funds that experience significant turnover of personnel. If not for a cogent explanation of the investment methods, the student-managed investment fund might have very different approaches and outcomes from year to year, even starting with the same inputs. In terms of cooking, this would be like trying to bake a cake and sometimes
ending up with a cake, sometimes bread, and sometimes a cookie. While the importance for a student-managed investment fund is clear, it would be dangerous to believe that an individual or other investment organization would not realize as much value from an investment process. Indeed, an investment process is just as important to an individual or professional investment firm. The investment process serves the role of providing for a consistent approach over time for an investment firm as employees come and go. For the individual, the process provides a consistent framework and helps to assure that approach has been purposefully and thoughtfully undertaken. These methods define the investment approach or strategy. Thus, a significant change in the methods represents a change in strategy. Baking from the same recipe typically takes time and expertise in perfecting. If you do not cook from the same recipe each time, then it is difficult to know what part of the recipe is responsible for a certain taste or outcome. Likewise, if the investment process methods vary through time, there is no way to use the investment outcomes to refine the investment approach.

Some of the methods utilized in the investment process can be and usually are proprietary to the individual or organization. Because of this, the full details of the investment process, especially those at the heart of the process, might not be publicly disclosed. However, most steps and methods can be part of a publicly disclosed investment process by simply excluding specific elements that make them proprietary. Returning to the cooking analogy, these items might be considered a baker's secret ingredient, a specific ratio of ingredients, or a specific technique in mixing the ingredients. But, just as ingredients are disclosed on food products, it is possible to disclose quite a bit of an investment process's inputs and methods without risking harm to its proprietary value.

The result of the heart of the investment process is the resulting target portfolio weights. Returning to Exhibit 1.7, the second and third paragraphs discuss the methods of the TCU-EIF in determining the resulting sector and security weights. For some investment approaches, this final result represents the ultimate goal and outcome, while perhaps not technically the end of the investment process. Returning to the baking example, the last step might be to bake the cake at 375 degrees Fahrenheit for 23 minutes. The implication is that the cake is finished at this point. In some sense, it is, but it probably is not in its final form that is to be presented to those who eat it. For the investment process, the target weights define the unadorned end product – perhaps even known as a model portfolio. These weights are ready to be implemented into an actual portfolio.

Implementation

The final step of the investment process is the implementation. This last step might be quite short and of have very little incremental value for some investment approaches or might be a key component of others. The end of the investment process should discuss how the target weights are converted into a real portfolio of security holdings. The implementation stage of the process might also include risk controls that are not integrated into earlier parts of the process. For baking, this might literally be the icing on the cake. That is, it describes how the cake is to be presented to those who actually eat it. This part of the investment process typically gives consideration to the direct and indirect costs of transactions and the trading methods used to affect such costs. For example, the final step might be to adapt the target weights to hold each stock in round lots of 100 shares each. An example of this is shown in the portfolio construction panel from Baylor's student-managed investment fund in Exhibit 1.8.

Finally, the end of the investment process discusses how the portfolio will be rebalanced or adjusted through time. In some cases, this part of the process might describe a specific rebalancing approach using the same target weights. In nearly all cases, rebalancing occurs as the result of a new iteration of the complete investment process. In this way, the end of the investment process directs us back to the beginning of the process, just as would occur in continuous loop.

Examples of Investment Process

Exhibit 1.9 shows examples of the investment process from the same investment firms whose philosophies are shown in Exhibit 1.2. Recall that these firms' philosophies motivate the quantitative approaches that these firms pursue. For example, LSV's philosophy discussed the opportunities that are created by human biases. It would be surprising,

Exhibit 1.8 Baylor University's Student Investment Fund Portfolio Construction

HANKAMER SCHOOL OF BUSINESS

Baylor**Business**

RISK MANAGEMENT

- Portfolio Construction
  - Minimize risk by not making sector bets
  - Aware of industry exposure
  - Avoid short-term, speculative investments
- Continuous monitoring of portfolio positions
- Strong sell discipline - we sell when:
  - Fundamentals deteriorate
  - Story changes
  - Our expectation of future earnings growth changes
  - Valuation is no longer attractive
  - Better opportunities exist

BAYLOR
UNIVERSITY

www.baylor.edu/business

therefore, if human judgment, subject to the same biases, were an integral part of the investment process. To wit, LSV's investment process outlines the key *quantitative* steps of the process that govern the selection of securities and their weights in the resulting portfolio. Similarly, DFA's investment process focuses on the steps to building diversified portfolios with targeted risk characteristics, as is consistent with the firm's investment philosophy.

Unlike quantitative firms' emphasis on quantitative methods and quantifiable variables, firms pursuing fundamental strategies must have processes that describe how economic conditions or company attributes are used to determine buy or sell decisions in the portfolio. Exhibit 1.10 shows the investment processes from the same firms whose philosophies are shown in Exhibit 1.3. As with quantitative firms, these firms' processes are consistent with their philosophies, which emphasize the particular opportunities these firms seek to realize. The Hotchkis & Wiley process is particularly thorough in discussing all aspects of the investment process, including a description of the personnel in whom certain responsibilities reside. Note how Alger's investment process is articulated with a chart, emphasizing the continuous nature of the process.

Exhibit 1.9 Investment Processes from Investment Firms with Quantitative Strategies

LSV Asset Management
Investment Process
LSV uses quantitative techniques to select individual securities in what would be considered a bottom-up approach. The investment process is similar for each of our investment strategies but is segmented into different capitalization ranges or regions.

A proprietary investment model is used to rank a universe of stocks based on a variety of factors we believe to be predictive of future stock returns. The process is continuously refined and enhanced by our investment team although the basic philosophy has never changed – a combination of value and momentum factors. We then overlay strict risk controls that limit the over- or under-exposure of the portfolio to industry and sector concentrations. We also limit exposures in individual securities to ensure the portfolios are broadly diversified, further controlling risk.

The competitive strength of this strategy is that it avoids introducing the process to any judgmental biases and behavioral weaknesses that often influence investment decisions.

Portfolio turnover is approximately 30% for each strategy.

Source: www.lsvasset.com (March 2013)

Dimensional Fund Advisors
Process/Management
Prudent investing is a rational process. It involves deciding how much risk to take, then choosing asset classes to match an investor's preferred risk-return trade-off. We build strategies designed to deliver precise risk dimensions to investors. But we are not a traditional investment manager – and traditional labels do not fit.

Structuring a strategy around compensated risk factors lends purpose to an investor's portfolio. Rather than analyzing individual securities, investing becomes a relatively simple matter of deciding how much to allocate to small, large, value, and growth stocks around the world – and how much term and credit exposure to target in fixed income. By focusing on what matters, Dimensional focuses your efforts.

Traditionally, managers do one of two things: they focus on picking individual securities, the antithesis of diversification, or they hold many securities but mimic arbitrary benchmarks.

Dimensional chooses a different path. It structures strategies based on academic research rather than on speculation or commercial indexes. Small cap strategies target smaller stocks more consistently. Value strategies target value returns with greater focus. As a result, investors can achieve more consistent portfolio structure.

Process/Engineering
Dimensional's portfolios are based on rigorous academic research on markets and the sources of higher expected return. We design strategies to offer consistent, fully diversified

exposure to the return sources we believe to be robust and reliable. Our flexible, innovative design offers potential to creatively enhance returns.

In Dimensional's view, the road to investment success lies in identifying the risks that bear compensation, choosing how much of these risks to take, and then striving to minimize the risks and costs imposed by traditional approaches. Research-based portfolio engineering makes this possible.

Dimensional seeks to design broadly diversified equity strategies that offer focused exposure to the sources of expected returns in the market. Unlike index funds that follow commercial benchmarks, Dimensional defines equity asset classes based on a security's market capitalization and book-to-market (BtM) ratio and actively applies our own eligibility rules. To gain the purest representation possible, we seek to exclude securities that do not exhibit the general characteristics of the defined asset class. We also seek to eliminate securities that lack sufficient liquidity for cost-effective trading.

Portfolio Construction: Equity Strategies
Engineering equity portfolios around broadly defined return sources generates opportunities for Dimensional traders to add value. Rather than replicate an index in mechanical fashion, we permit deviations from market cap weightings and allow for the integration of stocks among asset classes. This flexibility also allows us to reduce transaction costs caused by counterproductive trading. For example, for asset classes defined by size, a slightly higher hold or "buffer" range allows Dimensional to hold securities that a commercial index may be forced to sell, which reduces turnover and can increase returns.

Internal and External Uses of the Investment Philosophy and Process

The discussions of investment philosophy and process focus primarily on the internal value to an individual or organization in having a documented philosophy and process. For student-managed investment funds and investment firms, the internal benefits help promote the consistent application of an investment approach in an environment of personnel turnover. Most student-managed investment funds experience nearly 100% turnover every semester or at least every academic year. While the turnover in investment firms is lower than this, turnover does occur in any organization. The existence of the philosophy and process helps to assure a firm's clients that the strategy that is followed when the investment firm is hired is likely to be the same strategy that is followed in the future, regardless of turnover in firm personnel. Likewise, if a student-managed investment fund manages a portion of its university's endowment fund, the existence of the investment philosophy and process provides the endowment fund's board of trustees with some confidence that students will employ the same approach 5 years from now, even though none of those students will be involved in the fund.

Exhibit 1.10 Investment Processes from Investment Firms with Fundamental Strategies

Fred Alger Management, Inc.
Investment Process
Alger Analysts are the foundation of our investment process.

Through Bottom-Up Fundamental Analysis
Analysts scour their sectors for solid companies demonstrating Positive Dynamic Change

Differentiated View
Analysts interview with management and independent industry contact, conduct innovative surveys, study public documents, and build proprietary financial models

Multi-Scenario Analysis
Analysts develop Bull, Bear, and Base case analyses to understand investment risk/reward under different fundamental scenarios and test the conviction of their assumptions

Analyst & Portfolio Manager Dialogue
Analysts recommend best ideas to Portfolio Managers and engage in Socratic Dialogue to determine highest conviction ideas

Portfolio Construction & Risk Management
Portfolio Managers construct robust portfolios based on Analysts' best ideas across all sectors constantly optimizing the portfolios to minimize risk and maximize reward

Source: www.alger.com (March 2013)

Hotchkis & Wiley
Process
H&W subscribes to a team-oriented, five-stage process. The goal is to employ a consistent, repeatable approach and create a diversified portfolio that exhibits attractive risk/return characteristics.

Stage	Purpose	Responsibility
1. Idea Generation	Identify investment candidates and prepare initial review	Entire Team
2. In-Depth Evaluation	Prepare detailed assessment of investment opportunity	Analysts
3. Recommendation	Review analysis, assess risk/return profile	Analysts/Sector Teams

Stage	Purpose	Responsibility
4. Portfolio Construction	Buy, sell, and monitor	Portfolio Coordinators
5. Portfolio Review	Assess portfolio positioning and macro exposures	Entire Team

1. Idea Generation We source investment ideas from screens of financial databases and from our investment team.

Financial Database Screens

We use dynamic and flexible quantitative screens designed to filter a large universe of securities to identify those that appear to have attractive risk/reward characteristics. These screens evaluate similar risk and valuation criteria, but can be tailored for specific sectors/industries to emphasize the most relevant factors.

Investment Team

We augment our quantitative screens with ideas sourced from our Analysts and Portfolio Coordinators. Based on their industry knowledge, contacts, experience, and discussions within the Sector Teams, our investment team identifies opportunities that automated screens can miss due to data issues or other limitations inherent with screens.

Once investment ideas are generated, an initial review is conducted to highlight the key investment merits and risks, verify the validity of the characteristics that attracted us to the security in the first place, identify any obvious issues/warning signs that need to be addressed, and provide a rough estimate of the risk/return profile.

2. In-Depth Evaluation The in-depth evaluation stage of the process is by far the most vigorous and time-consuming. This stage involves detailed research at the industry, company, and security levels.

Industry

Analysts conduct industry research concentrated on determining long-run margins and returns on capital. We seek to understand the factors that influence changes in supply and demand in order to determine normal industry profitability. Competitive analysis, akin to a Porter's Five Forces approach, is also evaluated to obtain a better understanding of industry risks. Our analysts accumulate a body of knowledge over years that enable them to respond to dynamic markets quickly.

Company

Using the industry research as a backdrop, the Analyst conducts detailed fundamental research at the company level. We focus on the company's long-run normal earnings power, which is the sustainable cash earnings of a company under equilibrium economic and competitive market conditions. Company analysis focuses on full cycle profitability, capital intensity, free cash flow, and financial leverage. Analysts meet with company management to better understand the company's business model by its various divisions, capital allocation policy, return potential of current capital programs, shareholder orientation, and overall competence.

Next we do a risk assessment, which entails a variety of both financial and non-financial factors. We assess the company's ability to survive temporary, short-term distress without impairing the long-term value of its franchise. This includes a review of its financial leverage, historical cash flow volatility, available liquidity, access to capital, exposure to extreme events, and unusual profit concentrations. To augment the risk evaluation process we have developed a red flags analysis, which is a list of questions that helps identify subtle but potentially meaningful risks. The ultimate goal is to identify attractively valued companies with acceptable risk profiles.

Security

To quantify return potential, we employ an internally developed, three-stage dividend discount model ("DDM"), using market-derived discount rates. The first stage uses explicit earnings projections for years one through five, which are derived from the Analyst's financial model.

We assume that a company achieves normal earnings in year five. The second stage of the DDM reverts the company's returns to market averages over the next 15 years. The third stage determines the terminal value of the stock. We determine the present value (price target) by discounting these values back at the cost of equity. Next the analyst provides a risk assessment highlighting critical issues that could affect the company and its stock price. Finally, the analyst summarizes the recommendation with an investment thesis and recommended weight.

3. Recommendation Each step of the in-depth evaluation is subject to peer review. Peer review is organized through six Sector Teams composed of industry Analysts and dedicated peer reviewers. In addition to reviewing financial models and ensuring integrity/consistency, the reviewers play a devil's advocate role to challenge the thesis and modeling assumptions. The primary objective is to solidify our belief in valuation and security risk. Sector Teams also consider macroeconomic trends and the potential effect on the portfolio. Once ideas are thoroughly vetted, the Analyst and Sector Team jointly recommend a target weight.

4. Portfolio Construction We employ a bottom-up, risk-controlled portfolio construction process with the primary goal of generating attractive risk-adjusted returns. Portfolio Coordinators, who are embedded within the Sector Teams, assess recommendations within the context of the overall portfolio. They consider the relative attractiveness of opportunities and assess the complementary nature of new ideas with the existing portfolio. Portfolio Coordinators have the responsibility for creating and maintaining a target portfolio for the investment strategy, generating trades, and assuring compliance with client guidelines — buy, sell, and monitor.

5. Portfolio Review The investment team interacts on an informal basis constantly, which is our most important means of communication. Monthly, the entire investment team meets formally to discuss portfolio positioning and any macro events that could affect the portfolio. We discuss portfolio performance, trading activity, and economic/industry events. Team members are encouraged to voice any concerns or new ideas in this medium, whether it is security-specific or otherwise.

Source: www.hwcm.com (March 2013)

The external benefits of a clearly articulated investment philosophy and process are critically important in establishing a mutual understanding between an investment organization and its client. The disclosure of the investment philosophy to the organization's clients and prospective clients allows the clients to judge whether there is a shared outlook of the market and available opportunities. Moreover, it allows the client to determine its own confidence in the individual's or investment organization's capabilities. Very simply, if there is a mismatch between the prospective client's and the investment firm's philosophies, then the client should not employ the investment firm to manage investments on its behalf. Similarly, confidence in the investment organization's stated capabilities are required for a client to retain the services of the investment organization. Further discussion of this issue is found in Appendix B, which contains a reprint of "The Role of Investment Philosophy in Evaluating Investment Managers: A Consultant's Perspective on Distinguishing Alpha from Noise," by John Minahan of New England Pension Consultants.

The investment process helps in a different but no less important way to help manage the relationship between a client and an investment organization. The documented investment process provides the client with an understanding of the methods used in constructing the client's portfolio as well as the expected characteristics and range of outcomes from the resulting portfolio. The ultimate outcome that is the goal in hiring a portfolio manager is its performance (i.e., return on investment). However, return on investment over a given time period is a noisy indicator of whether an investment manager has diligently employed its own investment process. Indeed, the signal-to-noise ratio of most investment processes is very low. Therefore, investment returns should not be the only evidence that a client considers when evaluating whether a manager has done what it was hired to do. Rather, the client should consider whether the manager continues to employ the methods as set out in the investment process and whether those methods have resulted in the expected characteristics and range outcomes. Likewise, the manager must provide transparent communication to the client that establishes whether the methods are being followed and whether characteristics and the range of outcomes are consistent with the investment process. Thus, the investment process provides an important part of the transparency that is critical for the effective monitoring of investment managers.

To help understand the importance of the role of the investment process in the manager-client relationship, consider the following example of two investment managers who were hired by an endowment fund. Prior to being hired by the endowment fund, both managers had recorded very good performance compared to the S&P 500 index. Manager A provides very little detail in its investment process, and just discloses that it has a team of analysts who pick the stocks that they consider to be the best. Manager B, on the other hand, has a detailed, step-by-step description of its investment process that makes clear that it seeks to hold firms with high dividend yields, low P/E ratios, and solid growth prospects, as forecasted by a team of analysts. The process provides further details of how the analysts are trained in a specific type of fundamental analysis that was developed by the firm's founder. The founder is known to have long ago retired, but her approach remains a hallmark of the firm. The final fact is that each firm has lost about one quarter of its investment personnel, including those that make up their analyst teams.

A few years after hiring these two firms, the endowment fund's board of trustees feels pressure to make a decision on whether to retain or fire these firms, since each firm's investment returns have been below the benchmark return and far less than expected. Can the endowment justify retaining either firm? If so, on what basis? Both managers are likely to correctly point out that no investment process can yield outperformance every year, or even every three-year period. However, the board of trustees must have confidence in each manager's ability in order to make a decision to retain the firm. In the case of Manager A, the board of trustees has little to go on except the faith and hope that the "good" analysts who were responsible for the good performance long ago have not left the firm — or at least that they have been replaced by equally good analysts. In other words, the board must hope that the bad performance is not because the firm no longer has the talent that it once had. However, the board has little information to verify that the same investment process that had been followed before (during a period of good performance) is still being followed now (during this period of bad performance). In other words, it must try to distinguish if the underperformance is just noise. In contrast, Manager B can point to specific elements of its investment process that have led to specific characteristics of the portfolio. Manager B might point out that the average dividend yield and/or P/E ratio of the stocks in the portfolio remain very similar to what they were before the firm was hired by the endowment fund. Moreover, Manager B can point to how clear its investment process is in providing for the training of any new analysts to replace the analysts it lost. This training would still emphasize the same investment principles and approach that the firm has used throughout its history. Finally, Manager B can establish whether the return outcomes are consistent with its approach in the current market environment and the expected range of outcomes from such an approach. That is, there may be evidence to support the claim that the underperformance really is just a result of "noise." In summary, it is likely that the board of trustees has more reason to remain confident in the capability of Manager B to deliver good performance in the future, assuming that the board had this confidence to begin with. Therefore, the board is less likely to fire Manager B than it is to fire Manager A.

This example highlights the importance of an investment process in the decision to retain or fire an investment manager. However, it is easy to see that the investment process is equally important in hiring an investment manager. Indeed, the board of trustees in the example possibly should not have hired Manager A in the first place, because Manager A either lacks a proper investment philosophy and process or cannot articulate the investment philosophy and process in a way that gives a prospective client a clear understanding of how it invests.

For a student-managed investment fund, this example serves as a cautionary tale. No one seems to pay attention to a fund or its investment process when returns are good (even though they should!). When returns are "bad" (negative or below that of a benchmark), interested parties such as boards of trustees, alumni, and administrators, pay very close attention — and attention during times of underperformance is usually stressful and unpleasant. Consistent adherence to, implementation of, and good communication of a specific investment philosophy and process are crucial in maintaining a positive ongoing experience and represent best practices. In short, the student-managed investment fund should strive to meet the same standards as an institutional investment firm.

Finally, while this example also takes the perspective of the client, it could have easily taken the perspective of the investment firm. If the investment firm has a clearly thought-out investment philosophy and process, such as Manager B, then it is more likely to maintain its approach, even during periods in which the approach is not yielding the desired results. Again, this emphasizes that investing at a professional level requires a consistent and disciplined application of a process that is built on the foundation of a sound investment philosophy.

Summary of Key Points

- Diligent investing is not *ad hoc*.
- The investment philosophy describes the beliefs about the market environment, the opportunities that the firm seeks to exploit in their investment process, and the capabilities of the individual or organization that help to realize those opportunities.
- The investment philosophy facilitates a shared understanding of purpose, opportunity, and direction.
- The investment process describes the key inputs into investment decisions, the methods employed to refine those inputs to create portfolio weights, and the implementation procedures.
- The investment process helps to assure that a plan is in place to provide for a continuous and consistent investment approach through time, even in the presence of personnel turnover.

Exercises

1. Navigate the following links to investment philosophy and investment process. These are some examples of real investment firms' philosophy and process statements. Not all of them are very good in that they do not necessarily fit the requirements of stating a

(Continued)

Exercises (Continued)

philosophy or clearly articulating the process. However, they are informative as to the approach of well-established investment managers.

a. Alger: www.alger.com

b. Dimensional Fund Advisors: www.dfaus.com

c. INTECH: www.intechjanus.com

d. Invesco: www.invesco.com

e. Janus: www.janus.com

f. LSV: www.lsvasset.com

g. Perkins: www.perkinsinvestmentmanagement.com

h. Waddell & Reed: www.waddell.com.

2. Develop separate investment philosophy statements for each of the following starting points:

a. A market that is semi-strong-form efficient

b. A market that is weak-form efficient

c. A market that is not efficient

d. A market in which there is overreaction

e. A market in which there is underreaction.

3. Develop separate investment processes for of the following strategies:

a. A U.S. small cap index fund

b. A Eurozone large cap index fund

c. A global all cap index fund

d. An active U.S. mid cap value fund

e. An active growth fund.

4. Obtain a list of active managers employed by your university's endowment fund. Critique the investment philosophy statements of several managers. In cases in which you find the statements deficient, try to glean the information from other information about the manager and rewrite a statement to meet the standards of a good investment philosophy.

5. Obtain a list of active managers employed by your university's endowment fund. Critique the investment process statements of several managers. In doing so, identify the parts of the process that you believe are proprietary.

6. Critique your own university's student-managed investment fund investment philosophy and process.

Appendix A: Common Investment Strategy Classifications

Most investment strategies fit into commonly used classifications. While these classifications are useful for a quick, broad understanding of an investment approach, they are only "headlines" that help provide a hint at the details of the story that are revealed in the investment process.

The most basic level of classifications is that of its asset class, such as *equity*, *fixed income*, or *real assets* (such as real estate). Further refinement of the asset class might also be appropriate for some funds. Most of these refinements are along the lines of the specific characteristics of the assets. In the equity asset class, securities are typically categorized by size and style. The size refers to the market capitalization of the target securities. A *small cap* strategy would typically target the smaller stocks in the market, such as those found in the Russell 2000 Index. Some strategies that target the smallest stocks in the market are often referred to as *micro cap* strategies. Likewise, *large cap* strategies would hold the largest stocks in a specific market, while *mid cap* strategies would hold stocks in the middle capitalization range. We have purposefully not defined the capitalization ranges using dollar values because the dollar cutoffs of these ranges are ever-changing. More specifically, the ranges are all relative to the current market of securities. The style of a stock typically refers to whether the stock is considered a *growth* stock or a *value* stock. Unfortunately, these two styles lack precise definitions, but are commonly understood to break down as follows. Value stocks provide relatively high dividends, price-to-earnings ratios, and/or price-to-book ratios, among other measures. Growth stocks are those that do not have these features, but instead whose prices are relatively high compared to their earnings or book values presumably due to their growth prospects. As with size, the style classifications are relative to the current universe of stocks, not absolute.

In the fixed income class, refinements are typically made along the lines of default risk, issuer, and/or duration or term. For example, bond funds might fall into the categories of (federal) *government* or *government agency*, *municipal*, *corporate*, and/or *high yield corporate*. These fund classifications might also have a term or duration modifier, such as *short-term* corporate debt or *long-term* government debt. In short, many classifications reveal the category off securities held.

Geographic focus provides additional classification for an investment strategy. Unless otherwise noted, most strategies are assumed to be *domestic* in scope (e.g., *U.S.* for a U.S.-based investment organization). However, it is best to be specific in referring to the geographical scope of a strategy. For example, a fixed income portfolio that seeks to purchase debt of countries worldwide would be classified as *global* fixed income fund. Likewise, the geographic scope should be classified as narrowly as appropriate. It is common to see U.S. state-classified municipal bond funds, such as a New York municipal bond fund.

Finally, one of the most important classifications of a strategy is the breakdown between *active* or *passive*. A passive investment strategy seeks to have exposure to a specific asset class or perhaps even a narrower segment of the market. However, a passive approach only seeks to track but not outperform that segment of the market as a whole. Passive strategies are typically broadly diversified within the segment and individual security weights are typically based on market capitalization. For example, an S&P 500 Index fund is a passive strategy that tracks the S&P 500, capitalization-weighted index. An *active* strategy seeks to outperform passive benchmarks and accordingly hold securities in weights that are different from those found in the strategy's benchmark. The expected source of the outperformance from an active strategy should be discussed in the strategy's investment philosophy and the methods for choosing the active weights should be covered in the investment process. Actives strategies also are typically classified by their broad investment approach. Two commonly used broad classifications are *fundamental* or *quantitative*. Methods that include research by analysts who make growth forecasts or valuation decisions based on their own judgment and interpretation of the facts are a common part of a fundamental approach. When a specific computer model is employed to make those forecasts without human judgments (other than those that created the model or computer program!), the approach is usually considered quantitative. Quantitative models also make heavy use of factor-based models. Of course, some approaches can employ a mix of these two approaches and would not be classified as either purely quantitative or fundamental.

Appendix B: The Role of Investment Philosophy in Evaluating Investment Managers: A Consultant's Perspective on Distinguishing Alpha from Noise

John R. Minahan*

*John R. Minahan is director of research at New England Pension Consultants in Cambridge, MA. This article was previously published in The Journal of Investing, Summer 2006, Vol. 15, No. 2, pp. 6–11. It is reprinted here with permission.

It has long been noted that investment returns have a substantial random element, and that this elevates the importance of investment philosophy in evaluating investment managers.[1] Despite this seeming consensus on the centrality of investment philosophy to the task of evaluating managers, it is rare that I encounter a manager who can articulate a compelling investment philosophy. While most managers have an "investment philosophy statement," in my experience these statements are more often marketing slogans or product positioning statements than they are thoughtful encapsulations of the investment insights an investment process is designed to exploit.

I have come to the view that many investment managers are "alpha-pretenders." That is, I believe that generating positive ex-ante alpha is a secondary consideration for many investment management firms. The primary concern for such firms appears to be exploiting the fact that randomness in returns will at times cause a mediocre investment process to exhibit positive ex-post alpha. Pretending to be an alpha-generator while in fact selling noise can be a successful business strategy because it is very difficult for a prospective investor to sort out whether ex-post alpha was generated by ex-ante alpha or noise. Consequently, investors overweight the importance of past performance, and often select managers whose future alpha-generation prospects are no better than chance.

Yet it is reasonable to assume that not all investment managers are pretenders. If one wishes to retain a true alpha-generator — a manager that can reasonably be expected to generate alpha in the future — how does one use the concept of investment philosophy to distinguish the alpha-generator from the pretender?[2] This article addresses the question by defining the concept of investment philosophy and discussing, with illustrations from my consulting experience, how the concept can be applied to evaluating investment managers. The paper concludes that investment managers and consultants are both underutilizing the investment philosophy concept, and that many true alpha-generators — by not articulating their investment philosophies more explicitly — are passing up an opportunity to differentiate themselves from alpha-pretenders.

What Is an Investment Philosophy?

In a sense, successful active management is simple. All one has to do is discount the cash flows of an asset by an appropriate discount rate, compare the resulting value to the asset's price, buy if the price is below the value, and sell if the price is above the value. If the investors using this process produced reasonably consistent and positive results, investing wouldn't need to be a philosophical endeavor.

But failure breeds introspection, and, it turns out, successful investment isn't so simple after all. The following turns out to be important:

- No one knows what the cash flows of a risky asset will be.
- No one knows the right discount rate for a risky asset.
- Market prices tend to reflect information and points of view as that information and those points of view are traded upon.

These facts reframe the problem of active management, and make central the following question: Why has the market not discounted the information or point of view on which cash flow projections and discount rates are based?[3]

Answering this question requires that a manager have points of view (implicit or explicit) on how the market prices — and sometimes misprices — securities, and on what the manager's competitive advantage is in identifying and exploiting such mispricings. These points of view frame the problem of designing an investment process, and provide guiding principles for the execution of the investment process.

With this background, we can define an investment philosophy as follows:

- A set of beliefs regarding the security pricing mechanism and what it is about that mechanism that sometimes causes securities to be mispriced.
- A set of beliefs regarding the manager's competitive advantage in exploiting these mispricings.

- A thesis about how these beliefs can be exploited to generate alpha (an "alpha thesis").

We might go further and define a *sound* investment philosophy as one that:

- Knows where it stands with respect to capital market theory and evidence.
- Is *living*; that is, it wrestles with confirmation and disconfirmation as it is used in practice, and adapts as necessary.
- Has deep enough core principles that adaptation does not result in total change.

How Does Analysis of a Manager's Investment Philosophy Aid in Distinguishing Alpha from Noise?

I am not aware of any empirical studies establishing a link between investment philosophy and performance. Yet, there is broad acceptance of the idea that a sound investment philosophy is critical to generating ex-ante alpha. I look forward to future research on this topic, but in the meantime I will take on faith the idea that a well-thought-out active management strategy is more likely to generate alpha than is a haphazard approach.[4]

The investment philosophy concept suggests that managers are more likely to generate alpha if they:

1. *Have a clear thesis of how they generate alpha.* Managers are not likely to generate ex-ante alpha without having a very clear idea of what they do that generates alpha, what it is about the markets they invest in that provides the opportunity to generate alpha, and what their competitive advantage is in exploiting that opportunity.
2. *Put significant effort into understanding where their performance comes from.* Good managers recognize that they have as much at stake as anybody in understanding whether their performance is due to successful execution of the alpha thesis, benchmark misfit, or luck, and are therefore very thoughtful about evaluating their own performance.
3. *Have thought about whether their alpha-generation process will need to change over time.* In competitive capital markets, alpha-generation sources tend to be arbitraged away. Good managers understand this, and therefore monitor whether or not it is happening, and have a process for seeking out new alpha sources which lever the manager's competitive advantage.

   This suggests a set of questions to which an evaluator should seek answers when striving to judge whether positive ex-post alpha was generated by positive ex-ante alpha or noise. Together, these questions comprise what can be called the "investment philosophy test":
   - What is the thesis (or theses) of how the product generates alpha?
   - What is the conceptual basis of the alpha thesis?

- What is the manager's view about the security pricing mechanism that underlies the thesis?
- What is the relationship of this view to capital market theory?
- What is the manager's competitive advantage in executing the thesis?
- What is the evidence that alpha has been generated by successful execution of the alpha thesis and not a mismatched benchmark or luck? If evidence is lacking, how does the manager convince him- or herself that the thesis is sound?
- How does the manager think about the possible need for the alpha thesis to change over time?

It is not always fruitful to ask a manager these questions directly, particularly if the manager doesn't think in these terms. Yet, an evaluator should strive to be able to answer these questions for him- or herself by the end of an evaluation.

Common Ways of Failing the Investment Philosophy Test

The majority of managers I interview do not pass the investment philosophy test. Following are examples of common failings:

1. Managers Who Don't Have an Alpha Thesis

Many managers present themselves by describing what they do without ever offering an argument why one should expect the process to add value relative to a passive alternative. Perhaps these managers think that, if they have good performance, consultants will just assume that the performance came from ex-ante alpha rather than noise. Perhaps they are right in some cases. However, consultants following the approach outlined in this paper will assume the good performance is noise unless the manager can present a credible case otherwise. A key component of such a case is being able to articulate a thesis of how the investment process generates alpha.

Sometimes it is possible to tease an alpha thesis out of a manager who hadn't thought to articulate one; these are sometimes the clearest ones, since they are composed of the manager's real thoughts rather than a script. However, just as often, the manager gets uncomfortable and sometimes even defensive. It is not unusual for managers in such situations to accuse the evaluator of trying to oversimplify their investment process.

2. Managers Who Have an Alpha Thesis That Isn't Conceptually Grounded

I am amazed at all the managers who make an assertion of the type: "In the long run X always wins," where X could be dividend yield, earnings growth, quality of management, a quantitative factor or mix of factors, etc. — yet are unable cite a reason why X should be systematically underpriced by the market. The managers may be able to point to data suggesting that X has been associated with excess returns in the past, but without a plausible explanation of *why* X should outperform, such data do not convince me that X is likely to outperform in the future.

Sometimes managers present data purportedly in support of an alpha thesis, but the data don't connect with the thesis. My favorite example of this is when managers claim that because over half of the total return of the S&P 500 since 1926 has come from reinvested dividends, one should expect high dividend-paying stocks to outperform low dividend-paying stocks over long time periods. I don't know whether the managers making this argument really believe it or just think it sounds good, but either way, the argument is a testament to the low quality of thinking one sometimes finds in manager–consultant meetings.

3. Managers Who Don't Think Very Deeply About Where Their Performance Comes From

I also find it striking that many managers with good performance don't put much thought into figuring out whether their performance came from ex-ante alpha or noise. They seem to think that good performance speaks for itself, as if they didn't understand that the consultant's job is to figure out whether the good performance came from alpha or noise, and as if they didn't have an interest in knowing themselves where their performance comes from.

A good example of this is a manager who selects securities from a universe that is different from the market benchmark to which the manager is compared. There is nothing wrong with this, per se, as there is no reason to expect the universe within which a manager can add value to exactly coincide with a market benchmark. However, benchmark misfit adds an extra step to performance evaluation. The manager's alpha should be calculated relative to the selection universe, so in order to even know what the manager's ex-post alpha is, not to mention evaluate it, one needs to know the performance of the manager's selection universe.[5]

In my experience, most managers with benchmark misfit don't even think about the performance of their selection universes. This makes it difficult for them to convince me that they will add value relative to it.

4. Managers Who Don't Think About Whether Their Alpha Generation Process Is Based on Temporary Charactistics of the Markets

A good example is a currency manager I once interviewed who used technical analysis to ride currency trends. The manager's thesis seemed to be: "Currencies trend: Certain technical trading rules have successfully exploited trends in the past; therefore those rules should be expected to work in the future." The manager was unable to satisfactorily answer the questions: Why do currencies trend? Might the underlying cause of trending change over time? How do you monitor whether or not the underlying cause is still present? Why do your trading rules work? Why are they not arbitraged away?

I was open to being convinced of the manager's process, but not if the manager didn't have a thoughtful perspective on these questions. I was even willing to leave some questions unanswered as long as the manager had wrestled with them. But in this case and many others, managers seem to have a predisposition against really thinking through why their processes should be expected to add value in the future. This makes me wonder if these managers are afraid of something. Perhaps deep down they understand that they are not really alpha-generators but pretenders hoping that they can hook enough clients before luck turns against them.

Uncommon Ways of Passing the Investment Philosophy Test

Managers who have good answers to all the questions of the investment philosophy test are very rare. Less rare, but still uncommon, are managers who cannot answer all the questions but who do have a sound investment philosophy underlying their investment process.

To avoid inadvertently eliminating managers who have solid alpha-generation processes but haven't thought in terms of the investment philosophy test, an evaluator needs to let managers tell their stories on their own terms. By listening first, an evaluator may find ways to ask the investment philosophy questions that flow naturally from the way a manager thinks about adding alpha. In other words, the questions should not be seen as a checklist but as a tool for opening windows into a manager's thought process and game plan for adding value.

Following are examples of manager characteristics that make it more likely for me to get comfortable with a manager's investment philosophy, even when the manager is unable to articulate his or her philosophy in the terms I have laid out in this article:

1. Managers Who Measure the Success of the Steps of the Process and Not Just the Ultimate Outcome

For example, consider a bond manager who makes the claim that his or her credit research not only predicts upgrades and downgrades, but makes those predictions before the expectation of a rating change is reflected in the market price. This manager tracks every prediction to see if the market consensus (as reflected by price) and rating agencies come around to his or her view. I get comfort from the facts that (1) such managers know their views only have value if they are not only correct but different than consensus, and (2) they track how prices eventually come to reflect, or not reflect, their views. Similarly, managers who evaluate their own performance with strategy benchmarks designed to replicate their selection universe demonstrate they understand the importance of attempting to differentiate alpha from noise (see Kuenzi [2003]).

2. Managers Who Recognize That Every Strategy They Come up with Is Potentially Subject to Being Arbitraged Away

For example, consider a quantitative equity manager who plays many themes at once. Each theme is viewed as having a finite life, and the performance of each theme is isolated and monitored so as to observe the decay in the value of the theme. The manager considers his or her competitive advantage to be in the identification of new themes and in the technology for measuring the contribution of each theme to performance. A similar idea is presented in the adaptive market hypothesis of Lo [2001], where the market is always tending toward efficiency, but the types of trades needed to move it toward efficiency rotate and evolve over time.

3. Managers Who Claim They Exploit Inefficiencies and Identify the Specific Inefficiency They Are Exploiting with Every Position They Take

Most managers who say they exploit inefficiencies use this claim as a broad justification for their investment process, but are unable to identify the specific inefficiency they are exploiting in any given decision they make. Those who routinely specify how their information or point of view differs from that reflected in price are much more credible.

4. Managers Who Know Their Companies So Well That They Are Quicker to Interpret Change, Even Though They Have No Explicit Alpha Thesis

There is always an exception to the rule. Sometimes a manager is simply talented and cannot articulate an alpha thesis.

Despite examples such as these, it remains frustratingly difficult to distinguish between true alpha-generators and alpha-pretenders. I believe there is more that alpha-generators can do to distinguish themselves, and that consultants should be more insistent that they do it.

Concluding Thoughts: Implications for Managers and Consultants

The investment philosophy test is not easy for a manager who doesn't have answers. Even if a marketer were very creative in reverse engineering a story that seemed to answer the questions, it would be very unlikely for such a story to hold up under cross examination, especially if the evaluator cross-references the story with analysis of the manager's holdings.

Therefore, a good way for alpha-generators to differentiate themselves from alpha-pretenders is to develop answers to the investment philosophy questions. Or, if the questions seem to not be on-target, given the manager's particular approach, the manager should reframe the questions in a way that they can be answered. However the questions are framed, it ought to be the case that true alpha-generators find it easier to come up with coherent answers than do alpha-pretenders.

For several years I worked as a freelance consultant to investment managers, providing a variety of services related to product management, including helping managers prepare for consultant evaluations. My approach in helping a manager prepare started with trying to get the manager to answer the investment philosophy questions.

I generally found managers resistant to engaging these questions, not because they disagreed with them in any fundamental sense, but because they didn't believe that consultants really thought in terms of these questions. They would say to me things like: "John, the objective is not to prepare us for an evaluation by you, but for evaluations by the consulting community at large, which, as far as we can tell, does not employ the investment philosophy approach."

I agree that the investment philosophy approach as I have laid it out is not widely used by consultants, but not because consultants disagree with it. Rather, I believe it is not used because it is very difficult to get answers to the investment philosophy questions from managers. Thus, we appear to be in a situation where consultants don't use the approach because managers don't think in terms of it, and managers don't think in terms of it because consultants don't use it.

This situation does not serve clients well. Nor does it serve the interests of consultants or alpha-generators. The only group that benefits from consultants not being able to get answers to the investment philosophy questions are alpha-pretenders. How the rest of us let the pretenders get the upper hand I do not know. But it is time for clients and consultants to more forcefully insist that alpha-generators distinguish themselves from the pretenders. I would think that managers who really believe they have an alpha-generation process would support and encourage this development.

Endnotes

The views expressed in this paper are those of the author, and may or may not be those of New England Pension Consultants.

1. See Brinson [2005] for a recent articulation of this point.
2. There are, of course, quantitative approaches to distinguishing alpha from noise, including measuring the consistency of ex-post alpha through time and across a firm's products. This article, however, is focused on using a manager's investment philosophy to assess that manager qualitatively.
3. Some managers argue it does not matter why the market has not discounted the manager's point of view so long as it, in fact, has not. This is a little like not asking why a chess master has offered you a piece. It seems more prudent to assume that the winner's curse − the tendency of the highest bidder on an item of unknown value to be the bidder with the highest misestimate of value − is alive and well.
4. A valid criticism of this article is that I assert that investment philosophy can be used to identify alpha-generator yet offer no evidence. It appears that I am failing to practice what I preach. My response to this

criticism is: I agree that evidence would make my argument stronger. Yet, the idea that investment philosophy is important has a strong theoretical basis. Consider the alternative — that knowledge of how securities markets work is of no relevance in generating alpha. This borders on nihilism.

5.   See Kuenzi [2003] for a detailed discussion of this point.

References

Brinson, G.P., 2005. The future of investment management. Financ. Anal. J. July—August.

Kuenzi, D.E., 2003. Strategy Benchmarks. J. Portf. Manage. Winter.

Organization

Chapter Contents

The focus in the last chapter was on an individual's or organization's investment philosophy and process. Placing the investment philosophy and process first was intentional, as this is the proper focus for an individual or organization whose primary responsibility is to invest money. That is, the student-managed investment fund exists to invest. As such, its approach to investing should be its first consideration. The operational structure should follow from and be consistent with the investment approach. Most student-managed investment funds have two goals: (1) to enhance the finance and investment education of students by providing a hands-on learning experience and (2) to achieve investment growth (i.e., good performance or outperformance) in the fund's investments. By focusing on the latter, the former can be achieved. In this chapter, we consider an investment organization and the investment vehicles that facilitate the achievement of these two primary goals.

All of the organizational issues and many of the investment issues are typically discussed in the student-managed investment fund's operating guidelines. The Appendix to this chapter has an example of a complete set of operating guidelines from Baylor University's student-managed investment fund. Throughout this chapter, we will consider organizational issues that arise in both conceiving and operating a student-managed investment fund, offering

Trading and Money Management in a Student-Managed Portfolio.
DOI: http://dx.doi.org/10.1016/B978-0-12-374755-6.00002-9

both discussion and examples of various items along the way. Some of these issues are codified in operating guidelines, while others simply comprise the operating policies or practices of the organization.

Regardless of the organizational form within which the student-managed investment fund operates, the vehicle within which the portfolio is managed must be chosen, usually based on the source of the portfolio's assets under management. With respect to the organization, we place an emphasis on the student-managed investment fund as a type of investment organization. Specifically, we explore the organizational form in terms of its most common forms: a volunteer student club or organization versus a for-credit class. Within these two types of student-managed investment funds, the operational structure of the organization must be chosen.

Even in this discussion of organizational form and structure, we will emphasize the relevance of the investment approach. We take the approach of first discussing the ultimate goal of the organizational structure − answering the question, what structure facilitates the best implementation of the organization's investment philosophy and process? This provides a framework for understanding the key elements of an investment organization. We then discuss other organizational considerations, such as whether to have a student fund as a class or as a volunteer organization, and some of the organizational issues that present particular challenges to a student-managed investment fund. Finally, we discuss the fund structure − as opposed to the organizational structure − to explore the issue of the investment vehicle through which an organization offers its portfolio. As in the previous chapter, the diversity of investment approaches suggests diversity of organizational forms. Indeed, there are multiple ways to structure an organization to effectively deliver on any particular investment approach. Therefore, we will place an emphasis on the common elements of most organizations but also try to give examples of alternatives to or variations on a common theme.

First and foremost, a fund must put the interests of its beneficiaries ahead of all other considerations. By structuring the organization around the investment approach, the organization stays true to this primary focus on beneficiaries' interests. For ease of exposition (and to further the interest of thinking of student-managed investment funds as operating as real investment firms), we will call these beneficiaries "clients." We recognize that the "client" label will be perfectly appropriate for student-managed investment funds that manage money for their universities' endowment funds but might not apply so strictly to other funds. However, even when the fund's beneficiaries are the students themselves or other investors, the "client" label is likely to be useful.

Organizational Structure

The structure of any organization, and especially any business enterprise, should be clearly spelled out and transparent to both the organization's members and other stakeholders of the organization, such as clients or benefactors. The roles and responsibilities should be

Exhibit 2.1 Objectives of Student Investment Funds

Wright Fund (Rice University)
Educational Objectives
The primary educational objectives of the Wright Fund are to provide Rice MBA students with:

- A challenging and stimulating opportunity to learn, develop, and practice professional stock analysis and portfolio management styles and techniques.
- Exposure to practices employed by professional fund managers including sound investment research, diverse investment philosophies, and ethical investment management.
- Insights into the structure, culture, and career choices in the investment industry.

Investment Objectives
The Wright Fund's investment objectives are to:

- Achieve risk-adjusted returns superior to the Fund's benchmark.
- Award scholarships to Jones School students.
- Preserve capital and grow portfolio assets.

Cayuga Fund (Cornell University)
The Cayuga MBA Fund aims to: (1) provide a competitive rate of risk-adjusted return to its investors; and (2) enhance the educational and professional opportunities of Cornell Johnson School MBA students through experiential learning. The fund invests in stocks traded in the United States.

Student Managed Investment Fund (University of Connecticut)
The primary objective of the Fund is to provide participating students an opportunity to gain valuable hands-on experience in security research, valuation of risky assets, asset allocation, and portfolio management. While performance will remain the primary focus, and will be reviewed at regular intervals, we do not presume that the students will be able to beat the market on a consistent basis. Rather, this is another SBA endeavor to deliver high quality practical education in an area of considerable interest to students and employers alike. The fund will increase the marketability of SBA students in industries such as equity research, investment banking, commercial banking, and corporate finance.

A long-term benefit of the fund will be the enhanced reputation of SBA as a school offering challenging, integrated, analytical projects using real time capital market data. This should enable us to attract more academically gifted and motivated students to the SBA.

Student Managed Investment Fund (Butler University)
Educational Objective
The SMIF should strengthen students' skills and abilities in security and market analysis, financial research, oral and written communication, and teamwork. Further, the fund should provide the opportunity for students to gain exposure to administrators (i.e., the Endowment & Investment Committee), investment advisors, alumni, professional money managers, and other industry practitioners. As such, in all facets the SMIF should provide experiential learning consistent with the mission of Butler University.

Investment Objective

The SMIF is designated by the Endowment & Investment Committee (hereafter, Committee) as a large-capitalization portfolio. Given the nature of the SMIF, the Committee authorizes the SMIF to further concentrate investments in the largest, most well-known stocks, which are represented by the S&P 500 index. The benchmark for the portfolio will thus be the S&P 500 index. Although the goal of the SMIF is to meet or exceed the return of the S&P 500, the Committee recognizes the constraints (i.e., limited meeting time and research resources) associated with managing the SMIF in the context of an academic setting. Thus, the stated performance objective is to trail the S&P 500 by no more than 100 basis points per year.

Saluki Student Investment Fund (Southern Illinois University Carbondale)

Educational Objective

Provide students at Southern Illinois University Carbondale with hands-on experience in portfolio management and investment research.

Investment Objective

Manage a portion of the Southern Illinois University Foundation portfolio with a Midcap Core Strategy. Invest to maximize long-term capital appreciation relative to the benchmark as the primary objective.

---

consistent with the mission or objectives of the organization. Exhibit 2.1 provides examples of the mission or objectives of several student-managed investment funds. As noted above, the common elements of these objectives are two-fold: (1) to educate the participants in the fund and (2) to produce a fund that experiences good performance (as this is the goal of both the client and any firm that the students will work for after graduation). The organization must be structured with the proper roles in order to realize both of these objectives. Most roles and responsibilities are reflected at the first level in titles on an organizational chart. The titles should give hints to the responsibilities of the individual in that role. While most investment firms have a familiar hierarchical organizational structure, student investment firms might chose a similar structure or one that is "flatter." In all cases, the structure must start with the responsibilities for oversight and develop from there the roles and responsibilities for the student members.

Oversight

Oversight of a student-managed investment fund can take several forms. Most student-managed investment funds are overseen on a day-to-day basis by a faculty advisor. In addition, many universities rely on an advisory board, typically made up of alumni who have professional experience and expertise in the investment industry. In addition to oversight, advisory boards can provide important mentoring opportunities for students. These professionals can draw on their experience to help shape the organization, its investment approach, and its focus. As discussed below, the oversight might also depend on the structure of the actual fund in terms of the investment vehicle. For example, the oversight role of the advisory board might be replaced by the endowment fund's investment committee if the student-managed investment fund is managed as part of the university's endowment fund.

Bryant College's Archway Investment Fund, shown in Exhibit 2.2, provides an example of many of these attributes. The fund spells out the role for the advisory board. Notice the

---

Exhibit 2.2 Job Description for Archway Investment Fund Advisory Board Members (Bryant University)

Role of Advisory Board members

The primary role of Advisory Board members will be to:

- Validate and refine course design ideas to ensure that we create an experience for students that captures key aspects of working in the investments industry;
- Serve as a guest speaker from time to time if he/she has a specific area of expertise that is relevant to the operation of the fund;
- Serve on the panel that reviews the performance of student analysts and portfolio managers;
- Provide encouragement, advice, and access to ideas and opportunities that might otherwise be unavailable to students;
- Mentor individual students as the need or opportunity arises.

From time to time, Advisory Board members may also be asked to provide guidance to student managers by suggesting high level investment themes, commenting on proposed portfolio strategies, or proposed changes to the investment policy statement which specifies the guidelines under which student managers operate the Fund. Note, however, that in all cases this input is advisory in nature. Student managers are ultimately accountable to the Investments Committee of the Bryant University Board of Trustees, and in that sense they are the "client."

Key Meetings

- February or March — Annual Financial Services Forum hosted by Archway Investment Fund student managers. The annual meeting of the Advisory Board is normally held on the same day as this event.
- Early May — Spring Semester Report: Student managers report on first quarter performance.
- Early December — Fall Semester Report: Student managers report on first 3 quarters performance.

While it is understood that most Advisory Board members will not be able to attend all 3 of the meetings listed above, it is hoped that each member will be able to attend at least one event per year and participate in at least one of the roles/activities outlined in the previous section.

emphasis on the Bryant University Board of Trustees as the ultimate client and the additional oversight offered by way of the board's Investments Committee.

Roles and Responsibilities

The hierarchical structure is usually shaped like a pyramid, with reporting lines leading to the person or group with ultimate responsibility. With regard to the investment function only, the top of the pyramid is usually the role of portfolio manager or perhaps an investment committee, in whom all responsibility and authority rests for the final buy and sell decisions in the portfolio. Below the portfolio manager, there could be sector or asset class team leaders or managers, who direct the work of analysts. The hierarchical structure allows individuals to focus on specific tasks and to specialize on a specific set of skills. This can benefit an organization through efficient execution and even enhanced capabilities from specialization. The hierarchical structure also has the benefit of clear paths for growth or promotion. As such, it requires clear succession planning and methods to identify and develop future leaders.

Exhibit 2.3 Roles and Responsibilities in an Investment Organization

Role	Responsibility
Overall Firm	
Chief Executive Officer President	Overall strategy and operations
Investment Functions	
Chief Investment Officer	Overall investment strategy, decisions, and implementation
Portfolio Manager	Specific portfolio strategy and decisions
Chief Economist Economist	Macroeconomic analysis
Director of Research Research Analyst Sector Analyst Quantitative Analyst Research Support Analyst	Research on specific sectors, firms, or aspects of the economy
Client Portfolio Manager	Investment professional resource for clients
Chief Risk Officer Director of Portfolio Analytics Portfolio Analyst	Analysis of portfolio performance and risks
Head Trader Trade Clerk	Execution of trades

Role	Responsibility
Operations	
Chief Operating Officer	Overall firm operations
Director of Human Resources	Hiring and staffing
Business Analyst Operations Analyst	Firm operating planning and processes
Client Operations Specialist Client Reporting Specialist	Client reporting and operations resource
Chief Technology Officer Technology Analyst	Technology and information systems
General Counsel	Overall legal
Chief Compliance Officer Compliance Officers	Compliance with laws, regulations, and firm and client policies
Finance and Accounting	
Chief Financial Officer Corporate Accountant	Budgeting, financial management, and reporting
Portfolio Accountant	Portfolio accounting and reporting
Marketing, Sales and Client Service	
Director of Marketing	External communications and public relations
Director of Product Development	Development of products and services
Director of Sales and Distribution	Sales to new and existing clients
Director of Client Service Client Relations Manager Client Service Specialist	Client service

Typical roles and responsibilities are outlined in Exhibit 2.3. These roles apply to a generic investment organization or firm. As such, each role might be somewhat different in any particular organization or even non-existent in some. As indicated above, these roles should be consistent with the investment philosophy and process of the firm. For example, a firm with a top-down investment process that begins with an overall economic view would have significant human resources in the economist roles. In contrast, a firm that employs a bottom-up approach might not even have a Chief Economist. Likewise, a "quant" firm would have significant resources dedicated to technology. The list in Exhibit 2.3 is intended to be indicative of the industry, but might apply exactly to a student-managed investment fund. As such, we discuss below the relevance of each role to a student-managed investment fund. For example, many investment funds have significant resources in the organization dedicated to distribution (i.e., sales) and client service. Indeed, without clients, there is no portfolio to manage! Therefore, the client-facing roles are extremely important and many investment firms find it valuable to have very knowledgeable investment professionals in those roles. For a student-managed investment fund, it would be tempting to simply dismiss that functional area. However, as most student-managed investment funds do manage money for their colleges' or universities' endowment funds, it is often desirable to consider the fact that these funds do have clients and therefore should not neglect client service. Furthermore, the marketing role can help fulfill the objective of helping create opportunities for graduates of the fund by managing the organization's external image and public relations.

As illustrated in the Wright Fund's Overview of Structure in Exhibit 2.4, the fund at Rice University follows the hierarchical structure with clearly assigned responsibilities and expectations for each role. The officers represent the top of the pyramid, with the base of the pyramid composed of analyst groups. Consistent with the hierarchical structure, each analyst group has senior and junior analysts, conveying a clear sense of responsibility and succession. An important aspect of the organizational structure for the University of Tulsa Student Investment Fund, shown in Exhibit 2.5, is the inclusion of non-investment functions within the hierarchical structure. Indeed, critical elements of any investment organization are functions that support both the investment decisions and the operation of the organization. These functions include accounting, human resources (i.e., personnel or membership), operations (e.g., technology and information systems), marketing and external communications (e.g., public relations), and macroeconomic analysis, among others. These functions also provide an opportunity for students (e.g., from majors other than finance) who are not necessarily interested in investment decisions to earn valuable experience in a real business setting. These students can make significant contributions to the fund's success through their roles in managing other aspects of the organization.

A flatter organizational structure usually has decision-making authority shared or spread out across individuals or even teams. The decisions for purchases or sales in the portfolio might be allocated to a specific asset class or sector team, or be decided upon by a group vote. For example, the organizational structure of the Saluki Student Investment Fund (SSIF) at Southern Illinois University Carbondale is relatively flat, as shown in Exhibit 2.6. The SSIF's flat structure has sector teams sharing responsibility and authority for making buy and sell decisions. According to the SSIF investment process, each sector team has the authority to buy or sell any stock within its assigned sector, subject to the other provisions of the investment process. Because there are usually only a handful of students on each sector team, each individual has a significant voice in choosing the portfolio investments, without any single person having significantly more than another. In this way, the resulting performance of the portfolio is truly shared across members. In addition, other functions of the organization, such as writing annual reports, are shared among the sector teams in this flat structure. As can be

Exhibit 2.4 Overview of Structure of the Wright Fund (Rice University)

The Wright Fund curriculum is designed for students with a sincere interest in the markets who hope to pursue a career in securities research or investment management. The Fund is a two-semester commitment, with half of the approximately 25 enrolled students rolling off each semester to provide for continuity of the Fund. In the first semester, students perform intensive research and analysis of individual stocks, making transaction recommendations for the entire Fund's consideration. First semester students are called "junior analysts." Second semester Fund members serve as "senior analysts" and are effectively portfolio managers responsible for the allocation, strategy, and risk-return management of one or two equity sectors. Three of the second semester students serve as elected officers to manage the fund under the guidance of the Faculty Director.

Officers

The three elected officers of the Wright Fund and their primary responsibilities are listed below.

- Chief Investment Officer:
    - Manages and tracks the performance and risks of the Fund, including trade review and approval
    - Provides the Fund with weekly updates and two formal presentations
    - Prepares and delivers the mid-term board report and end-of-semester board presentation.
- Chief Operating Officer:
    - Designs and administers the course including syllabus preparation and agenda
    - Administers the application/interview and officer election processes
    - Oversees marketing needs and arranges guest speakers.
- Chief Economist:
    - Tracks economic trends and their impact on the Fund
    - Provides the Fund with weekly updates and two formal presentations
    - Makes allocation and trading decisions for the Fixed Income sector.

All officers are expected to keep up on the financial markets, to read all research reports written by other students, and to be involved in the application/interview process.

Analyst Groups

Non-officer students are divided into Analyst Groups ("AGs"), consisting of one or two Senior Analysts and one or two Junior Analysts, each of which focuses on one or two of the S&P industry sectors:

- Consumer Discretionary
- Financials
- Consumer Staples
- Healthcare
- IT/Telecom
- Energy/Utilities
- Industrials/Materials

The AG is responsible for tracking their assigned sectors and managing Fund holdings within those sectors as a portfolio. The AGs choose sector strategies, goals, risk/return parameters, and performance monitoring techniques, as well as conduct in-depth stock analysis resulting in buy, sell, or hold recommendations.

Exhibit 2.5 Organizational Chart for the Student Investment Fund (University of Tulsa)

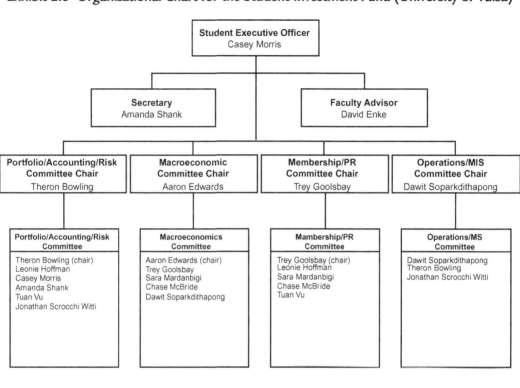

Exhibit 2.6 Organizational Chart for the Saluki Student Investment Fund (Southern Illinois University)

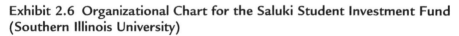
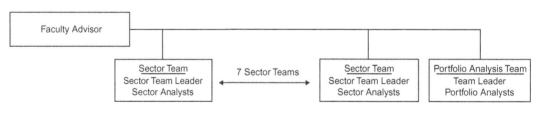

seen, even in this flatter organizational structure, some hierarchy exists in having team leaders. The role of the team leader exists to provide guidance and direction to each team from an experienced SSIF member, without implying seniority or increased authority. In this way, the structure facilitates continuity and succession, without imposing a hierarchical structure.

The flat organizational structure is rarer in actual investment firms for various reasons, including the benefits of having a single person with whom "the buck stops." However, given that the student-managed investment fund often has the luxury of focusing more exclusively on investment decisions, this type of structure can work. A cost can arise in a flatter organizational structure in that efforts might be duplicated, as the structure does not readily facilitate specialization. However, it also could have benefits in having members gain experience in accomplishing a broad spectrum of fund and organization activities.

The organizational structure must be rationalized to most effectively execute and implement the organization's investment process. Certain investment processes might give rise to a hierarchical structure, while others might suggest a flatter organization. An investment process that calls for very specialized skills might benefit more from a hierarchical structure than one that requires analysis across a large number of eligible securities. In this sense, it is convenient to think of the organizational structure as the shoe and the investment process as the foot. Putting the left shoe on the right foot might keep the foot dry, but it will be an awkward fit, at best. Over time, the wearing of the wrong shoe will adversely impact the foot and cause it to suffer. Therefore, the design of an organization's structure should start with a list of responsibilities that result from the investment process. These responsibilities should motivate specific roles, which help build a resulting organization chart. To conceive an organizational structure and then try to fit that on to an investment process risks orphaning or omitting some necessary functions and responsibilities. In summary, the investment philosophy and process should motivate the organizational structure, and not vice versa.

Student-Managed Investment Fund as a For-Credit Course or a Volunteer Student Organization

A key consideration at many universities is whether to offer the student-managed investment fund as a course or as a volunteer student organization. Under either structure, other considerations are made, such as whether to allow participation by permission (or selection) or whether to have open (unrestrictive) participation. This section discusses the pros and cons of such considerations in the context of the benefits and challenges that they create in an investment organization. As indicated elsewhere, this book takes the perspective of a student-managed investment fund having a goal to carry out its duties to the same standards of a professional investment management firm. Student-managed investment funds face specific organizational challenges that investment firms do not. These challenges are discussed below in the context of the both the organizational structure and the course credit/non-credit issue. Exhibit 2.7, "Challenges and Benefits of a Student-Managed Investment Fund at a Small Liberal Arts College," discusses how course credit issues were

Exhibit 2.7 The Challenges and Benefits of a Student-Managed Investment Fund at a Small Liberal Arts College

Founded in 1849, Austin College, located about 60 miles north of Dallas, Texas, provides a fairly traditional undergraduate liberal arts education for about 1400 residential students. The college does not have a business school but does have a seven-member department of Economics and Business Administration, which consistently graduates one of the largest numbers of majors on campus.

While a student-managed investment fund (SMIF), using a substantial amount of "real money," is somewhat common in business schools, it is rare in a liberal arts college. We detail below our experiences incorporating such a fund into our curriculum. We try to identify the benefits to the students and to the school as well as some of the ongoing challenges we face. Teams of undergraduate students, in concert with faculty and alumni advisors, have been managing a fund that began with $1 million in fall 2007. The potential benefits from this gift included not only introducing a group of undergraduate students to portfolio management using real money, but also creating additional scholarships with our investment gains. The timing for starting a new fund probably could not have been much worse. However, in addition to learning a great deal about investing, our student portfolio managers have outperformed the market.

Curriculum Considerations

Since this gift was not the result of a proposal that we had submitted, we had to start from scratch immediately upon being informed of the gift to design a program to incorporate a student-managed investment fund into our curriculum. Prior to receiving this funding, we had only two finance courses in the curriculum — a junior-level managerial finance course and a senior-level international finance course. We decided that we needed to add a junior-level capital markets course to our spring 2007 course offerings so that by fall 2007 we would have a critical mass of sufficiently knowledgeable students available to manage the fund. One of our concerns was that with our small size we might have difficulty maintaining enough students in the pipeline to participate in the fund's management. The initial prerequisite courses for students who wanted to be fund managers included financial accounting, managerial finance, and the capital markets course. We launched an SMIF program that effectively limited involvement to seniors.

Setting up the Fund

We decided to set up the fund as a course and give students ½ course credit per semester initially for successful participation in the fund's management with the expectation that students would be involved for a full year, both fall and spring semesters. The faculty member responsible for running the fund was given ½ FTE teaching credit per semester as well.

The SMIF Course

With the guidelines, the bylaws, and the account set up, the focus shifted to the structure and operation of the course. We decided to make each student responsible for only one sector of the S&P 500. The intent was to simplify the process and make the students' experience resemble more closely the specialized responsibilities of true money managers.

The initial design of the course was to meet weekly at the beginning of the fall semester for four weeks to get the new students oriented to the structure of the class, the investment guidelines, and the expectations with regard to their research, presentations, and recommendations. Subsequent to that, we would meet every two weeks, sometimes more often, if needed.

Challenges

Many of our challenges are the result of our small size and liberal arts mission. Our biggest concern at the present time is having enough qualified students involved in the course and the management of the fund to make the individual student workload manageable, as well as having a course that serves a reasonable number of students. To address our desire to have more continuity and attract more students earlier, we recently restructured the prerequisites to make it easier for juniors to get involved in the fund. During their junior year, students can enroll in the SMIF course while they are completing the prerequisite courses. As juniors, they act primarily as researchers and receive $\frac{1}{4}$ credit per semester for their involvement as researchers for a maximum of two semesters, or a total of $\frac{1}{2}$ credit. The following year they can become full-fledged managers. This adjustment appears to be getting more students involved in the fund for two full years, which gives the fund more continuity.

Given the workload and the time commitment involved, both the students and faculty thought that being a fund manager was worth more than the $\frac{1}{2}$ credit per semester, we had originally decided to give. The problem was that if we gave students more credit, the SMIF could comprise an unacceptably high percentage of the total major credits required for graduation. As a liberal arts institution encouraging breadth of education, we have to be careful not to give too much credit for involvement in the SMIF. With our recent revision to the curriculum, increasing fund manager credit to $\frac{3}{4}$, and adding the $\frac{1}{4}$ credit researcher category, a student who serves two semesters as a researcher and two semesters as a fund manager can receive a total of 2.0 credits toward the major, which requires 8−9 total credits for graduation.

Steve Ramsey and Jerry Johnson
Austin College

considered and dealt with at Austin College as they integrated a student-managed investment fund into the curriculum.

There are two key benefits of having the student-managed investment fund integrated into the curriculum, in general, and a portfolio management course, in particular. The most obvious benefit arises from the practical application of the course material to the management of the fund. This enhances the overall business education of the student by making the course material more tangible, more relevant, and likely more interesting than it might otherwise be. As such, this first benefit accrues primarily to the students enrolled in the course in comparison to a similar course offering that does not have such a practical component.

The second key benefit of having students participate in a student-managed investment fund through a formal course accrues primarily to the fund client. Specifically, the for-credit course structure usually requires that students earn a grade in the course. The course grade can be used by the course instructor as a form of currency with which to compensate students who participate in the management of the portfolio. It might seem controversial to think of course grades as currency. However, the point is that a grade provides an incentive mechanism that allows the interest of the student to be aligned with that of the fund's client. In real investment firms, monetary compensation is used to provide incentives to employees to do a good job on behalf of the investment firm and its clients. If an employee is not meeting the requirements of the job, the employee might not be paid a substantial bonus, or might even be fired, causing the employee to forgo future compensation. Likewise, an employee can earn a nice bonus, raise, or promotion by performing well in a job. If the student is not meeting the requirements of a job or role in the operation and management of the student-managed investment fund, then the grade can reflect this performance, with the harshest penalty being a failure to get credit for the course. Likewise, a student making an outstanding effort and a significant contribution to the management of the fund can earn a high grade in recognition of such performance. It should be noted that this notion of a course grade is consistent with the traditional notion of a course grade that reflects achievement in completing course requirements and mastery of course content, assuming that course content and requirements are relevant to the management of the portfolio. In summary, the for-credit course model of a student-managed investment fund can serve to make up for the lack of compensation and provide an additional mechanism for aligning the incentives of the student fund managers with the interests of the fund beneficiaries. These aspects highlight the important issues with respect to a student-managed investment fund in putting the client's interest first. Other goals, such as the education of student-managed investment fund members, can be mutually compatible with the primary goal being that of serving the needs of the client.

The most common forms of for-credit student-managed investment funds are one-semester or two-semester courses. Examples of such structures are shown in Exhibit 2.8. Other forms include "labs" or practicum credit for participating in the fund outside of a traditional course structure, though still with integration into the curriculum and multi-year programs which can provide continuity otherwise lacking in the one- or two-semester form.

Student-managed investment funds that are organized outside a formal for-credit course structure face a challenge in overcoming the potential cost of incentive alignment, which arises as it does in almost any volunteer organization. Specifically, an individual is beholden to a volunteer organization only by the individual member's own will. If the individual loses the will to actively participate, there is no direct cost to the individual. For student-managed investment funds, this can be especially important around certain times of the semester, such as exam times (e.g., final exams), social occasions (e.g., Homecoming or

---

Exhibit 2.8 Course Examples

Archway Investment Fund (Bryant College)

The Archway Investment Fund experience consists of a two course sequence with a securities analysis course in the first semester and a portfolio management course in the second semester. The progression of experiences that students are exposed to in these courses is intended to represent a mini "career path." Although the courses blend theoretical coverage of key topics with practical experience, heavy emphasis is placed on learning through experience. One objective of the course design is to replicate important elements of the look and feel of actually working in the industry.

Cayuga Fund (Cornell University)

Student Portfolio Managers are students officially enrolled in the Applied Portfolio Management class. Most student managers work in sector teams following an assigned economic sector. Others may be assigned to a quantitative research group or to investor relations/marketing or the student trader role. They are responsible for conducting thorough research of investment vehicles. They prepare and present proposed investment ideas to the class as a whole and positions are taken only after a 2/3 majority is achieved in a formal class vote. Student course grades are based on their formal reports, presentations, class participation, as well as portfolio performance relative to the sector benchmark.

Portfolio Practicum (Creighton University)

Portfolio Practicum is a two-semester "hands-on" undergraduate course in the College of Business at Creighton University. The class oversees a student-managed investment fund with approximately $2.7 million in equity investments for the Creighton University Endowment Fund. Eligible students apply for the class during the Spring semester of their Junior year. Applicants enter an interview process to gain acceptance to the class for the following academic year. The Fall semester of the class focuses on equity research and valuation techniques. Students also will revalue the existing stocks in the portfolio. In the Spring semester, students learn about the concepts central to portfolio construction and portfolio management. Students also present investments they believe would be good additions to the portfolio.

---

fraternity/sorority rush), or other extra-curricular activities (e.g., athletic tournaments). Student-managed investment fund members might find demands on their time from activities during these times that bring penalties (e.g., through lower grades or reduced social status) if they choose to divert attention away from those activities. This presents a challenge to the organization either to find means to mitigate these issues, to compensate members with other benefits that outweigh the costs associated with diverting time to the student-managed investment fund, and/or to attract and retain members for whom these issues are minor.

One of the primary forms of compensation in any student-managed investment fund is the wealth of knowledge and experience that the student gains from participating in the fund. This single factor helps mitigate much of the incentive alignment problem because a student who fails to devote the appropriate time and effort toward fund activities reaps little of the primary reward of such activities. Like anything else in life, the benefits that are realized from participating in a student-managed investment fund are proportional to the effort and energy put into it.

As discussed in the previous chapter, consistency of approach can be maintained in either a for-credit or volunteer format by maintaining the fund's identity through its investment philosophy and process. The volunteer structure can also have benefits compared to a for-credit course structure. In particular, because a volunteer structure is extracurricular, it does not count against (or toward) credit for other courses. In this way, it does not limit the participation of members to a specific time period, such as one or two semesters. Rather, the volunteer structure accommodates students who might participate in the fund for only one semester or even for the entirety of their college careers. Clearly, a first year college student might have much more to learn about investing than the more seasoned student who has taken courses in finance and investing. However, as in any organization, there are myriad ways to contribute to both the investment function and the operation of the organization without having specific finance knowledge or training. For example, first year students can contribute by preparing reports, auditing statements and account positions, reviewing trades for compliance with policies, managing proxy voting procedures, maintaining records, and preparing external communications. These functions simply require a bit of training of and diligence by the member. While duties such as these do not necessarily require in-depth finance knowledge, they are no less important to the operation of a fund. Moreover, these types of functions help initiate new members and provide them with training and education that can pay significant dividends for the fund as these members matriculate through the program and acquire more subject-matter knowledge. Thus, an open structure can help facilitate continuity in the fund over time and establish a depth and capacity in the organization.

Challenges to a Student-Managed Investment Fund

Regardless of a student-managed investment fund being organized as part of the curriculum in a for-credit course or as a volunteer organization, there are challenges that student-managed investment funds face by virtue of the fact that students are the primary participants in managing the fund. Among others, the primary challenges are the facts that students typically follow an academic calendar and successful students graduate and, therefore, leave the fund. It is tempting to suggest that these challenges are unique to student-managed investment funds — which would imply that investment firms do not face these challenges. However, this simply is not the case. All investment firms must make contingency plans for business disruptions and must deal with personnel turnover. While these challenging events might not be quite as numerous or regular in an investment firm compared to a student-managed investment fund, they are no less important. Indeed, these events can often have serious consequences for the investment firm, especially because, unlike in student-managed investment funds, these disruptions are often unscheduled and unexpected.

Personnel Recruiting and Turnover

A key determinant of the value of any organization is the people who comprise the organization. This is especially true of investment organizations. While the investment philosophy and process provide a basis for investment judgments, key decisions relating to the output of the organization are directly influenced by the organization's personnel. At an investment organization, it is important to attract and retain motivated, knowledgeable, and capable people. In a student-managed investment fund that emphasizes learning, the key is to attract motivated individuals who will approach the responsibility with the diligence that money management deserves. Because (good) students cannot be "retained" indefinitely, the student-managed investment fund must also find ways to manage the turnover in personnel. We begin by discussing the selection of new members and then turn to considerations that arise due to turnover or matriculation and graduation of student members.

Whether a student-managed investment fund is offered in a for-credit course format or as a volunteer organization, the membership is either "open" to anyone who chooses to sign up or it is "selective" in restricting access only to those who meet certain criteria. As with the other organizational issues that are discussed throughout this chapter, there are costs and benefits to either participation model. The selective organizational structure typically requires a specific course background (i.e., prerequisite courses), grade point average, or status (e.g., seniors only) to be eligible. This is especially true in the for-credit course that is part of a specific curriculum. In addition, many student-managed investment funds screen prospective members through an application process that often includes interviews. Exhibit 2.9 shows examples of the selection process at several student-managed investment funds and Exhibit 2.10 shows example applications. This structure resembles that of a real investment firm that would typically try to chose the "best of the best" to hire. This structure can serve to ration the opportunity in a situation in which there is significantly more interest in participating than there is availability of "seats" in the organization. In turn, this helps to motivate both current members and prospective members. Current members might consider participation to be an honor, thereby increasing their dedication to and effort in the student-managed investment fund. Likewise, prospective members might work harder to achieve the proper credentials in preparing for application to the student-managed investment fund. Potential costs to a selective organizational structure include the accessibility to the opportunity and direct and indirect costs of maintaining the application and selection process.

Exhibit 2.9 Interview and Selection Process

Interview Process (Rice University)
Each semester, first-year students are invited to apply and interview for 12 to 14 positions. The application/interview process occurs in two stages. In the first stage, candidates must submit an application, resume, and stock analysis. Qualified applicants are then invited to interview with Fund Officers and the Faculty Director. Interviews consist of a presentation/ pitch of the stock analysis completed in the first stage and a character/fit component. Strong preference is given to students pursuing careers in Investments fields.

Student Selection Process (Creighton University)
The selection of the students for the Portfolio Practicum begins in their junior academic year. Admission into the two-semester sequence is highly competitive. On average, 40 students apply for 16 positions. The application process includes a recommendation from a business professor, submission of a resume, a personal interview with the previous class participants and faculty members, and selection by a faculty committee. The Portfolio Practicum application requires that the prospective student get an application form (downloadable from the Portfolio Practicum section of Creighton University's website). The application form requires a signature from a College of Business professor. The student must submit a current resume. The student must also write a one-page letter of interest describing why s/he wants to be in the class. This size allows for individual consultation and has been very functional for forming groups of four members per team.

The Portfolio Practicum applicants must sign up and attend a personal interview during the selection process. Interview teams include a Finance professor and two or more members of the current portfolio class. Interviews are scheduled for 20 minutes each. Interviews are conducted on two consecutive evenings, Sunday and Monday, with two groups interviewing simultaneously for three to four hours each. (The questions used in this year's interviews are included in Appendix 1.) Students and professors rotate asking the questions and each interviewer makes an individual evaluation of the applicant. The selection process then reviews the evaluations of each applicant in a Portfolio Practicum class. The process typically identifies eight applicants who are very good applicants. The remaining four slots are then determined from a vote of the finance faculty with the top vote getters being selected.

In the class selection process we look to see the proportion of males and females. For example, one year the Portfolio Practicum only had one female member. That year, only one female student applied for the class. The next year we advertised the fact that female applicants for the class had a 100% acceptance rate and the number of female applicants has increased ever since that year. International students offer diversity of opinion and perspective to the class, so it is also considered. Varsity athletes are another category of students who add diversity to the class. We consider the majors of the students as well. In the course of the life of the Portfolio Practicum it has evolved from a pure finance class into a financial accounting course, to a College offering for all majors, to a heavily focused CFA-type class primarily for accounting students, to an accounting and finance focused class for exceptional majors from all areas.

Once the students for the class have been selected notifications go to all the applicants regarding whether they were selected for the class or not. The selected students are invited to attend classes with the graduating class. They listen to the Portfolio Practicum students present their financial analysis reports and their buy, sell, or hold recommendations. The selected students choose the sectors they want to follow during the next academic year. They are assigned stocks from our current holdings to track during the summer. They are given a summer reading list. In their Fin 325 Investment Analysis class they do a stock valuation report that is designed to get them experience with the top-down approach to fundamental analysis. The students typically gravitate to the sector they studied in that class.

Selection Process (Bryant College)

Students apply to be admitted to the first course in very much the same way that they would apply for a job. To start the process students are required to send in a resume and a cover letter by sometime around the middle of the semester preceding the one in which they wish to begin the first course. Interviews are held during the following week, and are conducted by an interviewing panel consisting of one faculty member and two or three students from the current classes. During the interview an attempt is made to gauge the candidate's level of focus, discipline, and level of passion for investment management. As one might expect, these traits tend to be highly correlated with grade point average, but although a simple GPA cutoff would be more efficient in many respects, and experience has shown that it would result in almost the same admitted group, we have resisted moving in that direction. There are several reasons for this choice. First, the interviews are good practice for the candidates and they send a very clear signal that it is time for them to have a polished resume and to be able to clearly articulate their career aspirations and their strategy for achieving them. Since many candidates are juniors when they apply for the first course, a little bit of a push in this direction sometimes helps to bring priorities into focus. Second, doing the interview provides the candidate with information about the standard of professionalism expected of students involved in the Fund-related courses. Third, the interviews provide useful information on candidate personalities and interests, which is helpful when putting together teams. Fourth, and finally, interviewing has often proven to be a transformative experience for students serving on the interviewing panel. They regularly report that experiencing the monotony and mental exhaustion that goes with interviewing demystifies the process for them and makes them much less apprehensive about their own job interviews, which are often taking place at around the same time. They also gain a much better understanding of the importance of standing out in the interviewer's memory, and this seems to cause them to take a much more serious approach to the process of preparing for interviews.

Fund Membership (University of Tulsa)

1.2 New Members — Students who wish to become members of TUSIF are required to fill out an application, which shall be reviewed by the Membership Committee. Applicants who are approved by the Membership Committee shall then be interviewed by that committee during a Membership meeting which shall be held prior to the enrollment period for the following semester. Following each applicant's interview, the Members shall vote Yea, Nay, or Abstention. The Membership Committee shall then present every applicant before the class along with their recommendation. The class will then vote on the acceptance of the individuals. A vote of 2/3 of the class must be received for an applicant to become a new member of the TUSIF.

1.2A In the event that there are more applicants than Member positions available, the assignments will be made in the following manner: The Members of the Membership Committee will individually rank the Applicants in ascending numerical order with the number "I" being the most preferable choice. The rankings for each individual will then be tallied by the Student Executive Officer. The lowest total scores will receive first assignment. In the event that Applicants are still tied in rank, a vote between the Student Executive Officer, the Membership Chair, and the Faculty Advisor shall determine the final selection.

Exhibit 2.10 Membership Applications

MBA Portfolio Practicum Class Application

Application for Student Managed Investment Fund

The University of Toledo
Student Managed Investment Fund
PLEASE TYPE OR PRINT CLEARLY *(All information is completely confidential.)*

Full Name:_____

Local Address:_____

_____

Local Phone:_____ E-Mail:_____

Major:_____ Minor:_____

Anticipated Graduation Date:_____

List your total credit hours in the following areas of study (including current semester):

Finance	
Accounting	
Economics	
Computer Information Systems	

List expected class schedule for next semester:

CLASS	CREDITS

Current GPA at UT:_____ Current GPA in Major:_____

Please answer the following questions on a separate piece of paper. Please limit your answer to no more than 100 words for each questions.

1. Why do you to be a member of the Fund?
2. What abilities and skills can you contribute to the succes of the Fund?
3. Attach a current resume.
4. Attach an unofficial copy of your undergraduate transcript. This can be obtained by logging onto the *myUT* web portal and clicking on the student self-service tab.
5. If you desire (not necessary), attach a faculty recommendation.

Your signature:_____ Date:_____

SIF Student Investment Fund
University of Tulsa

Student Investment Fund Membership Application

Name: _____ GPA: _____
E-mail: _____ Phone: _____
Majors(s)/Minor(s): _____
Expected Graduation Date: _____ Advisor: _____

Term for enrollment: □ Spring   □ Fall 2010

Classification: □ Freshman   □ Sophomore
                  □ Junior   □ Senior
                  □ Graduate   □ Other: _____

Finance Courses Completed:
(Undergrad):	□ Personal Investing	□ FOB Finances/Finance 3003
	□ Institution and Markets I	□ Institutions and Markets II
	□ Invest/Portfolio Mgt I (Required)	□ Invest/Portfolio Mgt II
	□ Portfolio Analysis	□ Adv Portfolio Mgt.
	□ Plan Cntrl/Capital Exp	□ Fin Analysis/Working Cap Mgmt
	□ Financial Statement Analysis	□ Int'l Business Finance
	□ Other: _____	

(Graduate):	□ Finance Concepts	□ Financial Admin 7003 (Required for Non-Finance Majors in Undergraduate Students)
	□ Portfolio Mgt	□ Advanced Portfolio Mgt I
	□ Investment Analysis & Mgt	□ Behavior Fin Mkts
	□ Long-Term Financial	□ Other: _____
	□ Decisions	

On which committees would you be interested in serving (Check all that apply)?:

Portfolio   MIS   Accounting   Economics
Membership   Capitations Public relations

Please list any offices you've held, awards you've received, or activities in which you are involved: _____
_____
_____

Please describe any related work or internship experience you've had: _____
_____
_____
_____

Please explain what attributes you will bring to the Fund: _____
_____
_____

Thank you for taking the time to fill out this application. Please return to the Finance Dept.
Office Use only

Date Received: _____
SIF initials: _____

March, 2009

Dear MBA students:

In This Job Market You Need an Edge

How about taking a professional quality analyst report on a company like Apple to your job interview? It's helped students over the years differentiate themselves from the pack. It can help you too. Whether you plan a career with an investment firm or hedge fund or just plan to take your MBA and get rich, hands-on experience in investments will be invaluable to your future success in managing someone else's or your own investments. In order to gain this knowledge, I encourage you to apply for the Portfolio Practicum class next year, FINA 6230/6231.

Get Experience Running a Live-Multi-million-Dollar Portfolio

I teach the MBA Practicum class and we manage a multi-million-dollar live portfolio that is part of the SMU endowment. We focus entirely on picking good stocks. The class functions like an institutional investment firm. You will be a stock analyst and you will come to the class with recommendations regarding the stocks you cover. You will learn techniques that I have used successfully at three of the largest money managers in the world: The Northern Trust, State Street Global Advisors, and Putnam Investments.

This Class Is Very Popular and Seats Are Limited

Please complete the attached information highlighting your grades, interests, and work history so you can make the best case for your participation. Please include information on your participation in the Buyside Club, if applicable.

I look forward to reviewing your application.

Director of the ENCAP & LCM Group Alternative Asset Management Center

Cox School of Business

MBA Portfolio Practicum Application
Fall 2009 FINA 6230/Spring 2010 FINA 6231
    Name/SMU ID#:_____
    Mailing Address:_____
    E-Mail:_____ Tel:_____

Please list courses taken in the areas of Economics, Finance, Investments, Valuation, and Financial Statement Analysis

Course #	Instructor	Grade	Hours/Semester Taken

Overall Cox GPA
    EXPECTED DATE OF GRADUATION:
    MBA PROGRAM (circle one): Full-time   Professional

Please return this completed form and attach:

- Required: A copy of your current resume
- Required: A one-page (maximum) typed statement explaining why you wish to participate in the course. Please include your career aspirations and any relevant experience in investments
- Optional: A copy of your transcript
- Optional: Up to three letters of recommendation

Please note that you must take this class BOTH semesters. Return this information IN HARD COPY to my mailbox in Fincher.

Deadline: Monday, March 30, 2009, at 5:00 PM

Most student-managed investment funds have a significant goal of enhancing financial and investment education through the practical, hands-on experience that comes with managing an actual portfolio. As such, an open membership policy has the potential to maximize the realization of this goal with the widest reach in bringing this educational opportunity to students. The open organization also can accommodate students from virtually any major, especially in a volunteer organization that is not offered as part of a specific curriculum. Students outside a business school can bring fresh perspectives and unique capabilities that can contribute to both the management of the portfolio and the value of the organization. For example, engineering majors might make insightful contributions to research into materials or industrial companies, while pre-med, biology, or biochemistry majors might have a valuable perspective for understanding certain aspects of biotech, pharmaceutical, or other healthcare companies. In such a setting, students can specialize based on their backgrounds (e.g., major subject matter) and learn to collaborate with fellow team members from diverse backgrounds. Like the selective organizational structure, the open organizational structure has costs that might mitigate some of these benefits. Like any organization, it is likely that the bulk of the work will be concentrated on the most dedicated members. However, this may be more equitable than it might appear on the surface, as those who do the most work and achieve the most in such an organization also reap the largest rewards in terms of acquiring knowledge and experience. As discussed above, the lack of direct incentives (e.g., grades) in an open, volunteer organization makes it difficult to engage some members and rely on their consistent efforts. If others are free to join or resign at any time, coordination costs might be imposed on the most diligent members of the group as turnover can create uncertainty as to who has responsibility for what. The other issue with an open structure is the potential lack of investment knowledge of students outside the business school. A chemistry major can understand pharma better then any finance major but may have almost no idea of how to research or value a stock. Any fund that utilizes non-finance students must be especially diligent in creating a structure that takes advantage of the diverse and specialized knowledge while compensating for the lack of basic investment knowledge.

All organizations must deal with turnover in personnel. While it might seem that turnover in a student-managed investment fund is more severe than in a typical investment firm, the issue might not be as clear as it seems. On the one hand, a student-managed investment fund will experience turnover due to matriculation or graduation of its members. In a for-credit course structure, the entire "staff" of the fund might turn over every semester or every academic year. Given this seemingly extreme turnover and lack of consistency in staffing, few investors would be comfortable investing with a firm that had such extreme turnover. On the other hand, the predictability and regularity of the turnover in a student-managed investment fund makes its impact on the fund potentially far less disruptive than the turnover of personnel in a real investment firm. Consider that a real investment firm experiences turnover of the following forms: (1) firm-initiated termination of an employee; (2) employee-initiated separation due to employment at another firm; (3) employee death; and (4) employee-initiated separation due to retirement. The turnover of personnel at a student-managed investment fund looks most like the last form of turnover at a real investment firm. As such, this form of turnover can be planned for and managed. Succession planning is an important element in any business and especially important for an investment management organization. The other forms of separation between firm and employee are no less important and, because the timing of such events usually is unanticipated, they are potentially more disruptive. As such, an investment organization must assume that such turnover will occur and plan accordingly.

As discussed in the previous chapter, the most important inoculations against disruption from personnel turnover are a clear and well-documented investment philosophy and investment process statements. Since the value of an investment organization is the service that it provides in a consistent and ongoing manner, the philosophy and process are all that remain when the firm experiences a change in personnel. For firms that lack a specific investment approach as expressed in the investment philosophy and process, personnel turnover can leave the organization with nothing − or, at least, nothing familiar. Of course, the survival of the investment organization does not rest alone on the investment philosophy and process. Other aspects of how the organization functions also must be memorialized in policies and procedures to help the organization continue to operate in a consistent manner through time. These policies and procedures should cover all aspects of the organizational structure, including roles and responsibilities and methods of operation. Furthermore, care should be taken to maintain organization-related documents and work products that are in the possession of the organization and, not of individuals who scatter far and wide after graduation. A central library or use of a computerized system like Blackboard can retain documents like analyst reports from year to year and maintain a history that simulates the knowledge retained in a typical investment firm.

Academic Calendar

At most U.S. colleges and universities, classes regularly meet during the academic year, consisting of fall and spring semesters or their academic quarter counterparts, starting around the end of August and lasting until around the beginning of May. While some institutions have summer classes, the number of students on campus, if any, is typically a fraction of the number attending during the academic year. Whether the student-managed investment fund is a voluntary organization or a for-credit course, this presents a challenge for the fund during semester breaks, such as the holiday between fall and spring semesters, and the lengthier summer break. Obviously, markets do not close and investment decisions are no less important during these times. The potential exists for significant information to come out about specific portfolio holdings, possibly posing a risk of a loss to the portfolio. Similarly, the risk of opportunity costs arises if information comes out that would have triggered a purchase of a security in the portfolio. These risks or losses could be in both absolute and relative (e.g., to a benchmark) terms. Generally, the more concentrated a portfolio, the larger the risk.

Plans must be made to manage the portfolio during these breaks in the academic calendar. As always, the way in which investment decisions are handled during these breaks should be consistent with the organization's investment philosophy and process. For a fund with a very long horizon and little turnover, the breaks are unlikely to require significant action. However, most funds would typically require at least some monitoring during the breaks to assure compliance with portfolio constraints and policies, and to respond to significant news that might trigger a decision to rebalance the portfolio. For example, a fund might have a policy that constrains individual security weights to a specific amount, such as 5% or 10% of the portfolio. The fund's duty is to enforce these policies regardless of whether classes are in session. Similarly, if a significant event affects one of the portfolio's current holdings, other actions might be necessary. For example, suppose that a fund has a policy not to hold firms that are implicated in wrongdoing by the U.S. Securities and Exchange Commission or other authority. If news emerges of such wrongdoing by a company held in the portfolio, then action would be necessary in the fund.

Fortunately, these scenarios have feasible solutions that take many forms. The most expedient solution might be to craft a fund policy that provides for action to be taken at the next earliest date when classes are in session. In essence, this creates two sets of rules: one set for when classes are in session and one set for when classes are not in session. While this type of policy would not likely be acceptable to a professional investment management firm, it addresses the issue in a transparent manner and sets the expectations of all parties as to how the assets of the fund are managed. This type of policy has the benefit of handling decisions in a deliberate manner. Another common approach is to liquidate individual stock holdings during extended breaks and move to a passive investment instrument, such as an index fund. As shown in Exhibit 2.11, Butler University specifies policies to cover its 4-week winter break period and the 20-week summer break period. In the shorter break case, the solution is to set limit order prices to transact based on the student-managed investment fund members' analysis of the individual securities. A passive approach is taken during the longer summer break.

An alternative approach is to establish explicit procedures for communication among student-managed investment fund members and, perhaps, the fund advisor during breaks. Modern technological conveniences, such as Skype, Face Time, Google Hangout, and teleconferencing can be used to facilitate meetings with participants who are not able to meet in the same physical location. In most cases, a simple exchange of e-mails might suffice to conduct the necessary business of the fund. Regardless of plans for communication, procedures require forethought and planning to assure that all participants understand their individual responsibilities and the logistics of how and with whom to communicate. In some cases, a "skeleton crew" might be appropriate, with certain responsibilities that normally rest with a team being delegated to an individual for a limited time period.

Exhibit 2.11 Academic Holiday Policies (Butler University)

Periods of Inactivity and Transition

Since the SMIF will operate in the context of a structured course that follows the academic calendar, there will be periods of time during which little oversight would exist. Specifically, Winter (~4 weeks) and Summer (~20 weeks) breaks represent the longest duration of inactivity. Further, when semesters end/begin, there will be a transition from one student team to another.

A. WINTER BREAK

   At the end of the Fall semester, the SMIF team will designate target selling prices (above and below the current price) for each security held. With these prices, the Faculty Advisor will institute good 'til cancelled stop orders that will automatically transact in the even the trigger price is reached. Further, the Faculty Advisor will monitor the account for unexpected market events. At the beginning of the Spring semester, the stop orders will be withdrawn and the new management team will assume control of the portfolio.

B. SUMMER BREAK

   Given the extended nature of the Summer break, SMIF holdings in individual company securities (and related derivatives) will be liquidated and invested in index funds that track the S&P 500. Exceptions may be made on a case-by-case basis with approval of the Faculty Advisor.

It is possible, as enrollment numbers increase, that sufficient interest may exist to offer a summer section of the SMIF course. If this occurs, transition from one academic period to the next will follow the rules designated under the Winter Break section.

Finally, it is also important to consider the access to information. We will discuss specific "tools of the trade" later in this book. However, many of those tools, such as Bloomberg Professional or proprietary databases, might have availability that is limited to a physical location on the college or university campus. As such, plans must be made to access similar information from remote locations. For example, if portfolio weights are typically monitored through an Excel Spreadsheet linked to Bloomberg, the same spreadsheet should be reworked to access up-to-date prices from another source, with holdings being manually updated or entered. Publicly available sources, such as Yahoo! Finance, Google Finance, and Morningstar offer some tools that might be useful for this purpose. Similarly, these services offer an array of business and company news that can be monitored from anywhere. As indicated above, the important aspect of this issue is to plan appropriately and have contingency plans in place.

Fund Structure

We conclude the discussion of organizational issues with a discussion of fund structure, or the actual investment vehicle through which the portfolio will exist. In addition to building a rational organizational structure in which the student-managed investment fund operates, decisions must be made as to the structure or form of the investment portfolio itself. In general, any investment strategy can be delivered in various forms, also known as "vehicles." The investment profession offers its services in two general vehicles to investors: separate accounts and pooled funds. Separate accounts (sometimes called "separately managed accounts," or SMAs) are often offered to institutional clients or very wealthy individuals. The key distinguishing feature of a separate account is that it has a single entity (individual or institution) as its beneficiary. Separate accounts are, therefore, usually a large enough dollar amount to justify their individual attention. Because there is a single beneficiary for each separate account, the oversight of the account is the sole responsibility of the beneficiary. An investment manager would be given discretion to trade a separately managed account according to that manager's investment process, but usually would not be given custody of the assets of the account.

Without having custody of the assets, the investment manager would direct sales and purchases of securities within the account, but would not be able to withdraw or otherwise divert the funds for its own use. Instead, the assets are usually held in an account at a brokerage firm or custodial bank in the name of the owner or beneficiary of the account. This structure of the account helps to provide some protection to the client that the investment manager cannot commit fraud or theft of the account's assets, while still facilitating the specific investment strategy of the manager. Having an account at a brokerage firm or a custodial bank so that the student-managed investment fund only directs trades in an account, but cannot otherwise access the assets for withdrawal, is a prudent organizational arrangement.

The management fee paid to the investment manager for a specific separate account is negotiated between the account holder and the investment manager and is typically set as a percentage of assets under management (AUM) in that account. Therefore, the investment management fee from a single investment manager might vary across separate accounts, usually being a decreasing function of the account's AUM. Brokerage and custodial fees are typically charged directly to the account.

Smaller accounts from either individuals or institutions are usually more efficiently offered through a pooled fund because they lack the scale to justify the cost of handling the accounts individually. A pooled fund is managed as a single account or fund by the investment manager, but the fund has multiple beneficiaries (i.e., shareholders) having a proportional claim on the assets, returns, and costs of the fund. In some cases, various share classes of the same underlying portfolio might exist to differentiate fees or costs, while in institutional pooled funds, like separate accounts, a client's fees are typically charged based on the AUM of that specific client. Because pooled funds have multiple, perhaps even numerous, shareholder or beneficiaries, funds other than those organized as unit investment trusts may have a board of trustees or board of directors. Boards have oversight responsibility on behalf of the fund's shareholders. For example, the Investment Company Act of 1940, under which publicly available mutual funds are organized, are required to have a board of directors who oversee the fund and make decisions on the fees paid to the fund's investment manager or advisor. The investment manager makes regular reports to both the fund's board and the fund's shareholders. The general types of investment vehicles are summarized in Exhibit 2.12.

Exhibit 2.12 Investment Vehicles

Separate Accounts
— Separately managed accounts.
Pooled Accounts
— Pooled or Collective Trusts (available only to qualified retirement plans, such as 401 (k) or defined benefit pension plans, regulated by the Office of the U.S. Department of Treasury/Comptroller of the Currency, no board of directors, trust account at a custodian or trust bank).
— Mutual Funds (Regulated by the SEC under the Investment Company Act of 1940, board of directors, restrictions on short-selling or use of leverage).
— Hedge Funds (SEC oversight but less regulation, may use leverage or short-sales, open to qualified investors only).

Student-managed investment funds can take either of the two main forms of fund structure. The source of the money for the fund usually dictates the fund structure. If the student-managed investment fund receives its assets under management from the university's endowment fund, then a separate account is typically the optimal structure. In this case, the student-managed investment fund is "hired" in the same manner as the endowment fund's other investment managers. The endowment fund's board of trustees, perhaps via an investment committee, provides oversight of the fund. In some cases, additional oversight might be established through a fund-specific board of advisors. Similarly, if a single sponsor or benefactor establishes a fund for students to manage, then a separate account is similarly appropriate. Again, oversight could be provided by the fund sponsor and/or through an additional board of advisors.

Some student-managed investment funds utilize a pooled structure to facilitate the addition of new investors and the "cashing out" of others. Some funds even create a pooled fund organized as a hedge fund or a mutual fund. In these cases, specific accommodations must be made for accounting to facilitate the issuance of new shares and redemption of old shares. Additionally, organizing documents would spell out the oversight of such a fund, usually with a board of trustees or board of directors to whom the student fund managers report on a regular basis. If the fund is organized under the Investment Company Act of 1940, then shares must be valued daily and policies regarding the pricing of the fund's underlying shares must be maintained. For most student-managed investment funds, a mutual fund structure is beyond what is feasible or practical.

Summary of Key Points

- Student-managed investment funds often have both educational and fund performance objectives. By focusing on the fund performance objective, the educational objective can be achieved.
- Because most student-managed investment funds perform the same primary function as an investment firm, it is useful to consider the structure of real investment firms.
- An investment organization's structure should be motivated by and consistent with the investment approach.
- The organization should have clearly defined roles and responsibilities.
- Regardless of whether a student-managed investment fund is a volunteer organization or part of a for-credit curriculum, incentives exist for students to diligently manage the fund on behalf of the fund's clients or beneficiaries.
- Continuity and consistency through time are critical and turnover in any organization is disruptive. Succession planning and processes should be in place to manage personnel turnover.
- Policies or procedures should exist for managing the fund during breaks in the academic calendar.
- The fund structure or vehicle should match the client's or beneficiary's needs.

Exercises

1. If a student-managed investment fund has only six (6) students who participate at any given time, what roles are critical? Does the answer depend whether the investment approach is top-down or bottom-up? What if the fund is purely quantitative or purely fundamental?

2. If a student-managed investment fund has 30 students who participate at any given time, what organizational structure might be most efficient? Be sure to discuss what roles would be included in the structure.

3. Suppose that a large business school offers a student-managed investment fund as a volunteer organization. In the Fall semester of its first year, it attracts 70 students. By the end of the first semester, only 45 students remain. By the end of the Spring semester, only 25 students remain. Why is this undesirable for the fund? Discuss what policies or procedures the fund might adopt in future years to protect the fund from having the same experience and discuss the potential cost/benefit tradeoffs of such policies.

4. Consider the following student-managed investment funds that have specific characteristics. For each fund, identify potential policies for managing the portfolio during short and extended semester breaks. What are the costs and benefits of the possible policies?
   a. Small-cap portfolio of 10 stocks, benchmarked to the S&P 400 index.
   b. Large-cap portfolio of 60 stocks, benchmarked to the S&P 500 index.
   c. Portfolio of 50 stocks, benchmarked to the Russell Midcap index.
   d. A balanced portfolio of mostly large-cap stocks and some government bonds.
   e. Tactical asset allocation strategy portfolio.
   f. Sector rotation strategy portfolio that holds sector ETFs.
   g. Hedged (long and short) portfolio with 40 open long and short positions.
   h. Large-cap portfolio with 25% turnover per year (or 4-year average holding period).

5. Identify and discuss the key advantages and disadvantages of offering a student-managed investment fund in a for-credit format.

6. Identify and discuss the key advantages and disadvantages of offering a student-managed investment fund in a volunteer (not for credit) format.

7. Identify and discuss the key advantages and disadvantages of being selective in restricting participation in a student-managed investment fund.

8. What roles might be appropriate for the following student with the given background?
   a. Freshman Accounting major.
   b. Sophomore Marketing major.
   c. Junior Finance major.
   d. Junior Marketing major.
   e. Junior Management major.
   f. Senior Finance major.
   g. Senior Economics major.
   h. Senior Education major.
   i. Psychology graduate student.
   j. Senior Chemistry major.

Appendix: Operating Guidelines for Philip M. Dorr and Alumni Endowed Investment Fund

Baylor University — Hankamer School of Business

Objective

The objectives of the Philip M. Dorr and Alumni Fund (henceforth, Fund) are: (1) to provide an investment fund by which business students can learn investment management principles and techniques by managing real money; (2) to provide scholarships out of the growth in market value of the Fund; and (3) to support the Southwest Securities Capital Markets Investments Center (henceforth, Center).

Education

Students involved in managing the Fund will gain valuable hands-on experience in securities research, valuation of risky assets, and portfolio management. In so doing, students will develop skills in evaluating economic, industry, and firm data and integrating such data into securities analysis. In addition, students will gain practice in effectively communicating their research results to others.

The performance of the Fund will be reviewed twice per year (at the end of the Fall and Spring semesters) and compared with the performance of the S&P 500 (the benchmark portfolio). The investment goal of the Fund will be to maximize the long-term rate of return consistent with prudent risk limits. The Fund's main objective, however, is to deliver high-quality practical education in securities analysis and portfolio management.

The Fund should increase the employment opportunities of participating students in areas such as equity research, investment banking, commercial banking, and corporate finance. In addition, over time the Fund should enhance the reputation of Baylor as a university offering challenging, integrated, hands-on investment management experience using real-time capital market data. This, in turn, should enable Baylor to attract more academically gifted and motivated students.

Distributions and Scholarships: Beginning 2007, the Fund's *Endowment Value* will be defined as the average market value of the Fund at the end of the prior four calendar years. (Through year-end 2006, the Endowment Value will be the market value of the Fund as of the prior year end.) Each academic year, the Board of Trustees (henceforth, Board) of the Fund will review the University's *distribution rate* and set the Fund's distribution rate for that fiscal year. The *distribution amount* is the distribution rate times the Endowment Value. The distribution amount goes first to meet the operating budget for the Center for that fiscal year as approved by the Board. The estimated operating budget for 2004–2005 is $100,000 and reasonable increases in this budget should be expected. Unusual increases or new budget items must be approved by the Board. Each year, the Board will set a *scholarship amount*, which will be based on the distribution amount less the Center's operating budget. The Chairman of the Board, after consulting with other Board members, will select a *distribution date* for liquidating assets and distributing the scholarship amount, but it shall not be later than May 31, the end of the University's fiscal year. It is anticipated that at least one scholarship will be reserved to recruit an outstanding MBA candidate who is interested in a career in investment management. Other scholarship recipients will be athletes who are pursuing a business school degree based on the following priority structure: football first, men's and women's basketball second, and other sports as funds permit.

Fund Amount

The initial endowment of the Fund was $250,000 contributed by Mr. Dorr and an additional $250,000 of matching contributions from Baylor alumni and friends. The University endowment contributed approximately $500,000 to match this initial seed money. A donor and his alumnus wife donated approximately $2.3 million specifically to support the operations of the Center. The donor has approved that the funds should be managed as part of the Philip M. Dorr and Alumni Endowed Investment Funds. The University endowment matched this contribution with a gift of $2 million. The Fund will remain open for additional contributions. Endowed funds will be deposited in an investment account under student management with oversight by the Board of Trustees of the Fund and an Investment Advisory Committee.

Operating Expenses

Operating expenses are expenses incurred by the Center, Practicum, and Department for such Practicum-related items as technical support, teaching payments, administrative personnel, director compensation, computers, data sources, equipment, accounting and legal fees, books, journals, research materials, speaker honorariums, travel, annual report production, and newsletter production. No fees will be paid by the Fund to any students, either in cash or in kind.

Investment Policy

Return Goal

The return goal is to obtain a long-term return (calculated on a five-year basis) as high as possible consistent with prudent risk limits, but at least as high as the return on the S&P 500 (with dividends reinvested). Since the Fund is exempt from federal and state taxation, the return goal is based on total return with no preference given to whether the return comes from dividends, interest, or capital gains. However, it is understood that the return on the Fund return will likely lag that of the benchmark portfolio in "up" markets due to the drag of lower returns on cash.

Risk Tolerance

The normal or target asset allocation calls for a large allocation to equities. In addition, even though each class of students will manage the Fund for only one semester, the Fund has an infinite time horizon and should be managed as such. Consistent with this time horizon and the target asset allocation, the Fund has a high tolerance for risk.

Asset Allocation

The Fund will be allowed to invest in any U.S. exchange traded securities of established firms. However, at no time will the Fund be allowed to use financial leverage. Consistent with the Fund's educational objective and goals, the target stock allocation should generally be 100%. The Fund's stock weight, however, may drop as low as 60%, permitting students to gain experience with other asset classes and to recognize that cash will exist after positions are liquidated. The purchase of derivative securities will not be allowed. Exchange traded funds, such as S&P Depository Receipts (SPDRs or "Spiders") and sector-specific exchange-traded funds such as sector Spiders, are acceptable investments. Mutual funds, too, will not be allowed for purchase except for investment of cash balances in a money market fund. Some liquidity must be maintained to provide cash for operating expenses. In addition, occasional liquidity will be needed to fund scholarship withdrawals.

Diversification

The Fund should be diversified across industry sectors and individual stocks. In general, each *sector's* weight in the Fund should be within either 50% of its weight in the S&P 500 or 5 percentage points of its absolute weight. Thus, a sector with a 20% weight in the S&P 500 could have a weight in the Fund of 10% to 30%, while a sector with a 3% weight in the S&P 500 could have a weight in the Fund of 0 to 8%. In addition, the maximum investment in any *one stock* should be no more than the larger of 7% or 5% in excess of its weight in the S&P 500. Thus, stocks with weights of 1% and 3% in the S&P 500 could have maximum weights in the Fund of 7% and 8%, respectively.

Exchange traded funds are not considered individual stocks for purposes of these calculations. However, the restrictions on industry weights and individual stock weights include the underlying exposure in ETFs. For example, suppose the Fund has $1 million and the technology sector's weight in the S&P 500 is 30%. The Fund could not invest $450,000 in technology stocks and the remaining $550,000 in S&P Depository Receipts (SPDRs). This would be an effective weight of $45\% + 55\% (0.30) = 61.5\%$, thus violating the restriction that the effective weight of the technology sector in the Fund must be between 15% and 45%.

Selection Emphasis

The selection process will focus on stocks that have the potential for good returns. Although the S&P 500 is the benchmark portfolio, investments can come from U.S. securities outside that index. However, restrictions on industry weights and individual stock weights will still apply, meaning that no more than 7% of the Fund can be invested in a single stock outside the S&P 500. In addition, no more than 20% of the Fund can be invested in all stocks outside the benchmark portfolio.

Fund Management

The Fund will be managed through a one-semester, three-hour Portfolio Management Practicum course (Practicum). The Practicum will be taught in the Fall and Spring semesters as a seminar open to graduate business students and senior undergraduate Finance majors. It is critical that at the close of the Fall and Spring semesters the Fund must satisfy the diversification requirements outlined above. The Fund will not be actively managed by the Practicum class between semesters. The Faculty Advisor and Chair of the Board of Trustees may liquidate investments during times that the Fund is not being managed by the Practicum class.

Class Structure

The Practicum will be taught using a combination of lectures, homework, readings, and research reports (using a template developed by the Faculty Advisor) prepared by the students working in sector Teams. For example, in a 15-student class there could be ten Teams, five with one student and five with two students. Each Team will be responsible for making presentations for stocks in its sector of the S&P 500. Although one Team will make the presentation for a given sector, all students are responsible for analyzing the stocks under consideration since all students vote for or against each stock recommendation.

The entire class will meet once a week to review the status of the Fund and discuss research reports and trade recommendations prepared by the various Teams on securities within their assigned sectors. Among these reports/recommendations will be an analysis every semester of each of the stocks in the Team's assigned sector(s) that are currently held in the Fund portfolio. Each recommended trade must be supported by a research report, which should be made available to non-team members of the class by Friday before the Monday night class. After discussion, the class will vote to execute the trade, not execute the trade, or postpone the decision.

At all times the class will make decisions consistent with maximizing the total return on the Fund through the avoidance of excessive transactions costs. In so doing, the class will be sensitive to the resulting costs associated with paying commissions and spreads from high turnover of the Fund's assets.

Student Fund managers may not hold themselves out, either privately or publicly, as *investment advisors* or *investment counsel* as defined by the Investment Advisors Act of 1970. Individual students, acting in their capacity as Fund managers, are specifically prohibited from using these descriptions in possible violation of state and federal regulations.

Execution of Trades

Final authority to execute trades rests with the Faculty Advisor. Trades can only be executed by the Faculty Advisor or his designated representative. All trades must be supported by a research report and minutes of the class meetings in which the recommended trade was discussed. These documents must be made available to the Faculty Advisor with sufficient time for him or her to review them prior to the trade. The Faculty Advisor must approve all trades.

Brokerage Account

All trades will be made through a brokerage account approved by the Board of Trustees of the Fund. The address of record of the brokerage account will be that of the Fund. The brokerage firm will provide to the Fund originals of all regular account statements and confirmations of all transactions made in the account on behalf of the Fund. In addition, the brokerage firm will be directed to provide duplicate statements to the Faculty Advisor and the University Investment Accounting Office.

End-of-Semester Report

At the end of Fall and Spring semesters the class will present a consolidated report to a meeting of the Board of Trustees of the Fund, outlining the results of the Fund to date. The report should discuss the performance of the Fund, especially relative to the return on the benchmark portfolio. Each Team will be responsible for reporting on its portion of the Fund portfolio.

Because of the important role of the Investment Advisory Committee (discussed below) in advising students about their stock selection process, members of this Committee will also be invited to attend these end-of-semester meetings. In addition, to provide continuity in managing the Fund from one semester to the next, students selected to take the Practicum during the succeeding semester will be asked to attend the last several class meetings, including the final class meeting, of the semester prior to their enrolling in the Practicum.

Oversight

Oversight of the Fund and the Practicum will be divided between the Board of Trustees of the Fund and an Investment Advisory Committee.

Board of Trustees

The Board of Trustees of the Fund will include the Chief Investment Officer of Baylor University, the Dean of the Hankamer School of Business, the Chair of the Department of Finance, Insurance, and Real Estate, the holder of the Pat and Thomas R. Powers Chair of Investment Management, the original Fund donor or his representative, and the Faculty Advisor. The holder of the Powers Chair of Investment Management will serve as Chair of the Board and will call meetings of the Board as necessary but at least once near the end of each semester to review the end-of-semester report prepared by the class.

The Board will make policy level and administrative decisions to accomplish the objectives of the Fund. Policy decisions include all the guidelines articulated in this document, including, for example, guidelines relating to Investment Policy and Fund Management. Administrative decisions include non-policy matters such as selecting the brokerage firm to handle trades for the Fund and determining an annual scholarship distribution amount.

Investment Advisory Committee

The Investment Advisory Committee will include the Faculty Advisor, who will serve as Chair of the Committee, select members of the Baylor faculty, and Baylor alumni and friends involved in professional money management. Committee members will serve strictly an advisory role, including advising Teams about their securities research and periodically attending class, either in person or via video- or tele conferencing, to discuss their securities-selection methods and other relevant investment topics.

Other Matters

Amended and Restated Agreement: The Operating Guidelines document set forth herein supersedes the previously executed agreement dated September 28, 2000, entitled Philip M. Dorr and Alumni Endowed Investment Fund.

Security Selection

Chapter Outline

The resulting product of a student-managed investment fund — indeed, of any investment manager — is a portfolio. A portfolio is a collection of securities, held at specific proportions or weights. As such, portfolio management can be considered as a combination of two activities: security selection and portfolio construction. This chapter focuses on the selection of the securities within the portfolio. The following chapter focuses on how those securities

Trading and Money Management in a Student-Managed Portfolio.
DOI: http://dx.doi.org/10.1016/B978-0-12-374755-6.00003-0

are combined to construct the portfolio. In most student-managed portfolios, the emphasis, the importance, and the majority of the time spent are on security selection. The amount of time spent on security selection versus portfolio construction should depend on the investment strategy as defined by the investment philosophy and investment process. In other words, the approach to security selection and portfolio construction should be governed by the investment philosophy and process. In some investment processes, security selection and portfolio construction might be mutually exclusive activities, while in others, there may be no discernible separation of the two. These chapters will treat security selection and portfolio construction separately, but attempt to point out areas in which dependencies and overlap exist between the two activities.

Security selection is made up of two separate activities: security analysis and quantitative modeling or screening. A good security selection process will feature both. For the majority of investment firms, the quantitative analysis comes at the beginning of the process. Below are the typical steps in building an equity portfolio.

1. Eligible Universe:
   a. Determine the appropriate benchmark.
   b. Pick a universe of stocks based on that benchmark.
2. Sector or Factor Allocation and Security Selection:
   a. Decide how to deal with macroeconomic or sector weightings.
   b. If actively weighting sectors, choose factors to research.
   c. Determine how to rank stocks within the portfolio or sector.
   d. Quantitative: Build a quantitative model:
      i. Determine factors that cause stocks to outperform.
      ii. Backtest those factors.
      iii. Use those factors to screen or rank stocks.
   e. Qualitative: Write a research report:
      i. Determine which factors cause stocks to outperform.
      ii. Do research into those areas/factors and determine criteria to compare them.
3. Portfolio Construction:
   a. Build the portfolio based on understanding the risks involved.
   b. Establish risk controls.
   c. Use an optimizer or a set of portfolio construction rules and guidelines.

Exhibit 3.1 shows a graphical representation of the steps of this type of process from the Tulane student-managed portfolio.

Like most solutions to complex problems, the above steps break a big problem into smaller pieces. It starts by narrowing down the scope of research and analysis from all possible securities to a specific universe of securities, usually based on the benchmark against which the portfolio is compared. It is important to note that the absence of a benchmark and some

Exhibit 3.1 Tulane Student-Managed Investment Fund Security Selection Process

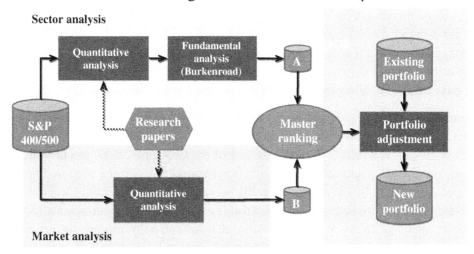

very broad benchmarks result in a very large eligible universe. The absence of a benchmark also creates issues for the fund in determining acceptable performance, as discussed in Chapter 6. Quantitative processes are especially adept at dealing with large numbers of securities, while fundamental processes that rely on a limited number of human analysts to conduct research must whittle the number of securities down to a manageable number. As such, fundamental approaches typically rely on at least some quantitative process to screen stocks in order to find a smaller set of candidates for further in-depth research in the security selection steps. In some processes, security selection might begin by carving the universe into separate pieces by sector or economic factor exposure, while other processes might consider all stocks together, regardless of sector or economic factor exposure. This chapter begins by looking at the first step of screening and modeling and then focuses on the analysis of securities in the second step, with the result being a long (hold or buy) or short (do not hold, sell, or short sell) decision. The final step of portfolio construction is discussed in detail in the following chapter.

Quantitative Analysis

The goal of quantitative analysis in a student-managed portfolio setting is to narrow down the universe of stocks for further in-depth research. Quantitative analysis is the activity of researching securities using characteristics, factors, or variables using quantitative models. As such, quantitative analysis relies on aspects of a security that are quantified or quantifiable, such as financial statement information, market price and trading activity, and historical stock return and risk characteristics. Some institutional investment processes are strictly quantitative. For example, of the investment philosophy and process examples in Chapter 1, LSV represents an investment manager that uses quantitative analysis exclusively. Recall that LSV's investment philosophy indicates that it believes opportunities exist because of traders' judgment biases. Its quantitative investment process specifically addresses these biases in human judgment by, among other things, not allowing human judgments to enter into its process.

Traditional fundamental processes often have quantitative components. In some cases, these quantitative components are blended with traditional fundamental analysis so that the investment process is a fully integrated mixture of the two approaches. In other investment processes, the role of quantitative analysis is to screen securities to be used in a primarily fundamental approach. Stock screens typically serve the purpose to reduce a set of stocks from a large number to a smaller number, resulting in a subset of securities for further fundamental analysis. In this way, quantitative analysis can help improve the efficiency of an investment process by focusing human research and analysis on securities with the most potential for added value within the portfolio. Exhibit 3.2 shows examples of security screening processes from two student investment funds. The first example in Panel A shows a screen used by a student in Southern Methodist University's SMIF to identify stocks

---

Exhibit 3.2 Examples of Stock Screens

Panel A: Southern Methodist University Student's Screening Process

1. To begin the screening process, I first compiled Market Cap, Beta, industry, LT and ST growth rates, PE, dividend yield, and analyst recommendations on all S&P 500 Consumer Staples firms.
   Companies Remaining: 42
2. From Consumer Staples sector averages, I eliminated companies with a PE above the sector average of 14.66.
   Companies Remaining: 22
3. Then I eliminated companies with dividend yields below the sector average of 2.81.
   Companies Remaining: 11
4. Finally, I eliminated companies with an analyst recommendation absolute minimum below "4."

   Companies Remaining: 5

Panel B: University of Houston Screening Parameters
Screening parameters include:

- Market capitalization
- Sector
- Risk metrics
- Discounted Cash Flow model

within the Consumer Staples sector. The screen narrows the sector's 42 stocks to five that the student would then use in further research and analysis. Panel B shows parameters used in the screening process in the University of Houston's student-managed investment fund.

Investment processes that are more heavily tilted to the quantitative side typically seek to rank stocks. The development of ranking models can be complex and time-consuming, requiring significant design and backtesting or historical analysis. For this reason, ranking models may not be as common among student-managed investment funds. Still, ranking models can be a useful tool by themselves, or in combination with traditional fundamental analysis.

The objective in a quantitative ranking model is to sort stocks from "best" to "worst." Ranking along one dimension appears quite simple: rank stocks according to the characteristic of interest. For example, suppose an investor believes in holding the most profitable stocks. The investor would find a source, such as Morningstar or Bloomberg, to determine the profit margin of each company. This list could then be sorted from highest to lowest. Of course, the quantitative analyst must take care to assure that the characteristic is measured consistently among the stocks that are being ranked. Furthermore, since the average measure of a characteristic such as profitability might vary significantly across industries or sectors, perhaps depending on how the measure is defined, ranking might be done only within a suitable set of peers (e.g., industry or sector). Alternatively, the analyst might want to adjust profitability by sector or industry. A popular method to standardize ranking measures is known as a "Z-score."

Z-Score

Suppose peer group (or sector) s has N_s securities as members of that peer group. The Z-score for characteristics c for each security i in the peer group can be calculated as

$$Z_{s,i} = \frac{c_{s,i} - \bar{c}_s}{\sigma_{c_s}}$$

$c_{s,i}$	Characteristic or factor of security i within peer group s.
$\bar{c}_s$	The average of characteristic c in peer group s, where

$$\bar{c}_s = \frac{1}{N_s} \sum_{i=1}^{N_s} c_{s,i}.$$

σ_{c_s}	The standard deviation of characteristics c in peer group s, where

$$\sigma_{c_s} = \sqrt{\frac{1}{N_s - 1} \sum_{i-1}^{N_s} \left(c_{s,i} - \bar{c}_s \right)^2}$$

As shown in the sidebar, the Z-score adjusts for both the mean (i.e., average) and standard deviation (i.e., variation) of a variable. More precisely, the Z-score provides a measure of the number of standard deviations above (positive) or below (negative) the mean for a particular observation. In the case of ranking along a single characteristic, the Z-score adjusts for differences in that characteristic across different subsets, such as industries or sectors. For example, in the case of profit margin, the quantitative analyst might use the Z-score to adjust for the average and standard deviation of the profit margin within each GIC sector. A Z-score of zero would indicate that a company is at the average profit margin for its sector. A Z-score of 1.00 would indicate that the company's profit margin is one standard deviation above its peer-group average and Z-score of −2.50 would indicate that a company's profit margin is 2.50 standard deviations below its peer group average. By standardizing by dividing by the standard deviation, two observations with the same Z-score are equally "extreme" within their peer group.

In general, ranking models attempt to combine multiple factors, characteristics, or dimensions to arrive at an overall ranking of stocks rather than just ranking along one dimension. The Z-score becomes especially important when trying to combine different measures into a single ranking. A common ranking process is to combine different factors by calculating a weighted average of the factors' Z-scores. The use of Z-scores assures that rankings are not disproportionately influenced by the variation (or lack thereof) within a single factor. The weights chosen by the quantitative analyst determine the importance of that factor in the ranking scheme. Exhibit 3.3 shows several examples of security ranking models. Panel A illustrates various weighting schemes and Panel B shows an example of a ranking model's results.

The results of a quantitative ranking model are entirely dependent on the formulaic analysis of data. Small errors in the programming of a spreadsheet or computer model can cause the output of the model to be totally unrelated to what was intended. As such, care must be

Exhibit 3.3 Examples of Quantitative Ranking Models

Panel A: Examples of Weighting Schemes within Ranking Models

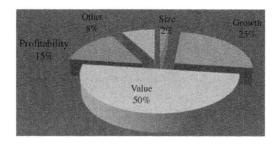

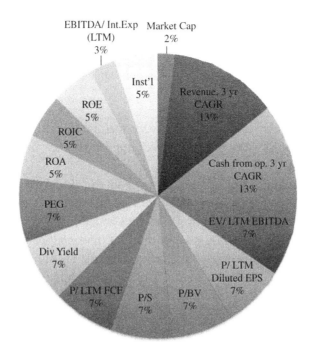

Factor	% Weight
ROE	6.00
ROA	6.00
PM	8.00
Dividend yield	10.00
Best Est. LTG	6.00
3 Yr Sales Average Growth	13.00
P/E	11.00
P/B	11.00
P/S	11.00
Market Cap	18.00

Panel B: Example of Ranking Model Output

Revised Financial Industry Ranking Model Comparables	Value				Growth		Momentum	Efficiency		Size	Score	Rank
	Trailing E/P Z	Forward E/P Z	S/P Z	Book / Price Z	Est. 2-Yr EPS	1m Upward EPS Analyst	12m Mom. Z	NI Margin Z	ROE Z	BV Z		
Hartford Financial Services Group Inc.	1.04	2.35	2.55	1.63	0.20	2.68	(0.22)	(0.12)	0.18	(0.10)	0.90	1
Capital One Financial Corp.	2.25	1.43	(0.04)	0.70	(1.10)	3.22	0.95	0.49	0.47	0.05	0.86	2
Prudential Financial, Inc.	1.16	1.49	1.53	0.71	(0.23)	3.22	0.18	(0.09)	0.39	0.22	0.82	3
Ameriprise Financial Inc.	0.50	1.05	0.15	(0.30)	0.24	2.68	1.79	0.03	0.54	(0.30)	0.79	4
Torchmark Corp.	1.50	1.75	(0.79)	0.09	(0.30)	1.05	0.55	2.34	0.71	(0.46)	0.73	5
Lincoln National Corp.	0.83	2.05	1.09	1.10	0.06	2.13	(0.16)	(0.05)	0.06	(0.27)	0.62	6
Principal Financial Group Inc.	0.43	1.23	0.50	0.36	(0.05)	2.13	0.82	(0.08)	0.07	(0.33)	0.56	8
Citigroup, Inc.	0.64	1.10	(0.20)	0.77	0.45	(0.04)	1.15	0.28	(0.04)	3.24	0.59	7
MetLife, Inc.	0.42	1.77	1.50	0.40	0.02	1.05	0.25	(0.22)	(0.05)	0.56	0.47	10
T. Rowe Price Group, Inc.	(0.38)	(0.09)	(0.82)	(1.43)	0.44	2.13	0.52	0.74	1.60	(0.49)	0.46	11
Wells Fargo & Company	0.46	1.00	(0.29)	(0.33)	0.68	(0.58)	(0.20)	0.30	0.36	2.37	0.25	24
The Goldman Sachs Group, Inc.	0.85	1.54	(0.21)	(0.01)	0.29	(0.58)	(1.05)	0.45	0.45	1.19	0.14	31

taken in checking (and double-checking) the formulas that comprise the model. In addition, the results are critically dependent on the input data. Care must be taken to maintain the quality and integrity of the data. Some common challenges and potential solutions are as follows:

- **Choice of factors.** There are many sources for factors. If an investment process does not have a stated bias toward growth, value, large, small, etc., then a balance of factors would be reasonable.
- **Missing data.** There must be a consistent procedure for handling missing data. When data are missing, many utilize an average for that factor for the security, peer group, or universe, depending on the data item. Be careful when doing this as missing data may be missing for a reason that could be negative and informational. Using the average is most appropriate when the reason for the missing data is unrelated to the actual conditions of the security and due to errors in the data sources.
- **Outliers.** The must be a strategy for dealing with outliers or extreme data points, which may or may not represent errors or inconsistencies in the data. It is sometimes desirable, though not always appropriate, to reduce the influence of outliers or extreme values. A good method for doing so is Winsorization, which sets values beyond the 5th (or 1st) percentile to the 5th (or 1st) percentile value.
- **Data integrity and consistency.** When buy and sell decisions are being made based on data about a stock, it is critical to ensure the data are as accurate as possible. Always double-check your data. Even with large, popular stocks listed in the United States, it is surprising how different data can be from one source to another. Try to find the best source of data and double-check the data when possible. Resolve any inconsistencies within or among sources with as many other sources as possible.
- **Standardization.** Z-scores are a way to deal with variables that are of various scales or magnitudes (see example above).
- **Consistent positives and negatives.** Make sure to score each factor so that the positives and negatives are in the right direction. For example, if high profitability and a low debt ratio are positives, then a highly profitable firm should rank high and a firm with low debt should rank high.
- **Timing of data.** Be sure to measure the data so that they are aligned in time. Since fiscal years are different for each firm, it is often necessary to assemble quarterly financial statements into yearly numbers rather than use fiscal year reports.
- **Weighting.** Decide on a weighting scheme for your factors. If there are no strong prior reasons for differential weighting, decision theory suggests that you should equal weight.
- **Refine the data.** There are too many data available. The key is to choose wisely the data used for the quantitative model.

Security Analysis

Security analysis, also referred to as fundamental analysis, is the key element resulting in security selection for many active investment strategies. Typically, its ultimate purpose is to identify mispriced securities by comparing the intrinsic value of the stock to its market price. As such, security analysis is only relevant in the context of an investment philosophy that articulates a belief that securities are not fairly priced at all times. In other words, security analysis is only relevant within the context of a strategy that seeks to exploit an inefficient market. As a practical matter, the belief that securities can be mispriced is only a necessary condition that motivates the use of security analysis. There must also be a mechanism by which mispricings lead to profits. A sufficient condition that provides for the realization of profits from security analysis is when market prices adjust toward intrinsic values (i.e., the market moves toward efficiency). Therefore, security analysis is often the central value-generating activity of a fundamental active strategy.

Security analysis is part science and part art. Many finance courses spend a substantial amount of time on the science aspect that includes ratio analysis, time value of money calculations, and estimation of the cost of capital and its components. While this chapter reviews some of the relevant science, we devote a substantial amount of time to discussing the role of the art in security analysis, as the art of security analysis is often the distinguishing factor between good and bad security selection. We note, however, that art by its nature is not subject to formulaic approaches or clearly identifiable steps that, when followed, will always lead to masterpieces. Rather, the art in security analysis resides in the creative choices, assumptions, or estimates that must be made to apply the science. The art arises because the science requires quantities from the future, such as future earnings, as inputs. As such, the art involves making calculated estimates about unknown quantities and often requires the analyst to quantify something that represents a subjective judgment.

Security analysis is a necessarily broad term and admits many specific methods. As such, we can consider security analysis to be a toolbox that holds many different tools. We cover below various tools or approaches and note how each is typically used. As with other chapters, we provide the basic theoretical motivation for the tools, but emphasize the practical application of these tools within the context of a student-managed investment fund. We provide an extended example from Texas Christian University's Educational Investment Fund at the end of the chapter to further illustrate the application of many of the tools discussed herein. In addition, the appendix to this chapter contains excerpts from *Analysts, Lies and Statistics* that discuss the role analysts play and information about some of the key financial information on which analysts make estimates. The Appendix is intended to provide valuable context to student-managed investment fund analysts who struggle with the same issues as Wall Street analysts.

Company Analysis

Before proceeding to the quantitative aspects of security analysis, it is important to recognize that a substantial part of security analysis is of a more qualitative nature, which we refer to as company analysis. Company analysis provides the context for the financial information and analysis that makes up the bulk of this chapter. Without this context, it is impossible to have a meaningful understanding of the business that generates the financial information. Revenues, costs, and capital expenditures, which will play key roles in the following valuation discussion, differ in character from industry to industry and business to business. It is the security analyst's job to know not only the numbers but also the story behind the numbers. In short, the analyst must know the company.

Company analysis involves researching any and all aspects of a company that affect its success, from its products and services to its leadership team. A key part of this research focuses on identifying sources of sustainable competitive advantages or value. That is, the company analysis aims to determine the key aspects of the firm's business that are likely to generate value.

The approach to analyzing the company depends on the investment philosophy and process. For example, in a top-down process that begins by identifying themes in the overall economy that represent investment opportunities, the role of company analysis is to first identify companies that are likely candidates to contribute to those economic themes. If there is a view that the market for new houses is about to boom, the analyst might make a list of all firms that are directly affected by such a boom and then a list of all firms that are indirectly but significantly affected by such a boom. In a bottom-up investment process, the analysts might seek an understanding of each company and its opportunities or risks.

Company analysis should also follow a process in terms of systematically developing an understanding of a firm's business. One approach might be to research a company from the standpoint of its financial statements. This approach is not necessarily concerned with specific numbers on the financial statements, but is concerned with the sources of those numbers. From the income statement, the analyst might start with the top line to determine the sources of the firm's revenues, answering questions such as, "Who are the firm's customers?," "What are the firm's major business/product segments?," "Where (in the world or in the country) are sales made?," "When (both in time and in economic conditions) are sales made?" In short, this aspect of company analysis concerns itself with the firm's marketing, sales, and distribution strategy. This might involve research on the firm's target market or current customer base. As will be seen later in this chapter, of particular concern here will be the opportunity for revenue growth. Therefore, the analyst would want to understand such opportunities and how the company is positioned to realize them. This often involves an analysis of the firm's position relative to competitors and an understanding of those competitors' businesses.

Moving down the income statement, the analyst would ask similar questions about the firm's costs and expenses throughout the production chain, including those about suppliers, opportunities to achieve cost efficiencies, or risks of increasing costs. Finally, the analyst might turn to the balance sheet and determine the strategy the firm uses to manage its assets and liabilities. Of particular importance is the firm's investment in assets and technology to help it increase its profits. Outside of the financial statements, analysts typically try to understand who the executives of the firm are and what strategy they have for the future of the firm. After all, the assets of the firm belong to the shareholders and the executive team is entrusted with managing those assets. Potential shareholders should understand who they are "hiring" to manage their assets when they purchase stock.

In some sense, company analysis is the qualitative side of security analysis. As such, it is the least technical aspect of security analysis. Student-managed investment funds can utilize student analysts who have had less exposure to accounting and finance courses to undertake basic company research and analysis and contribute such an understanding of the firm to a team in which others focus on the more technical or quantitative aspects.

A Good Company Versus a Good Investment

A good company is not the same thing as a good investment. Some people think that successful investing or stock picking is all about finding good companies. However, this seemingly commonsense approach ignores a simple fact: To earn a profit, an investor must not overpay for a stock. In other words, *price* and *value* are not necessarily the same things. The discussion that follows focuses on determining the value of a company and its stock.

There may be times when market participants "fall in love" with a company, its products, or its characteristics and bid its stock price up. While the market might be "right" that the company, its products, or its characteristics are very good, those who buy into the stock at a price above its true or intrinsic value are less likely to realize the expected benefits or profits from such a purchase. Conversely, there may be companies that fall out of favor in the market − a company whose stock price is beat down beyond what is justified. For example, this might happen to companies that suffer a scandal, a product liability claim, or simply bad press. Even if such a company might not be considered a "good company" by some measure, its market price might represent such a discount to its intrinsic value that it is a good stock.

We raise the point about a good company versus a good investment (or good stock) because there appear to be some who do not understand or appreciate this truth. Successful business-people understand it. Good investments are those that are worth more than the price paid for them. Whether or not a stock is a good investment depends on whether the value of the stock is greater than its current price within the context of the investment philosophy and process.

The following discussion reviews the underlying financial theory regarding the intrinsic value of a firm and provides tips for developing practical valuation models.

In focusing on the intrinsic value of the future cash flows of the stock or the firm as criteria for security selection, the discussion implicitly assumes that a stock's price and its intrinsic value can be different. That is, we implicitly assume that the market might not be efficient in that the price may not reflect the information used in the analysis. This assumption may not be consistent with every investment managers' investment philosophy. However, this implicit assumption is common among active managers who engage in security selection.

Valuation

Our discussion of valuation reviews the theory and application of several important valuation models. The common element among all valuation models is that they begin with the same first principle: The value of any asset is the present value of its future cash flows. That is, the scientific aspect of determining the intrinsic value of a stock is as simple as discounting the future cash flows from the stock. If its future cash flows and the appropriate discount rate are known, then the value of the stock is determined by the application of a time value of money principles. We start with this simple abstraction even though it relies on the naive notion that future cash flows are known.

We first review the Dividend Discount Model, which uses dividends paid to the company's shareholders as the key cash flow paid by a stock. Beyond its usefulness in its own right, the Dividend Discount Model offers an important conceptual framework upon which we will base the other models. We next discuss the DCF approach using the firm's cash flows that are available to equity-holders. This model considers the cash flows to the entire firm and, therefore, models the value of the entire firm. The company's stock represents the residual value available to equity shareholders after all senior claims, such as those of bondholders, are paid. Finally, we discuss the use of earnings or earnings per share as a measure of cash flow. While not technically a cash flow, the use of earnings in firm valuations has its virtues, primarily from a practical standpoint. We conclude this chapter with a discussion of commonly cited valuation metrics. Specifically, we emphasize the link between these metrics and the valuation models.

Dividend Discount Model

If an investor buys a stock and holds it indefinitely, the investors derives value from the stock's stream of dividends. The Dividend Discount Model (DDM), also known as the Gordon Growth Model, formalizes the valuation of a stock as follows.

Suppose a stock will pay dividend of D_1 a year from now. Subsequent dividends will grow at a rate of g_D and investors demand a required return of k_E. Today's price of the stock, V_0^{DDM}, is equal to the present value of this constant growth in perpetuity, given as

$$V_0^{DDM} = \frac{D_1}{k_E - g_D} \tag{3.1}$$

The assumptions underlying this valuation model seem to be quite restrictive. For starters, the model implicitly assumes that a stock currently pays dividends. Therefore, its use seems limited to only those stocks that currently pay dividends. Furthermore, the explicit assumption that dividends will grow at a constant rate in perpetuity seems almost certain to be violated for nearly every stock. Fortunately, the model's usefulness is not as restrictive as it might seem.

A more general form of the Dividend Discount Model allows for any pattern of dividends throughout time. In this case, the value of a stock today is just the infinite sum of all future dividends, as given by:

$$V_0^{DDM} = \sum_{t=1}^{\infty} \frac{D_t}{(1+k_E)^t} \tag{3.2}$$

or

$$V_0^{DDM} = \frac{D_1}{(1+k_E)} + \frac{D_2}{(1+k_E)^2} + \frac{D_3}{(1+k_E)^3} + \cdots + \frac{D_t}{(1+k_E)^t} + \frac{D_{t+1}}{(1+k_E)^{t+1}} + \cdots \tag{3.3}$$

Note that, by specifying D_1, D_2, D_3, etc., we are implicitly assuming these dividends must be individually forecast. Equations 3.1, 3.2, and 3.3 are equally "correct" from a theoretical perspective. However, applying this theory of valuation to practice requires either an assumption of constant growth rate for all future dividends (for equation 3.1), or a year-by-year forecast of all future dividends (for equation 3.2 or 3.3). Good security analysis balances the need for tractability and simplicity with the desire to capture critical details and complexities. Fortunately, the DDM's flexibility allows the analyst to balance such interests.

Before proceeding, we consider that the constant growth formula from equation 3.1 is relevant at any point in time after which dividends grow at a constant rate. In other words, if dividends grow at a constant rate g_D starting at time t, then the price at time t can be calculated using the constant growth of a perpetuity formula, given by:

$$V_t^{DDM} = \frac{D_{t+1}}{k_E - g_D} = \frac{D_t(1 + g_D)}{k_E - g_D} \tag{3.4}$$

Note that D_{t+1} appears in both equation 3.3 and 3.4. Indeed, if all dividends grow at a constant rate subsequent to time t, we can rewrite equation 3.3 as:

$$V_0^{DDM} = \frac{D_1}{(1+k_E)} + \frac{D_2}{(1+k_E)^2} + \cdots + \frac{D_{t-1}}{(1+k_E)^{t-1}} + \frac{D_t + V_t^{DDM}}{(1+k_E)^t} \qquad (3.5)$$

In this way, we now need only make forecasts of individual dividends between now and time t and then assume a constant growth rate of dividends beyond time t. Indeed, this version of the DDM, often referred to as the multistage Dividend Discount Model, allows for any pattern of dividends over the short term (even admitting the case of no dividends, where $D_1 = D_2 = 0$) and allows a simplifying assumption to be made about the level and growth rate of longer term dividends. That is, dividends D_1, D_2, D_3, ... in the near-term future periods, such as the next several years, can be individually forecast. Beyond those first few years, dividends can be assumed to grow at a constant rate, often referred to as the terminal growth rate. Those dividends get summarized into a single value or price according to equation 3.3, which we refer to as the terminal value. Together, the dividends and terminal value get discounted to the present according to equation 3.4.

Finally, we note that we have used the precise and seemingly restrictive language of referring to g as the constant growth rate of dividends. This need not be the only interpretation of g within this dividend discount model of valuation. In practice, we can consider g as the future *average* growth rate of dividends and still be precisely accurate and consistent with the theory.

In summary, the security analyst can value stocks using the DDM by applying the following steps:

Steps to Using the Multistage Dividend Discount Model

1. Forecast each year's dividend over the near term (e.g., the next 5 years).
2. Estimate an average terminal growth rate of dividends beyond the near future (e.g., beyond the next 5 years).
3. Estimate the appropriate discount rate for the stock.
4. Discount the dividends in step 2 to find the terminal value of the stock at the beginning of the terminal growth stage.
5. Discount the terminal value and the dividends during the abnormal growth stage to find the intrinsic value of the stock.

These steps are easily implemented or modeled using an Excel spreadsheet, as shown in the example in Exhibit 3.4. The exhibit distinguishes between cells that are inputs and those that are calculated. It is common practice to estimate the required return to equity (i.e., the firm's cost of equity capital) using a model of the fair expected return, such as the Capital

Exhibit 3.4 Example of Dividend Discount Model in Excel

Assumptions, Estimates, and Forecasts
1. Stock will pay a dividend of $0.60 next year.
2. The dividends per share over the following four years will be: $0.80 in two years; $0.96 in three years; $1.08 in four years; and $1.16 in five years.
3. The terminal growth rate will be 4% per year, starting after five years.
4. The discount rate will be calculated using the Capital Asset Pricing Model.
5. The risk-free rate is 3.5% per year.
6. The market risk premium is 5.50% per year.
7. The stock's beta, calculated from the last five years of monthly returns, is 0.92.

	A	B	C	D
1	**Dividend Discount Model**			
2	Risk Free Rate	3.50%		
3	Market Risk Premium	5.50%		
4	Equity Beta	0.92		
5	Required Return on Equity	8.56%		=B2+B4*B3
6				
7	Terminal Growth Rate	4.00%		
8				
9	Year	Dividend per Share ($)	Terminal Value ($)	
10	1	0.60		
11	2	0.80		
12	3	0.96		
13	4	1.08		
14	5	1.16	26.46	=B14*(1+B7)/(B5-B7)
15				
16	Year	Present Value ($)		
17	1	0.55		=(B10+C10)/(1+$B$5)^A17
18	2	0.68		=(B11+C11)/(1+$B$5)^A18
19	3	0.75		=(B12+C12)/(1+$B$5)^A19
20	4	0.78		=(B13+C13)/(1+$B$5)^A20
21	5	18.32		=(B14+C14)/(1+$B$5)^A21
22				
23	Intrinsic Value per Share ($)	21.07		=SUM(B17:B21)
24				
25	Inputs	Calculated		
26				

Asset Pricing Model (CAPM). Of course, the CAPM requires inputs of the risk-free rate, the market risk premium, and the stock's beta. The inputs should match the horizon of the model. Because the DDM values an infinite stream of future dividends, the risk-free rate and market risk premium are based on a long-term historical average of these values. There are numerous methods for estimating the beta of the firm's equity. If using historical data for the estimate, the analyst must decide on the horizon (e.g., 3, 5, 10, etc. years) for the data, frequency of the data (e.g., daily, weekly, monthly, etc.), and the market proxy (e.g., S&P 500, all U.S. stocks, all world) stocks. We note that a student-managed investment fund, and indeed any investment organization, should agree on these issues, as the required return model and its parameters should be the consistent across the analysis of every firm, since these are not firm-specific measures. That is, the risk-free rate and market risk premium assumption for one stock should be the same as those of every other stock, regardless of the analyst using the model. Otherwise, the results of the analysis are not comparable or compatible across analysts.

A correctly programmed spreadsheet model will perform these calculations flawlessly. However, the old adage applies: Garbage in, garbage out. In other words, the model's output is only as good as its inputs or assumptions. The inputs of the model shown in the exhibit must be estimated or forecasted by the analyst. Herein is the "part science, part art" aspect of security analysis. The science of the model requires forecasts of variables that are inherently unknown with any certainty. Therefore, analysts must develop their skills in the art of making forecasts and estimates of these inputs.

The DDM is deceptively simple when it comes to making estimates or forecasts of its inputs. Indeed, for a stock that currently pays a dividend, it appears that the dividend is effectively known with certainty. While it may be the case that a company's current dividend is known, a key issue is whether this known dividend currently reflects a large portion of the source of value from holding the stock. This issue is best understood by considering the source of a firm's dividends. In general, the source of a company's dividends is the company's earnings or profits. When the firm earns a profit, it has two choices as to what to do with those earnings: (1) it can pay the earnings out to shareholders as a return on the shareholders' capital; or (2) it can retain those earnings, effectively reinvesting them in the company. For a stock to be valuable, capital must eventually be returned to shareholders. Indeed, the stock of a company that never returns cash to its shareholders is worth nothing. Therefore, retained earnings must be paid back to shareholders eventually. In this sense, retained earnings can be thought of as capital that is reinvested on behalf of shareholders for the purpose of delivering a higher rate of return – or a higher rate of growth – when the capital is eventually returned. This highlights the importance of considering the dividend payout ratio when performing security analysis using the DDM.

The dividend payout ratio is calculated as the ratio of the per-share dividend paid to the per-share earnings of the company. The ratio indicates what proportion of the firm's capital is paid out to shareholders, with the remainder being what proportion is retained. In some cases, a low payout ratio might be considered good or desirable, as it might reflect the fact that a firm has valuable growth opportunities for which it needs to reinvest its earnings. Indeed, as is covered in many corporate finance courses, earnings could represent a relatively low-cost source of capital for the firm. A growing firm might benefit its shareholders by reinvesting earnings in high-return activities in order to pay out larger dividends in the future.

For companies in some industries or sectors, such as utilities or REITs, the payout ratio is typically a high proportion of earnings. For others, the ratio might be quite low. For those firms in which the dividend payout ratio is high, the dividends might be expected to grow at the same rate as the firm's earnings. Therefore, the security analyst might forecast the long-term average growth rate of the firm's earnings and assume that the dividends will grow at the same rate, implicitly assuming that the payout ratio will remain the same. For companies with low payout ratios, there is capacity for the stock's dividend to grow substantially, even if the earnings of the company do not grow. This implies that the growth rate can play a relatively larger role in the DDM for a stock with a low payout ratio than for a stock with a higher payout ratio, holding all other things constant. For these stocks, the security analyst must forecast the growth rate of earnings *and* the change (and its timing) in the payout ratio in order to forecast the growth in future dividends. In this way, there may be more uncertainty surrounding the DDM valuation for stocks that have low payout ratios. In the extreme circumstance of a company that does not currently pay a dividend, the DDM provides a particular challenge because of the added uncertainty surrounding the forecast of the timing and amount of the initial dividend. While we just described this as an "extreme circumstance," we note that it is hardly uncommon, as only 50.7% of the stocks in the Russell 3000 Index and only 22.6% of all U.S. actively traded stocks paid dividends in 2012, according to Bloomberg.

Discounted Cash Flow Model

The Dividend Discount Model considers the cash flows that accrue directly to the shareholder of a firm's stock in the form of dividends. An alternative method of valuing the stock of a company is to value the entire firm and then determine the amount of that value on which equity shareholders have a claim. We refer to this model as the Discounted Cash Flow (DCF) model or the Free Cash Flow model, because it discounts the firm's future free cash flows to determine the intrinsic value of the firm available to equity holders. The time-value-of-money calculations in the DCF model are nearly identical to those in the DDM. However, we replace the forecast of dividends with a forecast of the firm's total free cash flows. Another subtle difference is that the resulting present value reflects the value available to all of the firm's claimholders. Recognizing that equity holders represent residual claimants, we must first subtract the value of the firm's debt in order to determine the value of the firm's stock, accounting for the number of shares outstanding.

We derive the DCF model in a similar manner as we developed the calculations of the DDM. We begin by considering the stream of future cash flows available to an infinitely lived firm. The cash flow in year t is forecast to be FCF_t. Because we are valuing the entire firm and not just considering the value of the firm's equity, the weighted average cost of capital, denoted by k_{WACC}, represents the appropriate discount rate for the time-value-of-money calculations. The total value of the firm is just the present value of the infinite stream of cash flows, as given by:

$$V_0^{DCF} = \frac{FCF_1}{(1+k_{WACC})} + \frac{FCF_2}{(1+k_{WACC})^2} + \cdots + \frac{FCF_t}{(1+k_{WACC})^t} + \cdots \tag{3.6}$$

Notice the similarities between equations 3.6 and 3.3. As with the Dividend Discount Model, some simplifying assumptions are necessary to make this model tractable, since it would otherwise require the security analyst to forecast an infinite number of inputs. If we assume that free cash flows grow at terminal growth rate g_{FCF} beyond time t, then we can utilize the valuation formula for a constantly growing perpetuity. We reflect the value of all dividends beyond time t in a terminal value at time t as:

$$V_t^{DCF} = \frac{FCF_t(1+g_{FCF})}{k_{WACC} - g_{FCF}} \tag{3.7}$$

Equation 3.6 can be restated to create a multistage version of the DCF model, given by:

$$V_0^{DCF} = \frac{FCF_1}{(1+k_{WACC})} + \frac{FCF_2}{(1+k_{WACC})^2} + \cdots + \frac{FCF_{t-1}}{(1+k_{WACC})^{t-1}} + \frac{FCF_t + V_t^{DCF}}{(1+k_{WACC})^t} \tag{3.8}$$

Just as with the Dividend Discount Model, the multistage DCF model allows the analyst to forecast near-term year-by-year cash flows and then summarize the long-term cash flows through an assumed constant average terminal growth rate, resulting in a terminal value. An analyst can easily implement such calculations in an Excel spreadsheet, as shown in the example in Exhibit 3.5. Note that equation 3.8 results in a calculation of the intrinsic value of the overall firm. This valuation should be useful for both bond and stock analysts. Bond analysts could determine whether the company's value exceeds the value of the firm's debt. Equity analysts could use this model to determine the residual value of the firm, after debt holders are paid. To do so, the market value of the firm's debt can be subtracted from the firm value V_0^{DCF} to get the total value of the firm available to equity holders, V_0^{DCF}. Finally, the intrinsic per-share value of the firm can be determined by dividing V_0^{DCF} by the number of shares outstanding.

Steps to Using the Multistage Discounted Cash Flow Model

1. Forecast each year's cash flow over the near-term (e.g., the next 5 years).
2. Estimate an average terminal growth rate of cash flows beyond the near-term (e.g., beyond the next 5 years).

Exhibit 3.5 Example of Free Cash Flow to Equity Model in Excel

Assumptions, Estimates, and Forecasts

1. Stock will pay a dividend of $0.60 next year.
2. The dividends per share over the following four years will be: $0.80 in two years; $0.96 in three years; $1.08 in four years; and $1.16 in five years.
3. The terminal growth rate will be 4% per year, starting after five years.
4. The discount rate will be calculated using the Capital Asset Pricing Model.
5. The risk-free rate is 3.5% per year.
6. The market risk premium is 5.50% per year.
7. The stock's beta, calculated from the last five years of monthly returns is 0.92.

	A	B	C	D
1	Free Cash Flow to Equity Model			
2	Risk Free Rate	3.50%		
3	Market Risk Premium	5.50%		
4	Equity Beta	0.92		
5	Cost of Equity	8.56%		=B2+B4*B3
6				
7	Yield Spread on Firm Debt	1.20%		
8	Pre-Tax Cost of Debt	4.70%		=B2+B7
9	Effective Tax Rate	30%		
10	After-Tax Cost of Debt	3.29%		=B8*(1-B9)
11				
12	Market Value of Debt ($)	500,000,000		
13	Market Value of Equity ($)	4,306,000,000		
14				
15	Wtd Avg Cost of Capital	8.01%		=(B13/(B12+B13))*B5+(B12/(B12+B13))*B10
16				
17	Terminal Growth Rate	3.00%		
18				
19	Year	Free Cash Flow ($)	Terminal Value ($)	
20	1	240,000,000		
21	2	260,000,000		
22	3	280,000,000		
23	4	300,000,000		
24	5	320,000,000	5,928,057,554	=B24*(1+B17)/(B5-B17)
25				
26	Year	Present Value ($)		
27	1	221,075,903		=(B20+C20)/(1+$B$5)^A27
28	2	220,614,310		=(B21+C21)/(1+$B$5)^A28
29	3	218,850,996		=(B22+C22)/(1+$B$5)^A29
30	4	215,994,114		=(B23+C23)/(1+$B$5)^A30
31	5	4,143,771,968		=(B24+C24)/(1+$B$5)^A31
32				
33	Intrinsic Firm Value ($)	5,020,307,290		=SUM(B27:B31)
34	Intrinsic Value of Equity ($)	4,799,231,387		=SUM(B28:B32)
35	Shares Outstanding	190,000,000		
36				
37	**Intrinsic Value per Share ($)**	**25.26**		=B34/B35
38				
39	Inputs	Calculated		

3. Estimate the firm's weighted average cost of capital to be used as the discount rate.
4. Discount the cash flows in step 2 to find the terminal value of the firm at the beginning of the terminal growth stage.
5. Discount the terminal value and the cash flows during the abnormal growth stage to find the intrinsic value of the firm.
6. Estimate the market value of the firm's debt.
7. Subtract the market value of the firm's debt from the intrinsic value of the firm to get the intrinsic value of the firm's equity.
8. Divide the intrinsic value of the firm's equity by the shares outstanding to find the intrinsic per-share value of the firm's stock.

We illustrate these steps in Exhibit 3.5. Note that the DCF model requires more inputs and more steps than the DDM model in Exhibit 3.4. In particular, the calculation of the discount rate, the weighted average cost of capital (WACC), to be applied to the firm's cash flows requires both the cost of equity and cost of debt. The cost of equity follows the same approach of relying on the Capital Asset Pricing Model beta for the stock and the assumptions of the risk-free rate and market risk premium. In addition, the weighted average cost of capital utilizes the required return on the firm's debt. To get the required return on the firm's debt, there are at least two approaches. The first approach is to simply find the average yield to maturity on the firm's existing long-term debt. Alternatively, the yield spread on the firm's debt can be used and added to the risk-free rate. The latter approach has the benefit of utilizing a long-term measure of the cost of debt rather than one that is possibly influenced by abnormally high or low current interest rates. The final ingredient to calculating the WACC is the firm's mix of equity and debt. The example has an implicit assumption that the firm is currently at its optimal or long-term average capital structure. As such, it uses the current market value of the firm's equity and debt in the WACC calculation. An alternative approach would be to forecast and specify the firm's long-term target capital structure directly for this calculation. The Excel formulas that calculate the terminal value and the present values are identical to the DDM, given the inputs.

The security analyst must do a bit more research in order to implement the DCF model, as it requires the use of the firm's financial statements to calculate cash flows. In theory, cash flow is a straightforward measure of the change in a firm's cash over a period of time, accounting for all of the sources and uses of that cash. In practice, cash flow can have several different, but related, definitions. Each measure has its usefulness in specific applications. Because the DCF model is valuing the entire firm, it is useful to consider the cash flows independent of the firm's source of capital or its capital structure decisions, which could affect the overall cash flow. For this model, the common method of measuring a cash flow to the firm is the after-tax value of earnings before interest and taxes (EBIT), plus depreciation, minus capital expenditures and changes to working capital. This method of calculating cash flow reflects the operating cash flows to the firm because it begins with EBIT rather than using net income. While it might seem that this valuation gives no tax credit for an interest expense, we note that the tax benefit of debt is already reflected in the after-tax cost of debt component of the weighted average cost of capital. We add back the non-cash component of EBIT, depreciation, but subtract capital expenditures and changes to working capital. In doing so, free cash flow to the firm reflects that amount of cash the firm earns during a period, net of the cash it spends to assure the company's ongoing ability to conduct business.

Free Cash Flow to the Firm Calculation

$$FCF = EBIT \times (1 - t) + Depr - CapEx - \Delta WC$$

FCF	Free cash flow to the firm
EBIT	Earnings before interest and taxes
t	Marginal tax rate
Depr	Depreciation
CapEx	Capital expenditures
ΔWC	Changes or investments in working capital

The approach that the security analyst takes to making forecasts of the free cash flow to the firm can vary from analyst to analyst. At one extreme of sophistication (or, at least, complexity), the analyst might make forecasts of the components of every aspect of DCF, starting with the top-line revenue forecast, proceeding to the costs and its driving factors, and finishing with the ongoing capital investment needs of the firm. Each item might be subject to different influences. For example, the firm's revenues might depend on its product development plans and its competitive position in the product markets. The costs for one firm might be highly variable depending on quantities sold and/or on commodity prices, while another firm might have a high degree of operating leverage. The firm's capital investment plan might influence both costs and revenues. These forecasts might be made at the geographical, market segment, and/or product level. Clearly, a detailed model of a conglomerate has the potential to be quite elaborate. At the other extreme, an analyst might consider recent years' free cash flows to form the baseline to which future year's cash flow growth is applied. Analysis anywhere between the elaborate, complex model and the baseline model exists.

Two analysts (or analysts from two firms or student-managed investment funds) can both conduct valuation using a DCF model, yet apply the model in substantially different methods. Indeed, the differences are likely to depend on the differences in the investment philosophy and represent differences in the investment process. Whether the elaborate, the baseline, or some approach in between is the best depends many factors. The superiority of one over the other is impossible to establish. The usefulness is likely to depend on the type and structure of the firm's business, the quality of information available about the firm, and the analyst's ability. We caution that a higher level of complexity does not always lead to a higher level of accuracy. Making forecasts of the components of EBIT, for example, requires many different forecasts to be made. If each forecast is made with error, then the errors could compound each other in a way that is not readily apparent. On the other hand, if the forecast errors are independent of one another, then they might average out.

Free Cash Flow to Equity Model

A variant on the Discounted Cash Flow model is the Free Cash Flow to Equity (FCFE) model. As its name suggests, the FCFE model discounts future cash flows to equity holders, taking into account receipt of cash from or payment of cash to debt holders. Specifically, the free cash flow to equity starts with net income, which is the earnings available to shareholders after interest and taxes have been paid. Just as in the total free cash flow calculation, depreciation and amortization are added back because they are non-cash charges that decreased the net income. Likewise, investments in working capital (additions to current assets and decreases to liabilities) are subtracted out as uses of cash. Finally, new issues of debt less debt repaid is added to the cash available to equity holders. The sidebar shows the calculation of the free cash flow to equity, which can be compared with free cash flow to the firm calculation in the earlier sidebar.

We note that the free cash flows to equity account for the portion of cash flows that are to be paid to debt holders (via the interest expense) and are discounted by the required return on equity. As such, the FCFE mode results in the intrinsic value of the firm that is claimed by equity holders. Given consistent measurement of the inputs to the DCF and the FCFE models, they should result in the same valuations for the firm. Therefore, one or the other model is commonly chosen by a security analyst. We note, however, that the DCF model may be more appropriate in the analysis of the firm's debt and equity, as it provides for the overall firm value available to all security holders.

Sidebar: Free Cash Flow to Equity Calculation

$$FCFE = NI + Depr - CapEx - \Delta WC + \Delta Debt$$

FCFE	Free cash flow to equity
NI	Net income
Depr	Depreciation
CapEx	Capital expenditures
ΔWC	Changes or investments in working capital
$\Delta Debt$	Net new borrowing

Steps to Using the Free Cash Flow to Equity Model

1. Forecast each year's free cash flow to equity over the near term (e.g., the next 5 years).
2. Estimate an average terminal growth rate of free cash flows beyond the near term (e.g., beyond the next 5 years).
3. Estimate the firm's required return on equity.
4. Discount the cash flows in step 2 to find the terminal value of the firm at the beginning of the terminal growth stage.
5. Discount the terminal value and the cash flows during the abnormal growth stage to find the intrinsic value of the firm's equity.
6. Divide the intrinsic value of the firm's equity by the shares outstanding to find the intrinsic per-share value of the firm's stock.

Valuation Using Earnings

An earnings-based valuation model can be considered middle ground between the Dividend Discount Model and a Discounted Cash Flow model, such as the Free Cash Flow to Equity model. The earnings approach, which we will call the Earnings Model, focuses on the value of the firm's equity (or price per share), just as the DDM does. Like the FCFE model, the Earnings Model considers the intrinsic value deriving from the firm's ongoing business, not just from the cash flows paid out to shareholders. Indeed, under certain assumptions the Earnings Model is equivalent to the FCFE model. We consider the Earnings Model in its basic form for both simplicity and to show how common practical valuation metrics are derived from valuation principles.

The Earnings Model considers the relevant cash flow in a discounted cash flow model to the earnings (or earnings per share) of the firm, discounted to the present using the required return on the firm's equity. As such, the growth rates used in the model refer to the growth rate in the firm's earnings. The steps to calculate the intrinsic value of the firm's equity follow the derivations for both the DDM and DCF as shown in the above equations. The resulting Earnings Model value of the firm's stock, given earnings per share each period, a terminal growth rate of earnings g_E, and the required return on the firm's equity is given by:

$$V_0^E = \frac{E_1}{(1 + k_E)} + \frac{E_2}{(1+k_E)^2} + \cdots + \frac{E_{t-1}}{(1+k_E)^{t-1}} + \frac{E_t + V_t^E}{(1+k_E)^t}, \text{ where} \tag{3.9}$$

$$V_t^E = \frac{E_t(1 + g_E)}{k_E - g_E} \tag{3.10}$$

Just as in the DDM and DCF models, the Earnings Model requires the analyst to make forecasts of the key variables used in the analysis. Specifically, the analyst must forecast the amount and timing of earnings, their growth over time, and the discount rate appropriate to the firm's equity. For completeness, we list the steps of for using the Earnings Model of stock valuation below.

Steps to Using the Earnings Model

1. Forecast each year's earnings over the near term (e.g., the next 5 years).
2. Estimate an average terminal growth rate of earnings beyond the near term (e.g., beyond the next 5 years).
3. Estimate the firm's cost of equity capital to be used as the discount rate.
4. Discount the earnings in step 2 to find the terminal value of the stock at the beginning of the terminal growth stage.
5. Discount the terminal value and the earnings during the abnormal growth stage to find the intrinsic value of the firm's stock.

As with the Discounted Cash Flow and Free Cash Flow to Equity models, the forecast of the earnings can apply short- and long-term growth forecasts to baseline earnings based on the current year's earnings or an average of recent past years' earnings and apply short- and long-term growth forecasts. Alternatively, the Earnings Model's application can be more complex and detailed by building earnings forecasts from estimates of the various components of earnings. Of course, earnings forecasts rely on similar research and analysis that goes into the Discounted Cash Flow model and vice versa. As such, these models should result in consistent intrinsic values, assuming that the inputs and forecasts are consistent with one another. Indeed, the Earnings Model and the Discounted Cash Flow model will yield the same result if the market value of debt is calculated accurately and the after-tax value of the firm's depreciation is equal to value of the firm's capital expenditures over time. The interested reader can prove this algebraically by solving for the conditions that set the intrinsic value of equity in the Earnings Model equal to the intrinsic value of equity in the Discounted Cash Flow model.

Market Valuation Measures

Rather than modeling the value of the firm using the Discounted Cash Flow to Equity, Dividend Discount Model, or Earnings Model, some analysts utilize market valuation measures to judge a stock's valuation relative to other stocks. Indeed, the above discussion focuses on absolute measures of valuation and ignores the pragmatic view that portfolio management is often an exercise in relative judgments: one stock's valuation relative to another stock's valuation. Market valuation ratios, such as Price-to-Earnings (P/E), Price-to-Cash Flow (P/CF), and Price-to-Book (P/B) serve as valuable tools in judging such relative values. These measures are motivated by the valuation models discussed above. As such, market valuation ratios provide yet another tool for use in security analysis.

Price-to-Earnings

The most popular market valuation measure is the price-to-earnings ratio, often just referred to as the P/E. The P/E is best interpreted within the context of the Earnings Model. To facilitate the interpretation, we consider the simplification of the EM in which we have a forecast of next year's earnings, E, which are expected to subsequently grow at a constant rate g. Therefore, we can rewrite equation 3.9 simply as:

$$V_0^E = \frac{E_0(1 + g_E)}{k_E - g_E} \tag{3.11}$$

Before proceeding, we adapt our notation to emphasize that the remainder of the analysis will be used to infer the market's forecast of the inputs into the EM. Consider variables with "hats" to be the market's forecast of the variable, so that $\hat{k}$ is the market-determined discount rate, $\hat{g}$ is the market's forecasted long-term growth rate, and P_0 is the market price for the stock. We rewrite equation 3.10 as:

$$P_0 = \frac{E_0(1 + \hat{g})}{\hat{k} - \hat{g}} \tag{3.12}$$

To obtain the P/E ratio, we simply divide both sides of equation 3.12 by the earnings per share, to get:

$$\frac{P_0}{E_0} = \frac{(1 + \hat{g})}{\hat{k} - \hat{g}} \tag{3.13}$$

Equation 3.13 shows that the P/E ratio reflects the market's forecast of the growth rate of earnings and the required return on the firm's equity. In other words, the market is willing to pay more per dollar of earnings when it forecasts a higher growth rate of earnings and/or when it has a lowered required return on the firm's stock. The higher the expected growth, the higher the P/E ratio is, holding the required return on equity constant.

Equation 3.13 illustrates that the P/E ratio can also be thought of as a time-value-of-money multiplier that is applied to a year's earnings to determine the present value of a growing stream of earnings. Simply put, the required rate of return and growth rate combine to determine the P/E. Any terminal value that is calculated in equation 3.10 of an Earnings Model could be considered as the last year's earnings multiplied by some future P/E ratio that represents the appropriate combination of required return and long-term growth rate in earnings. As such, analysts can check their long-term growth forecasts and required return assumptions against the average market P/E for similar stocks. An analyst should question any forecast of a terminal growth rate relative to the required return that results in too high of a P/E compared to what is typical in the market.

Equation 3.13 is also useful when comparing the valuation of two stocks with similar characteristics. For example, stocks from the same industry or sub-sector might be assumed to have the same cost of equity capital. Assuming the same $\hat{k}$, the stock with the higher P/E ratio is the stock that has higher long-term growth prospects according to the market's expectation. The security analyst who evaluates these two companies might have a different view of which company has the better growth prospects, making one company appear undervalued relative to the other. In the case in which the security analysts shares the consensus of the market as to which stock has the higher growth prospects, then the issue of which stock represents the better relative value is less clear.

The security analyst who has a good forecast of the required return on equity can rearrange equation 3.13 to determine the market's implied long-term growth forecast of a stock, as given by:

$$\hat{g} = \frac{\frac{P_0}{E_0}\hat{k} - 1}{1 + \frac{P_0}{E_0}} \qquad (3.14)$$

By comparing the growth estimate from equation 3.14 with her own long-term growth estimate, the analyst can judge whether the market is too optimistic or pessimistic about a firm's future long-term growth. That is, rather than arriving at a price estimate for the firm, the analyst need only forecast the growth rate for the firm's earnings and compare it to the implied growth rate from the market price. Any stock for which the market's implied growth rate is too low is undervalued, while stocks with too high an implied growth rate are overvalued by the market. Together, equations 3.13 and 3.14 illustrate that security analysis and valuation depend critically on future long-term growth prospects. This is akin to calculating an implied volatility from an option premium and using that implied volatility rather than a calculated premium.

Price-to-Sales

The same approach as used in the analysis of the P/E ratio can be used in examining a firm's price-to-sales (P/S) ratio. P/S can be especially useful in comparing the valuations among companies that have comparable profit margins. Consider using the company's sales, S_0, and its net profit margin, π, to define earnings as $E_0 = \pi S_0$. We can rewrite equation 3.12 to express the firm's stock price in terms of the firm's sales per share, as given by:

$$P_0 = \frac{\pi S_0(1 + \hat{g})}{\hat{k} - \hat{g}} \qquad (3.15)$$

In this case, we might assume that the profit margin remains constant over the long term and any growth in earnings comes from a growth in sales. Therefore, the price-to-sales ratio can be expressed in terms of the firm's growth rate of sales, profit margin, and required return on equity, as given by:

$$\frac{P_0}{S_0} = \frac{\pi(1 + \hat{g})}{\hat{k} - \hat{g}} \tag{3.16}$$

Applying the same analysis as was applied to the P/E ratio, the growth rate becomes the key differentiator between the value of two companies that have similar profit margins and required rates of return. As discussed in the Appendix, the profit margins for some types of companies are found to be quite stable over time. This implies that growth in earnings, and perhaps even cash flows, are driven primarily by growth in sales. Therefore, some analysts view sales-driven valuation approaches, such as that reflected in the price-to-sales ratio, to have the virtue of reducing the valuation problem to its fundamental elements.

Price-to-Cash Flow

The price-to-cash flow (P/CF) ratio can be evaluated in the context of the Free Cash Flow to Equity model. As with the Earnings Model, we can simplify equation 3.7 by assuming a constant growth rate for the firm's cash flows. Since equation 3.7 relies on cash flows to the firm, we also simply the model by expressing cash flows on a per share basis. Using the latest cash flow, the firm's cost of capital, and the long-term growth rate, the value of the firm is given by:

$$V_0 = \frac{CF_0(1 + g_{CF})}{k_{WACC} - g_{CF}} \tag{3.17}$$

Again, we adapt the notation to emphasize that the remainder of the analysis will be used to infer the market's forecast of the firm's valuation. The variables with "hats" refer to the market's forecast of the variable, so that $\hat{k}$ is the market-determined cost of capital, ghat is the market's forecasted long-term growth rate, and P is the market price for the stock. We rewrite equation 3.17 as:

$$P_0 = \frac{CF_0(1 + \hat{g}_{CF})}{\hat{k}_{WACC} - \hat{g}_{CF}} \tag{3.18}$$

Dividing both sides of equation 3.18 by the per share cash flow results in the P/CF ratio, given by:

$$\frac{P_0}{CF_0} = \frac{(1 + \hat{g}_{CF})}{\hat{k}_{WACC} - \hat{g}_{CF}} \tag{3.19}$$

Notice the similarities between equations 3.18 and 3.13. While there are technical differences in the parameters on the right-hand side between the two equations, the interpretations of the parameters are essentially the same. While the weighted average cost of capital might be lower than the cost of equity (i.e., the required return on the firm's equity), the growth rate in cash flows might be expected to be equivalent to the growth rate in earnings. For the growth rates in earnings and cash flows to be different, there must be some long-term change in capital expenditures or non-cash items in proportion to the firm's earnings. As discussed earlier, these growth rates might also be considered equal to the long-term growth rate in the firm's cash flows, assuming a constant net profit margin. While these subtleties and technicalities are sometimes important, they can be minor when using these ratios to make relative valuation judgments across securities in related sub-sectors or industries.

Security Analysis Application

We illustrate the application of the security valuation models by discussing the equity valuation approach used in Texas Christian University's Educational Investment Fund (TCU-EIF). Chapters 4 and 5 also utilize the TCU-EIF example in demonstrating the role of security analysis in the construction of the overall portfolio and the importance of the written investment idea presentation, respectively. We thank Stanley Block, Larry Lockwood, and Ben Wyatt of the TCU-EIF for their significant contributions to this material.

Example: Texas Christian University's Educational Investment Fund

By Stanley Block and Larry Lockwood

Valuation

While the EIF employs various methods to value assets, we rely heavily on the Free Cash Flow to Equity (FCFE) and Dividend Discount Models (DDM). We believe that these models, especially the FCFE model, force the analyst to carefully consider all the factors that can affect firm value, including profitability, risk, working capital, debt, and capital expenditures.

Our analysis begins with the income statement in which we forecast revenues, expenses, and net income. While we follow a standard framework of analysis, we leave no stone unturned when deriving our pro forma forecasts and valuation estimates. While company guidance can be helpful, we tend to consider them with a healthy dose of skepticism.

We do not simply look at the bottom line numbers; instead we constantly stress the importance of the quality of earnings and attempt to identify any potential latent problems that may surface for the company in the future.

Much consideration is given to our projections as these figures are the main drivers of the DDM and FCFE values. To confirm our forecasts are reasonable, we report the annualized growth in forecasted earnings per share (EPS) and compare the growth rates to the past three years' EPS growth rate. After forecasting the income statement, the balance sheet and cash flow statements are projected.

After generating the pro forma statements for the next three fiscal years, we then forecast dividends and free cash flow to equity. To estimate the terminal stock price (for year 3), we use the P/E multiple method: We derive a forecast for the year 3 P/E and multiply it times the predicted year 3 earnings per share. To forecast the year 3 P/E, we consider determinants such as the company's historical P/E, industry average P/E, earnings growth, systematic risk, and key macroeconomic factors. For the DDM, we discount the projected dividends through year 3, along with the forecast year 3 stock price. For the FCFE model, we discount the projected FCFE through year 3, along with the forecast of the year 3 stock price.

For both the DDM and the FCFE, we discount the pertinent cash flows using the appropriate risk-adjusted discount rate based on the Capital Asset Pricing Model (CAPM). In our CAPM, we use the currently quoted 30-year U.S. Treasury bond yield as the risk free rate and the historical geometric average market risk premium (i.e., the historical geometric average market return less the 30-year Treasury bond return, which is equal to 5.7%). Geometric averages are a preferred metric for long-term asset comparisons. Individual stock betas are gathered from various sources, such as Bloomberg and Value Line, but are also compared against historical betas using regression analysis over the past 60 months. Fund members have the flexibility to choose a beta believed to best represent the company's systematic risk over the coming years. We also compare our CAPM projections against other models such as the bond build-up approach. In all our calculations, we emphasize reliance on intuitive understanding of models and their output, and not strict adherence to mathematical rules at the expense of good logic and common sense.

After forecasting the key cash flows and determining the appropriate risk-adjusted discount rate, we run sensitivity analyses based on different earnings per share and P/E forecasts. Through the sensitivity analysis, the members can see forecasts and valuations scenarios ranging from worst to best case. From here, the members can also obtain some understanding of the potential undervaluation or overvaluation of the evaluated stock. Comparisons between the valuations derived from the DDM and the FCFE models are made and considered when making buy (undervalued) and sell (overvalued) decisions.

Checks and Balances

We run our predictions through various checks and balances. For instance, we use stock price multiple comparisons such as price to earnings, price to book value, price to sales, price to cash flow, and price-to-EBITDA across similar competitors within the industry. Fund members use these comparisons to either support or refute the recommendation made by the (student) analyst. We also derive the present value of growth opportunities (PVGO) for each stock, equal to the current stock price minus the stock's zero growth value (current year forecast earnings divided by the discount rate). The PVGO calculation separates the existing earnings of the firm from investors' perception of future incremental earnings generated from the firm's growth opportunities. A high PVGO relative to current stock price is indicative of a growth stock. To justify the purchase of a high PVGO stock, fund members must be convinced of the high growth potential of the company's earnings.

DDM and FCFE Models: An Illustration

In this section, we provide a simplified example for both the DDM and FCFE models used by the TCU Educational Investment Fund. Our analytical framework relies heavily on the valuation principles established in the Chartered Financial Analysts program.

We present a condensed pro-forma income statement in Exhibit 3.6, in which we forecast key variables for the next three years, after which we estimate a horizon value for the stock. The analysis begins with revenue forecasts, which are derived after a thorough examination of main revenue drivers of the company. For our example, revenues are predicted to grow at 5%, 7%, and 9%. All dollar figures reported in the exhibit are in millions, except per share variables. Other assumptions are listed at the bottom of the exhibit.

To forecast earnings, we often rely on margin forecasts such as an operating profit (EBITDA) margin, and then proceed to the forecasts of interest, taxes, depreciation, and amortization. Key inputs when forecasting EBITDA include labor costs, operating leverage, inflation, and stage of the business cycle. For our example, predicted EBITDA margins equal 22%, 23%, and 24%, over the next three years, respectively.

We forecast depreciation and amortization, interest, and taxes separately, and subtract them from EBITDA to derive net income. Because depreciation generally rises and falls as a percentage of property, plant, and equipment, we generally predict depreciation after formulating our PP&E forecasts. In our example, depreciation is expected to grow 9%, 10%, and 12% for the next three years.

We forecast interest expense as a percentage (interest rate) of debt outstanding (e.g., increasing 5%, 10%, and 15%, over the next three years, respectively, in our example). Taxes are deducted, based on tax rates determined by current and anticipated tax

Exhibit 3.6 Pro Forma Income Statement

	2009	2010	2011	2012
Revenues	7,000.00	7,350.00	7,864.50	8,572.31
EBITDA	1,400.00	1,617.00	1,808.84	2,057.35
Depreciation & Amortization	200.00	218.00	239.80	268.58
Interest	70.00	73.50	80.85	92.98
Pre-Tax Profit (EBT)	1,130.00	1,325.50	1,488.19	1,695.80
Tax	169.50	265.10	312.52	373.08
Net Income	960.50	1,060.40	1,175.67	1,322.72
Shares Outstanding	500	500	500	500
Earnings/Share	$1.92	$2.12	$2.35	$2.65
Dividend/Share Assumptions	$0.77	$0.85	$0.94	$1.06
Revenue Growth		5%	7%	9%
EBITDA Margins	20%	22%	23%	24%
Depreciation & Amortization Growth		9%	10%	12%
Interest Expense Growth		5%	10%	15%
Effective Tax Rate	15%	20%	21%	22%
Capital Expenditure Growth		10%	10%	10%

legislation. Finally, after calculating net income, shares outstanding are forecast (often based on company guidance, or recent trends). For simplicity, in our example, we assume no changes in shares outstanding.

To predict dividends, we often apply a dividend payout rate (e.g., based on historical data or company guidance) against our net income forecasts. In our example, we use a 40% dividend payout.

After applying the growth and margin assumptions, predicted dividends equal $0.85, $0.94, and $1.06, for 2010, 2011, and 2012, respectively. To determine the intrinsic value for the stock using the dividend discount model, we discount the predicted dividends along with the predicted year 3 stock price. As explained earlier, we derive our year 3 stock price forecast by using the combined P/E and earnings model: 2012 stock price estimate equals predicted 2012 P/E ratio times predicted 2012 earnings per share.

Exhibit 3.7 presents our CAPM and P/E assumptions, and Exhibit 3.8 presents the DDM valuation. Assume that the fiscal year ends December 31, and that the current date is March 14, 2010 (80% of the year remains).

As explained earlier, we also rely heavily on the free cash flow to equity (FCFE) model, especially in cases for which dividends are either not paid by the company or show a weak

Exhibit 3.7 Capital Asset Pricing Model and P/E Assumptions

Risk Free Rate	4.50%
Risk Premium	5.70%
Beta	1.25
CAPM	11.625%
2012 Predicted EPS	$2.65
2012 Predicted P/E	12.0
2012 Predicted Stock Price	$31.80

Exhibit 3.8 Valuation Using the Dividend Discount Model

Year	Dividends	Period	Present Value
2010	$0.85	0.80	$0.78
2011	$0.94	1.80	$0.77
2012	$1.06	2.80	$0.78
	PV of Dividends	$2.33	
	PV of 2012 Stock Price	$23.34	
	Intrinsic Value		$25.67

relationship with the firm's profitability. To derive the FCFE, we begin with net income and subtract changes in net working capital, capital expenditures, and add non-cash expenses and net new borrowing.

Changes in net working capital (excluding cash) are derived after a thorough examination of accounts receivable, inventory, and accounts payable. An increase in accounts receivable and inventory result in a decrease in cash flow, while an increase in accounts payable results in an increase in cash flow.

Next, capital expenditures are predicted (often as a percentage of sales), and must be consistent with the student's growth forecasts for the company. For instance, if the company is in an expansionary phase, capital expenditures should exceed depreciation. Conversely, if the company is in a declining phase, capital expenditures should be less than depreciation. While the analyst usually focuses on the purchase of assets when discussing capital expenditures, also included in the figure would be any cash received from the sale of a fixed asset such as equipment.

Finally, net new borrowing is determined, often predicted by using the company's target capital structure (e.g., target debt ratio times capital expenditures net of depreciation). By including additional debt that would be needed to finance new capital expenditures, the analyst debt forecasts remain close to the company's target capital structure. Also included in net new borrowings would be any principal debt payments due within the year.

The FCFE intrinsic value of the stock equals the present value of the FCFE for the next three years, plus the horizon value. An illustration of the FCFE model is provided in Exhibit 3.9. We begin with our pro-forma net income presented in Exhibit 3.3. Once again, we assume the current date is March 14, 2010 (80% of the year remains).

Therefore, our analysis leads us to an intrinsic value of $27.26 using the FCFE model and to $25.67 using the DDM. We can rely on just one model or use a weighted average of the two depending on our relative levels of confidence in the two models.

Potential Variations

Clearly, there are many variations to our methods that we can consider. First, we could forecast individual year dividends or free cash flows for more than three years, presumably

Exhibit 3.9 Free Cash Flow to Equity

	2010	2011	2012
Net Income	1,060.40	1,175.67	1,322.72
Non-cash Charges	218.00	239.80	268.58
Total	1,278.40	1,415.47	1,591.30
Changes in Working Capital			
Accounts Receivable	(100.00)	(125.00)	(150.00)
Inventory	(50.00)	(100.00)	(150.00)
Accounts Payable	125.00	175.00	200.00
Total Changes in Working Capital	(25.00)	(50.00)	(100.00)
Operating Cash Flow	1,253.40	1,365.47	1,491.30
Capital Expenditures	(735.00)	(786.45)	(857.23)
Free Cash Flow to the Firm	518.40	579.02	634.07
Net New Borrowings	206.80	218.66	235.46
FCFE	725.20	797.68	869.53
Shares Outstanding	500	500	500
FCFE per Share	1.45	1.60	1.74
PV of FCFE per Share	1.33	1.31	1.28
Sum of PV of FCFE			$3.92
PV of 2012 Price			$23.34
Intrinsic Equity Value			$27.26

forecasting until the firm's competitive advantage ends, after which we would apply the industry average P/E to derive the horizon value. In our experience, however, it is exceedingly difficult attempting to forecast the period in which a competitive advantage will end. Consequently, we prefer to forecast dividends and free cash flows for three years and to then apply either a discount or premium P/E to reflect the firm's strength or weakness within the industry at year 3.

Second, we could forecast the horizon value using a constant growth assumption, rather than using the combined P/E and earnings method. Clearly, we could solve for the constant growth that would equalize the two methods. But we prefer the combined method because it forces the analyst to draw price-multiple comparisons, which many investors deem essential in their buy and sell decisions.

Third, we could use the free cash flow to the firm (FCF) rather than free cash flow to equity. In the FCF model, the weighted average cost of capital is used to discount the predicted FCF, equal to net income minus change in net working capital and capital expenditure, plus non-cash expenses and after-tax interest expense. In the FCF model, equity value equals the discounted value of the FCF minus the market value of the firm's outstanding debt. The FCF and FCFE procedures will give the same intrinsic value, and we feel the FCFE method is a more direct method for stock valuation purposes.

Summary of Key Points

- Security analysis is the driving force in security selection.
- The role of security analysis in an investment process should be consistent with the strategy's investment philosophy and process.
- Quantitative models can be used to screen securities for further research and analysis or to rank securities as part of a quantitative security selection model.
- Company analysis is a part of, but not equivalent to, security analysis. A good company is not necessarily a good investment.
- The goal of security valuation is to determine the intrinsic value of a firm or its securities.
- The value of any security is the present value of that security's future cash flows.
- The Dividend Discount Model uses a stock's dividends as the future cash flows that are relevant to the security's intrinsic value.
- The Discounted Cash Flow model and its variants use the future cash flows to the firm in calculating the intrinsic value.
- Market valuation measures, such as P/E, P/S, and P/CF are motivated by and related to theoretical valuation models.

Exercises

1. What key beliefs must be embedded in an investment philosophy for security analysis to be a valuable part of the investment process? That is, what conditions are necessary to believe that security analysis is a valuable activity?
2. What is the difference between a good company and a good stock?
3. Explain the difference between a firm's earnings and its cash flows.
4. Discuss the meaning of *relative value*.
5. This chapter focuses on stock valuation models. Using the valuation concepts in this chapter, explain how you would value a firm's bond and how you would value the firm's debt.
6. List all of the assumed or forecasted inputs to the Dividend Discount model. For each input, explain how the resulting calculated intrinsic value of the stock changes when the value of the input is increased.
7. List all of the assumed or forecasted inputs to the Dividend Discount model. Identify each input as either universal or firm-specific. Universal inputs take on the same value for all firms. Firm-specific inputs take on different values for different firms.
8. List all of the assumed or forecasted inputs to the Discounted Cash Flow model. For each input, explain how the resulting calculated intrinsic value of the stock changes when the value of the input is increased.
9. List all of the assumed or forecasted inputs to the Discounted Cash Flow model. Identify each input as either universal or firm-specific. Universal inputs take on the same value for all firms. Firm-specific inputs take on different values for different firms.
10. What conditions must be met (or assumptions made) for the calculated intrinsic value using the Discounted Cash Flow model to be equal to the intrinsic value using the Earnings Model for the same firm? Discuss your answer in words and show your answer algebraically.
11. Discuss the advantages and disadvantages of each valuation model.
12. Some security analysts utilize price-per-*unit* valuation heuristics, where examples of *units* are customer, subscriber, store, mile, acre, square foot, or hit (referring to the Internet, not organized crime).
    a. Relate these heuristics to the fundamental valuation models discussed in this chapter. Specifically, discuss how each heuristic could be considered equivalent to one of the valuation models.
    b. Discuss the implicit or explicit assumptions the make these heuristics useful.
    c. Are these heuristics more or less useful relative valuations? Why?
13. Suppose a firm has a negative long-term growth rate of earnings and/or cash flows. Does this firm have a positive intrinsic value? Why or why not?
14. Some are tempted to claim that the Dividend Discount Model is useless for stocks that do not currently pay dividends. Explain why this claim is not true.

Appendix: Cutting through the Hype

This material is excerpted from *Analysts, Lies, and Statistics: Cutting through the Hype in Corporate Earnings Announcements* by Brian Bruce and Mark T. Bradshaw with permission from the authors.

The Role of Analysts

A reasonable investor might ask, "What role do analysts serve? Why can't we get rid of them? At the very least, let's replace them with independent research firms and not rely on analysts tied to brokerage firms." In this Appendix we will show the critical function that analysts play in the flow of information from companies to investors.

Buy and Sell Recommendations

Recently, analyst recommendations have been subject to much scrutiny. The best place to start looking at those recommendations is at the overall recommendation from analysts. Each analyst issues a strong buy, buy, hold, sell or strong sell recommendation for each stock that they follow. What did each of three leading compilers of earnings estimate data show with their data recently?

Thompson Financial/First Call aggregated these recommendations in July of 2001 and found that almost 50% of all recommendations are buy while less than 1% were sell. A similar study done by Zacks Investment Research of over 8000 recommendations of stocks in the S&P 500 showed that only 29 were sells or less than one-half of one percent. This compared to 214 strong buy recommendations.

The third firm I/B/E/S had their data analyzed in a study by Li (2002) over time. It showed startling consistency across seven years and nearly a quarter million recommendations.

IBES Rating	Strong Buy	2	3	4	Sell	Total Recommendations
1994	25%	33%	37%	2%	3%	29,521
1995	27	32	36	2	3	30,854
1996	30	33	32	2	2	29,734
1997	31	37	29	1	2	30,350
1998	29	39	30	1	1	35,445
1999	30	40	28	2	1	37,318
2000	31	40	27	1	1	32,663
Average	29%	36%	32%	2%	2%	

Source: Li (2002).

This pattern cannot appear by chance. Consistently averaging 2% of all recommendations as sells is not because only 2% of all companies followed are worthy of that recommendation. What causes analysts to have such a significant bias in their recommendations?

The Analyst Cycle and the Critical Role of Analysts

To understand analyst recommendations, you first must understand the analyst cycle. This cycle is a description of all the forces that act on analysts in their making a recommendation. The first part is the source of much information to an analyst: company management. Company management provides financial projections about future earnings and allows the analyst to discuss the firm's prospects. In this part of the relationship, the analyst is a non-paying client of the company.

There is a second part to the relationship between company and analyst. Many analysts work for firms that are investment banks. Investment banks market to companies to do the companies' investment banking business like issuing bonds or a new class of stock for the company. The relationship now may be that the company is the client to the analyst and his firm. Since the analyst works for the firm, he must not get in the way of the investment banking marketing effort and, in fact, may be asked to help in that effort.

The next relationship is that of the analyst to the investor. The analyst provides the investor with critical information about a security that may be difficult to obtain by the investor. In return, the analyst needs the investor to trade with the analyst's firm in order for his/her firm to "get paid." Many times in a portfolio manager's career does he or she get a call from an analyst asking if the portfolio manager values the information that the analyst sends. If the portfolio manager answers yes, the analyst will generally ask for a certain level of trading commissions to flow to his/her firm. Many analysts are judged based on the amount of trading flow they bring into a firm.

Finally is the link back to the company. The investor will act on the information provided by the analyst (along with other information). This will affect the price, which is of great concern to company management. As stock options became more prevalent in the 1990s, the concern of senior management turned from earning a large cash bonus to getting lots of stock options and maximizing their value. This causes senior management of a company to be very concerned about what investors think about the company.

The Changing Nature of Analyst Estimates

Over the years, it has been the job of CFOs of major corporations to tweak the books in order to make earnings appear more stable than they really are. They did this because they believed that investors would reward them for predictability. Then came the internet mania and CFOs stretched the envelope even further in trying to show good results to investors.

So how do companies smooth out their earnings? Firms that issue credit can report higher earnings by adjusting their default rates on loans to levels that are too low, which pushes up earnings. Once the company is doing better, the default rate can be pushed up to bring earnings down. These actions in combination create a smoothed earnings pattern. Likewise, a company can push product out to dealers and distributors and book the revenue, even if the merchandise can be returned at a later date, bringing profits up. Later, when revenues have improved, the returns can be booked.

All of the above manipulations can occur within Generally Accepted Accounting Principles (GAAP). These are the numbers created by a firm's auditors and reported to the Securities & Exchange Commission. However, the 1990s popularized a new set of earnings numbers, the pro-forma earnings. These numbers are not regulated like GAAP earnings and allow firms to exclude such basic costs as marketing and interest. One famous pro-forma story is a firm who repainted their fleet of vehicles on a regular schedule. After deciding to paint the vehicles before their schedule date, the firm excluded the cost of painting, claiming that since it wasn't scheduled it was an extraordinary item and should not be included as an expense in their pro-forma earnings numbers.

Pro-forma has become such a fixture in the press that it was the subject of a column by Rob Walker on cnbc.com. An excerpt is illuminating:

PRO FORMA literally means "for the sake of form," but the Wall Street Journal sheds light on what the phrase means to corporations in America when it explains that "a growing number present their earnings on a 'pro forma' basis, 'as if' certain expenses didn't exist." This is not a scandalous idea; it's a delightful one.

On a pro forma basis, I'm having an outstanding year. In calendar year 2002 I've gone to the gym on a regular basis and expect this trend to continue and to have a material impact on my health going forward. Year-to-date, my health has improved by a solid 15 percent on an annualized basis.

BETWEEN THE LINES

These results do not reflect certain items. Loss of good health and potential mortality stemming from 62 consecutive quarters of above-plan intake of assorted spirits, tobacco, and other substances reliant on mouth-to-lung delivery systems, and miscellaneous off-book chemical and pharmaceutical substances, are addressed in a one-time write-down. Results also include the application of "good will" regarding those days, and in some cases weeks, when actual gym attendance was negatively impacted or curtailed by visits to the racetrack, where I ate oysters and drank Budweiser.

Finally, a recent post-workout lunch of a 22-ounce, bone-in rib steak at Smith & Wollensky and three shots of bourbon is treated here as a non-recurring expense. I'll never do that again! I encourage you to focus on these pro forma results as a truer portrait of the state of my health than "traditional measures," which suggest that I have been dead for at least a year.

The problems with pro-forma earnings have led the SEC to issue a warning to companies to stop using pro-forma earnings. Pro-forma earnings "can make it hard for investors to compare an issuer's financial information with other reporting periods and with other companies," the SEC wrote. The SEC warned investors to be especially careful looking at reports that contain alternative calculations of financial results, leave out non-recurring transactions, and vary widely from GAAP results.

Effect of Pro-forma versus GAAP Earnings on the Investor

The current gap between pro-forma and GAAP earnings are the widest in history. In, fact Standard & Poor's and First Call, both using pro-forma earnings, still estimated that earnings fell by 32% versus 17% in 2001 based mainly on how special items were treated. This caused a valuation difference that is significant. In looking at the price/earnings ratio of the S&P 500, it was approximately 36 using GAAP earnings, 24 using S&P earnings and 22 using First Call earnings. Looking at the chart below you can see how clearly the gap has widened between GAAP and pro-forma earnings for the S&P 500.

An exhaustive report on the subject by Keon (2001) looked at the differences. First, he found that a key difference was whether the ratio was calculated based on trailing or estimated earnings. Another difference was the way pro-forma earnings were calculated. Reported earnings "could be whatever the company could convince analysts were correct" according to Keon, a former executive at I/B/E/S. He speculates that when the gaps began they were driven by two changes in corporate practices: the merger and acquisition boom and the re-structuring movement. Due to a need to show the results from an acquisition or to deal with poor performance discontinued, many companies sold or cut back on marginal operations, thereby taking a one-time charge against earnings. By the 1990s companies like General Motors were taking charges due to how pension liabilities were accounted for. Since there was no change in the actual liability, companies excluded these charges from earnings. By the late 1990s internet firms had taken this practice to extremes, excluding marketing costs, shipping costs, and other normal expenses associated with doing business.

This has caused investors to push analysts to take a deeper look at pro forma earnings. In early 2002, Merrill Lynch told its analysts to use a variety of methods to judge financial performance rather than relying on pro forma earnings when reporting on a company. In an internal memo, Merrill is adopting in its research "the use of broad measures beyond pro-forma earnings to evaluate a company's quality of earnings with the objective of establishing an enhanced standard of accountability and transparency for our clients." The goal is to use the tougher GAAP standards more rigorously in evaluating firms.

Earnings Surprise

This section will focus on the topic of earnings surprise. What is earnings surprise? It is an earnings report that differs from what analysts were expecting. Earnings surprise often causes a substantial movement in the stock's price. Parts of the above description came from a web-based investment site. It shows how common the ideas of earnings surprise have become. In the 1960s, the concept of earnings surprise was limited to a few academics doing research on an effect that wasn't known to many sophisticated investors.

History

The relationship between corporate earnings information and stock prices has been an active area of financial research since the 1960s. The origins of this research can be traced to the notion of stock market efficiency, which implies that all publicly available information should rapidly get reflected in stock prices in an unbiased manner. Because of this security prices should quickly react to earnings numbers when they are released. The magnitude and direction of the market reaction should be related to the degree to which the information contained in earnings disclosures is new (unexpected). In an early study on this effect, Ball and Brown were able to document a significant pre-earnings announcement drift in the stock prices of the companies in their sample. Figure 3.1 shows that for two measures of unexpected earnings (variable 1: net income and variable 2: EPS), this drift was positive for companies that reported higher earnings than expected (an excess return of about 7% over the twelve months preceding the announcement), and negative for companies whose earnings came in below expectations (an approximate -9.5% excess return over the same period). Furthermore, companies that had the largest earnings deviations from the prior year (i.e., the biggest surprises) experienced the greatest reaction.

Two features of Figure 3.1 deserve further comment. First, consistent with the thesis of informational efficiency of the stock market, Ball and Brown found that about 85–90% of the market reaction to earnings announcements occurred in the months preceding the announcement and only 10–15% during the announcement month itself. This is consistent with the existence of analysts whose forecasts and forecast revisions cause prices to continuously move up (down) during the year, in accord with favorable (unfavorable) news. Subsequent studies obtained even stronger results. Brown, Griffin, Hagerman and Zmijewski (1987) attributed this improvement to the fact that analysts' forecasts are better predictors of actual earnings than mechanical forecasts of the type used by Ball and Brown because they are likely to incorporate the more timely and broader sources of information typically available to market participants. Their work led to the widespread use of analysts' forecasts as proxies for market expectations. The availability of large historical databases of analysts' forecasts in electronic form and readily accessible online updates to such data served to further popularize the use of analysts' forecasts in investment research and practice.

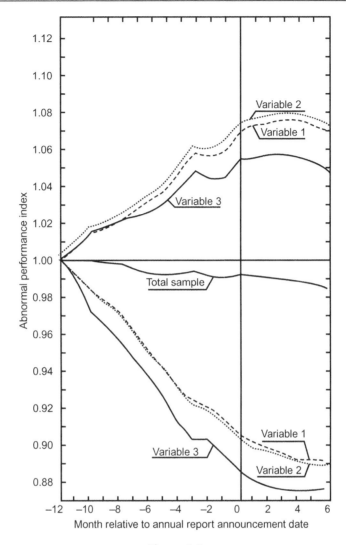

Figure 3.1
Abnormal Performance Indexes for Various Portfolios. Reproduced with permission from the
Journal of Accounting Research.

The second noteworthy aspect of Figure 3.1 is that the market reaction to positive and negative earnings surprises is not symmetric. Firms whose reported earnings fall below expectations appear to experience a larger negative reaction before, during and after the month of the earnings announcement than those that surprise on the upside.

Finally, as Figure 3.1 indicates, excess returns associated with extreme earnings surprises seemed to persist for several months after the earnings report. This implies that abnormal returns could be earned by forming portfolios based on the sign and magnitude of earnings surprises. This observation led to the use of standardized unexpected earnings (SUE) scores in stock valuation. We discuss SUE scores in the next section in context of our discussion of earnings surprise measurement.

Measurement Issues

As mentioned above, one key component in measuring the earnings surprise for a company is the analyst's forecast of earnings for the company. Unless the company is very small, it is likely to be covered by more than one analyst, and earnings forecasts issued by different analysts for the same company and fiscal period may differ. A conventional approach to incorporating the divergent views of multiple analysts is to construct a consensus forecast, such as a mean (or median) of all currently available forecasts. If one believes that each individual analysts' forecast of earnings measures the company's actual earnings with some error, but that these errors are idiosyncratic across analysts, this approach has the merit of reducing the error (noise) inherent in the individual forecasts.

Stock returns from an earnings surprise strategy depend on variation in the magnitude and direction of the surprises. The magnitude of the surprise cannot be measured in purely monetary terms, since the impact of an actual earnings report of ten cents a share by a company for which the mean analyst expectation was five cents (a 100% surprise) is likely to be much greater than the case where the analysts' forecast was one dollar and the company reported actual earnings of $1.05 per share (a 5% surprise). Note that in both cases, the actual reported earnings beat expectations by the same amount (5 cents per share). The example illustrates the need to account for differences in scale when studying the relation between earnings surprises and stock prices.

The earnings surprise number can be normalized by a variety of deflators, such as the actual or forecast earnings, as indicated in the above example. One problem with these approaches is that they tend to break down when the actual (or forecast) earnings are negative. An alternative is to use the absolute value of the actual or forecast earnings instead. Even so, difficulties can arise in cases where the earnings number used for scaling is very small. Deflators close to zero magnify the actual surprise, leading to large cross-sectional variations that are unrelated to significant differences between expectations and the actual outcomes. In such cases, the stock price at the time of the forecast is often used as a deflator.

The above discussion has focused on operational factors that can affect the robustness of earnings surprise measures. However, when constructing such measures, it is equally important to consider the reliability of the consensus earnings forecasts. The market reacts to a company's earnings announcement because it triggers a revision of beliefs about the company's future (e.g., its ability to grow or pay a certain stream of dividends). The extent of this revision depends on the strength (consistency) of investors' pre-announcement views about a particular earnings outcome. If the market is fairly certain about what the earnings for a company are likely to be, an earnings announcement that deviates from that expectation constitutes unambiguously good (or bad) news, and the resulting price reaction is likely to be sharp and swift. On the other hand, if there is considerable uncertainty about the earnings outcome, the announcement of earnings primarily serves to dispel uncertainty about future outcomes. A widely accepted measure of earnings surprise that incorporates this notion is the standardized unexpected earnings or SUE score proposed by Latane and Jones (1977). The SUE score is the difference between the actual earnings and expected earnings deflated by a measure of uncertainty in the earnings forecast. To calculate a stock's SUE, three items of data are needed: the company's latest reported earnings, the last consensus earnings estimate before the release of the actual earnings, and the standard deviation of the individual analysts' forecasts that make up the consensus. The SUE can then be calculated as:

$$SUE = \frac{\text{Actual earnings} - \text{Consensus earnings forecast}}{\text{Standard deviation of analysts' forecasts}}$$

The more extreme the value of the resulting number, the more likely it is that the company's earnings announcement will have a significant effect on its share price. The intuition underlying the SUE score follows from our earlier observation that the market reaction to the surprise associated with an earnings announcement depends not only on the magnitude of the surprise (captured in the numerator of the calculation), but also on the uncertainty inherent in the forecast of expected earnings. The denominator of the SUE score captures this uncertainty by directly gauging the extent to which analysts disagree about the earnings outcome for a company. However, as with other earnings surprise measures, caution needs to be exercised in the computation of SUE scores in cases where sufficient data is not available for computation. For small companies, the number of analysts following the company may be small (often one or two), making it difficult or impossible to compute the standard deviation of forecasts.

Clearly, the benefits of using any particular deflator are debatable, and much depends on one's view of what drives the stock price reaction to earnings surprises and the nature of the data available. If the time series process underlying earnings is considered stable, focusing on large percentage changes will capture the stock market effects of unusual earnings events. On the other hand, price deflation is appealing since it directly associates earnings changes with the valuation impact of those changes. SUE scores are intuitively pleasing because they allow us to incorporate not only the effect of extraordinary earnings reports, but also the characteristics of the forecasts themselves into the surprise metric in a logical fashion. This reason and the fact that SUE was the first published indicator of surprise have made the SUE scores the most commonly used measure of earnings surprise.

Earning Abnormal Returns from Earnings Surprises

In our discussion of the Ball and Brown (1968) study, we alluded briefly to the nature of the market reaction to earnings surprises around the time of the earnings announcement. In a pattern confirmed by several independent academic studies, Figure 3.1 (above) indicated that stocks with the largest positive (negative) surprises move higher (lower) before the earnings announcement, jump (drop) dramatically during the report week and then continue to drift up (down) during subsequent weeks. The pattern of market reaction to earnings surprises during and before the announcement month confirms our intuition that as the uncertainty about future earnings is gradually resolved during the year, the good or bad news should manifest itself in stock prices via continual revisions of forecasts by analysts, interim corporate disclosures, and leakage of information into the market through the information search activities of other market participants. However, the post-announcement reaction is counter-intuitive in that after earnings have been publicly announced, the information in the earnings release should be rapidly incorporated into market prices in an unbiased fashion, rather than continuing to drift up or down over a prolonged period. In the early 1970s some researchers examined this post-announcement drift in greater detail, noting that it was contrary to the notion of market efficiency. The post announcement drift persisted well into the 1990s and was subjected to rigorous academic research because it contradicted the notion of market efficiency. The anomaly could not be explained even after controlling for risk, size and a variety of other factors that could affect stock returns, and with investors eyeing potential short-term gains from trading on earnings surprises, SUE scores soon became a standard component of stock valuation models. SUE scores performed well from 1987 to 1998, displaying correlations of as much as 30% with one-month ahead stock returns and predicting the direction of subsequent stock price movements correctly over 83% of the time. Results for longer holding periods (two or three months) were similar and enabled investors to earn excess returns of 4–5%. However, of late the ability of SUE scores to forecast one-month ahead returns has begun to diminish. For example, in 1999, the correlation between the two was negative for six out of 12 months. To a large extent, this should have been expected, for discovery of information inevitably leads to its reflection in market prices. Indeed, what was surprising was the fact that the effect persisted for so long after its discovery and exploitation. However, two additional factors have contributed to the decline in the effectiveness of SUE scores: (1) the corruption of consensus estimates as a measure of market expectations over this period; and (2) the manipulation of reported earnings by corporate management, subjects to which we shall return at the end of this chapter.

Factors Affecting the Strength of the Earnings Surprise-Stock Return Relationship

The relationship between SUE scores and stock returns at and after the earnings announcement depends not only on the magnitude and direction of the reported surprise but also on the characteristics of the reporting companies. Companies with low P/E multiples (value stocks) tend to show greater reaction on the upside when the earnings surprise is positive, while those with high P/E ratios (growth stocks) experience greater negative fallout from an earnings report that disappoints. This is consistent with Stickel (1998) who finds that stocks with higher analyst ratings tend to have higher P/E ratios. The reasons for this phenomenon may be traced back to the earnings expectations life cycle discussed earlier. Recall that in the late part of the cycle, as the estimate revisions for positive surprise stocks turn positive, momentum investors pile into these stocks, causing their P/E ratios to go up. When expectations rise to unrealistic levels, subsequent negative surprises "torpedo" these very same growth stocks, causing them to "sink" rapidly at the time of the earnings announcement. Dreman suggests that the above relationship between P/E ratios and market reaction to earnings surprises can be used to earn abnormal returns, as depicted in the chart below:

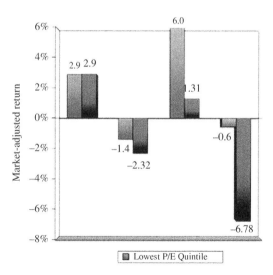

Another factor that affects this relationship is firm size. Bhushan (1989), has shown that smaller firms tend to have fewer analysts following their stock. If analysts are viewed as information intermediaries whose forecasting activities serve to incorporate value-relevant information into market prices, one would expect smaller firm size (lower analyst following) to be associated with larger earnings surprises. This is because in the case of smaller companies, less information is likely to have been impounded into its stock price prior to its earnings announcement. The quantity and quality of predisclosure information increase, earnings surprises, and the market's reaction to them, is smaller. They also report that the speed of stock prices adjustment following earnings surprises is greater when the quality and quantity of analysts' forecasts is high. There is an inverse relationship between the degree of prominence of a firm (as measured by the amount of coverage it receives in the financial press) and the market reaction to its earnings announcements. However, firm size can proxy for a variety of factors, such as risk, therefore any conclusions should be drawn with caution. For example, the level of institutional shareholding in a firm has been shown to vary directly with firm size.

Observed Earnings Distributions

Overall, the search for evidence of earnings management around specific corporate events and within specific accounts has resulted in somewhat mixed or weak evidence that managers manipulate earnings, with much of the evidence limited to a particular industry (e.g., banks) or corporate event (e.g., acquisition). Thus, one possible reason why evidence is somewhat mixed is that most of the studies focus on a small number of firms, which results in earnings management tests that have low power. In response to this, researchers have begun to look not at specific accounts or corporate events, but at overall distributions of earnings across large numbers of firms. By considering large numbers of firms, researchers are able to appeal to the "law of large numbers" that suggests that many distributions tend to be normal (i.e., the bell-curve).

In these studies of earnings distributions, it is hypothesized that managers dislike reporting negative earnings, and will avoid reporting negative earnings if they have the opportunity to exercise discretion and bump earnings up to positive earnings. Also, it is hypothesized that managers would prefer to exercise discretion to manipulate earnings upwards to avoid a decrease in reported earnings from an earlier fiscal quarter or year.

As an example of the results in these studies, we constructed the graph below. It plots the distribution of earnings before extraordinary items scaled by market value for all firms from 1976–2000. The figure presents the frequencies of reported earnings numbers (scaled by market value) for intervals of width 0.005 across the range −0.25 to +0.35. The overall shape of the distribution of earnings reflects the bell-curve that characterizes normal distributions. However, around earnings of zero, there is an unexplained kink in the distribution. There are fewer than expected frequencies of earnings just below zero, and more than expected frequencies of earnings just above zero. It appears that, barring some inexplicable property of earnings, managers who would have reported just slightly negative earnings intervened in the accounting process to produce earnings figures that were just above zero.

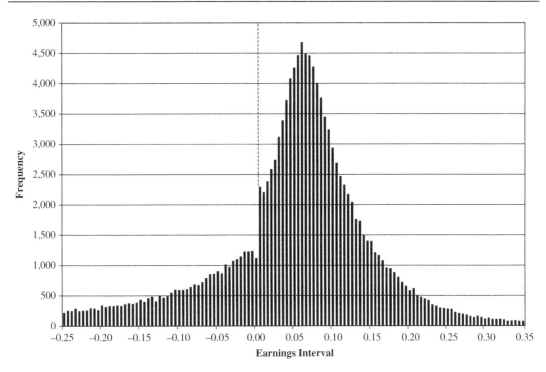

Source: Compustat.

Summary

It is a widely held belief that managers manipulate accounting earnings. These beliefs underlie a large number of academic studies where researchers attempt to uncover evidence of earnings management. While there are a number of studies that provide evidence that is consistent with earnings management, those results are sometimes sensitive to the way earnings management is measured. Although many studies interpret their analysis as evidence of earnings management, a fair number lack evidence of earnings management. The closest evidence we have to a "smoking gun" that earnings are managed is the analysis of overall distributions of earnings, which provide compelling evidence that managers avoid reporting slightly negative earnings or slightly decreasing earnings. This area remains interesting because of the unyielding beliefs that managers freely manipulate earnings.

Accruals vs. Cash Flows

How well does accrual accounting accomplish the objective of providing a better summary measure of performance than cash flows? Dechow (1994) studied the relative performance of cash flows and earnings at explaining stock returns. She first showed that as you lengthen the measurement interval, say several years, earnings and cash flows become more similar in their ability to measure a company's performance, i.e., explain stock returns. This makes sense, because over the life of a firm, the total earnings will equal the total cash flows. The key to her findings, however, is the analysis of earnings over shorter intervals, such as quarterly and annual earnings. For the shorter intervals, she shows that earnings dominate cash flows in their ability to explain stock returns. She concludes:

> *"[The results] demonstrate that cash flows are not a poor measure of firm performance per se. In steady-state firms, where the magnitude of accruals is small and cash flows and earnings are most similar, cash flows are a relatively useful measure of firm performance. However, when the magnitude of accruals increases, indicating that the firm has large changes in its operating, investment, and financing activities, cash flows suffer more severely from timing and matching problems. Therefore, as accruals increase in magnitude net cash flows' association with stock returns declines. Overall, the results are consistent with the hypothesis that accountants accrue revenues and match expenditures to revenues so as to produce a performance measure (earnings) that better reflects firm performance than realized cash flows."*

The evidence is compelling in favor of accrual accounting, and it is consistent with what we observe when we see analysts predominantly forecasting earnings rather than cash flows.

Accounting Numbers as a Measure of Performance

Even though accrual accounting leads to financial reports that provide better summary information than would a cash-flow based report, accruals can be too much of a good thing. That is, rather than accruals providing enhanced earnings figures, they do the opposite.

At the Harvard Business School, the core accounting class emphasizes that the best accounting can do is provide a picture of a company's true economics, but that discretion available in accounting rules makes accounting numbers fuzzy. As a heuristic for communicating this idea in class, the following representative formula is used.

$$\frac{\text{Accounting}}{\text{Numbers}} = \frac{\text{Economic}}{\text{Substance}} + \frac{\text{Measurement}}{\text{Error}} + \text{Bias}$$

The formula is suggestive rather than an attempt to partition accounting numbers into separate quantities. Accounting numbers constitute any of the numbers from any of the financial statements, but the most common number is earnings. Economic Substance is what accountants are trying to measure. For example, did a company generate value for its investors? Clearly, accountants would prefer that all Accounting Numbers reflect Economic Substance.

However, because accrual accounting requires that estimates be made (e.g., the estimated life of a machine, its expected salvage value, etc.), the resulting accounting numbers will often be wrong, reflecting misestimates. This "noise" in the Accounting Numbers is labeled

Measurement Error. Some measurement is expected and tolerable, but the hope is that overestimates from one period will be offset by small underestimates from another period, leading to just a small amount of Measurement Error.

Unfortunately, because managers are aware that accountants and financial statement users understand and tolerate some measurement error, they turn this to their advantage. Rather than provide estimates that increase the correspondence between Accounting Numbers and Economic Substance, dubious managers with incentives to overstate Accounting Numbers can infuse Bias into those numbers. For example, managers can intentionally overestimate the useful lives of machinery, resulting in lower periodic depreciation charges.

This bias cannot go on forever, because of the disciplined nature of double-entry accrual accounting. If a manager intentionally overstated the useful life of a machine, then the lower depreciation expense would result in an asset that is likely overstated. When the firm sells or disposes of the asset, it will likely record a loss on the sale or disposal. Such a loss is the "catch-up" for the under-depreciation that resulted from the manager's intentional bias.

Another source of bias is actually built into accounting by accountants themselves. Despite the fact that the FASB does not actively seek conservative accounting methods, most of the rules that it issues are inherently biased towards being conservative (e.g., recognizing unrealized losses but not unrealized gains). Thus, the conservative nature of accounting rules serves as an additional source of bias. If we generally believe that managers have incentives to bias accounting numbers upwards, then the conservative nature of accounting rules provides some offset.

Accruals Are Sometimes Not So Good

The subjective nature of accruals recorded by managers makes them a dangerous thing. If managers are upstanding and transparent, then accruals enhance the financial statements' ability to convey the economic condition and performance of the firm. If, however, managers have less than noble objectives, then accruals are an easy to use tool to artificially modify the financial reports in some desired direction (usually up). We will see a detailed discussion of this in the next chapter.

By way of introduction, in this chapter we want to simply visit accounting accruals from the perspective of their time-series behavior. It is useful to consider a simple example to appreciate further how accruals work.

Consider a simple sale of $100,000 to be booked by a company. A customer places an order for products, and the company ships them to the customer. The customer receives them, and agrees to pay for the products within 30 days. Even though the accountant sees no cash coming in the door, the financial statements are nevertheless adjusted to reflect this transaction. In other words, accrual accounting is employed to better reflect the economic substance of the sale of products to a customer.

The accountant would record an account receivable asset for the amount that the customer owes the company, and would also go ahead and recognize the sales revenue for the sale of the products. The increase in the accounts receivable asset goes on the balance sheet and will stay there until the customer pays off their account.

Suppose further that nothing else happened during this year. The increase in accounts receivable represents an "income increasing" accrual. Nothing is wrong with income-increasing accruals per se. However, a small dose of healthy skepticism will trigger a concern that unscrupulous managers might abuse their discretion. In a real company, there is not just one sales transaction per year, but often thousands. With all the transactions, what is to keep a manager from bumping up the amount recorded as sales by some artificial amount? Auditors come in at the end of the year and spot check transactions recorded by managers, but they cannot view all transactions. As it turns out, most of the Accounting Enforcement Actions issued by the Securities and Exchange Commission, in which companies are admonished for fraudulent accounting, reveal that fictitious or overstatement of sales is usually the violation.

Note that we are not arguing that all managers "bump up" the amount of revenues beyond that which is justified. Instead, we wish to provide a simple exposition of how accruals impose discipline on managers through the reversing process. To that end, we are introducing the possibility that accruals might be recorded at the wrong amounts initially, but that this will work its way back out of the accounting system eventually.

To provide a contrasting example to the account receivable accrual, suppose also that the company discussed above rewards its sales staff with paid vacations in the year following a big sale, and that the sales agent who made the $100,000 sale gets vacation time during which the company will pay her $1000. The company would record the cost of this paid vacation in the current period during which the sale was recorded. This would require the company to record an expense and a corresponding accrued vacation liability. This is an example of an "income decreasing" accrual.

Neither the income increasing nor the income decreasing accruals can continue indefinitely. They eventually reverse when the company either collects the account receivable or pays the employee her vacation time. However, over short periods of time, it should be clear that managers could adjust too much for income increasing accruals and too little for income decreasing accruals.

Now back to the sales example. Suppose that the manager decided to record the sale at $120,000 rather than $100,000. Eventually, the customer will pay but will only pay what was invoiced to them – $100,000. This leaves an uncollectible $20,000 account receivable on the books. Sooner or later, the manager will have to clean out that receivable. To make things simple, suppose that when the manager writes off the bogus account receivable they have to record some kind of "loss." The loss decreases earnings in the period recorded. And, the amount of the loss is exactly equal to the amount by which sales were initially "overbooked." It is important to again restate that we do not believe or mean to imply that the overbooking of revenues or the underbooking of expenses is routine.

Thus, if a manager overbooked revenue in the first year leading to an overstatement of income in that year, the undoing of that overbooked revenue would come in the second year when the useless account receivable had to be written off. This provides a stylized example of a basic fact: All else equal, income increasing accruals in one period are generally followed by reversals in later periods. Similarly, income decreasing accruals in one period are generally followed by reversals in later periods.

Where to Look

How is an investor to keep track of accruals made by managers? Fortunately, the statement of cash flows provides an investor with such information summarized nicely. For example, contrast the two excerpts from the operating section of the cash flow statements of Ebay and E-Trade:

Ebay			
	2001	2000	1999
Net Income	$90,448,000	$48,294,000	$10,828,000
Depreciation	$89,732,000	$45,191,000	$25,331,000
Adjustments to Net Income	$113,023,000	$54,245,000	$6,522,000
Changes in Accounts Receivables	($50,221,000)	($48,862,000)	($28,884,000)
Changes in Liabilities	$2,310,000	$42,055,000	$68,103,000
Changes in Other Operating Activities	$6,820,000	($40,775,000)	($15,336,000)
Cash Flows from Operating Activities	$252,112,000	$100,148,000	$66,564,000

E-Trade			
	2001	2000	1999
Net Income	($241,532,000)	$1,353,000	$19,152,000
Depreciation	$188,268,000	N/A	$97,638,000
Adjustments to Net Income	($241,495,000)	N/A	($140,719,000)
Changes in Accounts Receivables	N/A	N/A	($3,586,689,000)
Changes in Liabilities	$20,738,000	N/A	$3,306,275,000
Changes in Other Operating Activities	$19,327,000	N/A	$165,651,000
Cash Flows From Operating Activities	($254,694,000)	$40,911,000	($138,692,000)

The operating section of the cash flow statement reconciles net income to cash flows from operating activities. The reconciling items reflect accruals recorded under GAAP. For Ebay, the reconciling items indicate a predominance of income-decreasing activities, because the net of the adjustments is positive. In contrast, for 1999 and 2001, the net adjustments for E-trade are negative, indicating that accounting accruals during those years were, on average, income increasing. These two companies are symbolic of an average phenomenon that characterizes the behavior of future earnings conditional on accruals, which is discussed next.

Accruals and Earnings Behavior

Sloan (1996) investigated the time-series properties of earnings unconditionally, and conditional on the level of accruals embedded in earnings in the base year. He found that extreme earnings that contain a large amount of income increasing accruals tend to revert towards lower levels in the future years at a much quicker rate than extreme earnings unconditionally revert. However, extreme earnings levels that contain a disproportionately low level of income increasing accruals (which is another way of saying the earnings reflect a high level of cash flows), persist for longer periods before reverting.

The following graph was constructed based on net income scaled by total assets (ROA). We ranked firms into deciles according to ROA, then tracked ROA in the years prior to and after the ranking period.

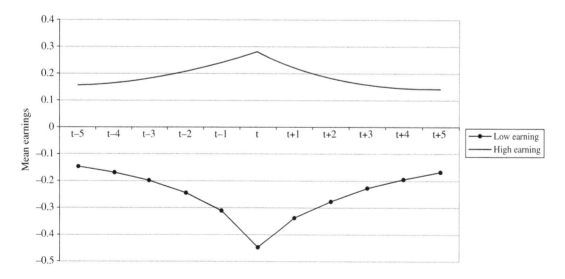

The figure demonstrates the well-known mean reversion in earnings levels. The next figure was similarly constructed and tracks the level of ROA as well. However, in period $t = 0$, the ranking variable was accruals scaled by total assets, not net income scaled by total assets.

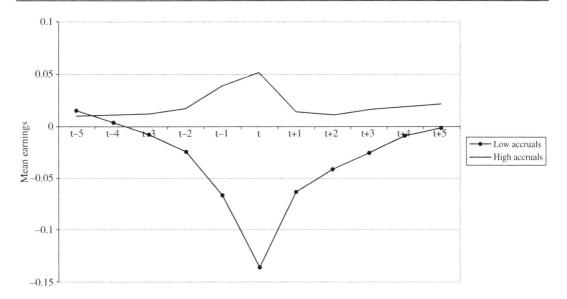

Clearly, the rate of mean reversion in earnings for extreme levels of accruals is much greater. This is a manifestation of the reversing nature of accounting accruals discussed in the stylized examples earlier.

Another way to construct the figure is to initially rank on the level of cash flows scaled by assets and track the mean reversion in levels of earnings.

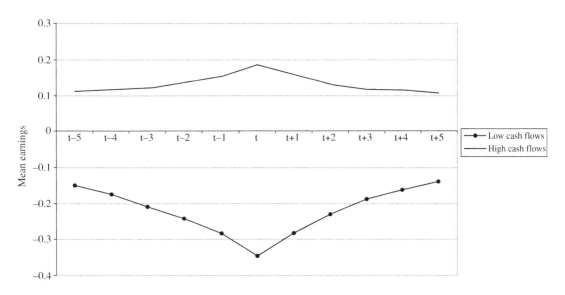

This figure provides complementary evidence to the second figure. However, when extreme levels of earnings are largely supported by underlying cash flows, the earnings levels, although reverting on average, tend to revert at a much slower rate than earnings that largely reflect accounting accruals.

Sloan (1996) documented that the stock market apparently does not appreciate these patterns in earnings. The following data covers the period 1988–1998 and reflects annual raw returns, value-weighted market adjusted returns, and size-decile adjusted returns for the three years subsequent to a portfolio formation year, across deciles formed on the basis of the level of accruals (e.g., as in the second figure above).

Rank	Raw Returns			Market-Adj. Returns			Size-Adj. Returns		
	t + 1	t + 2	t + 3	t + 1	t + 2	t + 3	t + 1	t + 2	t + 3
Low	0.203	0.249	0.217	0.037	0.076	0.038	0.048	0.073	0.025
2	0.211	0.229	0.235	0.049	0.060	0.060	0.064	0.065	0.048
3	0.183	0.185	0.227	0.022	0.018	0.056	0.038	0.021	0.049
4	0.161	0.165	0.187	−0.002	0.000	0.019	0.010	0.006	0.017
5	0.141	0.158	0.176	−0.019	-0.009	0.007	−0.002	−0.001	0.004
6	0.154	0.173	0.153	−0.006	0.006	−0.018	0.013	0.017	−0.025
7	0.152	0.175	0.213	−0.009	0.008	0.038	0.011	0.016	0.036
8	0.146	0.192	0.185	−0.017	0.024	0.012	0.000	0.033	0.010
9	0.117	0.149	0.219	−0.047	−0.017	0.041	−0.031	−0.012	0.033
High	0.080	0.147	0.210	−0.082	−0.023	0.034	−0.063	−0.018	0.025
Nc	35,956	28,608	22,429	35,956	28,608	22,429	35,107	27,951	21,932

The figure replicates the original findings of Sloan. Companies reporting high levels of accruals in a base year realize substantially lower returns in the following two years. On the other hand, companies with the lowest levels of accruals realize substantially higher levels of accruals in the subsequent two years. Together, these observed patterns in stock returns suggest a market that is either pleasantly or unpleasantly surprised when subsequent earnings either increase (after low and typically income decreasing accruals) or decrease (after high and typically income increasing accruals).

Resources and Bibliography

Accruals versus cash flows:
Dechow, P.M., 1994. Accounting earnings and cash flows as measures of firm performance: the role of accounting accruals. J. Account. Econ. 18 (1), 3–42.
Accruals:
Bhushan, R., 1989. Firm Characteristics and Analyst Following. Journal of Accounting and Economics. 11 (2–3), 255–274.
Bradshaw, M.T., Richardson, S.A., Sloan, R.G., 2001. Do analysts and auditors use information in accruals? J. Account. Res. 39 (1), 45–74, June.
Sloan, R.G., 1996. Do stock prices fully reflect information in accruals and cash flows about future earnings? Account. Rev. 71 (3), 289–315, July.

The classic paper on this topic was written by Lang Wheeler and included in Brian's earlier book "The Handbook of Corporate Earnings Analysis."

Wheeler, L., 1994. Changes in consensus earnings estimates and their impact on stock returns. Handb. Corp. Earnings Anal.

Morgan Stanley's earnings revisions study is:

Whither Analysts Revisions?, December 2001. Global Equity and Derivative Markets Quantitative Strategies.

Other useful papers include:

Angwin, J., Peers, M., November 1, 2001. Cold Calls: AOL May Be Snubbing Merrill, Wall Street Journal.

Bagnoli, M., Beneish, D., Watts, S., 1999. Whisper forecasts of quarterly earnings per share. J. Account. Econ.

Bernstein, R., January 16, 2001. Five-year growth rates haven't budged, Merrill Lynch Quantitative Strategy Update.

DeBondt, W., Forbes, W., 1999. Herding in analyst earnings forecasts: evidence from the United Kingdom. Eur. Financ. Manage. 5 (2).

DeBondt, W., Thaler, R., May 1990. Do security analysts overreact?, AEA Papers and Proceedings.

Dechow, P., Skinner, D., 2000. Earnings management: reconciling the views of accounting academics, practitioners, and regulators. Account. Horiz. 15 (2).

Dreman, D., 1998. Contrarian Investment Strategies: The Next Generation. Simon and Schuster.

Edmonston, P., 2001, Focus on Whisper numbers fades as pundits sidestep the informal targets, Wall Street Journal, July 26.

Healy, P.M., Wahlen, J.M., 1999. A review of the earnings management literature and its implications for standard setting. Account. Horiz. 13 (4).

Jha, V., Mozes, H., April 2001. Forecasting changes in consensus earnings estimates, working paper.

Keon, 2001. What's the P/E Ratio of the S&P 500? Prudential Equity Res.

Li, X., 2002, Career concerns of analysts: compensation, termination and performance, Vanderbilt University working paper.

Lauricella, T., September 4, 2001, Analyst reports pressures of employer's trading, Wall Street Journal.

Schipper, K., 1989. Commentary on earnings management. Account. Horiz. 3 (4).

Williams, N., February 21, 2002, The quality and quantity of earnings: both are cyclical, Goldman Sachs Global Portfolio Strategy.

In this Appendix, we limited our definition of earnings management to what we termed "classical" earnings management. We omitted discussion of several related areas such as fraud, accounting choices, and operating decisions. The following papers and their included references address fraud through an analysis of Accounting and Auditing Enforcement Releases by the SEC.

Beneish, M.D., 1999. Incentives and penalties related to earnings overstatements that violate GAAP. Account. Rev. 74 (4), 425−457.

Bonner, S.E., Palmrose, Z.V., Young, S.M., 1998. Fraud type and auditor litigation: an analysis of SEC accounting and auditing enforcement releases. Account. Rev. 73 (4), 503−532.

Dechow, P., Sloan, R.G., Sweeney, A.P., Causes and consequences of earnings manipulation: an analysis of firms subject to enforcement actions by the SEC Contemp. Account. Res., 13 (1), 1−36.

Feroz, E.H., Park, K., Pastena, V.S., 1991. The financial and market effects of the SEC's accounting and auditing enforcement releases. J. Account. Res. 29 (Suppl.), 107−142.

Additionally, the following summary papers discuss the evidence regarding management accounting method choices, and to a lesser extent, operating decisions that impact reported income.

Fields, T.D., Lys, T.Z., Vincent, L., 2001. Empirical research on accounting choice. J. Account. Econ. 31 (1−3), 255−307.

Holthausen, R.W., Leftwich, R.W., 1983. The economic consequences of accounting choice − implications for costly contracting and monitoring. J. Account. Econ. 5 (2), 77−117.

For an analytical model supporting the notion that current shareholders demand earnings management, see:

Dye, R., 1988. Earnings management in an overlapping generations model. J. Account. Res. 26, 195−235.

The Jones model and several of its subsequent modifications may be found in the following papers:

Dechow, P.M., Sloan, R.G., Sweeney, A.P., Detecting earnings management. Account. Rev., 71 (2), 193−227, April.

Jones, J., 1991. Earnings management during import relief investigations. J. Account. Res. 29 (2), 193−228.

The following references are a very limited sampling of studies investigating specific accruals.

Ayers, B.C., Deferred Tax Accounting Under SFAS No. 109: An empirical investigation of its incremental value-relevance relative to APB No. 11. Account. Rev., 73 (2), 195−212.

Beatty, A., Chamberlain, S., Magliolo, J., 1995. Managing financial reports of commercial banks: the influence of taxes, regulatory capital and earnings. J. Account. Res. 33 (2), 231−261, Autumn.

Beaver, W.H., Engel, E.E., 1996. Discretionary behavior with respect to allowances for loan losses and the behavior of security prices. J. Account. Econ. 22 (1−3), 177−206, August−December.

Elliott, J.A., Hanna, J.D., 1996. Repeated accounting write-offs and the information content of earnings. J. Account. Res. 34, 135−155.

Francis, J., Hanna, J.D., Vincent, L., 1996. Causes and effects of discretionary asset write-offs. J. Account. Res. 34, 117−134.

Miller, G.S., and D.J. Skinner, Determinants of the valuation allowances for deferred tax assets under SFAS No. 109. Account. Rev., 73 (2), 213−233.

Petroni, K.R., 1992. Optimistic reporting in the property casualty insurance industry. J. Account. Econ. 15, 485−508.

Petroni, K.R., Ryan, S.G., Wahlen, J.M., 2000. Discretionary and non-discretionary revisions of loss reserves by property-casualty insurers: differential implications for future profitability, risk and market value. Rev. Account. Stud. 5, 95−125.

These studies examine the manipulation of earnings in order to affect compensation:

Gaver, J., Gaver, K., Austin, J., 1995. Additional evidence on bonus plans and income management. J. Account. Econ. 18, 3−28.

Guidry, F., Leone, A., Rock, S., 1999. Earnings-based bonus plans and earnings management by business unit managers. J. Account. Econ. 26, 113−142.

Healy, P., 1985. The effect of bonus schemes on accounting decisions. J. Account. Econ. 7, 85−107.

See the following studies for examinations of earnings management to avoid debt covenant violations:

DeFond, M.L., Jiambalvo, J., 1994. Debt covenant effects and the manipulation of accruals. J. Account. Econ. 17, 145−176.

Healy, P., Palepu, K.G., 1990. Effectiveness of accounting-based dividend covenants. J. Account. Econ. 12 (1−3), 97−124.

Incentives and results surrounding management buyouts are found in these papers:

DeAngelo, L. Accounting numbers as market valuation substitutes: a study of management buyouts of public stockholders. Account. Rev., 41, 400−420.

Perry, S.E., Williams, T.H., 1994. Earnings management preceding management buyout offers. J. Account. Econ. 18 (2), 157−180.

Stock-for-stock acquisitions and the existence of earnings management are addressed in the following papers:

Erickson, M., Wang S., Earnings management by acquiring firms in stock for stock mergers. J. Account. Econ., 27 (2), 149−176.

To read more about the anomalous distributions of earnings and earnings changes, see the following papers:

Burgstahler, D., Dichev I., Earnings management to avoid earnings decreases and losses. J. Account. Econ., 24 (1), 99−126.

Degeorge, F., Patel, J., Zeckhauser, R., 1999. Earnings management to exceed thresholds. J. Business. 72 (1), 1−33.

Portfolio Construction

Chapter Contents

A security's portfolio weight is the proportion of the portfolio's value that is allocated to that security. Securities' portfolio weights define the portfolio and determine the portfolio outcomes and performance. Portfolio construction is the process through which the weights are set and maintained. As such, portfolio construction is typically viewed as dealing primarily with a portfolio's risk, while security analysis selection deals primarily with the portfolio's return.

Once a security is selected, its weight must be determined. As discussed in the last chapter, these activities often are not mutually exclusive. Indeed, the selection of a security to be held in the portfolio results in the stock having a non-zero weight. However, there can be a meaningfully different outcome from holding a specific security at a weight of 1% compared to a weight of 5%, though both are non-zero weights. While the previous chapter discussed how security analysis results in the selection of securities in the portfolio, this chapter focuses on the determination of the weights of those selected securities and how the portfolio is rebalanced to maintain the security weights.

As with security analysis and selection, portfolio construction should be a clearly articulated component of the investment process. As such, portfolio construction should be motivated by

Trading and Money Management in a Student-Managed Portfolio.
DOI: http://dx.doi.org/10.1016/B978-0-12-374755-6.00004-2

and consistent with the investment philosophy and contribute to the overall objective of the investment process. In some investment processes, security selection and portfolio construction might be fully integrated and inseparable components, while they might be mutually exclusive activities in others. Moreover, the emphasis within the investment process might be heavily tilted toward one or the other activity or evenly split. That is, security selection and portfolio construction both contribute to value of an investment process. Therefore, the methods that yield the resulting portfolio weights should be clear in any investment process.

This chapter covers numerous aspects of portfolio construction and the contribution of portfolio weights to portfolio performance. We use the term "performance" broadly to mean the portfolio performance outcomes. As such, performance will at times refer to the expected or realized average returns, while at other times it will refer to the risk or distribution of returns. We begin with a review of basic portfolio mathematics. While the review might be unnecessary for many readers, we also use this review to introduce the notation that we will use for the remainder of this book.

Portfolio Weights and Returns

Consider a portfolio worth a total of $V_{p,t}$ dollars at time t. Suppose for each stock i, the portfolio holds S_i shares at a price per share of $P_{i,t}$ at time t. The weight of the stock in the portfolio is given by:

$$w_{i,t}^p = \frac{S_{i,t} \times P_{i,t}}{V_{p,t}} \tag{4.1}$$

The superscript on the weights identifies the weights as belonging to portfolio p. The weights of the N securities in the portfolio must sum to one at every point in time, so that:

$$\sum_{i=1}^{N} w_{i,t}^p = 1 \tag{4.2}$$

Note that we have explicitly included time subscripts for the number of shares, stock price, weight, and portfolio value. Holding the number of shares constant, a stock's portfolio weight will change over time if the price of the stock changes and/or the value of the portfolio changes. In the latter case, the weight of the stock might change when other securities' prices change, even if there is no change in the number of shares held in the portfolio. For convenience, we will often drop the time subscript from our notation if the time over which these are measured is unambiguous. However, we retain the time subscript for now and note that a time subscript on the number of shares is required if the number of shares changes over the time periods of interest.

The return for a stock over time t is defined to be its percentage change in value from the end of the previous period to the end of the current period, as given by:

$$r_{i,t} = \frac{P_{i,t} - P_{i,t-1}}{P_{i,t-1}} \tag{4.3}$$

A portfolio's return is similarly defined:

$$r_{p,t} = \frac{V_{p,t} - V_{p,t-1}}{V_{p,t-1}} \tag{4.4}$$

Combining equations 4.1, 4.3, and 4.4, a portfolio's return is a weighted average of the returns of the securities in the portfolio, as given by:

$$r_{p,t} = \sum_{i=1}^{N} w_{i,t-1}^{p} \times r_{i,t} \tag{4.5}$$

The equations make clear that two portfolios that hold the same securities at different weights are different portfolios and have different realized returns. For example, a value-weighted portfolio of 500 stocks will perform differently from an equally weighted portfolio of the same 500 stocks. Likewise, two portfolios that have different rebalancing schemes will have weights that evolve differently through time as a result of the number of shares changing. Therefore, an equally weighted portfolio that is rebalanced on a quarterly basis will perform differently from an equally weighted portfolio that is rebalanced on a daily basis, even ignoring transaction costs. In either case, there is a direct impact on portfolio performance resulting from portfolio construction.

Relative Returns and Active Weights

An investment strategy that aims to beat a specific benchmark's return is often referred to as a *relative return* strategy. This reflects that fact that the portfolio's absolute return is less important than its return relative to or against the benchmark return. For example, an investment manager who is hired by his or her client to manage a large cap core mandate with the S&P 500 Index as the benchmark is likely to be evaluated exclusively against that benchmark. The absolute performance of the portfolio is of little concern. If the portfolio has a 15% return in a given year, this may be viewed by the firm's clients as a terrible year if the S&P 500 experiences a 25% return. Likewise, if the portfolio loses 5% in a year, this may be celebrated by the client if the S&P 500 loses 12% that year.

The selection of securities and their weights distinguish one benchmark from another. The most popular benchmarks used in institutional portfolios in the United States are the S&P (e.g., S&P 500, S&P 400, and S&P 600) and Russell (e.g., Russell 1000, Russell 2000, and Russell 3000) equity indexes and the Barclays (e.g., Barclay's Aggregate and Barclay's U.S. Treasury). The FTSE (e.g., FTSE All World) MSCI indexes (e.g., MSCI EAFE and MSCI EM) are among the popular non-U.S. and global indexes. Exhibit 4.1 lists popular benchmarks, organized by asset class. In general, good benchmarks are those that clearly define the set of securities and weights so that a passive investment in the benchmark is feasible. The benchmark should be consistent with the portfolio's target asset class mix and style. Finally, the benchmark for any active strategy should be declared in advance so that outcomes can be measured against the benchmark.

Exhibit 4.1 Benchmarks

Equity	
FTSE All World	Global Large/Mid Cap
FTSE Global All Cap	Global All Cap
FTSE All World ex-U.S.	Non-U.S. Large/Mid Cap
FTSE Global All Cap ex-U.S.	Non-U.S. All Cap
FTSE Shariah Global	Global Shariah-compliant Large/Mid Cap
FTSE Emerging	Emerging Markets
MSCI World	Developed Market All Cap
MSCI ACWI	Global All Cap
MSCI EAFE	Europe, Asia and Far East Developed Large Cap
MSCI EM	Emerging Markets
Russell 1000	U.S. Large Cap
Russell 1000 Growth	U.S. Large Cap Growth
Russell 1000 Value	U.S. Large Cap Value
Russell 2000	U.S. Small Cap
Russell 2000 Growth	U.S. Small Cap Growth
Russell 2000 Value	U.S. Small Cap Value
Russell 3000	U.S. All Cap
Russell Midcap	U.S. Mid Cap
Russell Midcap Growth	U.S. Mid Cap Growth
Russell Midcap Value	U.S. Mid Cap Value
Russell Global Large Cap	Global Large Cap
Russell Global Small Cap	Global Small Cap
Russell Europe	Europe Large/Mid Cap
S&P 500	U.S. Large Cap
S&P 500 Growth	U.S. Large Cap Growth
S&P 500 Value	U.S. Large Cap Value
S&P 400	U.S. Mid Cap
S&P 400 Growth	U.S. Mid Cap Growth
S&P 400 Value	U.S. Mid Cap Value
S&P 600	U.S. Small
S&P 600 Growth	U.S. Small Growth
S&P 600 Value	U.S. Small Value

Equity	
S&P Global Broad Market (BMI)	Global All Cap
S&P Global 1200	Global Large Cap
Commodity	
Dow Jones-UBS	Global Energy, Industrial Metals, Precious Metals, Agriculture, and Livestock
S&P GSCI	Global Energy, Industrial Metals, Precious Metals, Agriculture, and Livestock
Hedge Fund	
Credit Suisse Hedge Fund	Global Multistrategy
HFN Aggregate	Global Multistrategy
HFRX Hedge Fund	Global Multistrategy
Fixed Income	
Barclay's Global Aggregate	Global Hedge Fund
Barclay's Global Treasury	Global Inv. Grade Government Intermediate to Long Term
Barclay's Global Corporate	Global Inv. Grade Corporate
Barclay's Global High Yield	Global Government and Corp. High Yield
Barclay's U.S. Aggregate	USD-denominated Inv. Grade
Barclay's U.S. Corporate	USD-denominated Inv. Grade Corporate
Barclay's U.S. Corporate High Yield	USD-denominated Corp. High Yield
Barclay's U.S. Municipal	U.S. State and Local General Obligation, Revenue, Insured, and Prerefunded
Barclay's U.S. TIPS	U.S. Treasury Inflation Protected
Barclay's U.S. Treasury	U.S. Treasury Intermediate to Long Term
Barclay's U.S. Universal	USD-denominated Inv. Grade, Corp. High Yield, Emerging Market and 144A
Barclay's Sterling Aggregate	GBP-denominated Inv. Grade
Barclay's Euro Aggregate	EUR-denominated Inv. Grade
Barclay's Asian-Pacific Aggregate	Asian-Pacific Investment Grade

We can express a portfolio's relative return in terms of a weighted average of the underlying security's relative returns. Defining $rr_{i,t} = r_{i,t} - r_{b,t}$ to be the relative return on security I relative to the portfolio's benchmark, the portfolio's relative return is given by:

$$rr_{p,t} = r_{p,t} - r_{b,t} = \sum_{i=1}^{N} w_{i,t-1}^{p} \times rr_{i,t} \qquad (4.6)$$

Thus, the higher the weight on securities with higher relative returns, the higher the relative return of the portfolio. This is just one way to express the relative return of the portfolio. It is also useful to consider alternative forms of calculating the portfolio's relative return. Specifically, we can use the fact that the benchmark is simply a portfolio that has a specific weight on each constituent security, and zero weights on non-constituent securities. Therefore, the benchmark's return can be written as:

$$r_{b,t} = \sum_{i=1}^{N} w_{i,t-1}^{b} \times r_{i,t} \tag{4.7}$$

Using the securities' benchmark weights and the portfolio weights, the portfolio's relative return can be written in terms of the securities' portfolio and benchmark weights and the securities' returns, as given by:

$$r_{p,t} - r_{b,t} = \sum_{i=1}^{N} w_{i,t-1}^{p} \times r_{i,t} - \sum_{i=1}^{N} w_{i,t-1}^{b} \times r_{i,t}$$
$$= \sum_{i=1}^{N} (w_{i,t-1}^{p} - w_{i,t-1}^{b}) \times r_{i,t} \tag{4.8}$$

In this calculation, the number of securities, N, refers to the number of securities in the benchmark plus any non-benchmark securities that are held in the portfolio. More generally, N could represent all securities in the market, with the portfolio and the benchmark having significant numbers of securities with zero weights.

The difference between the portfolio's weight and the benchmark's weight is known as a security's active weight. We define $\delta_{i,t-1}^{p} = w_{i,t-1}^{p} - w_{i,t-1}^{b}$ as the *active weight* in portfolio p on security i at time $t-1$. Therefore, the relative return on an actively managed portfolio is a sum of the product of all portfolio and benchmark securities' active weights and returns, as given:

$$r_{p,t} - r_{b,t} = \sum_{i=1}^{N} \delta_{i,t-1}^{p} \times r_{i,t}, \text{ where} \tag{4.9}$$

$$\sum_{i=1}^{N} \delta_{i,t-1}^{p} = 0 \tag{4.10}$$

Notice that the portfolios' active weights sum to zero. Clearly, a passive portfolio that mimics the benchmark exactly would have a zero active weight for every benchmark security. Any other portfolio has at least some non-zero active weights, while still having the property that the active weights sum to zero. Active weights that are positive are known as overweighted securities, or just overweights. Likewise, those securities with negative active weights are known as underweighted securities, or just underweights. Another interpretation of overweights and underweights is to think of them as *long* positions and *short* positions, respectively, relative to the benchmark. Indeed, any benchmark security that is not held in the portfolio is short relative to the benchmark. Furthermore, the amount by which the non-held security is short is its benchmark weight. Any other security in which the portfolio weight is less than the benchmark weight is also short relative to the benchmark by the difference between the benchmark weight and the portfolio weight.

The framework of a relative return strategy as given above is useful in both security analysis and portfolio construction. This framework reveals that value can be added in a relative return strategy from overweighting good securities and/or underweighting bad securities. That is, both picking winners and avoiding losers within the target benchmark contribute to the outperformance of a portfolio relative to its benchmark. Thus, a strategy need not actually short sell securities on an absolute basis to benefit from the ability to identify underperforming securities. Rather, such a strategy benefits relative to its benchmark by underweighting securities that underperform.

Furthermore, the above framework is flexible in its application to securities or groups of securities. Heretofore, we have focused the discussion on security weights and returns. However, this framework can be applied to weights and returns of groups of securities, such as groupings based on asset class, sector, characteristic, or factor. For example, the S&P 500 Index can be split among GICS sectors. Exhibit 4.2 provides the definitions for the GICS sectors. For a portfolio that has N_s securities from group s, the portfolio's weight in group s is the sum of the weights of the securities in group s, as given by:

Exhibit 4.2 Global Industry Classification Standard (GICS) Sector Definitions

Energy Sector — The GICS Energy Sector comprises companies whose businesses are dominated by either of the following activities: The construction or provision of oil rigs, drilling equipment, and other energy-related service and equipment, including seismic data collection. Companies engaged in the exploration, production, marketing, refining, and/or transportation of oil and gas products.
Materials Sector — The GICS Materials Sector encompasses a wide range of commodity-related manufacturing industries. Included in this sector are companies that manufacture chemicals, construction materials, glass, paper, forest products and related packaging products, and metals, minerals, and mining companies, including producers of steel.
Industrials Sector — The GICS Industrials Sector includes companies whose businesses are dominated by one of the following activities: the manufacture and distribution of capital goods, including aerospace and defense, construction, engineering and building products, electrical equipment, and industrial machinery. The provision of commercial

services and supplies, including printing, data processing, employment, environmental, and office services. The provision of transportation services, including airlines, couriers, marine, road and rail, and transportation infrastructure.

Consumer Discretionary Sector — The GICS Consumer Discretionary Sector encompasses those industries that tend to be the most sensitive to economic cycles. Its manufacturing segment includes automotive, household durable goods, textiles and apparel, and leisure equipment. The services segment includes hotels, restaurants and other leisure facilities, media production and services, and consumer retailing.

Consumer Staples Sector — The GICS Consumer Staples Sector comprises companies whose businesses are less sensitive to economic cycles. It includes manufacturers and distributors of food, beverages, and tobacco and producers of nondurable household goods and personal products. It also includes food and drug retailing companies.

Health Care Sector — The GICS Health Care Sector encompasses two main industry groups. The first includes companies who manufacture health care equipment and supplies or provide health-care-related services, including distributors of health care products, providers of basic health care services, and owners and operators of health care facilities and organizations. The second regroups companies primarily involved in the research, development, production, and marketing of pharmaceuticals and biotechnology products.

Financials Sector — The GICS Financial Sector contains companies involved in activities such as banking, consumer finance, investment banking and brokerage, asset management, insurance and investment, and real estate, including REITs.

Information Technology Sector — The GICS Information Technology Sector covers the following general areas: first, Technology Software and Services, including companies that primarily develop software in various fields such as the Internet, applications, systems, and/or databases management, and companies that provide information technology consulting and services; second, Technology Hardware and Equipment, including manufacturers and distributors of communications equipment, computers and peripherals, electronic equipment and related instruments, and semiconductor equipment and products.

Telecommunications Services Sector — The GICS Telecommunications Services Sector contains companies that provide communications services primarily through a fixed-line, cellular, wireless, high bandwidth, and/or fiber optic cable network.

Utilities Sector — The GICS Utilities Sector encompasses those companies considered electric, gas, or water utilities or companies that operate as independent producers and/or distributors of power. This sector includes both nuclear and non-nuclear facilities.

$$w_{s,t}^p = \sum_{i=1}^{N_s} w_{i,t}^p \tag{4.11}$$

where each i is a member of group s. Note that Equation 4.11 can also be written in active weight terms along the lines of equations 4.9 and 4.10. As such, group weights and active weights combine with group returns to generate portfolio returns and relative returns. Specifically, a portfolio might generate relative performance from overweighting and underweighting specific sectors, smaller stocks, or growth-oriented stocks. For a fixed income portfolio, such relative performance might originate from active weights to a particular duration or credit risk.

An example of group weightings appears in the TCU EIF investment process. Recall that the TCU EIF investment process was discussed in Chapter 3 regarding its approach to security selection and analysis. Of importance here is how the TCU EIF constructs its portfolio with specific allocation to asset classes and sectors within the equity class as

---

Exhibit 4.3 Texas Christian University Educational Investment Fund Top-Down Balanced Portfolio Construction Approach

The TCU-EIF is a well-diversified balanced fund, investing across multiple asset classes. The fund's long-term strategic asset allocation is 70/25/5 percentage allocations to stocks, bonds, and cash, respectively. Exposure to real estate and international assets is also encouraged. Tactical asset deviations from the strategic allocations are exercised within limits. For instance, equity allocations can range between 60 and 80% depending on shorter term capital market forecasts of the fund members.

At the beginning of the semester, the Fund's Chief Economist provides a state of the global economy address. Key macroeconomic variables discussed include gross domestic product, industrial production, capacity utilization, inflation, unemployment rates, default risk spreads, maturity risk spreads, intermediate Treasury bond rates, federal debt as a percentage of GDP, U.S. dollar strength relative to key foreign currencies, retail sales, fiscal and monetary policy, housing prices, and foreclosure rates. We use these and other leading indicators to proactively move assets to favorable sectors, evaluate businesses within those sectors using appropriate valuation techniques, and finally, to make investment decisions on individual companies.

After the economist's presentation, the class spends one week examining individual sectors. Class members are assigned to examine specific sectors and then to make formal presentations to the class, after which sector allocation targets are established for the semester. Targets are established by majority vote of fund members. Active sector allocations for equities are made relative to the S&P 500 equity industry sector allocations. Allocations can deviate up to 25% relative to the S&P 500 weightings. For instance, if 20% of the S&P 500 is allocated to the information technology sector, the EIF target weight to the sector can range anywhere from 15% to 25%, depending on the funds expectations for the sector.

Tactical decisions also are made to equities segmented by capital appreciation (dividend yields less than 2%), income and capital appreciation (dividend yields between 2% and 4%) and income (dividend yields over 4%) stocks. The fixed income portion of the portfolio is invested primarily in fixed income mutual funds, which are monitored by the fund's fixed income analysts. Fixed income deliberations focus on maturity and quality sector weightings. Key factors include interest rate movements, business cycle projections, duration, and convexity.

described in Exhibit 4.3. Notice that the TCU EIF portfolio construction specifically contemplates the benchmark weights in setting sector weights. In this way, they group makes an explicit consideration of active sector weights in constructing the fund.

Expected Returns

The expected return of a portfolio is the weighted average of the expected return of the portfolio's securities. In short, if the investment manager selects securities with high expected returns, the portfolio should have a high expected return. As such, the expected return is largely determined by the security selection and analysis that is covered in Chapter 3. However, the resulting portfolio expected return is also impacted by the choice of portfolio weights. We show this by taking statistical expectation of Equation 4.5 to get the portfolio's expected return. Assuming that portfolio weights are constant, the expected return on the portfolio is given by:

$$E[r_p] = \sum_{i=1}^{N} w_i^p \times E[r_i] \tag{4.12}$$

where $E[r_i]$ is the expected return on asset i.

Similarly, we can determine the average portfolio return using the average of the portfolio securities' returns by taking the average of Equation 4.5. Assuming constant portfolio weights, the arithmetic average portfolio return is given by:

$$\bar{r}_p = \sum_{i=1}^{N} w_i^p \times \bar{r}_i \tag{4.13}$$

where $\bar{r}_i$ is the expected return on asset i. We discuss the geometric average return later in this chapter.

The assumption that weights are constant is unlikely to be true. Indeed, other than extreme coincidence, weights are constant only if the portfolio is rebalanced to the same weights at least as often as, or more often than, the data are observed. For example, to use Equation 4.13 to calculate the average return of an equally weighted portfolio using monthly returns, the portfolio must be rebalanced at least monthly to maintain the equal weights. If the portfolio is not rebalanced monthly, the security weights drift away from their starting values due to price changes. Consequently, the average return of a rebalanced portfolio can differ from the average return of a portfolio that is not rebalanced, even if both portfolios start with the same security weights.

Using portfolios of four stocks, Exhibit 4.4 illustrates how portfolio weights drift unless the portfolio is rebalanced and how the returns between a rebalanced and non-rebalanced portfolio can differ. Each portfolio begins the example period with weights of 40% in AAPL, 30% in CNP, 20% in DDS, and 10% in ROK. The portfolio with constant weights is rebalanced back to the same weights at the end of each month (ignoring transaction costs). Each month's portfolio return is calculated according to Equation 4.5, using the same weights each month, of course. The average of the monthly returns of this portfolio is 2.70%. Note that the average monthly portfolio return is equal to the weighted average of the average monthly stock returns, as given in Equation 4.13. The portfolio with no rebalancing begins with the same set of weights as the portfolio with constant weights, but those weights drift away from their initial values over time. As each stock experiences a return in a month, all stocks' weights change as well. The weight on AAPL starts at 40%, but exceeds 50% during the year, while the weight KO dwindles from an initial 30% to only 23.5% of the portfolio. The variations in weights each month cause the weights used in Equation 4.5 to differ each month, resulting in a portfolio return that differs from the return to the portfolio with constant weights. In this example, the rebalanced portfolio earns a higher rate of return over the year than the portfolio that is not rebalanced. However, this is not always the case, as a different pattern of stock returns might result in the rebalanced

Exhibit 4.4 Four Stock Portfolio Average Return Example

	Portfolio with Constant Weights (Rebalanced Monthly)					
	AAPL	CNP	DDS	ROK		
Weights:	40.0%	30.0%	20.0%	10.0%	Portfolio	Portfolio
Month		Stock Returns			Value ($)	Returns
Dec–02					100,000	
Jan–03	0.21%	–10.04%	–5.42%	11.30%	97,117	–2.88%
Feb–03	4.53%	–31.78%	–7.00%	0.54%	88,308	–9.07%
Mar–03	–5.80%	52.79%	–7.10%	–10.04%	98,107	11.10%
Apr–03	0.57%	3.82%	8.20%	10.14%	102,058	4.03%
May–03	26.23%	16.88%	–4.43%	4.45%	117,485	15.12%
Jun–03	6.18%	–15.94%	1.12%	0.80%	115,132	–2.00%
Jul–03	10.60%	–2.74%	11.88%	8.39%	122,766	6.63%
Aug–03	7.26%	4.49%	0.40%	5.98%	128,817	4.93%
Sep–03	–8.36%	9.07%	–7.34%	–3.56%	125,667	–2.45%
Oct–03	10.47%	1.32%	15.67%	18.29%	137,664	9.55%
Nov–03	–8.65%	–0.98%	4.21%	7.62%	134,702	–2.15%
Dec–03	2.20%	–5.35%	–2.08%	7.07%	134,119	–0.43%
		Average return per period:				
	3.79%	1.80%	0.68%	5.08%		2.70%

(Continued)

Exhibit 4.4 Four Stock Portfolio Average Return Example (Continued)

Portfolio with No Rebalancing

Month	\multicolumn{4}{c}{Stock Positions* ($)}	Portfolio Value ($)	Portfolio Returns
	AAPL	KO	DDS	ROK		
Dec–02	40,000	30,000	20,000	10,000	100,000	
Jan–03	40,084	26,988	18,916	11,130	97,117	–2.88%
Feb–03	41,898	18,410	17,591	11,190	89,090	–8.27%
Mar–03	39,470	28,129	16,343	10,067	94,009	5.52%
Apr–03	39,693	29,204	17,684	11,088	97,669	3.89%
May–03	50,105	34,134	16,900	11,582	112,720	15.41%
Jun–03	53,203	28,695	17,089	11,675	110,662	–1.83%
Jul–03	58,842	27,907	19,119	12,654	118,522	7.10%
Aug–03	63,112	29,161	19,195	13,411	124,880	5.36%
Sep–03	57,837	31,807	17,787	12,933	120,363	–3.62%
Oct–03	63,894	32,227	20,573	15,298	131,992	9.66%
Nov–03	58,367	31,911	21,439	16,463	128,179	–2.89%
Dec–03	59,651	30,204	20,993	17,627	128,475	0.23%
				Average return per period:		2.31%

Month	\multicolumn{4}{c}{Stock Positions* (Portfolio Weights)}
	AAPL	KO	DDS	ROK
Dec–02	40.0%	30.0%	20.0%	10.0%
Jan–03	41.3%	27.8%	19.5%	11.5%
Feb–03	47.0%	20.7%	19.7%	12.6%
Mar–03	42.0%	29.9%	17.4%	10.7%
Apr–03	40.6%	29.9%	18.1%	11.4%
May–03	44.5%	30.3%	15.0%	10.3%
Jun–03	48.1%	25.9%	15.4%	10.5%
Jul–03	49.6%	23.5%	16.1%	10.7%
Aug–03	50.5%	23.4%	15.4%	10.7%
Sep–03	48.1%	26.4%	14.8%	10.7%
Oct–03	48.4%	24.4%	15.6%	11.6%
Nov–03	45.5%	24.9%	16.7%	12.8%
Dec–03	46.4%	23.5%	16.3%	13.7%

*Positions are as of the end-of-month.

portfolio having lower returns. In general, the rebalancing frequency can affect the returns to a portfolio. For the constant weight formula in Equation 4.12 to work exactly, the frequency of rebalancing must match the frequency with which returns are measured.

The constant weight formulas also apply to the calculation of relative returns. The expected relative return of a portfolio is the expected portfolio return minus the expected benchmark return,

$$E[r_p] - E[r_b] = E[r_p - r_b] = \sum_{i=1}^{N} w_i^p \times E[r_i - r_b] = \sum_{i=1}^{N} w_i^p \times E[rr_i] \tag{4.14}$$

Likewise, the average relative return of the portfolio is given by:

$$\overline{rr}_p = \overline{r}_p - \overline{r}_b = \sum_{i=1}^{N} w_i^p \times (\overline{r}_i - \overline{r}_b) = \sum_{i=1}^{N} w_i^p \times (\overline{r}_i - \overline{r}_b) \tag{4.15}$$

These equations illustrate that the portfolio's expected or average relative return depends on securities' portfolio weights and their relative returns. The higher the weight on securities with higher relative returns, the higher the portfolio's average relative return.

We can also express a portfolio's average relative return in terms of each security's average relative return, as given by:

$$\overline{r}_p - \overline{r}_b = \sum_{i=1}^{N} w_i^p \times (\overline{r}_i - \overline{r}_b) = \sum_{i=1}^{N} w_i^p \times (\overline{r}_i - \overline{r}_b) \tag{4.16}$$

Total Risk of a Portfolio

A common measure of total risk in a portfolio is the portfolio's variance of returns. It is also common to use standard deviation, which is the square root of the variance. The return variance of a constant weight portfolio depends on the variances and covariances of the portfolio's underlying securities. Denote the covariance between security i and security j as $\sigma_{i,j}^2 = Cov(r_i, r_j)$ and the variance of security i as $\sigma_i^2 = Var(r_i) = Cov(r_i, r_i) = \sigma_{i,i}^2$. For a portfolio of N securities, the $N \times N$ covariance matrix has off-diagonal (i.e., when $i \neq j$) elements of $\sigma_{i,j}^2$ and diagonal (i.e., when $i = j$) elements of the covariance matrix are σ_i^2. The portfolio variance is given by:[1]

$$Var(r_p) = \sigma_p^2 = \sum_{i=1}^{N} \sum_{j=1}^{N} w_i^p w_j^p \sigma_{i,j}^2 \tag{4.17}$$

The covariance between two securities is also be defined as the product of the correlation between two securities and those securities' standard deviations, or $\sigma_{i,j}^2 = \sigma_i \sigma_j \rho_{i,j}$, where $\rho_{i,j}$ is the correlation coefficient. The correlation coefficient measures the extent to which two securities, returns move with one another. Unlike the covariance, which also measures the

---

[1] Using matrix notation, we can define the N-dimensional vector of security weights as **w** and the covariance matrix as **V**, so that portfolio variance is **w′Vw**.

relationship between securities' returns, the correlation coefficient is standardized and is bounded between -1 and 1. Therefore, it is sometimes more convenient or meaningful to analyze the co-movement or relationship between two securities' returns in terms of the correlation, rather than the covariance. Using correlation, the portfolio variance can also be written as:

$$\sigma_p^2 = \sum_{i=1}^{N}\sum_{j=1}^{N} w_i^p w_j^p \sigma_i \sigma_j \rho_{i,j} \tag{4.18}$$

The standard deviation of the portfolio is, of course, given by:

$$\sigma_p = \sqrt{\sigma_p^2} \tag{4.19}$$

The formula for the portfolio variance illustrates that the portfolio risk increases when more weight is placed on securities with (1) higher variances and (2) higher covariances with other portfolio securities. Total risk is often important when the portfolio is considered as an investor's only portfolio or investment.

Exhibit 4.5 Return Covariance Matrix and Correlation Matrix

Correlation of Monthly Returns (2003 – 2007)

	MSFT	DELL	AAPL	ORCL	IBM	KO	WFC	DDS	ROK	CNP	
MSFT		0.37	0.24	0.15	0.27	0.22	−0.08	0.14	−0.05	0.06	
DELL	0.37		0.29	0.27	0.34	0.19	0.00	0.36	0.34	0.02	
AAPL	0.24	0.29		0.35	0.25	0.16	0.05	0.17	0.44	0.05	
ORCL	0.15	0.27	0.35		0.38	0.15	0.16	0.18	0.32	−0.12	
IBM	0.27	0.34	0.25	0.38		0.17	0.23	0.02	0.19	0.15	
KO	0.22	0.19	0.16	0.15	0.17		0.11	−0.15	0.02	0.20	
WFC	−0.08	0.00	0.05	0.16	0.23	0.11		0.14	0.14	0.06	
DDS	0.14	0.36	0.17	0.18	0.02	−0.15	0.14		0.35	0.06	
ROK	−0.05	0.34	0.44	0.32	0.19	0.02	0.14	0.35		−0.10	**Overall**
CNP	0.06	0.02	0.05	−0.12	0.15	0.20	0.06	0.06	−0.10		**Average**
Average	0.15	0.24	0.22	0.20	0.22	0.12	0.09	0.14	0.18	0.04	0.16

Correlation of Monthly Returns (2008 - 2012)

	MSFT	DELL	AAPL	ORCL	IBM	KO	WFC	DDS	ROK	CNP	
MSFT		0.59	0.55	0.66	0.38	0.41	0.49	0.58	0.45	0.35	
DELL	0.59		0.48	0.63	0.52	0.22	0.33	0.33	0.56	0.38	
AAPL	0.55	0.48		0.48	0.49	0.26	0.15	0.55	0.45	0.34	
ORCL	0.66	0.63	0.48		0.54	0.23	0.35	0.47	0.53	0.35	
IBM	0.38	0.52	0.49	0.54		0.31	0.23	0.45	0.42	0.36	
KO	0.41	0.22	0.26	0.23	0.31		0.35	0.46	0.32	0.44	
WFC	0.49	0.33	0.15	0.35	0.23	0.35		0.47	0.46	0.09	
DDS	0.58	0.33	0.55	0.47	0.45	0.46	0.47		0.45	0.33	
ROK	0.45	0.56	0.45	0.53	0.42	0.32	0.46	0.45		0.44	**Overall**
CNP	0.35	0.38	0.34	0.35	0.36	0.44	0.09	0.33	0.44		**Average**
Average	0.49	0.45	0.42	0.47	0.41	0.33	0.32	0.45	0.45	0.34	0.42

Average Correlations (2003 – 2007)

	Info. Tech.	Other
Info. Tech.	0.29	0.14
Other	0.14	0.08

Average Correlations (2008 – 2012)

	Info. Tech.	Other
Info. Tech.	0.53	0.38
Other	0.38	0.38

Covariance of Monthly Returns (2003 – 2007)

	MSFT	DELL	AAPL	ORCL	IBM	KO	WFC	DDS	ROK	CNP	
MSFT	0.0033	0.0015	0.0014	0.0006	0.0008	0.0006	−0.0002	0.0008	−0.0002	0.0003	
DELL	0.0015	0.0046	0.0021	0.0012	0.0011	0.0005	0.0000	0.0023	0.0017	0.0001	
AAPL	0.0014	0.0021	0.0111	0.0025	0.0013	0.0007	0.0002	0.0017	0.0034	0.0005	
ORCL	0.0006	0.0012	0.0025	0.0045	0.0013	0.0004	0.0004	0.0012	0.0016	−0.0008	
IBM	0.0008	0.0011	0.0013	0.0013	0.0025	0.0004	0.0004	0.0001	0.0007	0.0008	
KO	0.0006	0.0005	0.0007	0.0004	0.0004	0.0019	0.0002	−0.0006	0.0001	0.0009	
WFC	−0.0002	0.0000	0.0002	0.0004	0.0004	0.0002	0.0012	0.0005	0.0003	0.0002	
DDS	0.0008	0.0023	0.0017	0.0012	0.0001	−0.0006	0.0005	0.0087	0.0024	0.0006	
ROK	−0.0002	0.0017	0.0034	0.0016	0.0007	0.0001	0.0003	0.0024	0.0054	−0.0008	Overall
CNP	0.0003	0.0001	0.0005	−0.0008	0.0008	0.0009	0.0002	0.0006	−0.0008	0.0104	Average
Average	0.0009	0.0015	0.0025	0.0013	0.0009	0.0005	0.0003	0.0018	0.0015	0.0012	0.0012

Covariance of Monthly Returns (2008 – 2012)

	MSFT	DELL	AAPL	ORCL	IBM	KO	WFC	DDS	ROK	CNP	
MSFT	0.0054	0.0049	0.0042	0.0040	0.0016	0.0015	0.0044	0.0081	0.0041	0.0017	
DELL	0.0049	0.0127	0.0057	0.0058	0.0032	0.0013	0.0047	0.0071	0.0080	0.0028	
AAPL	0.0042	0.0057	0.0110	0.0041	0.0029	0.0014	0.0020	0.0111	0.0060	0.0023	
ORCL	0.0040	0.0058	0.0041	0.0068	0.0025	0.0010	0.0035	0.0074	0.0055	0.0019	
IBM	0.0016	0.0032	0.0029	0.0025	0.0031	0.0009	0.0016	0.0048	0.0029	0.0013	
KO	0.0015	0.0013	0.0014	0.0010	0.0009	0.0027	0.0023	0.0045	0.0021	0.0015	
WFC	0.0044	0.0047	0.0020	0.0035	0.0016	0.0023	0.0155	0.0112	0.0071	0.0008	
DDS	0.0081	0.0071	0.0111	0.0074	0.0048	0.0045	0.0112	0.0363	0.0107	0.0041	
ROK	0.0041	0.0080	0.0060	0.0055	0.0029	0.0021	0.0071	0.0107	0.0158	0.0037	Overall
CNP	0.0017	0.0028	0.0023	0.0019	0.0013	0.0015	0.0008	0.0041	0.0037	0.0044	Average
Average	0.0040	0.0056	0.0051	0.0042	0.0025	0.0019	0.0053	0.0105	0.0066	0.0025	0.0048

Average Covariances (2003 – 2007)

	Info. Tech.	Other
Info. Tech.	0.0014	0.0007
Other	0.0007	0.0004

Average Covariances (2008 – 2012)

	Info. Tech.	Other
Info. Tech.	0.0039	0.0039
Other	0.0039	0.0048

Exhibit 4.5 shows the correlation and covariance matrixes using monthly returns for ten stocks during the period 2003 through 2012. These ten stocks were constituents of the S&P 500 as of the end of 2012. We report the correlation and covariance matrixes in each 5-year period within the entire 10-year period to allow us to consider how correlations, variances, and covariances change through time. Note that five of the ten stocks are from the Information Technology sector: MSFT, DELL, AAPL, ORCL, and IBM. We would expect these stocks to be more correlated with one another (i.e., to covary more with one another or to have higher covariances) than with stocks in other sectors. The other five stocks are from different sectors: KO from Consumer Staples; WFC from Financials; DDS from Consumer Discretionary; ROK from Industrials; and CNP from Utilities.

The "heat map" color coding is intended to aid in visually comparing stocks' covariances and correlations. Notice that the Information Technology stocks in the top-left quadrant of the correlation matrix for both 2003 through 2007 and 2008 through 2012 are coded as "warm" (i.e., yellow, orange, and red), indicating that they are among the highest correlations among these ten stocks. The correlations in the other three quadrants have a mix of green, yellow, and red, indicating that there is a mix of relatively high and low correlations. The summary matrixes show that the average correlations among the Information Technology sector stocks are higher in both 5-year periods, compared to the average correlation of Information Technology stocks with stocks in other sectors and the average correlation among those other sectors' stocks. Indeed, the correlations among Information Technology stocks average 0.29, but the correlations between Information Technology stocks from other sectors average 0.14 in the 2003 through 2007 period. Correlations are generally higher in the 2008 through 2012 period, but the tendency for stocks to have higher correlations with stocks in their own sector remains.

Similarly, the Information Technology stocks have covariances that tend toward yellow and orange, indicating that they are in the mid-to-high covariances among these ten stocks. In contrast, the covariances between Information Technology stocks and stocks outside the Information Technology sector tend toward green and yellow, indicating that they are among the lower covariances of these ten stocks. The average covariances for 2003 through 2007 indicate that these five Information Technology stocks have an average return covariance of 0.0014 with each other (excluding stocks' own variances from the average), while they have an average return covariance of 0.0007 with stocks in other sectors.

Interestingly, the results are somewhat different in the 2008 through 2012 period, as Information Technology stocks' return covariances with each other are roughly equal to their return covariances with stocks from other sectors. This provides evidence that covariances can change through time. However, we note that there is considerable similarity in the average covariance between the two time periods. In particular, DELL, AAPL, DDS, and ROK are in the top 5 covariances in both periods, leaving 4 stocks in the bottom 5 for both periods. Likewise, KO's average covariance with all other stocks is either the lowest or next-to-lowest in each time period, while DDS is either the highest or next-to-highest in each time period. These ten stocks comprise a very limited sample. For this reason, we caution against drawing strong conclusions from this example. However, persistence in return variances and covariances seems likely to be similar from time period to time period, since businesses are often exposed to the same or similar risk factors through time.

The portfolio variance calculation is readily accomplished in Excel with at least two methods. The first method, which we refer to as the "matrix method," builds a return covariance matrix and a calculation matrix. The return covariance matrix appears in Exhibit 4.5 and uses the $=$ COVAR() function in Excel.[2] We create a second "calculation matrix" that allows us to calculate the double-sum in Equation 4.17. For the calculation matrix, we create a row of portfolio weights as shown in Exhibit 4.6. References to these weights are made in the column to the left of the calculation matrix, so that we have a row of weights and a column of weights that create the top and left blue borders of the calculation matrix. In terms of the formula, the weights for security i appear across the top and weights for security j appear down the left side. We add a cell that sums the weights. This sum should always equal one and is there to confirm that our portfolio weights are properly defined. For each entry in the body of calculation matrix, we multiply the w_i^p from that entry's row by the w_j^p from that entry's column and by the two securities' covariance, $\sigma_{i,j}^2$, which appears in the same matrix position in the return covariance matrix. That is, we create the product, $w_i^p w_j^p \sigma_{i,j}^2$, in each cell of the calculation matrix. After the first formula is entered into the upper-left cell of this matrix, it can be efficiently copied across and down to fill the table.[3] To calculate the portfolio variance, we sum the entire calculation matrix to accomplish the double-sum in Equation 4.17. Note that we can change the row of weights and Excel automatically calculates the new portfolio variance and standard deviation.

A second method for calculating the portfolio variance is to use the time series of security returns to create a time series of portfolio returns. The variance is then calculated directly from the time series of portfolio returns. We refer to this method as the "time series" method. In this method, we must have a set of weights, as shown in Exhibit 4.6. In each month, we utilize Equation 4.5 to create that month's portfolio return. This is easily accomplished with Excel's $=$ SUMPRODUCT() function that takes the array of weights and array of returns in a given month as the arguments to the function, being careful to use

[2] The $=$ COVAR() function in Microsoft Excel 2007 is the population covariance. However, it is more common to use a sample covariance calculation. Therefore, we get the sample covariance by making the simple adjustment of multiplying Excel's population covariance by N/(N-1), where N is the number of periods in our sample. All calculations in this Exhibit use this adjustment where necessary. Note that the $=$ STDEV() and $=$ VAR() functions are sample standard deviation and variance function, respectively. Therefore, no adjustment of these functions is necessary.

[3] The formula can be copied and pasted across and down as long as care is taken to put the appropriate absolute references (using the "$") in place, as shown in the exhibit.

Exhibit 4.6 Excel Calculation of Portfolio Variance and Standard Deviation

Calculation Matrix Method

Calculation Matrix Method

	B197		▾	fx	=B$196*$A197*B167						

	A	B	C	D	E	F	G	H	I	J	K	L	M
165						Covariance of Monthly Returns (2003 - 2007)							
166		MSFT	DELL	AAPL	ORCL	IBM	KO	WFC	DDS	ROK	CNP		
167	MSFT	0.0033	0.0015	0.0014	0.0006	0.0008	0.0006	-0.0002	0.0008	-0.0002	0.0003		
168	DELL	0.0015	0.0046	0.0021	0.0012	0.0011	0.0005	0.0000	0.0023	0.0017	0.0001		
169	AAPL	0.0014	0.0021	0.0111	0.0025	0.0013	0.0007	0.0002	0.0017	0.0034	0.0005		
170	ORCL	0.0006	0.0012	0.0025	0.0045	0.0013	0.0004	0.0004	0.0012	0.0016	-0.0008		
171	IBM	0.0008	0.0011	0.0013	0.0013	0.0025	0.0004	0.0004	0.0001	0.0007	0.0008		
172	KO	0.0006	0.0005	0.0007	0.0004	0.0004	0.0019	0.0002	-0.0006	0.0001	0.0009		
173	WFC	-0.0002	0.0000	0.0002	0.0004	0.0004	0.0002	0.0012	0.0005	0.0003	0.0002		
174	DDS	0.0008	0.0023	0.0017	0.0012	0.0001	-0.0006	0.0005	0.0087	0.0024	0.0006		
175	ROK	-0.0002	0.0017	0.0034	0.0016	0.0007	0.0001	0.0003	0.0024	0.0054	-0.0008	Overall	
176	CNP	0.0003	0.0001	0.0005	-0.0008	0.0008	0.0009	0.0002	0.0006	-0.0008	0.0104	Average	
177	Average	0.0009	0.0015	0.0025	0.0013	0.0009	0.0005	0.0003	0.0018	0.0015	0.0012	0.0012	
178													
179						Covariance of Monthly Returns (2008 - 2012)							
180		MSFT	DELL	AAPL	ORCL	IBM	KO	WFC	DDS	ROK	CNP		
181	MSFT	0.0054	0.0049	0.0042	0.0040	0.0016	0.0015	0.0044	0.0081	0.0041	0.0017		
182	DELL	0.0049	0.0127	0.0057	0.0058	0.0032	0.0013	0.0047	0.0071	0.0080	0.0028		
183	AAPL	0.0042	0.0057	0.0110	0.0041	0.0029	0.0014	0.0020	0.0111	0.0060	0.0023		
184	ORCL	0.0040	0.0058	0.0041	0.0068	0.0025	0.0010	0.0035	0.0074	0.0055	0.0019		
185	IBM	0.0016	0.0032	0.0029	0.0025	0.0031	0.0009	0.0016	0.0048	0.0029	0.0013		
186	KO	0.0015	0.0013	0.0014	0.0010	0.0009	0.0027	0.0023	0.0045	0.0021	0.0015		
187	WFC	0.0044	0.0047	0.0020	0.0035	0.0016	0.0023	0.0155	0.0112	0.0071	0.0008		
188	DDS	0.0081	0.0071	0.0111	0.0074	0.0048	0.0045	0.0112	0.0363	0.0107	0.0041		
189	ROK	0.0041	0.0080	0.0060	0.0055	0.0029	0.0021	0.0071	0.0107	0.0158	0.0037	Overall	
190	CNP	0.0017	0.0028	0.0023	0.0019	0.0013	0.0015	0.0008	0.0041	0.0037	0.0044	Average	
191	Average	0.0040	0.0056	0.0051	0.0042	0.0025	0.0019	0.0053	0.0105	0.0066	0.0025	0.0048	
192													
193													
194						Portfolio Variance Calculation Matrix (2003 - 2007)							
195		MSFT	DELL	AAPL	ORCL	IBM	KO	WFC	DDS	ROK	CNP	Sum	
196	Weights	0.10	0.10	0.10	0.10	0.10	0.10	0.10	0.10	0.10	0.10	1.00	
197	0.10	3.3E-05	1.5E-05	1.4E-05	5.8E-06	7.7E-06	5.5E-06	-1.5E-06	7.5E-06	-2.2E-06	3.5E-06		
198	0.10	1.5E-05	4.6E-05	2.1E-05	1.2E-05	1.1E-05	5.5E-06	1.0E-07	2.3E-05	1.7E-05	1.2E-06		
199	0.10	1.4E-05	2.1E-05	1.1E-04	2.5E-05	1.3E-05	7.3E-06	1.8E-06	1.7E-05	3.4E-05	4.9E-06		
200	0.10	5.8E-06	1.2E-05	2.5E-05	4.5E-05	1.3E-05	4.3E-06	3.6E-06	1.2E-05	1.6E-05	-8.0E-06		
201	0.10	7.7E-06	1.1E-05	1.3E-05	1.3E-05	2.5E-05	3.7E-06	3.9E-06	7.9E-07	7.0E-06	7.5E-06		
202	0.10	5.5E-06	5.5E-06	7.3E-06	4.3E-06	3.7E-06	1.9E-05	1.7E-06	-5.9E-06	5.2E-07	8.9E-06		
203	0.10	-1.5E-06	1.0E-07	1.8E-06	3.6E-06	3.9E-06	1.7E-06	1.2E-05	4.6E-06	3.5E-06	2.1E-06		
204	0.10	7.5E-06	2.3E-05	1.7E-05	1.2E-05	7.9E-07	-5.9E-06	4.6E-06	8.7E-05	2.4E-05	6.1E-06		
205	0.10	-2.2E-06	1.7E-05	3.4E-05	1.6E-05	7.0E-06	5.2E-07	3.5E-06	2.4E-05	5.4E-05	-7.8E-06		Portfolio
206	0.10	3.5E-06	1.2E-06	4.9E-06	-8.0E-06	7.5E-06	8.9E-06	2.1E-06	6.1E-06	-7.8E-06	1.0E-04	Variance	0.0012
207												St. Dev.	3.52%
208													

(Continued)

Exhibit 4.6 Excel Calculation of Portfolio Variance and Standard Deviation (Continued)

Time Series Method

Time Series Method

	A	B	C	D	E	F	G	H	I	J	K	L	M
				Function Library							Defined Names		
	M3	▾		f_x	=SUMPRODUCT($B$135:$K$135,B3:K3)								
1							Monthly Returns						
2	Month	MSFT	DELL	AAPL	ORCL	IBM	KO	WFC	DDS	ROK	CNP		Portfolio
3	200301	-8.20%	-10.77%	0.21%	11.39%	0.90%	-7.71%	1.07%	-5.42%	11.30%	-12.66%		-1.99%
4	200302	0.21%	12.99%	4.53%	-0.58%	-0.13%	-0.59%	-3.63%	-7.00%	0.54%	-33.29%		-2.69%
5	200303	2.15%	1.30%	-5.80%	-9.29%	0.62%	1.19%	-0.79%	-7.10%	-10.04%	53.76%		2.60%
120	201210	-4.10%	-6.24%	-10.76%	-1.02%	-6.23%	-1.98%	-2.43%	6.47%	2.17%	1.74%		-2.24%
121	201211	-5.94%	4.33%	-1.24%	3.52%	-1.86%	2.68%	-1.37%	15.47%	12.17%	-8.02%		1.97%
122	201212	0.36%	6.02%	-9.07%	4.12%	0.78%	-4.40%	3.54%	-0.10%	5.99%	-2.43%		0.48%
123													
124	2003-2007												
125	Avg.	0.96%	0.08%	6.20%	1.46%	0.77%	0.86%	0.75%	0.77%	2.44%	2.09%		1.64%
126	Variance	0.0033	0.0046	0.0111	0.0045	0.0025	0.0019	0.0012	0.0087	0.0054	0.0104		0.0012
127	St. Dev.	5.76%	6.77%	10.56%	6.72%	5.02%	4.36%	3.43%	9.35%	7.34%	10.21%		3.52%
128													
129	2008-2012												
130	Avg.	-0.01%	-0.80%	2.26%	1.04%	1.27%	0.66%	1.21%	4.57%	1.32%	0.84%		1.23%
131	Variance	0.0054	0.0127	0.0110	0.0068	0.0031	0.0027	0.0155	0.0363	0.0158	0.0044		0.0048
132	St. Dev.	7.34%	11.27%	10.50%	8.22%	5.56%	5.15%	12.46%	19.06%	12.58%	6.62%		6.95%
133													
134		MSFT	DELL	AAPL	ORCL	IBM	KO	WFC	DDS	ROK	CNP	Sum	
135	Weights	0.10	0.10	0.10	0.10	0.10	0.10	0.10	0.10	0.10	0.10	1.00	
136													

absolute references for the weights so that the formula can be copied and pasted to all months. We leave it to the reader to verify that each method results in the same portfolio variance and standard deviation when using the same set of portfolio weights.

Returning to our analysis of the relationship between securities' covariances and portfolio variance and standard deviation, we begin with an equally weighted portfolio (i.e., each stock has a weight of 10%), which we label P1. Applying the equal weights using the matrix method or the time-series method, we calculate the portfolio variance over the 2003 through 2007 period to be 0.001237 and the portfolio standard deviation to be 3.52%, as shown in Exhibit 4.7. With the 2008 through 2012 period being one of higher variances and covariances, the equally weighted portfolio's standard deviation is consequently higher at 6.95%. Portfolio P1 is diversified among ten stocks, but is relatively concentrated in a single sector, with 50% of the portfolio weight on the five Information Technology stocks.

Exhibit 4.7 Portfolio Weights and Standard Deviations

Portfolio	Portfolio Weights										Standard Deviation	
	MSFT	DELL	AAPL	ORCL	IBM	KO	WFC	DDS	ROK	CNP	2003 – 2007	2008 – 2012
P1	10%	10%	10%	10%	10%	10%	10%	10%	10%	10%	3.52%	6.95%
P2	5%	5%	5%	5%	5%	25%	25%	5%	5%	15%	2.97%	6.28%
P3	5%	5%	5%	5%	5%	5%	5%	25%	25%	15%	4.39%	9.04%

It seems that better diversification is possible. Indeed, the covariance matrix reveals that KO and WFC have the lowest average covariance among these ten stocks in 2003 through 2007. Therefore, placing more weight in these stocks is expected to decrease the overall portfolio variance during that period. Portfolio P2 places a weight of 25% on KO and WFC, 15% on CNP, and 5% on all other stocks, resulting in a portfolio standard deviation of 2.97% in 2003 through 2007. In contrast, DDS and ROK have among the highest average covariances among the stocks outside the Information Technology sector during both periods. Constructing portfolio P3 to have a weight of 25% on DDS and ROK and setting KO and WFC each to 5% results in a portfolio standard deviation of 4.39% and 9.04% in 2003 through 2007 and 2008 through 2012, respectively. In summary, the example illustrates that portfolio construction, or the choice of weights, combines with the characteristics of the portfolio securities as reflected in the return covariances, to determine the total risk of the portfolio.

Tracking Error and Relative Risk

Tracking error is the risk of the portfolio's returns relative to its benchmark. This measure of relative risk is often important when the mandate for the investment manager is to outperform a specific benchmark, but to also have a similar exposure to that benchmark's asset class. For example, a client might grant an active U.S. small cap core mandate to an investment manager with either the Russell 2000 Index or the S&P Small Cap 600 Index as a benchmark. The client might expect the investment manager's portfolio to outperform the Russell 2000 Index over time, but to generally track the index's ups and downs. Tracking error is a measure of how poorly the portfolio tracks the benchmark. More precisely, tracking error is the standard deviation of the portfolio's relative returns versus the benchmark index. As such, the average relative return of a portfolio does not count as tracking error. Rather, the variation around the average relative return counts as tracking error.

Exhibit 4.8 Portfolio Returns and Tracking Error against a Benchmark

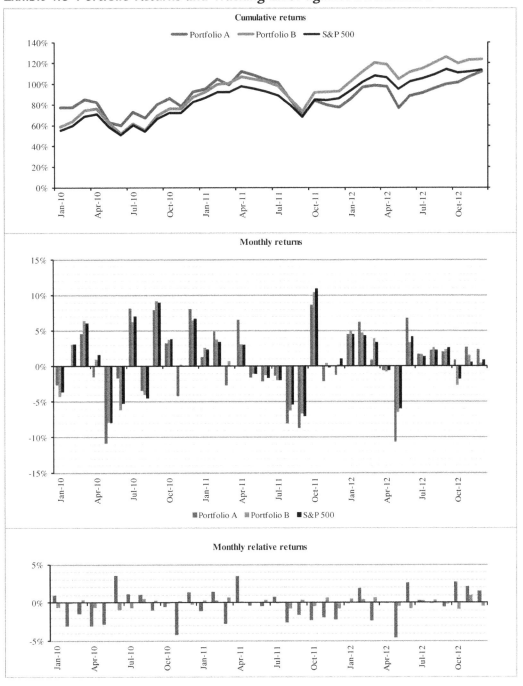

Before proceeding to the mathematical analysis, we illustrate tracking error using two actively managed portfolios, Portfolio A and Portfolio B, benchmarked to the S&P 500 index. The cumulative returns for these two portfolios along with the benchmark S&P 500 are shown in Exhibit 4.8 for a three-year period ending in December 2012. These portfolios take active risk by holding securities at weights different from the capitalization weighted S&P 500, but generally track the large cap benchmark in it moves up and down. That is, the two portfolios generally track the S&P 500 as it rises from around August 2010 through April 2011, and then track its decline over the subsequent 5 months. Portfolio A appears to deviate a bit more from the track of the S&P 500, while Portfolio B mimics the movements of the index quite closely. The two portfolios and the S&P 500 generally have the same direction and similar magnitude of monthly returns as shown in the second graph. However, there is some deviation from the S&P 500 from month to month, as more clearly shown in the graph of monthly relative returns. Recall that relative return each month is simply the return of the portfolio minus the return of the benchmark (the S&P 500, in this case). The relative returns of Portfolio A are more volatile than those of Portfolio B, showing that Portfolio A has more tracking error – it deviates more from the S&P 500 in each month.

Finally, the distribution of monthly returns and relative returns for the 10-year period ending December 2012 for these two portfolios is shown in the set of histograms in Exhibit 4.9. The distribution of the S&P 500 and the two portfolios' returns appear to have a similar spread or width, as confirmed by their having similar overall standard deviations. Specifically, the standard deviation of monthly returns for the S&P 500 is 4.26%, while the standard deviation for portfolios A and B is 4.61% and 4.12%, respectively. Because it is common to use annualized numbers, we also report the annualized standard deviation as calculated from the monthly returns.[4] The widths of the relative return distributions are very different, with Portfolio B's monthly relative returns being distributed more closely around the mean compared to Portfolio A's monthly relative returns. Indeed, the tracking error (i.e., the standard deviation of relative returns) of Portfolio A is approximately three times as large as the tracking error of Portfolio B.

Mathematically, the tracking error of asset i relative to benchmark b (i.e., the relative return variance of security i) is defined to be $\tau_i = \sqrt{\tau_i^2}$, where $\tau_i^2 = Var(r_i - r_b)$. Again, the tracking error is simply the standard deviation of relative returns. Similarly, define the covariance of relative returns between securities i and j to be $\tau_{i,j}^2 = Cov(r_i - r_b, r_j - r_b)$. Note that the covariance of relative returns between two securities is a function of the

---

[4] We employ the common practice of using the "square root of time" rule when annualizing standard deviations by multiplying the monthly return standard deviation by the square root of 12. The "square root of time" rule has an implicit assumption that the sub-period (e.g., monthly) returns are uncorrelated through time, which may not be accurate. However, this common practice provides a nice approximation for our purposes here. The same approach is used in annualizing tracking error.

Exhibit 4.9 Distribution of Returns, Standard Deviation, and Tracking Error

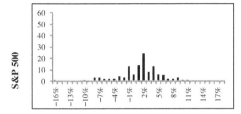

Monthly Standard Deviation = 4.26%
Annualized Standard Deviation = 14.77%

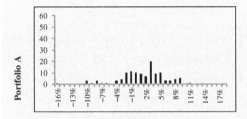

Monthly Standard Deviation = 4.61%
Annualized Standard Deviation = 15.97%

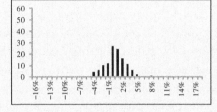

Monthly Tracking Error = 2.09%
Annualized Tracking Error = 7.23%

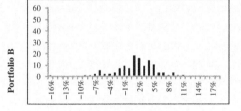

Monthly Standard Deviation = 4.12%
Annualized Standard Deviation = 14.27%

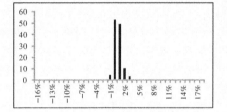

Monthly Tracking Error = 0.70%
Annualized Tracking Error = 2.42%

covariance of the securities' returns, their covariances with the benchmark, and the benchmark's variances, as given by:

$$Cov(r_i - r_b, r_j - r_b) = Cov(r_i, r_j) - Cov(r_i, r_b) - Cov(r_j, r_b) + Var(r_b) \qquad (4.20)$$

or:

$$\tau_{i,j}^2 = \sigma_{i,j}^2 - \sigma_{i,b}^2 - \sigma_{j,b}^2 + \sigma_b^2 \qquad (4.21)$$

Note that this means that a security's relative return variance can also be written as a function of the security's own variance, the benchmark's variance, and the security's covariance of returns with the benchmark returns.

With these preliminaries in mind, we can write the tracking error of a portfolio in several different ways. First, the variance of the portfolio's relative return can be expressed as a function of the portfolio securities' weights and variances and covariances of relative returns, as given by:

$$Var(r_p - r_b) = \tau_p^2 = \sum_{i=1}^{N} \sum_{j=1}^{N} w_i^p w_j^p \tau_{i,j}^2 \tag{4.22}$$

This formula should look familiar, as it is nearly identical to the portfolio variance formula in Equation 4.17. Indeed, the relative return variance formula (Equation 4.22) replaces the plain covariance matrix in the portfolio variance formula (Equation 4.17) with the relative return covariance. With portfolio variance, we are confident that most securities have positive covariance with one another. As such, portfolio variance cannot be diversified away or reduced to zero because of securities' average positive covariance. With relative return variance or tracking error, the intuition changes a bit. Because we are now dealing with relative or residual risk, we should expect some securities' relative returns to be negatively correlated (i.e., to covary in a negative way), with the average covariance of relative returns being approximately zero. Equation 4.22 illustrates that tracking error in a portfolio can be reduced in two ways: (1) placing more weight on securities that lower tracking error; (2) placing more weight on securities whose relative returns have a negative covariance with one another. That is, there is a possibility of achieving a relatively low tracking error with a subset of the benchmark securities.

We extend our previous example of ten stocks to consider tracking error relative to the S&P 500 Index. Exhibit 4.10 shows the relative return correlation and covariance matrixes. The summary matrixes show the average covariances and correlations for two groups of stocks: Information Technology stocks and the five stocks that are not in the Information Technology sector. In Exhibit 4.5, notice that 10 (or 10%) of the return covariances are negative in 2003 through 2007 and none are negative in 2008 through 2012. In Exhibit 4.10, 52% of the relative return covariances are negative in 2003 through 2007 and 46% are negative in 2008 through 2012. Furthermore, the relative return covariances are generally lower, having an average relative return covariance of near 0.0005 in both periods, compared to an average return covariance of 0.0012 in 2003 through 2007 and 0.0041 in 2008 through 2012. The same comparisons hold for the relative return correlations compared to the return correlations.

Overall, the heat map of the relative return covariance matrix is very similar to the heat map for the return covariance matrix in 2003 through 2007. However, the relative return covariance matrix heat map looks quite different from the return covariance matrix heat map during 2008 through 2012, indicating that there can be meaningful differences in the patterns of covariances when using relative returns compared to plain returns. This indicates that portfolios constructed to have low total risk or standard deviation might not have low tracking error. In other words, the portfolio must be constructed in consideration of the specific type of risk that is targeted.

Exhibit 4.11 shows the tracking error for the same portfolios that appear in Exhibit 4.7. Not surprisingly, the resulting portfolio relative return variances and tracking errors shown in Exhibit 4.11 are smaller compared to the return variances and standard deviations in Exhibit 4.7. Also, given the similarity in the ranking of stocks' return covariances and relative return covariances in 2003 through 2007, the pattern of resulting tracking errors is similar to the pattern of standard deviations across different sets of portfolio weights during that period. Specifically, the equally weighted portfolio, P1, has a tracking error that is larger

Exhibit 4.10 Relative Return Covariance Matrix and Correlation Matrix

Correlation of Monthly Relative Returns (2003 – 2007)

	MSFT	DELL	AAPL	ORCL	IBM	KO	WFC	DDS	ROK	CNP	
MSFT		0.24	0.10	−0.05	0.07	0.06	−0.25	0.03	−0.21	−0.06	
DELL	0.24		0.15	0.06	0.11	−0.06	−0.27	0.26	0.22	−0.13	
AAPL	0.10	0.15		0.22	0.06	−0.04	−0.17	0.07	0.36	−0.06	
ORCL	−0.05	0.06	0.22		0.16	−0.13	−0.12	0.05	0.18	−0.30	
IBM	0.07	0.11	0.06	0.16		−0.13	−0.04	−0.19	−0.01	−0.01	
KO	0.06	−0.06	−0.04	−0.13	−0.13		−0.08	−0.35	−0.18	0.07	
WFC	−0.25	−0.27	−0.17	−0.12	−0.04	−0.08		0.00	−0.02	−0.09	
DDS	0.03	0.26	0.07	0.05	−0.19	−0.35	0.00		0.27	−0.02	
ROK	−0.21	0.22	0.36	0.18	−0.01	−0.18	−0.02	0.27		−0.23	Overall
CNP	−0.06	−0.13	−0.06	−0.30	−0.01	0.07	−0.09	−0.02	−0.23		Average
Average	−0.01	0.07	0.08	0.01	0.00	−0.09	−0.11	0.01	0.04	−0.09	−0.01

Covariance of Monthly Relative Returns (2008 – 2012)

	MSFT	DELL	AAPL	ORCL	IBM	KO	WFC	DDS	ROK	CNP	
MSFT		0.19	0.16	0.25	−0.15	0.03	0.10	0.10	−0.21	−0.03	
DELL	0.19		0.14	0.29	0.04	−0.31	−0.05	−0.10	0.22	−0.02	
AAPL	0.16	0.14		0.04	0.07	−0.19	−0.31	0.24	0.03	−0.03	
ORCL	0.25	0.29	0.04		0.07	−0.31	−0.13	−0.04	0.00	−0.07	
IBM	−0.15	0.04	0.07	0.07		0.16	−0.28	−0.22	−0.28	0.18	
KO	0.03	−0.31	−0.19	−0.31	0.16		−0.05	−0.17	−0.34	0.37	
WFC	0.10	−0.05	−0.31	−0.13	−0.28	−0.05		0.17	0.11	−0.33	
DDS	0.10	−0.10	0.24	−0.04	−0.22	−0.17	0.17		0.08	−0.22	
ROK	−0.21	0.22	0.03	0.00	−0.28	−0.34	0.11	0.08		−0.05	Overall
CNP	−0.03	−0.02	−0.03	−0.07	0.18	0.37	−0.33	−0.22	−0.05		Average
Average	0.05	0.04	0.02	0.01	−0.05	−0.09	−0.08	−0.02	−0.05	−0.02	−0.02

Covariance of Monthly Relative Returns (2003 – 2007)

	MSFT	DELL	AAPL	ORCL	IBM	KO	WFC	DDS	ROK	CNP	
MSFT	0.0029	0.0008	0.0005	-0.0002	0.0002	0.0001	-0.0004	0.0001	-0.0008	-0.0003	
DELL	0.0008	0.0036	0.0009	0.0002	0.0003	-0.0001	-0.0005	0.0014	0.0009	-0.0008	
AAPL	0.0005	0.0009	0.0098	0.0013	0.0002	-0.0002	-0.0006	0.0006	0.0024	-0.0006	
ORCL	-0.0002	0.0002	0.0013	0.0035	0.0004	-0.0003	-0.0002	0.0002	0.0007	-0.0017	
IBM	0.0002	0.0003	0.0002	0.0004	0.0018	-0.0002	-0.0001	-0.0007	0.0000	-0.0001	
KO	0.0001	-0.0001	-0.0002	-0.0003	-0.0002	0.0015	-0.0001	-0.0012	-0.0005	0.0003	
WFC	-0.0004	-0.0005	-0.0006	-0.0002	-0.0001	-0.0001	0.0011	0.0000	0.0000	-0.0003	
DDS	0.0001	0.0014	0.0006	0.0002	-0.0007	-0.0012	0.0000	0.0079	0.0016	-0.0002	
ROK	-0.0008	0.0009	0.0024	0.0007	0.0000	-0.0005	0.0000	0.0016	0.0047	-0.0015	**Overall**
CNP	-0.0003	-0.0008	-0.0006	-0.0017	-0.0001	0.0003	-0.0003	-0.0002	-0.0015	0.0096	**Average**
Average	0.0003	0.0007	0.0015	0.0004	0.0002	-0.0001	-0.0001	0.0010	0.0008	0.0004	0.0005

Correlation of Monthly Relative Returns (2008 – 2012)

	MSFT	DELL	AAPL	ORCL	IBM	KO	WFC	DDS	ROK	CNP	
MSFT	0.0025	0.0008	0.0007	0.0007	-0.0003	0.0001	0.0005	0.0008	-0.0010	-0.0001	
DELL	0.0008	0.0075	0.0010	0.0014	0.0002	-0.0013	-0.0004	-0.0014	0.0017	-0.0001	
AAPL	0.0007	0.0010	0.0067	0.0002	0.0002	-0.0008	-0.0026	0.0030	0.0002	-0.0001	
ORCL	0.0007	0.0014	0.0002	0.0031	0.0002	-0.0009	-0.0008	-0.0004	0.0000	-0.0002	
IBM	-0.0003	0.0002	0.0002	0.0002	0.0021	0.0004	-0.0013	-0.0016	-0.0012	0.0005	
KO	0.0001	-0.0013	-0.0008	-0.0009	0.0004	0.0026	-0.0003	-0.0014	-0.0016	0.0011	
WFC	0.0005	-0.0004	-0.0026	-0.0008	-0.0013	-0.0003	0.0106	0.0028	0.0010	-0.0020	
DDS	0.0008	-0.0014	0.0030	-0.0004	-0.0016	-0.0014	0.0028	0.0245	0.0012	-0.0021	
ROK	-0.0010	0.0017	0.0002	0.0000	-0.0012	-0.0016	0.0010	0.0012	0.0085	-0.0003	**Overall**
CNP	-0.0001	-0.0001	-0.0001	-0.0002	0.0005	0.0011	-0.0020	-0.0021	-0.0003	0.0037	**Average**
Average	0.0007	0.0013	0.0008	0.0006	0.0002	0.0000	0.0008	0.0003	-0.0001	-0.0001	0.0004

Avg. Relative Return Correlations (2003 – 2007)

	Info. Tech.	Other
Info. Tech.	0.11	-0.04
Other	-0.04	-0.06

Avg. Relative Return Correlations (2008 – 2012)

	Info. Tech.	Other
Info. Tech.	0.11	-0.06
Other	-0.06	-0.04

Avg. Relative Return Covariances (2003 – 2007)

	Info. Tech.	Other
Info. Tech.	0.0006	0.0000
Other	0.0000	-0.0002

Avg. Relative Return Covariances (2008 – 2012)

	Info. Tech.	Other
Info. Tech.	0.0005	-0.0003
Other	-0.0003	-0.0002

Exhibit 4.11 Portfolio Weights and Tracking Error

Portfolio	Portfolio Weights										Tracking Error	
	MSFT	DELL	AAPL	ORCL	IBM	KO	WFC	DDS	ROK	CNP	2003 – 2007	2008 – 2012
P1	10%	10%	10%	10%	10%	10%	10%	10%	10%	10%	**2.23%**	**2.54%**
P2	5%	5%	5%	5%	5%	25%	25%	5%	5%	15%	**1.79%**	**2.80%**
P3	5%	5%	5%	5%	5%	5%	5%	25%	25%	15%	**3.43%**	**4.69%**

than when more weight is placed on KO and WFC, which have the lowest average relative return covariances among these ten stocks. However, the tracking error results in 2008 through 2012 show a different pattern across portfolios than the standard deviation results. Specifically, both P1 and P2 have higher tracking errors than the equally weighted portfolio. This illustrates the usefulness of the relative return covariance matrix to an investment manager who wishes to construct a portfolio with tracking error risk management as one of the portfolio goals. We discuss more thoroughly the full optimization of a portfolio using the information in the return and relative return covariance matrixes later in this chapter.

Tracking Error and Relative Risk Using Active Weights

Alternatively, we can use active weights to calculate the portfolio tracking error. Using the active weights and security's return variances and covariances, the portfolio's relative return variance is given by:

$$\tau_p^2 = \sum_{i=1}^{N} \sum_{j=1}^{N} \delta_i^p \delta_j^p \sigma_{i,j}^2 \qquad (4.23)$$

Note that the number of securities in Equation 4.23 is greater than or equal to the number of securities in Equation 4.22. Equation 4.22 need only consider the securities held in the portfolio at a non-zero weight, while Equation 4.23 must consider all securities that appear in both the portfolio and the benchmark. Equation 4.23 provides the viewpoint that a portfolio can achieve a low tracking error by underweighting securities with high covariances and overweighting securities with low covariances.

Finally, we can express the portfolio's relative return variance in terms of both active weights and relative return covariances, as given by:

$$\tau_p^2 = \sum_{i=1}^{N} \sum_{j=1}^{N} \delta_i^p \delta_j^p \tau_{i,j}^2 \tag{4.24}$$

As with Equation 4.23, the securities counted in Equation 4.24 include all portfolio and benchmark securities. In this case, the tracking error decreases by having lower active weights or underweights on securities with high relative return covariances and higher active weights or overweights on securities with low relative return covariances.

Expressing the relative return variance in terms of the active weights of the portfolio is also convenient in showing that tracking error derives from the general scale of the active weights of a portfolio. To demonstrate this, consider a reference portfolio with an active weight of δ_i^r in security i. This reference portfolio's relative return variance is:

$$\tau_r^2 = \sum_{i=1}^{N} \sum_{j=1}^{N} \delta_i^r \delta_j^r \tau_{i,j}^2 \tag{4.25}$$

As discussed earlier, each active weight represents a view or a "bet" on security i. A negative active weight is a negative or bearish view and a positive active weight is a positive or bullish view on the security. Now consider a portfolio that has the same view on each security, but only differs in the magnitude of this view. That is, scale the active weight in the reference portfolio to arrive at the portfolio's active weight. Therefore, the portfolio's active weight in security i is given by $\delta_i^p = a_s \delta_i^r$, where a_s is the scale factor for the active weights. This portfolio's relative return variance is:

$$
\begin{aligned}
\tau_p^2 &= \sum_{i=1}^{N} \sum_{j=1}^{N} \delta_i^p \delta_j^p \tau_{i,j}^2 \\
&= \sum_{i=1}^{N} \sum_{j=1}^{N} a_s \delta_i^r a_s \delta_j^r \tau_{i,j}^2 \\
&= a_s^2 \sum_{i=1}^{N} \sum_{j=1}^{N} \delta_i^r \delta_j^r \tau_{i,j}^2 \\
&= a_s^2 \tau_r^2
\end{aligned}
\tag{4.26}
$$

Taking the square root reveals that $\tau_p = |a_s| \tau_r$. That is, the tracking error of a portfolio scales with its active weights. An alternative way to think about this result is to consider an overall portfolio that invests in two assets: the reference portfolio and the benchmark portfolio. In this case, a_s represents the proportion of the overall portfolio that is invested in the reference portfolio and $1 - a_s$ is the proportion invested in the benchmark portfolio. Clearly, if $a_s = 0$, there is no tracking error. If $a_s = 2$, the tracking error is doubled. In general, the larger (in magnitude) the active weights, the higher the tracking error.

In summary, the portfolio's relative return variance, and hence its tracking error, can be expressed as a function of the portfolio's securities' weights and relative return variances and covariances or the portfolio's securities' active weights and return or relative return variances and covariances. The variance and covariance structure of the market can be quite complex, though some general relationships tend to hold in theory and in practice. Securities within the same category (e.g., country, asset class, size group, sector, or factor) tend to be more highly correlated with each other than with securities in different categories. An active portfolio that seeks to be neutral to categories but to achieve abnormal performance through security selection can diversify within categories and achieve relatively low tracking error. This would result by placing relatively large weights on securities with relatively low (even negative) relative return covariances in Equation 4.22. In contrast, a strategy that diversifies within a category but is concentrated along limited dimensions might still have a high tracking error. Cremers and Petajisto (2009) distinguish between these two sources of active management by developing a measure of a how active a portfolio is. They call this measure the portfolio's *active share*.[5] Active share is measured as:

$$ActiveShare = \frac{1}{2} \sum_{i=1}^{N} |\delta_i^p| \tag{4.27}$$

Intuitively, active share is another measure of the "distance" of a portfolio from the benchmark. The farther away from the benchmark, the larger the active weights. This means a portfolio is more active or less passive. As discussed above, the tracking error will increase with an increase in active share unless the portfolio is constructed in such a way so that larger active weights are placed on securities that have lower relative return covariances. Similarly, a portfolio can have a lower active share with higher tracking error if the active weights are focused on companies that share similar factor exposures and, therefore, covary more with one another. Cremers and Petajisto summarize this in the figure depicted in Exhibit 4.12.

Portfolio Optimization

In its strictest sense, portfolio optimization is a solution, in the form of portfolio weights, to a specific formal mathematically stated portfolio problem or objective. As we discuss in several examples below, even this seemingly scientific exercise is subject to considerable "art" in its implementation. Of course, portfolios are optimized according to the objectives reflected in the individual or organization's investment process. Formalized optimizations are typically characterized by either maximizing or minimizing a portfolio measure.

---

[5] See Cremers, K. J. M., and A. Petajisto, "How Active Is Your Fund Manager? A New Measure That Predicts Performance," *Review of Financial Studies*, 2009, Vol. 22, No. 9, pp. 3329–3365.

Exhibit 4.12 Active Share and Tracking Error

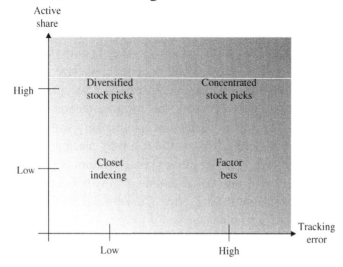

Source: Cremers and Petajisto (2009)

However, portfolio optimization can be considered less formally and more generally to be the setting of portfolio weights according to overall goals or rules, without a formal mathematical solution. In this sense, portfolio optimization involves setting portfolio weights to achieve a general orientation in the portfolio. Some portfolio goals may not have unique solutions that lend themselves to mathematical solutions. In either case, portfolio mathematics governs the resulting portfolio performance and provides the framework for portfolio optimization. As such, portfolio optimization can be the central step in portfolio construction, resulting in a set of portfolio weights.

Minimize Total Risk

One example of a formal objective for setting portfolio weights is the minimization of the portfolio's total risk. This objective seeks a set of weights to achieve the lowest possible portfolio volatility. Many readers will recognize the resemblance of this objective to the minimum variance portfolio that is discussed in many introductions to portfolio theory. It is important to note that this portfolio is similar to the minimum variance portfolio in its solution method, but is likely to differ in a very meaningful way. Specifically, the portfolio optimization for an investment process is generally done in combination with other security selection methods, while the minimum variance portfolio represents the portfolio of all market securities that achieves the least possible variance. In other words, the resulting portfolio here seeks to find the lowest risk portfolio among a set of securities which represent a subset of the overall universe of securities.

While we repeat some of the discussions of the minimum variance portfolio, our focus is on the practical implementation of such an objective. We begin with the simplest form of the optimization by stating our objective in terms of total portfolio risk as given in Equation 4.1. The mathematical problem is:

$$\underset{w_i^p}{Min} \quad \sum_{i=1}^{N}\sum_{j=1}^{N} w_i^p w_j^p \sigma_{i,j}^2 \quad s.t. \quad \sum_{j=1}^{N} w_i^p = 1 \tag{4.28}$$

In words, this expression reflects that we are minimizing the portfolio variance function by choosing the portfolio weights, subject to the constraint that the weights sum to one. The minimization of the portfolio's total variance (or standard deviation) is the objective function. Other than the restriction that the weights sum to one, this optimization is seemingly unconstrained. As noted above, however, we have constrained this problem to the N securities that make it to this step of the investment process — to the point of having the weights optimized. If there were prior steps that screened securities or otherwise narrowed the universe of securities, then this problem has effectively constrained the excluded securities to have zero weight.

This problem can be solved analytically to arrive at a formula for each security weight. Conceptually, each security weight is a function of the portfolio securities' covariances or covariance matrix. In practice, this problem is usually solved numerically with computer-based "optimizers." Some investment firms maintain clusters of custom-built workstations with proprietary algorithms to solve such optimization problems. While such technology might be unavailable to student investment funds, there are optimization tools that are well within reach. Microsoft Excel has a useful optimization tool, known as the "Solver" and we will demonstrate its use in several examples below.

We return to the ten stock example shown in Exhibits 4.4 through 4.6. Recall that a portfolio constructed with more weight on stocks KO and WFC results a lower standard deviation compared to a portfolio that places more weight on stocks DDS and ROK. We now seek to optimize this example by finding the set of portfolio weights that results in the

Exhibit 4.13 Microsoft Excel 2007 and 2010 Solver Add-In

Excel 2007

Excel 2010

lowest standard deviation, given the covariance matrix of these ten stocks. We utilize the Solver in Microsoft Excel to solve this optimization.

With the spreadsheet set up to calculate the portfolio standard deviation using the matrix method or the time series method, as shown in Exhibit 4.6, the key is to have Excel solve for the set of weights that minimize the portfolio variance. To do this, we use the Excel add-in Solver. The Excel Solver, shown in Exhibit 4.13, looks slightly different between Microsoft Excel 2007 and Microsoft 2010, but both versions allow us to set the following items in minimizing the portfolio variance or standard deviation:

Set Target Cell:	A reference to the cell that has the portfolio variance.
Equal to:	Choose Min, since we want to minimize the variance or standard deviation in the target cell.
By Changing (Variable) Cells:	A reference to the row of portfolio weights.
Subject to the Constraints:	A constraint must be added that sets the cell with the sum of the portfolio weights to one. Other constraints are discussed below.

In Excel 2010, there is a check box to make unconstrained variables non-negative. We leave this box unchecked for now, allowing negative portfolio weights in the solution. Once we hit "Solve," Excel uses a numerical algorithm to change the set of weights until it finds a minimum for the variance in the target cell, always making sure that the constraint that the weights sum to one is satisfied. Exhibit 4.14 shows the resulting portfolio characteristics and weights for minimizing the portfolio standard deviation in the 2003 through 2007 period. We label this portfolio as MSD2007U (to indicate the objective to Minimize the Standard Deviation of the portfolio using data ending in 2007, Unconstrained other than the requirement that the weights sum to one). The optimized portfolio standard deviation is 2.44%, which is substantially lower than the equally weighted portfolio's 3.52% standard deviation. The Solver's solution puts 44% in WFC and 22% in KO. As discussed above, the Solver favors these stocks because of their low covariance with the other portfolio stocks. Among the other weights, note that the Solver places a negative weight in AAPL in order to minimize the portfolio standard deviation. The short position in AAPL is likely due to its having the highest covariance with the other portfolio stocks during this period.

Before proceeding further in discussing the use of optimizers, we caution that optimizers are inherently "dumb" in that they do not have an innate knowledge of a specific problem, its context, or the data being used. As such, an optimizer does not know whether a solution is reasonable or unreasonable. The optimizer simply arrives at a solution according to the problem, parameters, and input data that are provided by the user. It is up to the optimizer's user to understand the problem, parameters, and input data and judge the reasonableness of

Exhibit 4.14 Effects of Optimization and Constraints

Portfolio	Weights										Standard Deviation		Objective and
	MSFT	DELL	AAPL	ORCL	IBM	KO	WFC	DDS	ROK	CNP	2003 – 2007	2008 – 2012	Constraints
EW	0.10	0.10	0.10	0.10	0.10	0.10	0.10	0.10	0.10	0.10	3.52%	6.95%	Equal Weights
MSD2007U	0.16	0.00	–0.03	0.03	0.06	0.22	0.44	0.02	0.08	0.03	2.44%	7.64%	Min. St. Dev.
MSD2007C1	0.15	0.00	0.00	0.02	0.06	0.21	0.44	0.02	0.07	0.03	2.46%	7.64%	Min. St. Dev. Weight >= 0.00
MSD2007C2	0.08	0.05	0.05	0.05	0.05	0.18	0.39	0.05	0.05	0.05	2.64%	7.43%	Min. St. Dev. Weight >= 0.05
MSD2007C3	0.11	0.05	0.05	0.05	0.09	0.25	0.25	0.05	0.05	0.05	2.72%	6.42%	Min. St. Dev. Weight >= 0.05 Weight <= 0.25
MSD2007C4	0.15	0.05	0.05	0.05	0.14	0.20	0.20	0.05	0.06	0.05	2.83%	6.23%	Min. St. Dev. Weight >= 0.05 Weight <= 0.20
MSD2007C5	0.15	0.05	0.05	0.08	0.15	0.15	0.15	0.05	0.09	0.08	2.99%	6.22%	Min. St. Dev. Weight >= 0.05 Weight <= 0.15

Portfolio	Weights										Tracking Error		Objective and
	MSFT	DELL	AAPL	ORCL	IBM	KO	WFC	DDS	ROK	CNP	2003 – 2007	2008 – 2012	Constraints
EW	0.10	0.10	0.10	0.10	0.10	0.10	0.10	0.10	0.10	0.10	2.23%	2.54%	Equal Weights
MTE2007U	0.10	0.04	0.00	0.09	0.12	0.21	0.29	0.04	0.06	0.05	1.32%	3.13%	Min. Trk. Err.
MTE2007C1	0.10	0.04	0.00	0.09	0.12	0.21	0.29	0.04	0.06	0.05	1.32%	3.13%	Min. Trk. Err. Weight >= 0.00
MTE2007C2	0.08	0.05	0.05	0.06	0.11	0.21	0.29	0.05	0.05	0.05	1.41%	3.08%	Min. Trk. Err. Weight >= 0.05
MTE2007C3	0.08	0.05	0.05	0.07	0.12	0.22	0.25	0.05	0.05	0.05	1.42%	2.75%	Min. Trk. Err. Weight >= 0.05 Weight <= 0.25
MTE2007C4	0.10	0.05	0.05	0.09	0.15	0.20	0.20	0.05	0.05	0.06	1.47%	2.34%	Min. Trk. Err. Weight >= 0.05 Weight <= 0.20
MTE2007C5	0.14	0.05	0.05	0.11	0.15	0.15	0.15	0.05	0.07	0.08	1.63%	2.08%	Min. Trk. Err. Weight >= 0.05 Weight <= 0.15

the optimizer's solution. For this reason and others discussed below, optimizers must be used carefully and constrained responsibly.

One particular problem is that the optimizer treats the input data as the Truth. Indeed, in the example of minimizing the portfolio standard deviation during the period 2003 through 2007, the Solver had the true data for that period and arrived at an accurate solution of the problem it was given. In practice, however, we do not have the luxury of using the true data to solve for weights, since we construct portfolios for the future, not the past. The Solver in the example above found a solution for what portfolio *should have been held* in order to minimize portfolio risk. Of course, an investment manager would want to know what portfolio to hold going forward, not what portfolio she should have held. The Solver cannot solve the real problem unless it is provided with data from the future. Since this is clearly not possible, we must rely on historical data, forecasts, or estimates that might (or might not!) be informative about the future. Note that forecasts or estimates using historical data will only represent the true data with error. Being "dumb," the optimizer treats these errors as facts. Therefore, an investment manager must operate the optimizer in a way that takes into account the fact that the optimizer cannot find the best solution because it is not being provided with the true parameters or data. The key solution to this problem is the use of constraints.

Constraints to the optimization use the investment managers' *a priori* knowledge about the problem and the characteristics and behavior of the portfolio securities to help the optimizer find a practical solution. In theory, constraints cause optimizations to find worse solutions, not better. Indeed, if we add a constraint to the 2003 through 2007 standard deviation minimization problem above, it would defy logic for the optimizer to arrive at a better solution in the form of a lower portfolio standard deviation *during that period*. Had the lower standard deviation been available, the optimizer would have been free to choose that solution in the absence of the constraint. It is impossible to constrain an optimizer and arrive at a better solution when using true data or parameters. It is this logic that leads some people to view constraints in an investment process negatively. However, it is critical to understand that these seemingly ill effects of constraints apply to theoretical situations in which the true data and known parameters are being used in the optimization. In practice, well-chosen constraints can, and generally do, result in better portfolio outcomes since the true (future) data and parameters are never known at the time of the optimization.

Returning to the results for MSD2007U in Exhibit 4.14, we have provided the standard deviation of this portfolio during the 2008 through 2012 period. This illustrates a feasible portfolio strategy that an investor could have followed. Specifically, an investor could have constructed a portfolio at the end of 2007 from an optimization that uses monthly data from the previous five years. The investor could have held this portfolio over the following five years (2008 through 2012) and achieved the performance indicated in the exhibit. For comparison, we provide the performance of an equally weighted portfolio, labeled EW, which represents a naïve portfolio of the same ten stocks that is also clearly feasible. It is interesting to note that the equally weighted portfolio has a lower standard deviation in 2008 through 2012 compared to the portfolio that used historical data to optimize its weights. This could indicate that these ten stocks' historical data from 2003 through 2007 are not informative enough about their covariances during 2008 through 2012 to be useful in optimizing a portfolio. Alternatively, perhaps the optimizer was not adequately constrained and allowed to place too much weight on stocks that appeared to have very desirable attributes and too little weight on stocks with seemingly undesirable attributes based on the historical data.

To illustrate the effect of constraints, we begin by adding a short selling constraint to the Solver that requires all weights to be non-negative (i.e., greater than or equal to zero). We label the resulting portfolio MSD2007C1. Still using the data from 2003 through 2007 as inputs into the Solver, the short-selling constraint causes there to be no negative weights – notice that AAPL no longer has a negative weight. The standard deviation of MSD2007C1 in 2003 through 2007 increases slightly to 2.46% compared with 2.44% for the unconstrained portfolio MSD2007U. The portfolio standard deviation for 2008 through 2012 does not change measurably. We next add a constraint that each of the ten stocks must have a weight of at least 5%, labeling this portfolio as MSD2007C2. Again, the standard deviation for the optimized portfolio increases to 2.64% in 2003 through 2007, but decreases to 7.43% in 2008 through 2012. Adding constraints on the maximum weight in each stock results in a further decrease in the optimized portfolio's standard deviation during the 2008 through 2012 period. For portfolio MSD2007C3, we add a constraint of a maximum weight of 25%. The resulting portfolio has a lower standard deviation than the equally weighted portfolio in 2008 through 2012. This suggests that when properly constrained, the historical data from 2003 through 2007 is informative enough about the covariance in 2008 through 2012 to reduce the standard deviation in a portfolio of these ten stocks by using a constrained optimization. That is, an investment manager could have constructed a portfolio at the end of 2007 to achieve lower standard deviation during 2008 through 2012 than that of an equally weighted portfolio by using historical data in a constrained optimization.

Minimize Tracking Error

Many investors, especially institutional investors such as pension and endowment plans, are more concerned with the tracking error of a particular investment strategy or mandate. This type of client might be concerned with the total risk of its overall portfolio, but hires a specific investment manager in an asset class or sub-class, such as long-term corporate debt or U.S. small cap equity. The client would expect the investment manager to be exposed to the same risks as the underlying passive benchmark.

If a portfolio is mandated to track a particular underlying benchmark or index, the tracking error of the portfolio might be more important than the total risk of the portfolio. The tracking error of a portfolio can be optimized in a similar manner as the portfolio standard deviation. In this case, the objective function becomes the tracking error. Because the minimization of the variance of portfolio relative returns is equivalent to the minimization of tracking error, we state the minimization problem in terms of relative return variances, as given by:

$$Min_{w_i^p} \quad \sum_{i=1}^{N} \sum_{j=1}^{N} w_i^p w_j^p \tau_{i,j}^2 \quad s.t. \quad \sum_{j=1}^{N} w_i^p = 1 \tag{4.29}$$

Of course, this minimization problem is nearly identical to the minimization of portfolio variance and standard deviation, except that the securities' covariances are measured using their relative returns against the underlying benchmark. As with minimization of portfolio variance, we can solve this problem with the help of an optimization routine, such as Excel's Solver. The setup of the Solver is identical, except that the Target Cell is set to the formula for the portfolio's tracking error.

Using Excel's solver, minimize the tracking error over the 2003 through 2007 period in order to construct a portfolio of the ten stocks from our earlier example. We use the S&P 500 as the benchmark index against which relative returns and tracking error are calculated. As with the example for minimizing the portfolio standard deviation, we begin with an unconstrained optimization, allow the Solver to choose negative weights, should it want to, labeling this portfolio as MTE2007U in Exhibit 4.14. The optimizer's solution in this case involves no short selling (even though it could have short sold stocks). The resulting tracking error during the 2003 through 2007 period is 1.32%. As in our earlier example, we consider the possibility that an investment manager would use the 2003 through 2007 data to construct a portfolio to be held starting in 2008. The tracking error of this portfolio during 2008 through 2012 is 3.13%, which is higher than the equally weighted portfolio's tracking error of 2.54%. As discussed above, the practical results from optimizers can usually be improved by constraining them in recognition of the fact that the input data into the optimizer are estimates and, therefore, subject to forecast errors. Exhibit 4.14 also shows the results from adding constraints to the weights in the Solver. When each security's weight is constrained to at least 5% and no more than 20% (portfolio MTE2007C4), the tracking error of the optimized portfolio in 2008 through 2012 is 2.34%, which is less than that of the equally weighted portfolio. Further constraining the weights by setting a maximum weight of 15% yields an even lower tracking error in the post-optimization period. As with the portfolio standard deviation, the constrained optimization using historical data from 2003 through 2007 appears to achieve a better result than a naïve equally weighted portfolio.

Such an optimization is feasible, even for a student-managed fund. For example, Southern Illinois University's Saluki Student Investment Fund's (SSIF) began using an optimization in the portfolio construction step in its investment process in 2011. Its objective is to minimize the tracking error relative to its S&P 400 Midcap Index benchmark. The stocks for the SSIF portfolio are selected from its benchmark using fundamental analysis along the lines discussed in Chapter 3. The SSIF believes that these stocks give the portfolio its opportunity to outperform the S&P 400. That is, it expects its "alpha" to come from its stock selection skills. It attempts to manage risk relative to the benchmark using the tracking error minimization process. The SSIF built an optimizer using an Excel spreadsheet to accomplish this task. In this optimizer, returns from the prior five years are collected and recorded in the spreadsheet. A hypothetical portfolio over this historical five-year period is constructed by referencing a set of weights in the spreadsheet. The tracking error relative to the benchmark S&P 400 index is calculated for the hypothetical portfolio. Using the Solver, the SSIF minimizes this historical tracking error in order to arrive at the portfolio weights. The underlying assumption is that the historical relative return covariances of the stocks contain information that helps minimize the tracking error in the future. That is, there is an implicit belief that the historical relationship among the portfolio stocks' relative returns provides a good estimate of the future relationship among these stocks.

Recognizing that the historical data are being used to estimate the future covariance relationships, the SSIF also incorporates practical risk controls that include the number of portfolio securities and security and sector weight constraints.[6] Specifically, the SSIF's portfolio, worth just over $1 million at the end of 2012, typically holds around 50 stocks. The optimizer sets a constraint in the Solver to set the sum of each sector's weight equal to the benchmark's weight in that sector. Finally, the Solver is constrained to set each stock's target weight to a minimum of 1% and a maximum of 3%. Since implementing a tracking error minimization into its investment process, the SSIF's annualized tracking error has been 2.22%, compared to 5.57% over the prior two years, using monthly data in the calculations. It is difficult to determine whether the tracking error reduction is due primarily to the optimization, the constraints, or any other specific aspect of the investment process. Indeed, it is often dangerous to try to assign too much success or failure to any specific element. The minimization by the Solver might work well in many markets, as there may be times when historical data provide very good estimates of future data. However, there will undoubtedly be times when relationships among stocks deviate from their historical norms. In these situations, practical risk controls that have a priori meaning, such as diversification constraints that restrict the minimum and maximum weight in a specific security or sector, can help to reduce the realized risk. This is like having both seatbelts and airbags in a car. One or the other might be more effective in specific circumstances, but because we do not know what kind of crash we might have, we are often safer having both.

Maximize Sharpe Ratio

Our optimization discussion so far has focused on minimizing risk. Of course, risk minimization is not the only objective in portfolio management. In general, investors attempt to maximize some reward-to-risk ratio, trading off risk in order to get more reward.

---

[6] Another risk control that precedes the portfolio construction step is that the SSIF requires 75% of the holdings to be drawn from the benchmark index.

The most prominent theoretical reward-to-risk tradeoff is the Sharpe Ratio. The Sharpe Ratio for a portfolio divides the portfolio's excess return (i.e., its return net of the risk free rate) by the portfolio's standard deviation, as given by:

$$\frac{\bar{r}_p - r_f}{\sigma_p} \tag{4.30}$$

To construct a portfolio using the Sharpe Ratio, the investor would optimize the set of weights by maximizing the objective function. Because portfolio average returns enter into the objective function, the maximization must utilize an estimate of securities' average or expected returns, in addition to estimates of securities' covariances. The expected return estimates may be generated as part of security analysis and security selection, discussed in the prior chapter. The optimization would favor stocks with relatively high expected returns and low covariances with other securities. We caution that expected returns are especially difficult to forecast. As discussed above with regard to the inputs to risk minimization, the optimizer treats errors as the Truth. If a security in a Sharpe Ratio optimization has a very large expected return compared to other securities, the optimizer is susceptible to "falling in love" with the security and placing a very large weight on it. Constraints become even more important in such situations.

An alternative form of constraints that can be useful in optimizations such as those involving the Sharpe Ratio is to constrain the estimated inputs rather than the optimized weights. For example, consider an investment manager engaged in a fundamental stock selection process that wishes to maximize the Sharpe Ratio. After screening the universe of securities, the investment managers' analysts arrive at a "short list" of securities that are deemed to be future outperformers. However, the analysts do not have precise enough expected return estimates for the short-listed securities to allow them to confidently rank these securities. In essence, the analysts view these chosen securities like parents would view their children: they love them all and cannot say which one they love more than another. If this investment manager wants to maximize the Sharpe Ratio, then a reasonable assumption would be to set all of the chosen securities' expected returns to be the same. This way, the numerator of the Sharpe Ratio is the same, regardless of the set of weights chosen. Assuming these expected returns are positive, the maximization of the Sharpe Ratio is equivalent to a minimization of the portfolio standard deviation. That is, minimizing the denominator of a fraction (the Sharpe Ratio, in this case) maximizes the fraction when the numerator is held constant.

The maximization of the Sharpe Ratio through risk minimization can also be viewed as a constraint on the optimization. This might work well when there is relatively high confidence in the covariance estimates of the securities, but relatively low confidence in the expected return estimates. This avoids the problem of the optimizer "falling in love" with securities whose estimated expected returns are high. If these estimated expected returns are known to have large errors, then this effectively constrains the optimizer from treating these errors as Truth. Other constraints discussed above can also help. However, we caution that when there are a few securities with very large expected returns, the optimizer is likely to want to put a very large weight on those securities, usually placing the constrained maximum weight on them.

Maximize Information Ratio

The Information Ratio is the relative return equivalent to the Sharpe Ratio. The Information Ratio is the portfolio's average relative return, $\bar{r}_p - \bar{r}_b$, divided by the tracking error, τ_p, as given by:

$$\frac{\bar{r}_p - \bar{r}_b}{\tau_p} \tag{4.31}$$

As with the Sharpe Ratio, the Information Ratio can be maximized by minimizing the tracking error if the expected relative return of each portfolio security is the same. The Southern Illinois University Saluki Student Investment Fund, as discussed above, is an example of such an optimization. The SSIF recognizes that their estimates of expected returns are very noisy. While they have confidence in their chosen securities, they have very little confidence in ranking the expected returns of securities relative to one another. One factor that contributes to the difficulty in ranking or differentiating securities' expected returns is the organizational structure of the SSIF, in which analysts are assigned to sector teams for in-depth research. Therefore, the uncertainty surrounding intra-sector rankings gets compounded with the uncertainty of inter-sector ranking, resulting in very low confidence in forecasting one chosen security to have a higher expected relative return than another chosen security. By using the objective function of tracking error minimization, the SSIF is effectively maximizing the portfolio's Information Ratio.

Trading and Rebalancing

Once portfolio target weights are set, the portfolio must be implemented and maintained through transactions in securities markets. We adopt the term "trade" to refer to the new purchase or full sale of a security (commonly referred to as a "name") in the portfolio. For example, a portfolio that holds 500 shares of AAPL and 0 shares of GOOG might sell 400 shares of AAPL for 200 shares of GOOG in a trade. In this sense, investment decisions are viewed as trades. Presumably, the investment manager perceives the value of GOOG in the portfolio to be greater than the value of AAPL. The trade requires transactions in both securities: AAPL is sold for cash and then GOOG is bought for cash.

All transactions involve costs. The clearest transaction costs are the commissions and fees paid to the broker and custodian for handling the transaction. Commissions can be fixed per transaction or depend on the number of shares or the dollar value of the transaction. Regardless, they are clearly disclosed by the broker. If the account is maintained at a custodial bank, there typically are "ticket" charges or fees for each transaction. While these commissions and fees can be between $5 and $50 for each transaction, they may represent either a negligible or a significant cost as a percentage of the transaction value. For example, a $10 commission on a $1000 transaction requires a 1% return to break even on paper and a 2% appreciation to break even on the entire round-trip (purchase and sale) transaction, even ignoring other costs. In cases in which commissions are fixed, larger transactions may be more beneficial as the transaction costs become a smaller proportion of the value of the transaction.

Other costs are less clear, but can be significant in certain circumstances. Price impact and effective bid-ask spreads can raise the effective cost of a transaction, especially for large transactions. Price impact occurs when a trader attempts to buy (or sell) a large number of shares and "moves the market." If the order to buy or sell is large enough, it might be split into several transactions. For example, an order to sell 100,000 shares of AAPL might occur in several transactions, each at a lower price. The price impact is the effect of achieving a lower price for the last shares sold compared to the first shares sold. The lower price is effectively a cost. This cost is more likely in less liquid securities. We leave a more in-depth discussion to the measurement of such costs to Chapter 6. However, we mention it here as it could impact the policies regarding how a portfolio is traded and rebalanced.

Rebalancing transactions occur when partial sales of position or additional purchases of a position are made. This might occur if the portfolio weights have deviated from their target levels. To bring the portfolio closer to its target weights, shares of existing positions are bought or sold, without trading names (entirely) into or out of the portfolio. The same transaction cost considerations apply to rebalancing transactions. As such, rebalancing and trading decisions represent a trade-off of the benefits of the transaction against the transaction costs. In a theoretical world of zero transaction costs, portfolios might be rebalanced continuously. However, in real portfolios, the transaction costs must be weighed against the costs of not trading. The cost of not trading is the opportunity cost or the risk of having a portfolio that deviates from its targets. Unfortunately, such costs are difficult or perhaps impossible to measure. Therefore, many portfolio managers adopt policies to conduct rebalancing transactions only when security, sector, or factor weights deviate significantly from their targets.

Practical Considerations

There is a popular story that tells of the U.S. Space Program's discovery in the early days of space flight that a ballpoint pen would not write in the zero gravity environment of space. After years of research and analysis costing millions of dollars, a ballpoint pen was developed that could write in a zero gravity. Meanwhile, the Russians sent their cosmonauts to space with pencils. While the veracity of this parable is questionable, the lesson is no less valuable. Sometimes, common sense is far more valuable than complex analysis. This chapter has covered many of the technical aspects of portfolio construction and described methods for completing quantitative optimizations - much of it for the sake of risk management. At times, we have discussed the possible hazards in relying too much on quantitative methods. We take this opportunity to emphasize the virtues of common sense and practical considerations.

As discussed above, quantitative methods work very well in theory. However, real portfolio management occurs in the real world, not in the theoretical world. The mathematics of portfolio theory are known ... and known to work when all of the parameters are known. Two key issues that arise in the real world that are not problems in the theoretical world are (1) parameter uncertainty and (2) human error. We discuss above how constraints can help

Exhibit 4.15 Examples of Portfolio Policies

Security, Sector, and Factor Weight Constraints	Minimum and/or maximum weights or active weights for individual securities, sectors, and factors.
Factor or Characteristic Exposure Targets	Target or target ranges for exposures, such as average betas or characteristic ratios.
Security, Sector, and Factor Weight Tolerances	Tolerances for deviations of portfolio weights from targets to determine when a rebalancing transaction is necessary.
Minimum Trade Sizes	Minimum number of shares or dollar value for a rebalancing transaction.
Number of Holdings	Minimum and/or maximum number of portfolio holdings.
Diversification Requirements	Minimum and/or maximum number of holdings, weights, factors, or characteristics.
Prototyping	Applying a method or model to a small model portfolio prior to deploying on a live portfolio.
Redundancy and Error Checks	Have multiple people use independent sources, methods, and/or platforms for analysis. Build automated error-checks where possible.
Reasonableness Checks	Check that outputs match expected results and reconcile any discrepancies.
Documentation	Document methods, protocols, and procedures so that any work can be replicated without additional instruction.

limit the problem of parameter uncertainty. In some cases, however, there is so much parameter uncertainty that it is not advisable to use such parameters at all, even in conjunction with constraints. In such circumstances, proportional weighting (e.g., equal weighting) within a sector or factor group might result in as good of a realized outcome as an optimized approach.

We summarize practical portfolio policies in Exhibit 4.15 that may be appropriate depending on the portfolio objectives, investment philosophy, and investment process. As many of these items are discussed above, we do not repeat their discussion here. However, this list also includes policies aimed at reducing the likelihood and impact of human error. Our failure to emphasize these considerations until now should not be taken to mean that they are of little importance. To the contrary, these considerations are essential in any investment process, especially those that make use of a quantitative optimization. We begin with prototyping to assure that a process works well on a small scale prior to deploying it on a larger scale. For example, it is helpful to do calculations by hand using only two or three securities while also programming an optimizer to do the same calculations. Doing these calculations at least once by hand checks that an optimizer, such as Excel's Solver, is set up to solve the desired problem correctly. In many cases, optimizations can become quite complex. Simplicity is often the friend of a robust outcome. Therefore, extra caution is required when building complex, elaborate, and unwieldy models. In some cases, a simpler model can achieve most of the benefit at a far lower fraction of the cost or risk of error. When possible, build a model multiple times, by multiple people, and/or on multiple platforms. This redundancy again helps assure that the solution is consistent and accurate.

Redundancy is costly, but reaps large benefits. Any data being added to a model or optimizer should be checked by at least two people. Again, the redundancy of having different people utilize different sources of data can also help reduce the likelihood that errors affect the outcomes. Check every solution for reasonableness. Are constraints met? Is the process placing the most weight on securities that were expected to get the most weight, given the objectives? If not, these issues should be resolved and reasoned to make sure that the result is accurate. Finally, document every step of the process, including revisions to the process and requirements for maintenance, updates, and input data. As turnover in a student-managed investment fund is a particular challenge, documentation becomes even more important to successfully maintaining the investment process.

Summary of Key Points

- Security selection determines which securities are included in the portfolio. As such, security selection largely determines the performance of the portfolio.

(Continued)

Summary of Key Points (Continued)

- Portfolio construction determines the weight of each security in the portfolio. As such, portfolio construction largely determines the risk of the portfolio.
- Portfolio risk is absolute and relative. Absolute risk is usually measured by the standard deviation of portfolio returns. Relative risk is usually measured by the tracking error of the portfolio relative to a benchmark.
- Portfolio weights and security returns combine to create portfolio returns and risk. Generally, the higher the total weight on securities with lower covariance with one another, the lower the portfolio variance and standard deviation.
- Portfolios with a specific objective function can be optimized using readily available tools, such as Excel's Solver.
- Optimizers treat all input data and parameters as the Truth. Constraints can help optimizers achieve better realized outcomes.
- Practical risk control and policies should be established in the construction of portfolios according to the investment objective, investment philosophy, and investment process.

Exercises

1. Suppose a student-managed investment fund is mandated to invest 60% in Large Cap U.S. Equity, 10% in Small Cap U.S. Equity, and 30% in U.S. Investment Grade Corporate Bonds. Develop an appropriate benchmark for this portfolio using the benchmarks listed in Exhibit 4.1.
2. Choose four stocks and create an Excel spreadsheet that has their capitalizations (shares outstanding multiplied by price) and returns for each month in the past three years.
   a. Create a benchmark of these four stocks by calculating a capitalization-weighted portfolio. From these weights, calculate the monthly returns for the benchmark according to Equation 4.7.
   b. Calculate each stock's monthly relative returns using the capitalization-weighted portfolio as a benchmark.
   c. Create an equally weighted portfolio of the four stocks. Calculate this portfolio's monthly returns and relative returns according to equations 4.5 and 4.6, respectively. Using the monthly portfolio returns and relative returns, calculate the equally weighted portfolio's average return and average relative return.
   d. Calculate the equally weighted portfolio's return standard deviation and tracking error by taking the standard deviation of the monthly returns and relative returns, respectively.
   e. Calculate the average returns and average relative returns of the four stocks.
   f. Calculate the equally weighted portfolio average return and relative return according to equations 4.13 and 4.16. Check that these match with the averages you calculated in part c.

(Continued)

Exercises (Continued)

   g. Create a covariance matrix of returns for these four stocks. Note footnote 2 in this chapter for adjusting the $=$ COVAR() function to match the $=$ VAR() function in Excel.

   h. Create a covariance matrix of relative returns for these four stocks. Note footnote 2 in this chapter for adjusting the $=$ COVAR() function to match the $=$ VAR() function in Excel.

   i. Calculate the equally weighted portfolio's standard deviation and tracking error according to equations 4.17 and 4.22, respectively. Note that these calculations make use of the covariance matrices in parts g and h. Check that portfolio standard deviation and tracking error match the values you found in part d.

3. Choose four stocks and create an Excel spreadsheet that has each stock's monthly returns for a ten-year historical period (e.g., 2003–2012).

   a. Create an equally weighted portfolio of the 10 stocks by calculating the equally weighted portfolio's (EWP) return in each month during the ten-year period.

   b. Create a series of monthly portfolio returns using the Time Series Method in Exhibit 4.6. To do this, create a set of weights in one row of the spreadsheet and reference these weights and each month's returns in the $=$ SUMPRODUCT() function to calculate the monthly return. Verify that changing these weights changes the portfolio's monthly returns. We will refer to this portfolio as P1.

   c. Calculate the average and standard deviation of the monthly returns and the Sharpe Ratio for the stocks and the portfolios (EWP and P1) for the "First Half" of the ten-year period (i.e., the first five years). Calculate the average and standard deviation of the monthly returns and the Sharpe Ratio for the stocks and the portfolios (EWP and P1) for the "Last Half" of the ten-year period.

   d. Are the stocks with the highest standard deviations in the Last Half the same as the stocks with the highest standard deviations in the First Half? What about average returns and Sharpe Ratios?

   e. Using Excel's Solver as in Exhibit 4.13, find the set of weights that sets the "First Half" standard deviation to its minimum for P1.

   f. Examine the P1 weights for the stocks resulting from the Solver in part d. Can you determine why each stock received the weight that it did? That is, which stocks received the most weight? Why?

   g. Compare the standard deviation during the "Last Half" for P1 with EW. Which is lower? Is this what you would have expected? Why?

   h. Redo parts e. and g., but add constraints that the minimum weight in each stock must be at least 5% and/or that the maximum weight in each stock must be no greater than 15%. How does this change your response to part f.?

4. Redo parts e. through h. of question 3, but use the object to maximize the Sharpe Ratio in the First Half.

5. Theoretically, a constraint always results in a worse solution according to mathematics. Why are constraints important in using optimizers to construct portfolios?

(Continued)

Exercises (Continued)

6. In general, which portfolio would you expect to have a lower tracking error against the S&P 500: an equally weighted portfolio of 20 large cap stocks or an equally weighted portfolio of 40 large cap stocks? Why?
7. In general, which portfolio would you expect to have a lower tracking error against the S&P 500: an equally weighted portfolio of 40 large cap stocks or an equally weighted portfolio of 40 mid cap stocks? Why?
8. In general, which portfolio would you expect to have a lower tracking error against the S&P 500: an equally weighted portfolio of 40 large stocks or a portfolio of 40 large cap stocks that has the same sector weights as the S&P 500, assuming stocks are equally weighted within sectors?
9. What are some advantages and disadvantages to constraining a portfolio to be sector neutral (i.e., have the same sector weights as the benchmark)?

Presentations

Chapter Contents

Reports and presentations are a part of any business. Nearly all business units make internal reports and presentations as a way to share information or support a decision. Client-facing business units also make external presentations as part of their efforts to develop new business (i.e., sell products or services) and provide service or support to existing business relationships. At their best, presentations provide information in its most useful form by distilling a thorough understanding of the subject matter into its most relevant points for a particular situation or audience. This chapter provides a discussion of the various types of presentations and reports that are prepared and made by investment organizations in general and student-managed investment funds in particular.

We classify presentations into two general groups: internal presentations and external presentations. Internal presentations are those targeted primarily at constituencies within the organization, such as reports or presentations within a team or by a team for the rest of the organization. Internal presentations, especially within a student-managed investment fund, often serve the purpose of sharing information with the goal of making a key business or investment decision, such as the purchase or sale of a security. External presentations are those targeted at external constituencies, such as clients, prospective clients, oversight boards, or, in the case of student-managed investment funds, interested alumni. As stated above, external presentations often have the purpose of gaining or retaining business or otherwise affecting the organization's external image and future opportunities.

Among the most important internal presentations for a student-managed investment fund are those involving security selection and portfolio construction decisions. As such, this chapter builds on important aspects of the material discussed in the previous two chapters. External presentations can encompass all activities of an investment organization, including its organization structure, but usually have a particular emphasis on the organization's

Trading and Money Management in a Student-Managed Portfolio.
DOI: http://dx.doi.org/10.1016/B978-0-12-374755-6.00005-4

investment philosophy and process, security selection and portfolio construction, and performance. Performance analysis and reporting are important both internally and externally − so important that the material merits the sole attention of the next chapter.

The practice and experience in making professional presentations in a business setting are among the key benefits to any student participating in a student-managed investment fund. Though this chapter focuses on presentations that support the business of investment organizations, the presentation skills and experience are applicable to any business, not just investment firms. While the substance of the presentation is derived from the activities involved in managing a portfolio, the lessons from the development and delivery of such reports and presentations are universal.

Internal Presentations

For most student-managed investment funds, internal reports and presentations are a key step in making a decision to buy or sell a security. Indeed, some funds require votes under majority rules prior to making a trade. These votes are typically taken at some point after an analyst's report is filed and/or a presentation is made. Given their prominent role, we discuss the elements of such presentations and provide several examples. As discussed earlier in this book, it is important that the content of such presentations be motivated by and consistent with the investment organization's investment philosophy and process. Specifically, most fundamental investment processes should not have reports or presentations that contain quantitative analysis of stock price trends or discussion of elaborate factor models. Rather, reports from such processes would emphasize the fundamental elements that contribute to the investment thesis within the framework of the organization's investment philosophy and process.

We begin by discussing the research report, which is also commonly referred to as an analyst report. Such reports are typical among investment organizations that employ a fundamental investment approach. Tulane University's program employs an interesting twist on the student-managed investment fund through their Burkenroad Reports program. The primary activity of the program is to publish stock research reports. In essence, these reports provide research to support the selection of portfolio securities. The program is described in Exhibit 5.1, with additional notes about the program from the program's faculty advisor, Prof. Peter Ricchiuti. We refer readers to the numerous examples from Burkenroad Reports that are available on the website listed in the exhibit.

Exhibit 5.2 shows an overview of the requirements for security reports as part of the Practicum in Portfolio Management to support Baylor University's student-management investment fund, the Philip M. Dorr Alumni and Friends Endowment Investment Fund. Guidelines such as those in Exhibit 5.1 help assure consistency across securities, fund

Exhibit 5.1 Tulane University's Burkenroad Reports

BURKENROAD REPORTS is the nation's first university-sponsored securities analysis program. Each year 200 students from Tulane's Freeman School of Business are put into teams of five and assigned to one of 40 small-cap, underfollowed public companies headquartered in Alabama, Florida, Georgia, Louisiana, Mississippi, and Texas. These "stocks under rocks" are generally overlooked by Wall Street securities analysts.

Students meet with top management, visit company sites, design financial models, and publish investment research reports which are distributed to nearly 20,000 individual and institutional investors. BURKENROAD REPORTS has been featured in *The Wall Street Journal*, *The Washington Post*, *Investor's Business Daily*, *The New York Times*, *BARRONS*, *Kiplinger's*, and *Fortune* as well as on *CNN*, *CNBC*, and the National PBS programs of *Wall Street Week* and *The Nightly Business Report*. In 1996 we started the BURKENROAD REPORTS Investment Conference. This annual event features presentations from company management to more than 500 investors.

On December 31, 2001, Hancock Bank created the Burkenroad Mutual Fund (HYBUX) that utilizes the research reports created by our students.

The Fund now has more than $45 million in assets and has outperformed 99% of the nation's equity mutual funds over its first seven years.

This program has benefited all involved. Since its inception in 1993 nearly 500 students have graduated from the program onto careers in the investment field. BURKENROAD REPORTS has generated a great deal of attention for the Freeman School, created a valuable experiential learning experience and offered the region's public companies a vehicle with which to connect to the financial markets. Information about the program, as well as recent research reports, is available at www.burkenroad.org.

Additional Notes from Professor Ricchiuti

The class runs for one semester and students receive three credits. The class meets for an hour each week. The students also have several team meetings (each team is made up of five students) as well as a minimum of five two-hour meetings with our accounting professor, Pam Shaw, to develop the pro-forma financial models.

Each team has a full day trip to meet management and company sites.

One Saturday during the semester we have an all-day workshop featuring presentations from alumni in the investment business.

Each year I select two associate directors of research to oversee the program (these are second-year MBAs who excelled as analysts as first-year MBAs. There are also 10 Investment Research Managers who oversee two analysts' teams each semester. Both of these jobs are paid positions.

Each week a different section of the report is turned in and reviewed by me and my student leaders. We utilize a number of information systems including Bloomberg, Reuters, Hoover's, and Thomson One Banker.

The year culminates at our annual investment conference which features presentations from the management of each of the 40 companies we follow. The event is free and open to the public and is usually attended by about 500–600 individual and institutional investors. The conference is held at a big hotel near the French Quarter and features stacks of reports done by the students.

After the conference all of the reports are available on our website www.burkenroad.org.

Finally, our Burkenroad Mutual Fund trades on the public market under the ticker symbol HYBUX and now has more than $60 million in assets. Over its first 8 years its price has more than doubled and the fund has outperformed more than 99% of the nation's 4000 + equity mutual funds.

---

members, and time within the same organization. Most investment and investment banking firms have such guidelines for reports by their employees. Standards such as these also help share information efficiently, as members of the organization know where certain information will be in the report.

Exhibit 5.2 Baylor Project Guidelines

Remember: A picture says a thousand words. Always be looking for concepts that can be displayed graphically in the form of a table, chart, or graph. Also, follow the page counts listed here. Do not exceed 8 pages plus appendices. Part of a good research report is making your case concisely.

Page 1

Always use the cover page found on the class web page!

Company Description

A short description of the company's basic business or businesses. Should be 3 to 7 lines in length. Should be exclusively factual and should offer no opinions about the company. What do they do?

Bullet Points

Look at the cover page example on the web page. Except for Bullet #4, these should be very general and should touch only on the broadest and most important points. Few specific details should be given, as these will appear later on in the report. The goal of Bullet points 1–3 is to tell the most important reasons why a potential investor might want to read the rest of the report or invest in the company. Why is this a good idea?

Bullet point #4 should be similar to every other Bullet #4 in all of our research reports. This gives basic valuations, earnings estimates, the method for valuing the stock, and a price target. See language from example on the web page.

Page 2
Investment Opinion

This should be about one page in length, and should expand on the first 3 Bullet points. This section should introduce new ideas about the potential investment merits of the company, as well as giving more specific details about some points already introduced in Bullet points 1–3. In general, this section should be starting to give more specific details about the most important points to the story. However, the focus of this section should continue to be on the main reasons why an investor should invest in the company or industry.

Page 3
Valuation

This section should be 1/3 to 1/2 of a page, and should expand on the fourth bullet point. This should include valuations based on price/book, price/sales, price/earnings, and/or price/cash flow, PEG ratio, equity duration, earnings growth rate estimates, ROE, historical earnings growth, historical trading range, ROA, insider trading, % of insider and institutional holdings, along with earnings revisions and earnings surprise, if possible. These must be compared to the company's industry/SIC code and the appropriate benchmark — i.e., S&P 500 or Russell 2000. Can also compare to other stocks within the industry. This may also include a price target.

Company Background

This section should be 1/3 to 1/2 of a page, and should also be very similar to other Company Background sections in our other research reports. This should include details on when the company was formed, the company's IPO, any secondary offerings, private placements or other financings, merger and acquisition activities, and/or spin-offs.

Page 4
Company Overview

This section should be one page in length. This section is the heart of the report and includes virtually all details about the company and any operating divisions/subsidiaries. Often included are subsections describing each clearly segmented division. These subsections can include separate pro-formas projecting the financial results for each subsidiary. This section should include discussion of competitive (dis)advantages, barriers to entry, international opportunities, clients, suppliers, distribution system, seasonal or cyclical trends, proprietary technology, the company's long-term growth strategy, etc.

Page 5
Competition

If the company has several publicly traded competitors, this should be a separate section. This section should include a brief 1/3 to 1/2 page description of the competition and a table of their relative valuations. If there are no good comparison companies, a brief description of the competition can be included in the company overview section.

Shareholders

This table should include the holdings of key management and employees. This can be found in the proxy statement. This should also include options or warrants outstanding, as well as major institutional shareholders.

Management

This should include a brief 3–5 line description of the background of the key management members. A one-line description of each member of the Board is also preferred. This information can generally be found in the proxy statement or the annual report.

Page 6
Industry Overview

Depending on the company, this section should be one page in length. This should include a fairly detailed description of the trends in the industry, such as consolidation, or other driving factors. This should include the impact of competing or new technology, competition, consumer behavior, etc.

Page 7
Income Statement Comments

This section should give descriptions of the most recent quarterly period that has been reported, unless it was the fourth quarter, and/or descriptions of the most recent fiscal year end. The focus of this discussion should be to highlight items that are not obvious at first glance. These include reasons for increases (decreases) in sales, one-time gains or losses, reasons for increases/decreases in expenses, etc. This section should also include a discussion of these same concepts that are in the projected results (e.g., if a large one-time gain is expected or a description of the assumptions underlying the earnings estimates). The language should be fairly dry, and should be similar to our other research reports. The information can be obtained from the annual reports, 10-K, or 10-Q.

Balance Sheet Comments

This section should be very brief, and should only include a discussion of anything that is out of the ordinary. This includes loans to officers, low levels of cash or working capital, high debt, etc. Many times, no discussion about the balance sheet is needed.

Page 8
Key Growth Drivers

A minimum of 1/2 page should be devoted to an analysis of why you believe the current analyst forecast for earnings growth is accurate or inaccurate. This should be done by examining what drives the growth in the forecast and your assessment of whether that growth can be accomplished.

Risks of Investing in This Security — What Can Go Wrong?

Much of this information is generic to small cap stocks, such as the risk of the loss of a key management member. Many of these will be the same for all companies, and can be taken directly from our other reports. A discussion of risks that are specific to the company or industry should also be included. A prospectus from a recent IPO or secondary offering is the best place to get ideas of the major risks to a story.

Appendix
Financial Statements

In general, the report should contain a quarterly income statement, an annual income statement, and a balance sheet.

The balance sheet should contain only the line items found in the company's 10-K, and should include two years of audited year-end information (most recent 10-K) and the most recent unaudited quarterly information (most recent 10-Q). If the last period reported was a year-end, it should contain three years of audited year-end information.

The quarterly income statement should include a full year of historical quarterly information, the current year (including estimates), and a future year of quarterly projections. We do not normally project more than 4 quarters in the future, so the periods presented are subject to change depending on where the company is in its fiscal year. The 4Q for historical periods is derived by subtracting the results through the IS nine months (3Q 10-Q) from the year-end totals (10-K).

The annual income statement should contain at least 3 years of historical information and 2–3 years of projections. This should also include an abbreviated cash flow statement (cash flow net income + depreciation/amortization/non-cash expenses) and an abbreviated free cash flow statement (free cash flow = cash flow − capital expenditures).

All of these cash flow figures can be found in the statement of cash flows in the 10-K.

We also note that the guidelines emphasize the importance of being concise. Einstein was known to say, "If I had more time, I would have written a shorter letter." A similar idea applies to all presentations and reports. Even complex ideas can be distilled into their most important elements. Likewise, the investment thesis should be focused on the key elements that lead to the buy, sell, or hold decision. Finally, the report is organized in a clear manner that provides a summary early in the report, along with supporting information throughout the report. By summarizing the investment thesis early on, readers are able to see how the later information helps justify the investment thesis.

Before proceeding to a discussion of specific student-managed investment fund presentations, we discuss considerations in preparing and making such presentations. The list below is purposefully general and primarily stylistic. As such, the suggestions apply to most business presentations. However, these suggestions should not be dismissed or minimized because they focus on style. To the contrary, by following these suggestions, the substance of the presentation should be clearer and more effectively communicated to the audience.

General Presentation Style and Delivery Guidelines

1. There should always be (1) an introduction; (2) a body; and (3) a conclusion. The key point of the presentation should be made in each of the three sections. Some describe this rule as, "Tell 'em what you're going to tell 'em. Tell 'em. And then tell 'em what you told 'em." People remember things that are repeated and this makes clearer to the audience what the presenter thinks his or her key points are. Telling the audience a summary of the key points up front allows the audience to know what to look for in the presentation. By telling them what the key points are (or were) again at the end of the presentation, it leaves them with a reminder.
2. Have clear "takeaways" or "messages" for each presentation. If someone sees and hears the presentation, what are the three or four main points that you want them to realize and remember? Have those points been made clearly in the presentation? Have other points that are not important been made that can be dropped or otherwise minimized? Even if there is a related point that can be made, the decision of whether to include it should be made based on whether the point contributes to the main points of the presentation. This rule can also apply at the section, page, or paragraph level of a report or at the slide level of a presentation. That is, the takeaway or point of each slide should be clear, or the relevance of the slide should be questioned.
3. Slides should . . .
    a. be clean and not cluttered.
    b. be easy to read from the back of the room. Make sure the font size is large enough, especially on tables and figures that are important.
    c. have bullet points, not long sentences and/or paragraphs.
    d. have a specific purpose or point to make in the presentation.
    e. have a simple and consistent color scheme. More colors are not necessarily better. Also, follow traditional norms with color. Green is usually used to denote a positive

value, an upward movement, or something "good." Red usually indicates a negative number, downward movement, etc. Yellow or orange often convey caution. It is best not to report numbers in all red or all green. Color can help add emphasis and should be used accordingly, not for color's sake alone.

f. have a simple and consistent format. Titles should appear in the same place consistently throughout the presentation. Likewise, the location and formatting of summary or highlight points should be consistent. For example, callout boxes highlighting points might always appear in the right margin. One or two fonts should be chosen that are easy to read. One font can be used for regular text; the other font can be used for emphasis or for special text, such as quotations.

g. have page numbers. Even when slides are projected and under the control of the presenter, page numbers allow the audience to refer to a specific slide for a question or clarification.

4. Observe the rules of proportionality. Spend time and space on a slide or in the presentation in proportion to the importance of a point or topic. If something is not very important in a 10-minute presentation, then do not spend 5 minutes on it. If something is one of the three key points, then it should have roughly a third of the presentation's time spent on it. By spending too much time on an unimportant point, the audience might infer that the point is more important than it is. By spending too little time on a point, the audience might infer that the point is of less importance than it is.

5. Be on time. This means many things. Of course, be on time for the presentation. But also be on time in ending the presentation without having to rush at the end (or in the middle, or at the beginning). If the presentation is too long, do not just try to go faster. Instead, whittle the presentation down to its most important aspects or points. Prepare the presentation so that it is concise and to-the-point.

6. Do not read the slides to the audience. This does not mean one or two bullet points or quotes cannot be read verbatim for special emphasis of a point. Keep in mind that the audience can read. It is up to the presenter to fill in the blanks with meaningful discussion, added detail, clarification and emphasis relating to what is on the slide.

7. Give a presentation, not a speech. A presentation involves *sharing* what the presenter understands and what is in his or her head, not what is on a note card or a script. Sharing is an interactive exercise between at least two parties. The audience is important in this exercise and cues should be taken from them. The slides should serve as the presenter's outline, reminding the presenter of the intended talking points. The presenter should know everything else and be able to say what needs to be said from memory, without having memorized specific sentences. Audience feedback, both direct (e.g., questions) and indirect (e.g., body language), can help to steer a presentation. The presenter has the flexibility to alter the delivery of the presentation to best communicate with a particular audience.

8. Keep everyone on the same page. It is common to give a business presentation to an audience that is following the presentation on paper without the benefit of a projected

image. In these cases, the audience usually would have a hard copy of the presentation (e.g., in a spiral-bound book or packet). The presenter should, in such cases, explicitly refer to the page number, especially when moving to a new page. For example, the presenter might say, "Turning to page 6, we list the portfolio holdings as of . . ." or "The graph at the top of page 3 depicts . . ." or "As indicated in the three bullet points on page 12, ..." Be aware if the audience is confused about a slide. Unless later slides help clarify the point, try to resolve the confusion before moving on.

Exhibit 5.3 shows the guidelines for reports in TCU's Educational Investment Fund. The report and its accompanying presentation that are described in this exhibit reflect the investment process discussed in the extended example of security analysis and selection from the TCU-EIF in Chapter 3. Notice that the TCU and Baylor report guidelines both emphasize a discussion of the company and its competitors or competitive environment. The TCU-EIF report also calls for the assumptions used in valuing the security to be explicitly spelled out. As discussed in Chapter 3, the assumptions that go into a valuation model are key in determining the resulting valuation of the security. By having the assumptions clearly stated in the report, readers can judge whether they agree with the valuation in large part based on whether they believe that the inputs and assumptions are reasonable. Both TCU and Baylor utilize an appendix for more detailed information that might be relevant to some readers or consumers of the report.

Finally, the TCU guidelines provide a discussion of the presentation that supports the research report. The guidelines explicitly contemplate and encourage discussion among the EIF members through questions and answers. The presentation culminates in a vote on the recommendation contained in the report and supported by the presentation. As such, the report and the presentation are the key inputs into the fund's investment decisions. Returning to Baylor's fund, Exhibit 5.4 shows an outline for internal presentations. Again, the existence of a standardized presentation outline assures consistency within the organization. Furthermore, the outline provides a useful checklist that the fund members can use in security analysis and research.

The outline in Exhibit 5.4 is implemented in the presentation shown in Exhibit 5.5. This extended example documents the security selection on stocks from various sub-sectors within the Financials sector in Baylor's fund. There are many noteworthy aspects of this presentation. First, note that presentation generally adheres to many of the applicable stylistic guidelines above. Specifically, the presentation utilizes a consistent style and format. Second, the presentation progresses through the selection of securities in several sub-sectors within the Financials sector. This allows the audience to clearly follow the investment process steps as securities are screened or filtered to arrive at a short list. Once the list has narrowed to two or three securities, specific information is presented about each one.

Exhibit 5.3 Texas Christian University's Educational Investment Fund Written Report and Presentation Guidelines

By Stanley Block and Larry Lockwood

The Written Report
Elements of the written report include the following:

Original Purchase Rationale: If the stock is an existing holding within the portfolio, the report explains the rationale employed by the student analyst at the time of the purchase. Also, this section is used to see if the factors influencing the original purchase have changed since the original purchase.

Portfolio Considerations: The written report describes how the stock fits into the portfolio from a diversification perspective (e.g., lists the current allocation of the fund to the equity sector of the stock, compares current allocation versus the fund's equity sector target).

Industry Overview: This section of the student's report discusses recent events within the industry with particular focus on changing trends.

Porter Competitive Analysis: The competitive forces governing the industry are examined and explained in detail using Porter's Five Forces (power of buyers, sellers, substitutes, potential entrants, and existing competitors). The model allows for the members to see any potential headwinds the company might face going forward. While the "forces" are always changing, an understanding of what the company faces going forward allows for a better feel for future performance. This section provides an overall view of the strength or fragility of the industry and constituent company earnings sustainability.

Company Overview: This section begins with a brief discussion of the company's history. Then we examine data related to the company's business segments. We include recent news events, especially those that had significant effects on stock valuation, including recent quarterly performance. This section includes the investment recommendation of the student analyst, along with a discussion of the pros and cons to the recommendation, the latter of which force the analyst to consider factors that move counter to his or her investment recommendation.

Pro Forma Income Statements: This section includes the forecasts of all key income statement variables for the next three years, along with a discussion of the assumptions used when deriving the forecasts. The discussion of the assumptions must be specific and quantifiable.

Ratio Analysis: These include ratios indicating liquidity (current ratio, quick ratio, accounts receivable), asset utilization (accounts receivable turnover, inventory turnover, total asset turnover), debt utilization (long-term debt to equity, total debt to equity, times interest earned), profitability (gross profit margin, ROE, ROA), valuation ratios (P/E, price-to-book ratio, price-to-cash flow, etc.). We present the ratios for each of the past 3 years for the company under consideration and for the most appropriate competitor and for the industry average in which the subject company operates.

DuPont Analysis: We include a separate section reporting the net profit margin, asset turnover, financial leverage, and return on equity. We use averages of all balance sheet numbers in our DuPont Analysis to adjust for companies that might have experienced large changes in assets during the year. The Dupont Analysis allows a nice comparison of the drivers of profitability across time and across competitors.

Valuation Assumptions: This section includes a listing of the risk-free rate, market risk premium, beta, and forecasts of earnings per share, dividends, P/E, and free cash flow to equity. Valuation of the stock and sensitivity analyses for the valuation also are presented. Indication of whether the stock is overvalued or undervalued according to the analysis is provided in this section.

Statistical Appendix: An appendix is included for all other valuation considerations including but not limited to historical regression results over the past 60 months, calculation of PEG ratios, alpha, PVGO, earnings growth rates over the past 3 years, and price-to-sales, price-to-cash flow, price-to-book value, and price-to-EBITDA comparisons.

The Presentation

After the financial model and the written report are prepared and distributed to fund members (at least two days in advance), the student analyst presents his or her findings and recommendation to the class members. The presentation lasts approximately 20 minutes and is followed by a 20-minute question and answer period in which each fund member is expected to participate. After the Q&A, a vote is taken and the recommendation either passes or fails based on a majority rule.

Exhibit 5.4 Baylor University's General Presentation Guidelines

The presentations should cover the following material plus any other material information particular to that stock — e.g., lawsuits, etc.

1. Outline of presentation.
2. List current holdings in sector and weight in Dorr Portfolio.
3. List current weight of sector in S&P 500.
4. Filters to reduce stocks in your sector to perhaps eight.
5. Reduce stocks using to one stock (or two if you recommend purchasing two) usually based on fundamental analysis.
6. Company overview.
7. Description of the firm's business model.
8. Discussion of firm's major areas and discussion of prospects and plans.
9. Price chart(s). See BigCharts.com.
10. Ratios including P/E, P/Book, P/CF, P/Sales; long-term projected growth rate; and a PEG ratio. The P/E should be P/forward earnings. These ratios for the firm should be compared to similar ratios for S&P 500, sector or industry, and the firm's major competitors.
11. List of earnings revisions and the up–down ratio probably for the past 30 days.
12. Perhaps the earnings surprise for the most recent quarter.
13. Discuss the CEO or management team.
14. List of growth drivers.
15. List of risks for the stock.
16. Advisor's input.
17. Your recommendation. Hold, sell now, or sell later if we find a better stock.

Exhibit 5.5 Financials Sector Presentation from Baylor University

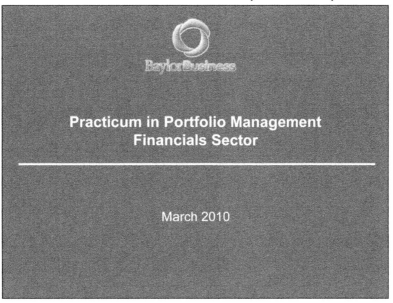

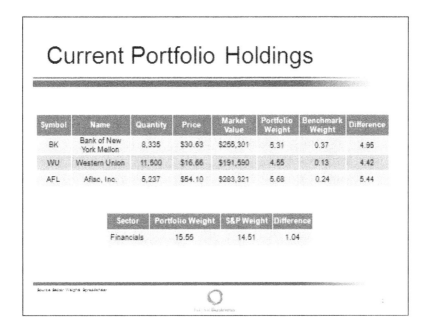

Agenda

- Basic Filter Methodology
- Security Comparisons
  - Individual Filters
  - Qualitative Factors and Final Selection
  - Current Stock Summary
  - New Stock
  - Comparison

Filter Methodology: Overview

- Large Cap Financials
  - Limit S&P 500
- Diversification Opportunities
  - Financial Services (WU, BK)
  - Insurance (AFL)
  - Banks ( )
- Earnings ⟶ Valuations ⟶ Financial Stability
- Qualitative Factors

Filter Methodology: Advisor's Comments

"The financial sector has been among the most volatile throughout the recent crisis…many analysts are expecting a sideways trending market due to slow, anemic growth in the economy.

As such, it is important to diversify your asset…across subsectors with management teams who are capable of managing through the downturns and/or have the ability to capture market share/increase revenue. Moreover, the risk affecting these different subsectors varies greatly…spread that potential risk as thin as possible."

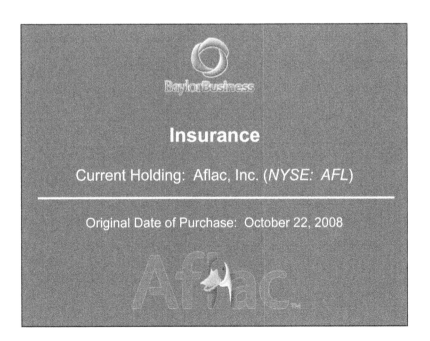

Filter Methodology: Insurance

- Valuation/Earnings Potential
  - >Median FY1 and FY2 Potential
  - <Median P/E
- Yield
  - Dividend Yield was Larger
  - <PEGY
- Qualitative Factors

Insurance

Methodology	Result
Median Earnings Growth - FY1	4.01
Median Earnings Growth - FY2	4.32
Median P/E	9.06
Median PEGY	64.57

Source: Bloomberg

Insurance: Filter

Passed FY1 & FY2	Passed P/E	Passed PEGY
Aflac, Inc.	Allstate	American International Group
Allstate	American International Group	Assurant Inc.
American International Group	Assurant Inc.	MetLife Inc.
Assurant Inc.	MetLife Inc.	
Chubb Corp.	Torchmark Corp.	
Loews Corp.		
MetLife Inc.		
Prudential Financial		
The Travelers Companies Inc.		
Torchmark Corp.		

9

Security Selection

AIG

- Irreparable Reputation
- Reluctance to Sell AIG's Products
- Concentrated Bets in Mortgage Markets
- Massively Diluted Shares from Gov't Aid

AIZ

- Strong Relationship with Bankrupt Circuit City
- Large Majority of Customers are Major Firms with Pricing Power

MET

- Significant Cross-Selling Opportunities
- Differing and Strong Brand and Distribution Channels
- "Sticky" Relationships with Customers
- Conservative Hedging Programs

10

Industry Overview MetLife

- Insurance, Accident and Health
  - Policies are marketed to pay cash benefit following an accident or health problem
    - Intent is to protect wealth, not build it
  - Revenue is generated in two ways
    - Collection of premiums
    - Investment Income
  - Regulated by state government, with review by the National Association of Insurance Commissioners (NAIC)

Source: Morningstar, Aflac 2008 10K

Baylor Business

11

AFL: Overview

Statistics	
Price	$53.65
52 Week Range	$15.72 - $55.00
Market Cap	$25.71B
Enterprise Value	$25.91B
P/B	2.83
Beta	1.74
Avg Dividend Yield	1.60%

Source: ThomsonOne, Yahoo Finance

Baylor Business

12

Original Purchase

- Considered a "recession proof" company
- Solid history of consistent growth
- High quality portfolio of investment grade securities

MET: Overview

MetLife

- Largest life insurance company in the US
- Also provides group non-medical insurance and some financial service

Statistics	
Price	$41.67
52 Week Range	$20.42 - $43.63
Market Cap	$34.77B
P/B	1.09
Beta	2.08
Avg Dividend Yield	0.9%

Products & Services
Auto Insurance
Banking
Deferred Annuities
Dental Insurance Center
Disability Income
Financial Planning
Home Insurance
Income Annuities
IRAs
Life Insurance
Long-Term Care
Mutual Funds & Brokerage

Source: ThomsonOne, MetLife.com

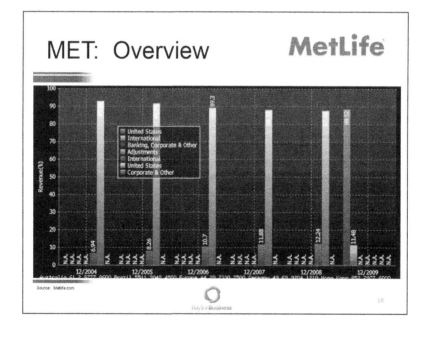

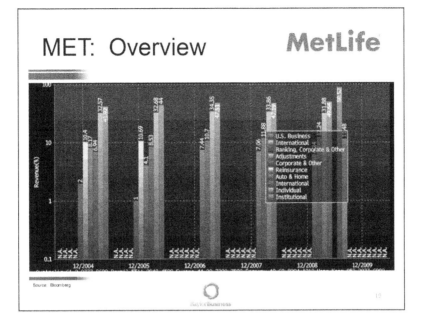

MET: Growth Drivers

- Purchase of ALICO from AIG
  - Acquisition is part of MetLife's international expansion strategy
  - Cost of $15.5B will be funded with $6.8B cash and $8.7B of equity (with lock ups and voting restrictions)
  - Expected to close late this year

Source: Metlife.com

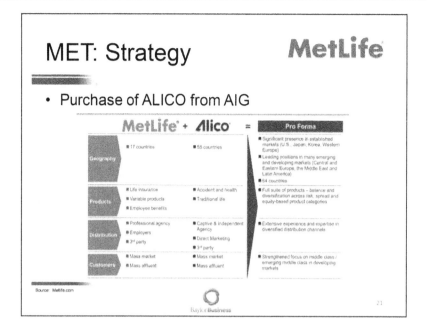

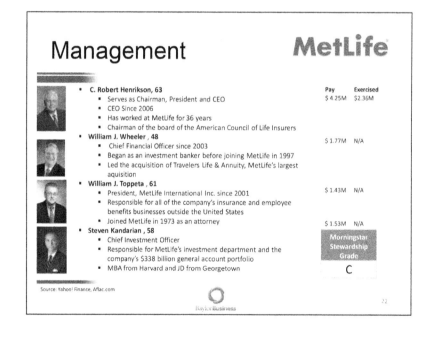

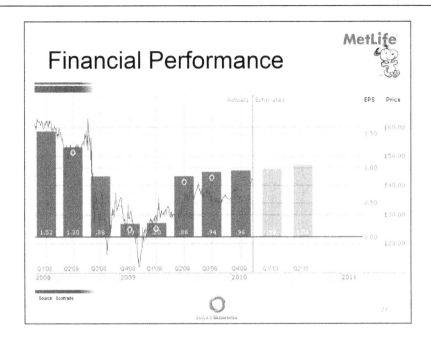

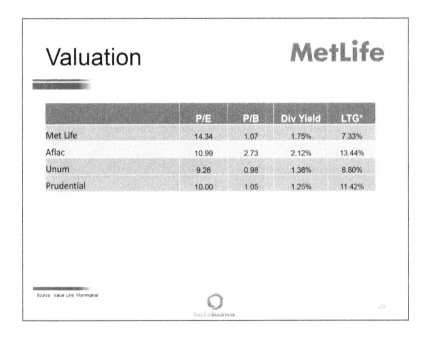

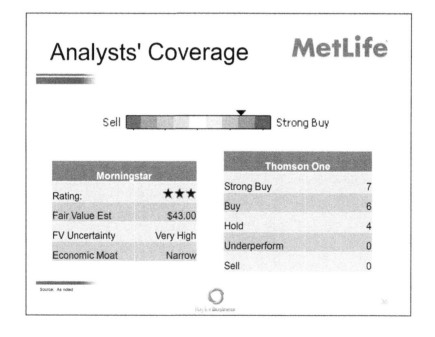

Forecasts

MetLife

Year	Earnings Estimate	P/E	Price	Growth
FY 1	4.056	10.254	41.59	--
FY 2	4.900	10.254	50.24	20.81%

Source: Bloomberg

31

MET: SWOT

MetLife

- Strengths
  - Provides insurance for 90% of the Fortune 100
  - Large scale, recognition and product line provide freedom to choose where to invest more resources
  - Offers more diversified products
  - Large presence in Japan (like Aflac) but international revenues are more diversified
  - Price is cheap in terms of P/E, price-to-book, price-to-sales, and price-to-cashflow

- Weaknesses
  - Scale provides no distinct competitive advantage over peers
  - 2009 NI was -$2,368
  - Officers own less than 1% of common stock
  - Large debt-to-equity ratio (503.3/32.3 = 15.58, compared to AFL = 8.33)

Source: Value Line; Morningstar

32

MET: SWOT

MetLife

- **Opportunities**
  - International Expansion
  - Acquisition of ALICO
  - Company-wide mission to reduce expenses by $400 million
  - Better economy means more hiring, more policies, more premiums

- **Threats**
  - 30% of common shares owned by policy holders trust, controlled by board
    - 819M shares outstanding
    - 233M shares in trust
  - Faces same risk of Japan Post privatization as Aflac
  - Commoditization of insurance products in US
  - Exposure to mortgage backed securities

Source: Value Line; Morningstar

Baylor Business

33

MET vs AFL

MetLife

Valuation	MetLife	Aflac	Variance
Earnings - FY1	4.056	5.346	-1.29
Earnings - FY2	4.900	5.866	-0.97
P/E	14.341	10.992	3.35
PEGY	130.97	75.96	55.00
Tier 1 RBC	9.21%	3.3%	5.91%

Baylor Business

34

MET vs AFL

MetLife

MetLife

Strengths
- Business & Geographic variety

Weaknesses
- Management not aligned with investor interests

Aflac

Strengths
- Less risk from healthcare reform
- Consistent growth

Weaknesses
- Concentration of revenues in Japan

MET vs AFL

MetLife

MetLife

Opportunities
- International Expansion
- ALICO Acquisition

Threats/Risks
- Exposure to healthcare reform

Aflac

Opportunities
- Product Innovation
- Consistently lowering benefit ratio

Threats/Risks
- Competition and Deregulation in Japan

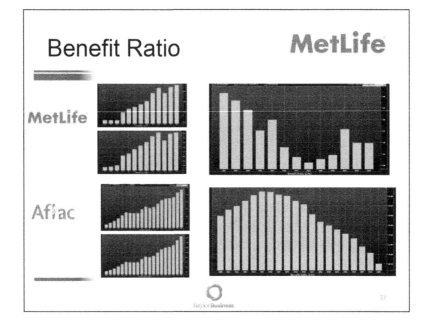

MET vs AFL: Rationale MetLife

- Stronger Fundamentals
- Less Uncertainty With Health Care Reform
- Stronger Benefit Ratio

Baylor Business

Advisor's Thoughts

- Organic growth prospects look weak for large caps as they are likely going to have to acquire mid caps to support revenue growth

- Variable annuity product is out of favor and demand is unlikely to come back

- Fundamentals remain intact for holding Aflac, although they lack diversity among product base, management has worked to consistently decrease their payout ratio, improving margins

Recommendation

 HOLD

 PASS

Filter Methodology: Financial Services

- Valuation/Earnings Potential
  - >Median FY1 and FY2 Potential
  - <Median P/E
- Financial Strength
  - >Median Tier 1 RBC
- Qualitative Factors

Financial Services

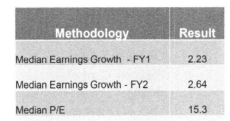

Methodology	Result
Median Earnings Growth - FY1	2.23
Median Earnings Growth - FY2	2.64
Median P/E	15.3
Median Tier 1 RBC	15.0%

Source: Bloomberg

Financial Services: Filter

Passed FY1 & FY2	Passed P/E	Passed Tier 1 RBC
Ameriprise Financial Inc.	Ameriprise Financial Inc.	Goldman Sachs Group
Bank of New York Mellon	Bank of New York Mellon	Morgan Stanley
CME Group Inc.	Goldman Sachs Group	State Street Corp.
Equifax, Inc	Morgan Stanley	
Franklin Resources	State Street Corp.	
Goldman Sachs Group		
IntercontinentalExchange Inc.		
Mastercard, Inc.		
Morgan Stanley		
State Street Corp.		
T. Rowe Price Group		
Visa		

Security Selection

Goldman Sachs	Morgan Stanley	State Street
• "Fat Trimming" for ROA	• Current Lawsuits	• Lack of Integration of Acquisitions
• 2008 Compensation	• Off BS Activities	• Legal Issues
• Competition Restructuring	• Expense Control (M&A)	• Very Poor Balance Sheet Management
• Decreasing Risk	• Lack of Qualitative Measures in Compensations	
	• <Desirable Financial Health	

Source: Morningstar

Baylor Business

45

Goldman Sachs vs. Bank of New York

Methodology	Sector Median	GS	Variance
Median Earnings Growth - FY1	2.23	18.49	16.25
Median Earnings Growth - FY2	2.64	20.53	17.89
Median P/E	15.3	8.58	-6.73
Median Tier 1 RBC	15.0%	15.0%	0.0%

Source: Bloomberg

Baylor Business

46

BK: Overview

- Top 10 Global Asset Managers
  - Over 1 Trillion in Assets Under Management

Statistics	
Price	$30.63
52 Week Range	$33.62 - $21.99
Market Cap	$36.18B
Enterprise Value	$-7.91B
P/B	1.24
Beta	0.61
Avg Dividend Yield	1.20%

Source: www.BNYMellon.com, Bloomberg

Original Purchase

- The Good
  - Aggressive 2008 Markdown of Investment Portfolio
  - $38 Billion Securities Portfolio
  - BK Claimed Little Credit Risk in 2008
  - Over $58 Billion in Cash
  - $4.1 Billion MTM Losses, 12/31/08
- The Bad
  - White Downs in OTTI Continued
  - Dividends Cut and New Equity Issued for TARP

Source: 2009 Presentation

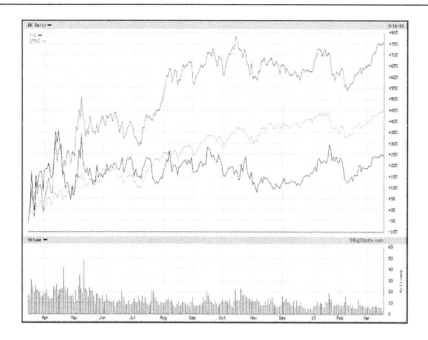

GS: Overview

- Founded in 1869

- Global Investment Firm

- Strong Reputation

- Savvy Management

Statistics	
Price	$177.90
52 Week Range	$193.60 - $72.78
Market Cap	$90.15B
P/B	1.44
Beta	1.43
Avg Dividend Yield	0.9%

Source: US Bancorp.com, Value Line, Morningstar

Stryker Business

50

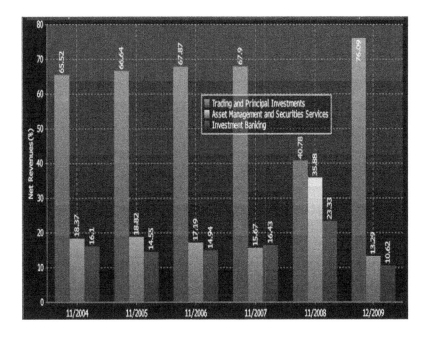

Management

Goldman Sachs

Mr. Lloyd C. Blankfein , 55 Chairman, Chief Exec. Officer and Managing Director	$ 600.00K	$ 0
Mr. J. Michael Evans , 52 Vice Chairman, Managing Director and Chairman of Asia Operations	$ 600.00K	$ 0
Mr. Gary D. Cohn , 49 Pres, Chief Operating Officer, Managing Director	$ 600.00K	$ 0
Mr. David A. Viniar , 54 Chief Financial Officer, Managing Director, Exec. VP and Head of the Operations, Technology & Fin. Division	$ 600.00K	$ 0
Dr. Ruth J. Simmons , 64 Chairwoman of Advisory Board For 10 000 Women Initiative	N/A	N/A

Morningstar Stewardship Grade
B

Source: Yahoo! Finance

53

Ownership

Goldman Sachs

Breakdown	
% of Shares Held by All Insider and 5% Owners:	5%
% of Shares Held by Institutional & Mutual Fund Owners:	75%
% of Float Held by Institutional & Mutual Fund Owners:	79%
Number of Institutions Holding Shares:	1084

- Top Institutional Owners
  - AXA, Barclay's, State Street
- Top Fund Holders
  - Vanguard, SPDR, College Retirement Equities

Source: Yahoo! Finance

54

Growth Drivers

- Past Growth Fueled By:
  - Leverage
  - Risk Taking
  - Pledging Firms Own Capital
- Future Plans
  - Seek More Moderate Risk and Above Avg Returns

Financial Performance

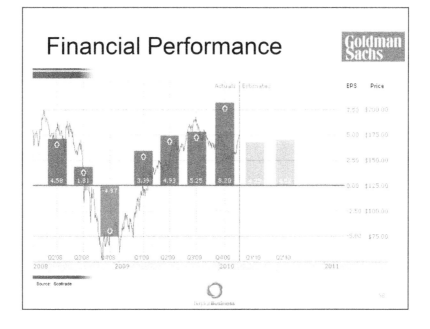

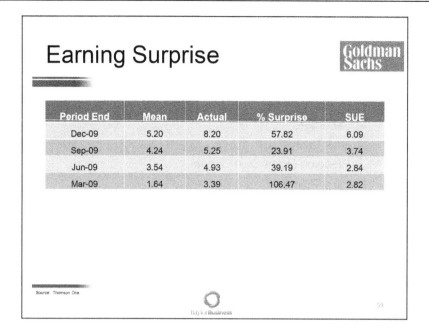

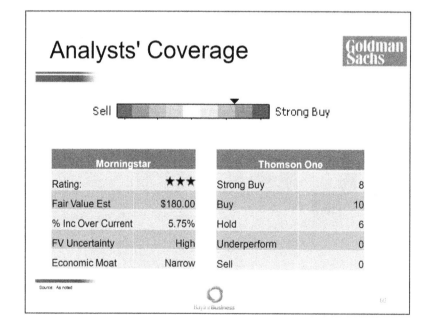

Price Forecast

Year	Earnings Estimate	P/E	Price	Growth
FY 1	18.49	8.58	175	--
FY 2	20.53	8.58	194	10.97%

Source: Bloomberg

S.W.O.T.

Strengths
- Savvy Management
- Impeccable Reputation
- Reduced Risk in Balance Sheet

Weaknesses
- Correlation with Capital Markets and Trading Volumes

Opportunities
- Increased ST Funding and Solvency
- Ability to Grow Deposits

Threats/Risks
- Change to Holding Company
- Chance of Not Hitting Such High Estimates
- Health of Capital Markets

Source: Morningstar; Value Line

GS vs BK

Valuation	Goldman Sachs	Bank of New York	Variance
Earnings - FY1	18.49	2.36	16.13
Earnings - FY2	20.53	2.8	17.73
P/E	8.58	12	-3.42
PEGY	80	94	-14
Tier 1 RBC	15%	12%	3%

Source: Bloomberg

63

GS vs BK

Strengths
- Savvy Management
- Impeccable Reputation
- Reduced Risk in Balance Sheet

Weaknesses
- Correlation with Capital Markets and Trading Volumes

BNY MELLON

Strengths
- Strong Economies of Scale
- Trimmed to Core Competencies

Weaknesses
- Cross-Selling with Mellon Corp Yet To Be Realized
- Tied to Capital Markets

Source: Morningstar, Value Line

64

GS vs BK

Opportunities
- Increased ST Funding and Solvency
- Ability to Grow Deposits

Threats/Risks
- Change to Holding Company
- Chance of Not Hitting Such High Estimates
- Health of Capital Markets

BNY MELLON

Opportunities
- Balance Sheet Growth Through Cheap Deposits

Threats/Risks
- Customer Dissatisfaction

Source: Morningstar, Value Line

GS vs BK: Rationale

- Better Fundamentals
  - Greater EPS Estimates, Lower P/E, Lower PEGY, Higher Tier 1 RBC
- Stronger Management
- BK: Analysts Doubt Returns Will Bounce Back
- GS Stronger Balance Sheet and Solvency
  - Decreased Financial Risk

Advisor's Thoughts

"Both are faced with regulatory risk. Goldman fundamentals are stronger and P/E valuation is low versus BNY and other companies within Financial Services."

"Converting to a commercial bank holding company has forced them to de-lever the balance sheet and increase their Tier 1, making them more attractive on a risk/return basis."

Recommendation

BNY MELLON   SELL

 BUY

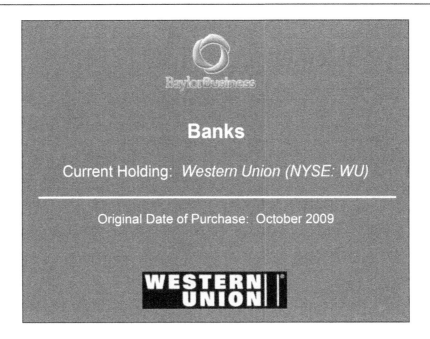

Industry Overview

- Regulation
  - Dodd Bill v Corker Bill
    - Curb in Proprietary Trading and Hedge Funds
    - "Too Big to Fail" No More
    - Limitation of Size of Firms
- Profitability
  - FDIC Assisted Acquisitions
  - Organic and Acquisition Based Growth

Source: CNN Money, Google Finance

Industry Overview

"Regional banks should do well in 2010. There will be significant opportunities for many of them to benefit from FDIC-assisted transactions of banks in attractive growth markets,"

- Frank Barkocy, Director of Research, Medon Capital Advisors

Source: CNBC.com

71

Advisor's Thoughts

"Community banks continue to face pressure and there is data to support the potential for as many as 800 failures, presenting opportunities for regional banks to increase their geographical presence and capture market share at discounted prices."

"With a few exceptions, the larger banks are focused on improving their personal balance sheets or operational issues; furthermore, the smaller transaction sizes associated with a community bank purchase are likely to fall under their radar screen.

72

Filter Methodology: Banks

- Regional Banks
- Valuation/Earnings Potential
  - >Median FY1 and FY2 Growth
  - <Median P/E
- Financial Strength
  - >Median Tier 1 RBC
- Qualitative Factors
  - Quality Loan Portfolio and Healthy Reserves

Regional Banks

Methodology	Result
Median Earnings Growth - FY1	-.037
Median Earnings Growth - FY2	1.31
Median P/E	19.9

Source: Bloomberg

Banks: Filter

Banks	Regional	Passed FY1 & FY2	Passed P/E
Bank of America Corp.	BB&T Corporation	BB&T Corporation	BB&T Corporation
BB&T Corporation	Comerica Inc.	Comerica Inc.	Fifth Third Bancorp
Citigroup Inc.	Fifth Third Bancorp	Fifth Third Bancorp	U.S. Bancorp
Comerica Inc.	Huntington Bancshares	U.S. Bancorp	
Fifth Third Bancorp	KeyCorp		
First Horizon National	Regions Financial Corp.		
Hudson City Bancorp	SunTrust Banks		
Huntington Bancshares	U.S. Bancorp		
JPMorgan Chase & Co.			
KeyCorp			
M&T Bank Corp.			
Marshall & Ilsley Corp.			
Northern Trust Corp.			
People's United Bank			
PNC Financial Services			
Regions Financial Corp.			
SunTrust Banks			
U.S. Bancorp			
Wells Fargo			
Zions Bancorp			

Baylor Business

75

Security Selection

U.S. Bancorp

- Wide Economic Moat
- ROE Consistently >20%
- Prudent Underwriting and Conservative Assets Reducing Charge Offs
- Loss Guarantees from FDIC
- Two Large Fee-Base Income Streams
- Tight Cost Control and Fee Income Pad ALLL

BB&T Corporation

- High Portion of Income is Insurance
- Strong Presence in Atlanta, D.C., etc Where Losses are Substantial
- Strong Balance Sheet
- Co-Acquirer of Colonial
- Higher Expected Credit Losses than USB

Fifth Third

- Poor Credit Standards and Loan Quality
- Over 4% of Portfolio Non Performing
- Highly Dependent on Auto Industry for Loans and Deposits

Source: Morningstar, Value Line

Baylor Business

76

US Bancorp vs. Western Union

Methodology	Sector Result	USB	Variance
Median Earnings Growth - FY1	-.037	1.6	2.32
Median Earnings Growth - FY2	1.31	2.3	1.01
Median P/E	19.9	15	4.4

Source: Bloomberg

77

WU: Overview

- Money Transfer Services
  - Consumer to Consumer
  - Consumer to Business
  - Business to Business
- Other Services
  - Money Orders, Prepaid Cards, etc.

Statistics	
Price	$16.66
52 Week Range	$20.64 - $11.18
Market Cap	$11.40B
Enterprise Value	$12.9B
P/B	32.83
Beta	1.46
Avg Dividend Yield	0.4%

Source: Bloomberg

78

WU: Strategy

- Superior Service
  - Monitoring and Controlling Systems
- Cost Advantages Due to Size
- Well Known Brand Key Differentiator
  - Speed, Trust, and Reliability

Source: Western Union Annual Report

Original Purchase

- Strong Earnings Surprise
- Expected Growth and Stable Earnings Growth
- Because of Recession WU Undervalued

Source: 2009 Report

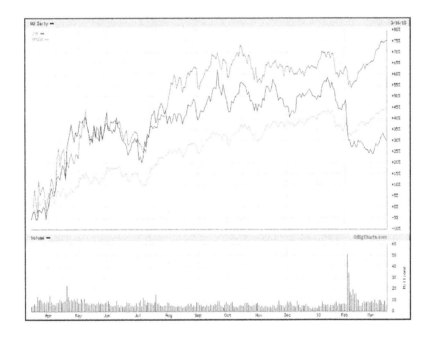

US Bancorp: Overview

- Founded in 1863

- $281B in Assets

- Parent of US Bank

- 3,015 Offices and Over 5,000 ATMs

Statistics	
Price	$26.14
52 Week Range	$26.84 - $8.42
Market Cap	$47.67B
Enterprise Value	$105.88B
P/B	1.93
Beta	1.05
Avg Dividend Yield	2.5%

Source: US Bancorp.com, Value Line

Baylor Business

US Bancorp: Business Model [US]bancorp

- **Consumer and Wholesale Banking**
  - About 60% of Top Line Income
  - Prudent Underwriting = Lower Charge Offs

- **Fee Based Income – Wide Moats**
  - Payment Processing – 27%
    - Debit/Credit Cards, Merchant Processing, etc
    - Highly Scalable
    - Distinct Growth and Profitability Characteristics
  - Wealth Management – 13%

Source: US Bancorp.com, Morningstar

Baylor Business

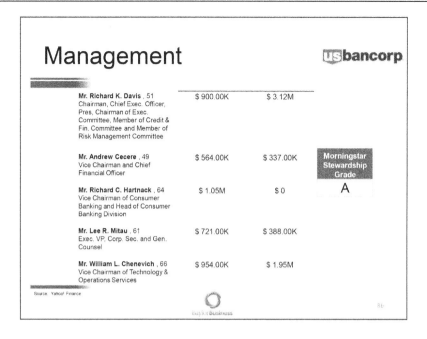

Management

USbancorp

Mr. Richard K. Davis , 51 Chairman, Chief Exec. Officer, Pres, Chairman of Exec. Committee, Member of Credit & Fin. Committee and Member of Risk Management Committee	$ 900.00K	$ 3.12M
Mr. Andrew Cecere , 49 Vice Chairman and Chief Financial Officer	$ 564.00K	$ 337.00K
Mr. Richard C. Hartnack , 64 Vice Chairman of Consumer Banking and Head of Consumer Banking Division	$ 1.05M	$ 0
Mr. Lee R. Mitau , 61 Exec. VP, Corp. Sec. and Gen. Counsel	$ 721.00K	$ 388.00K
Mr. William L. Chenevich , 66 Vice Chairman of Technology & Operations Services	$ 954.00K	$ 1.95M

Morningstar Stewardship Grade

A

Source: Yahoo! Finance

Baylor Business

86

Ownership

USbancorp

Breakdown	
% of Shares Held by All Insider and 5% Owners:	0%
% of Shares Held by Institutional & Mutual Fund Owners:	67%
% of Float Held by Institutional & Mutual Fund Owners:	67%
Number of Institutions Holding Shares:	907

- Top Institutional Owners
  - Capital World, State Street, Barclay's
- Top Fund Holders
  - WAMU, American Balanced Fund, Fundamental Investors, Vanguard 500
- Berkshire Hathaway owns 3.6%

Source: Yahoo! Finance

Baylor Business

87

Growth Drivers

- Acquisitions
  - Co-acquisition of Colonial with BB&T
  - FDIC Assisted Acquisitions
    - Seemingly risky acquisitions but with FDIC guarantee, USB can expand with little risk to its core
- Organic Growth
  - Fee Based Income Strong Cash Flow Support
  - High Credit Standards

Source: Morningstar

Baylor Business

88

Financial Performance

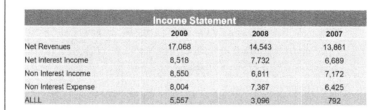

Income Statement			
	2009	2008	2007
Net Revenues	17,068	14,543	13,861
Net Interest Income	8,518	7,732	6,689
Non Interest Income	8,550	6,811	7,172
Non Interest Expense	8,004	7,367	6,425
ALLL	5,557	3,096	792

Source: Bloomberg

Baylor Business

91

Financial Performance USbancorp

Statement of Condition	2009	2008	2007
Net Loans	190,329	181,715	151,769
Total Assets	281,179	265,912	237,615
Total Deposits	183,242	159,350	131,445
Total Liabilities	254,515	239,612	216,569

Ratios	2009	2008	2007
Loan to Deposit	96%	88%	87%
Tier 1 Capital	9.60%	10.60%	8.30%

Source: Bloomberg

Financial Performance USbancorp

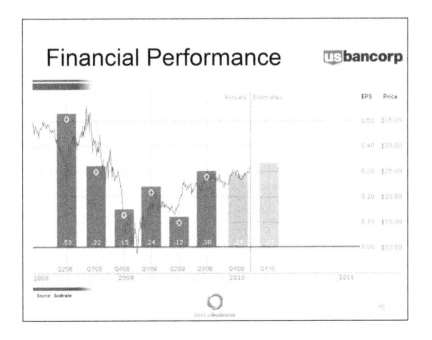

Source: Scottrade

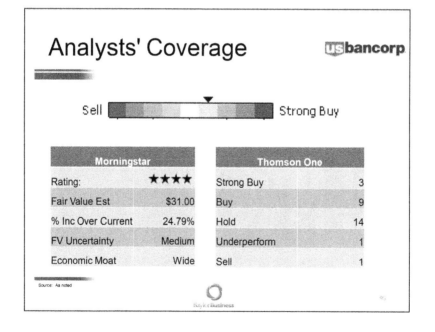

Forecasts

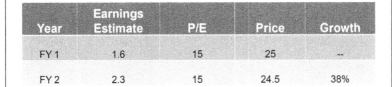

Year	Earnings Estimate	P/E	Price	Growth
FY 1	1.6	15	25	--
FY 2	2.3	15	24.5	38%

Source: Bloomberg

S.W.O.T.

Strengths
- Credit Standards
- Fee Income

Weaknesses
- Lower Equity Values Hurt Assets Under Management

Opportunities
- Potential for Organic and Acquisition Growth
- Lower Impact of Potential Regulatory Risk
- FDIC Assisted Acquisitions for Cheap/Low Risk $

Threats/Risks
- Regulatory Risk
- Potential for Continued Increase in ALLL

Source: Morningstar, Value Line

WU vs USB

Valuation	US Bancorp	Western Union	Variance
Earnings - FY1	1.6	1.32	0.28
Earnings - FY2	2.3	1.45	0.85
P/E	15	12	3.0
Dividend Yield	0.89%	0.32%	0.57%

Source: Bloomberg

98

WU vs USB

US bancorp

Strengths
- Credit Standards
- Fee Income

Weaknesses
- Lower Equity Values Hurt Assets Under Management

Strengths
- Size and Reputation Gives Strength
- Transfer Monitor Systems

Weaknesses
- Very Narrow Moat (disagree with Morningstar)

Source: Morningstar, Value Line

99

WU vs USB

Opportunities
- Potential for Organic and Acquisition Growth
- Lower Impact of Potential Regulatory Risk
- FDIC Assisted Acquisitions for Cheap/Low Risk $

Threats/Risks
- Regulatory Risk
- Potential for Continued Increase in ALLL

Opportunities
- Innovative Transfer Tools Could Maintain Their Advantage

Threats/Risks
- High Unemployment and Low Immigration Predictions
- Regulators Closely Monitor

Source Morningstar, Value Line

100

WU vs USB: Rationale

- Stronger Fundamentals
  - Higher EPS Estimates, Higher Div Yield
  - Although Higher P/E
- Growth Opportunities
  - USB: Organic and Acquisition
  - WU: Must Be Innovative
- Strength
  - USB: Financially Stable and Poised to Gain Market Share
  - WU: Must Rely on Size and Reputation

101

Advisor's Thoughts

"For diversification benefits and the potential growth in regionals, I think USB is a good opportunity. Furthermore, market sentiment has shift against the banking sector and valuations appear reasonable."

"Much of WU revenue is derived from sending money across borders, typically migrant workers, with unemployment levels in double digits and expectations from analysts that unemployment will remain high in the near (2017 before 5%-normal – unemployment levels are reach in some studies) is appears revenue growth will be challenging."

102

Recommendation

 SELL

 BUY

103

The presentation in Exhibit 5.5 is also careful to point out recent developments, financial data, and valuation information before presenting a SWOT analysis of the candidate securities. SWOT stands for Strengths, Weaknesses, Opportunities, and Threats. SWOT analysis is a useful framework for summarizing important return and risk considerations when selecting a security. The strengths and weaknesses of a company relate to its ongoing business and existing products and/or services. These aspects are typically internally focused and considered to be under the control of the firm itself. The opportunities and threats assess the interactions of the company with the economy, marketplace, or industry that represent potential for gains or losses. After summarizing the rationale and providing input from the faculty advisor, the presentation makes a clear recommendation to buy, hold, pass, or sell the subject securities. By making a clear recommendation, the presentation sets the stage for further discussion and a final vote.

Exhibit 5.6 contains three examples of meeting summaries that were created to memorialize internal presentations, such as the one presented in Exhibit 5.5. Minutes or meeting reports

---

Exhibit 5.6 Examples of Baylor University's Discussion Summaries

Summary of Discussion for Potential Stock Purchase
Sector: Consumer Cyclicals
Recommendation: Starwood Hotels & Resorts (HOT)

1. Summary of Presentation
- Discussed industries within Consumer Cyclicals sector
- Discussed why I chose Starwood Hotels
- Explained Starwood background, competitive strengths, and management
- Covered the state and the risks associated with the lodging industry, and discussed competitors
- Mentioned balance sheet and income statement highlights
- Touched on 4Q00 highlights
- Had the valuation discussion, thoroughly discussing value, hybrid, and growth criteria
- Discussed key growth drivers, future projections, and analyst opinions for Starwood

2. Summary of Discussion
- Discussed many of the above topics thoroughly
- Asked questions including:
  - What are the profit margins for others in the industry?
  - What are the occupancy rates for competitors?
  - What do you perceive as the two most relevant risks for Starwood? (Responded the state of the economy in general on the industry, and tax risks associated with possibly not qualifying as REIT)
  - Do you know how much revenue each country/region generates? (Top five included North America, Europe, Asia, Latin America, and Africa)
- Explained concerns about ROE and ROA, including explanation about historical ROEs, purchase of ITT in 1998, price paid for ITT, impact on stock price and overall profitability, how the acquisition is currently impacting profitability, and projections about future ROE

3. Summary of Voting
- 7 students voted for the purchase of HOT
- 1 students voted against the purchase of HOT
- 1 student abstained from voting
- 3 remaining students were absent

Summary of Cendant "Sell" Discussion

Sector: Industrials
Recommendation: Sell Cendant (CD)

1. Summary of Presentation
- Recommendation: Sell Cendant (CD) and Buy General Dynamics (GD)
  - Voted to sell CD if we found a better stock on October 4, 2004
- Cendant:
  - Foremost provider of travel and real estate services in the world
- Industry Overview:
  - Companies in this sector are diverse
  - Performed better in 2004 after lagging margins
  - Ranks in top half of timeliness ranking
- Company Overview:
  - World's largest real estate brokerage franchiser
  - Own and operate 920 Coldwell Banker locations
  - One of the largest vehicle rental operations in the world with Avis and Budget
- Acquisitions
  - Recently purchased Orbitz on September 29, 2004
    - Purchased at a 35% premium for $1.25 billion in cash
    - Previously owned by top 5 US airlines
  - Planning to purchase Ramada Hotel and Resorts
- Risks:
  - Pending trials of 1998 Accounting fraud
  - Possibility of heightened terrorism may reduce travel
  - Higher than anticipated interest rates could affect real estate–related business
  - Increasing oil prices increase travel costs

2. Summary of Discussion
- Is this stock cheap for a reason?
  - Currently underperforming the market
  - Lower PE ratio yet lacking a promising outlook
- Purchasing of Orbitz
  - Will this easily integrate in Galileo International?
  - Is it worth the premium price?
  - Growth potential

3. Summary of Voting
- 8:4 for selling the security

Summary of General Dynamics "Buy" Discussion

Sector: Industrials
Recommendation: Buy General Dynamics (GD)

1. Summary of Presentation
- Recommendation: Sell Cendant (CD) and Buy General Dynamics (GD)
  - Voted to sell CD if we found a better stock on October 4, 2004
- General Dynamics:
  - Uniquely qualified to engineer, manufacture, and integrate complex land, air, and maritime platforms with leading-edge information technology
- Industry Overview:
  - Signs of pickup in jetliner demand
  - Military budget expected to rise 6% in 2005
  - Concentrate on stocks with timeliness of 2 or better
- Reasons for Selection:
  - ValueLine timeliness ranking of 2, safety ranking of 1
  - FWD PE less than the industry
  - Market Capitalization greater than $5 billion
  - Diversification of revenues
- Acquisitions
  - Recently agreed to purchase Alvis of Britain
    - Maker of Challenge II battle tank
    - Positions GD to win combat vehicle orders in US, Britain, and Sweden
- Veridian Corporation:
  - Provider of network security and enterprise protection
- Creative Technology:
  - Supports intelligence community and Department of Defense
- Risks:
  - Foreign currency exchange rate risk
    - Inter-company transactions in foreign currencies
- Environmental Laws:
  - Indirectly/directly involved in the release of hazardous materials at former sites
  - In some cases, rely on 1 or 2 sources of supply for their product
  - Possibility of terminated projects

2. Summary of Discussion
- GD's business jet division on the rise
  - World's leading producer of mid-size and intercontinental business jet aircraft
- Conservative stock for the future
- Diversifies Dorr Portfolio
- Good finances and strong free cash flows project future acquisitions

3. Summary of Voting
- 7–6 for purchasing security

provide important documentation of the discussion surrounding the presentation. While these are not transcripts of the meetings, these reports note significant issues or questions that are raised during the presentation. As indicated elsewhere in this book, saving such reports, presentations, and summaries provides for the "institutional memory" for an organization that would otherwise have little. As discussed in Chapter 7, there are tools available to store and share such documents within an organization. It is important to facilitate access to this documentation for future members of the student-managed investment fund so that they can learn from past members, understand the original rationale behind the purchase of portfolio securities, and evaluate the investment process.

External Presentations

In addition to the internal reports and presentations that investment organizations produce to make organizational and portfolio decisions, reports and presentations must be made to communicate with external constituents and stakeholders. External presentations by investment managers are usually produced for two purposes: client service and business development. A client service presentation's primary objective is to retain a current client, while business development presentations aim to attract new clients or new money from existing clients. As such, the focus of external presentations differs somewhat from internal presentations. External presentations tend to focus more on the overall organization, portfolio, and performance and less on the details surrounding a specific buy or sell decision.

We consider presentations to oversight boards to fit into the client service category, though some presentations to oversight boards might have elements of internal presentations. For example, reports and presentations by mutual fund advisors (investment managers) to the mutual fund's board of directors would generally be considered client service presentations, since the board represents the interests of the mutual fund's shareholders, who are the ultimate client of the investment manager's services. However, boards also typically have authority for decisions regarding how the portfolio is managed. Therefore, such presentations might share some elements of the internal presentations discussed earlier. Furthermore, oversight boards for student-managed investment funds typically have shared interests with the investment managers beyond that of the portfolio's performance. Specifically, a student-managed investment fund's board typically would not choose to "fire" the managers by dissolving the fund in the same way a pension fund client might decide to fire an investment manager. Moreover, some SMIF oversight boards play an active role in investment decisions by participating in some of the internal presentations discussed above.

A key differentiating factor between internal and external presentations is that the audience of an external presentation is unlikely to be as familiar with or conversant in the content of the presentation. That is, members of an investment organization live and breathe the methods and data used in making portfolio decisions. The investment philosophy and process and their implications are dealt with in detail every day. External constituents, such as clients, typically have multiple investment managers who each have their own investment philosophy and process. The clients might be familiar with each of their manager's investment philosophies and processes, but they only focus on any specific investment process during those few times per year that they interact with that particular investment manager. Therefore, it is important that each external presentation seizes the opportunity to remind the audience of the framework in which the investment manager operates. Depending on the specific purpose of the presentation, it should almost always include a review of the organization, its purpose, and its investment philosophy and process in order to provide context for other content within the presentation.

Some content from internal presentations, especially those used to discuss security selection or portfolio construction, might be appropriate to include in external presentations. Indeed, such content can provide further clarification and detail regarding the investment process. However, such content should be presented in a way that recognizes the external audience's potential lack of familiarity with and context for the details and complexities of the investment process.

An investment manager's report or presentation to an existing client, also called a "client review," is typically provided on a quarterly basis. The primary purpose of a client review is to update the client on the performance of their assets that have been entrusted to the investment manager. It is the investment manager's responsibility to go beyond the performance numbers to provide insight into the performance of the assets so that the client understands why the performance is good or bad. As discussed above, an understanding of the performance is best achieved through an understanding of the investment process. An example of such a client review is show in Exhibit 5.7, in which Jill Foote discusses Rice University's Wright Fund report and presentation to its oversight board. Because of its top-down investment process, the Wright Fund's strategy is best understood in the context of

---

Exhibit 5.7 External Presentation Example from Rice University's Wright Fund

By Jill Foote

The Wright Fund reports to an Oversight Board consisting of Rice University's Vice President for Investments and Treasurer; the Dean of the Jones Graduate School of Business; and prominent investment professionals. The Board typically meets three times per year: twice at the end of each school semester to hear a formal presentation by Fund Officers on performance and activities, and once otherwise to discuss strategic initiatives and curriculum changes.

Oversight Board Reporting

Each semester, the Fund Officers issue a short (2-page) mid-term Board Report and provide a formal end-of-semester presentation to the Oversight Board.

The end-of-semester Board presentation will typically cover the following agenda items:

- Semester strategy
  - Economic and market strategies
- Performance/Results
  - Performance vs. benchmark for fund and sectors
  - Best and worst stock performance
  - Attribution analysis
  - Risk metrics

- Events and initiatives
  - Conferences, speakers, and initiatives
- Awards and achievements
  - Scholarship winners
  - Best reports and Best Analyst Group

Source: Fall 09 WF Board Presentation.

Strategy

The strategy segment of the Board presentation typically follows the WF's top-down approach. Both the Chief Investment Officer (CIO) and the Chief Economist (CE) will provide macro-level views on the economy and the market overall. Then the CIO will give an overview of the Fund strategy pursued for the semester, and typically changes to the strategy from the previous semester. Included in the strategy section will be asset allocation among Equities, Fixed Income, and Cash; and overweighting/underweighting of sectors.

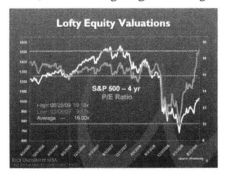

Source: Fall 09 WF Board Presentation.

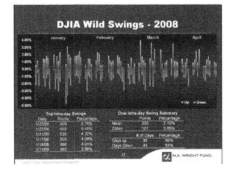

Source: Spring 08 WF Board Presentation.

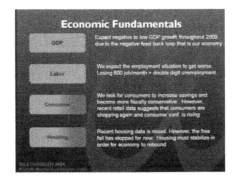

Source: Spring 09 WF Board Presentation.

Source: Spring 08 WF Board Presentation.

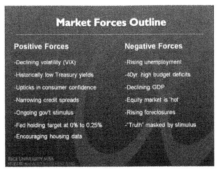

Source: Fall 09 WF Board Presentation.

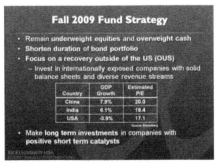

Source: Fall 09 WF Board Presentation.

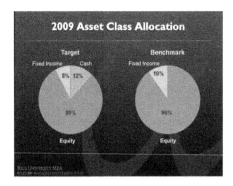

Source: Fall 09 WF Board Presentation.

Sector	S&P Weight	Delta	WF Target Weight
Overweight			
Energy/Utilities	15.6%	4%	19.6%
Industrials/Materials	13.5%	4%	17.5%
Equalweight			
IT/Telecom	21.6%	0%	21.6%
Consumer Discretionary	9.1%	0%	9.1%
Consumer Staples	11.4%	0%	11.4%
Underweight			
Financials	15.1%	-4%	11.1%
Healthcare	13.6%	-4%	9.6%

Fall 2009 Sector Allocations

Source: Fall 09 WF Board Presentation.

Performance/Results

Both risk and return are covered in the performance section. Continuing with a top-down approach, the usual flow of the presentation section first covers overall Fund performance (both for the semester and one or more longer terms of performance, such as YTD and 5-year performance), followed by sector performance, and then individual stock performance, usually best and worst performers. Attribution analysis, discussing the contribution to performance by allocation, selection, and interaction effects, is included. Risk measures such as portfolio Beta, Sharpe Ratio, and Value at Risk are reviewed. Depending on the goals of the presenting officers, sometimes other material, such as a styles analysis, will be included.

Source: Fall 09 WF Board Presentation.

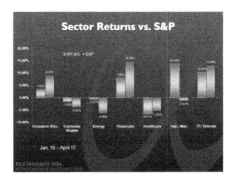

Source: Spring 09 WF Board Presentation.

Attribution Analysis

Sector	Allocation Effect	Selection Effect	Interaction Effect	Alpha
Consumer Disc.	0.00%	(0.10%)	0.00%	(0.10%)
Consumer Staples	0.00%	(0.28%)	0.00%	(0.28%)
Energy	0.02%	(0.06%)	(0.02%)	(0.05%)
Financials	0.37%	0.49%	(0.13%)	0.73%
Healthcare	(0.04%)	0.15%	(0.03%)	0.08%
Ind. / Mat.	0.08%	0.65%	0.14%	0.87%
IT / Telecom	0.00%	(2.52%)	0.00%	(2.52%)
Total	0.43%	(1.67%)	(0.03%)	(1.27%)

Source: Fall 09 WF Board Presentation.

Source: Fall 09 WF Board Presentation.

Portfolio Metrics

	Wright Fund	S&P 500
Forward P/E	13.17x	14.47x
Price/Book	2.55x	2.43x
ROA	7.04%	8.48%
ROE	20.58%	22.13%
Average Market Cap ($mil)	34,237	56,126
	Wright Fund	Benchmark
Beta	0.87	1.00
Sharpe Ratio (as of 04/18/2008)	0.86	0.91
Sharpe Ratio (as of 04/27/2007)	1.51	1.37

All values YTD April 18, 2008

M.A. WRIGHT FUND.

Source: Spring 08 WF Board Presentation.

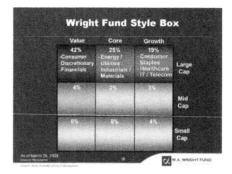

Source: Spring 08 WF Board Presentation.

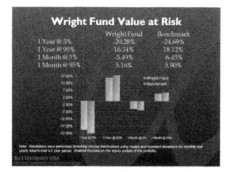

Source: Spring 09 WF Board Presentation.

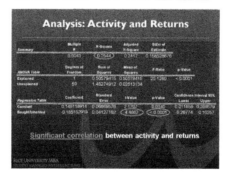

Source: Fall 09 WF Board Presentation.

Forward View/Looking Ahead
In similar fashion to the strategy, often the CIO and CE will present their forward looking view after the Performance/Results Section. The Oversight Board members have expressed an interest in hearing the forward view of the officers at the point in time when they are most knowledgeable (at the end of their term).

Sector Presentation – Best Performer
The Board presentation includes a few slides by one or two sectors that performed particularly well on either an absolute or a relative basis. The presenting AGs are judgmentally chosen by the Officers and the Faculty Director.

Source: Fall 09 WF Board Presentation.

Events and Initiatives
In addition to performance reporting, the Fund Officers also present a few slides on events in which the WF was involved including training, speakers, conferences, and volunteerism in the Houston community. Initiatives, such as improvement in tools, new or updated assignments, and fund raising, are also covered in this section.

A Q&A session is held after Events and Initiatives, but before Awards are announced, so that the presentation can end after Awards.

Awards and Achievements
For the past few years, the Wright Fund has recognized individual and analyst group (AG) achievement with several awards. These awards, along with WF scholarship recipients and any WF students receiving other recognition (such as winning competitions at conferences or receiving CFA Institute scholarships) are announced at the finale of the Oversight Board presentation.

Best Report
For each of the major report assignments, the WF Officers and Faculty Director agree on the "best report." This individual or team is recognized both to the Fund at the time and to the Oversight Board. Copies of the winning reports are shared with Oversight Board members.

AG Award
At the end of the semester, an AG award is voted on by the entire class. Votes are cast with the following in mind: sector strategy, sector performance, quality of presentations and class participation by AG members, and excellent on-going communication with the Fund. Analysts are not permitted to vote for their own AG. Each member of the winning AG receives a prize of "incalculable value."

Concluding with awards and achievements makes for a nice finale to the presentation.

the economic and market environment, which is reviewed at the beginning of the presentation. The economic discussion provides relevant context for further details about the fund's performance. While we discuss performance reporting and analysis in the next chapter, we note that a presentation of performance and analysis that reveals further insights into the sources of out- and under-performance is a critical element of reports and presentations to clients and oversight boards.

Beyond discussing the investment process and its recent performance, the client review typically provides an update on the organization. Any significant changes to the organization, especially turnover in key personnel or changes in ownership and control, would be presented to the client to assist the client in their continued due diligence responsibility. The organizational update also provides an opportunity for notifying the client of enhanced product or service capabilities. In the case of student-managed investment funds, this section of the presentation can be appropriately used to provide a review of student and organizational achievements, such as awards, competitions, or job placements. As noted in the exhibit, the Wright Fund's presentation concludes with recognition of student awards.

We conclude this chapter with a discussion of business development presentations. Most investment firms have a "pitchbook" that highlights the firm's capabilities in terms of products and services, explains the firm's investment philosophy and process, and provides an overview of the organizational structure. The overlap in content between the pitchbook and the client review is purposeful. The client review should contain the same message about the firm as the pitchbook. That is, the implicit promise provided in the pitchbook as to how the client's assets *will be* managed should be consistent with the client review's report as to how the client's assets *have been* managed. In this sense, the business development and client service presentations simply have different objectives and, therefore, emphasis. Business development presentations are more forward-looking in highlighting the benefits of a given investment strategy. Client service presentations are necessarily a mixture of looking back in reporting performance and looking forward in providing confidence to the client that the organization retains its ability to continue to successfully manage the client's assets.

Business development presentations by student-managed investment funds are likely to be used primarily at the start-up of the fund or when trying to expand the fund. As with the other presentations discussed above, business development presentations provide an opportunity for SMIF members to practice important presentation skills. Specifically, business development presentations must provide a clearly articulated view of the organization's competitive advantages and motivate the value proposition for the prospective client. As with any external presentation, this requires not only an understanding of the organization's own capabilities, but an appreciation for the client or prospective client's needs.

Exhibit 5.8 provides an interesting example of an external presentation. In this business development presentation, the University of Minnesota's Carlson Funds Enterprise uses a prospectus format to attract donors to benefit its student-managed investment fund. The prospectus provides an overview of the organization, including its history, and then makes the case for the benefits of "buying" into the fund.

Exhibit 5.8 University of Minnesota's Carlson Fund External Presentation

CARLSON *FUNDS* **ENTERPRISE**

Common Stock, 70,000 shares, $100 per share

Minimum Purchase $100

$7,000,000 Total Offering Proceeds

The Carlson Funds Enterprise (CFE) is an experiential learning opportunity offered to select graduate and undergraduate students who want to pursue careers in investment management, investment banking, and corporate finance. Using discounted cash flow analysis, students analyze existing and potential investments in the Carlson funds. While the CFE and its students benefit from the generous contributions of time from many members of the local investment community, students take control of all management issues with respect to the $25 million of assets under management.

One hundred percent of the proceeds from the sale of Common Stock (without reduction for any marketing or other expenses) will be used to expand and remodel the Financial Markets Lab, to fund a CFE fellowship program, to invest in investment management and accounting systems, and to provide an endowment at the University of Minnesota Foundation to cover the annual operating expenses of the CFE.

THE PROCEEDS FROM ANY PURCHASES OF "COMMON STOCK" WILL BE GIFTS TO THE CFE. SHARES OF COMMON STOCK ARE NOT REDEEMABLE, NOR DO THEY ENTITLE THE PURCHASER TO ANY INVESTMENT RETURNS FROM THE CFE, THE CARLSON SCHOOL OF MANAGEMENT OR THEIR AFFILIATES, OR ANY OTHER ATTRIBUTES OF A SECURITY OR AN INVESTMENT. ALL PROCEEDS FROM THE SALE OF COMMON STOCK WILL BE USED TO BENEFIT THE CFE, INCLUDING THE BUILDING OF AN ENDOWMENT TO ALLOW IT TO BECOME MORE SELF-SUSTAINING.

Carlson School of Management

University of Minnesota

May 1, 2008

Table of Contents
Prospectus Summary
Summary Consolidated Financial Data
Risk Factors
Use of Proceeds
Management's Discussion & Analysis of Financial Condition
Management
Organization

Prospectus Summary

The Carlson Funds Enterprise (CFE) is an educational organization offering select graduate and undergraduate students an opportunity to learn real as well as theoretical aspects of the investment management business through the management of two funds: the Carlson School Growth Fund and the Carlson School Fixed Income Fund.

The CFE was founded in 1998 by a group of Twin Cities financial executives and Carlson School professors. Founding members include Bill Dudley, Al Harrison, Lou Nanne, and faculty members Tim Nantell and David Runkle. The Carlson Funds consist of two Limited Liability Companies run by MBA students and selected undergraduates. The Carlson School Growth Fund (formerly the Golden Gopher Growth Fund) began operations on May 4, 1998. Initial contributors included Alliance Capital Management (through a gift to the University of Minnesota Foundation), Ameriprise Financial, U.S. Bancorp, and Wells Fargo. Since then, the fund has gained four additional participants including Securian, Piper Jaffray, and two individuals. The Carlson School Growth Fund now totals $11 million. On March 1, 2003, the Carlson School Fixed Income Fund was funded by six institutions (Ameriprise Financial, Securian, the Regents of the University of Minnesota, Thrivent Financial, U.S. Bancorp, and Wells Fargo). In 2007, Allianz Life joined as a contributor, and the balance in the Fixed Income Fund is now $15 million. The CFE is unique among our peers in that our participants are institutions and individuals (not an investment club or university endowment).

Capitalization

To date, the CFE has received invaluable financial and in-kind assistance from the following individuals and corporations:

Individuals	Corporate
William Dudley	Ameriprise Financial
Herbert Hanson	Bridge Information Systems
Al Harrison	RBC Dain Rauscher
Ira Hersch	Faegre & Benson
Thomas Juda	KPMG
John King	Kopp Investment Advisors
Malcolm McDonald	Alliance Bernstein, Mpls. Partners
Thomas Morrison	Wells Fargo
Lou Nanne	Rosemount Office Systems
Hollis Rademacher	State Farm Insurance
Mort Silverman	
Joan Smith	
Arch Spencer	
Irv Weiser	
William Westhoff	
Richard Whiting	

Performance

Carlson Growth Fund

The Carlson School Growth Fund (CGF) has generated a strong performance record since its inception in 1998. The fund's benchmark index is the Russell 2000 Growth Index. From inception through December 2007, the CGF net asset value per share has risen 165% as compared with a 36% increase in the benchmark index. On a compound annual rate, the CGF has increased at

10.6% per year, while the index has returned 3.2% per year. If it were a fund manager, this performance would cause the CGF to be ranked within the top quartile of all domestic small cap growth fund managers for almost all time periods as illustrated in the following chart.

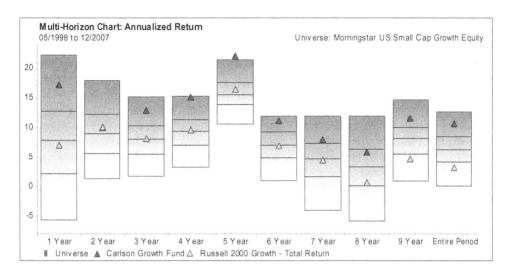

Carlson Fixed Income Fund

The Carlson School Fixed Income Fund (CFIF) has also performed successfully. Since October 1, 2006, the fund's benchmark index has been the Lehman Intermediate Government Credit Index (prior to this date, the benchmark index had been the Lehman Intermediate Aggregate Index). A change to the benchmark was recommended by the advisory board to reflect a change in the fund's focus to credit analysis, and away from investment in structured products. Since inception through December 2007, the CFIF has risen 20.2% on a gross basis (17.3% on a net basis) as compared with an increase in the benchmark index of 21.6%. The fund's performance on a gross and net of fees basis is shown in the following graph.

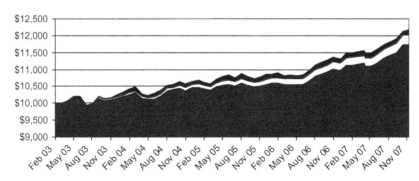

Performance Against the Benchmark
Growth of $10,000

Vision

The CFE's goal is to be recognized as the best student-run investment management program in the country. We will accomplish this goal when investment management firms around the country aggressively recruit our students.

Mission

The mission of CFE is to leverage the Carlson School's combination of faculty and financial community resources to create a real-time learning environment, immersing students in strategic and financial analyses of companies from top to bottom. The program builds on financial concepts learned in traditional classroom settings and provides students with real money to manage and real experience in investment management. The CFE combines classroom concepts, hands-on experience, and industry mentoring to prepare students for real-world jobs. Much of this work takes place in the School's Financial Markets Lab which is equipped with the same on-line market data services used by investment professionals. For the financial industry, the program provides a pool of highly trained Carlson School graduates who can "hit the ground running" and help their firms prosper. For the Carlson School, the fund enhances the institution's status, strengthens ties to the business community and helps attract top-notch students and faculty — providing a continuing cycle of ever-improving financial education.

Advisory Board

The Carlson Funds Enterprise has an active advisory board comprised of senior representatives of the investment management industry and industry service providers with close affinities with the Carlson School of Management (CSOM). The Board meets three times per year and reviews the general operations of the funds. The Board's functions are modeled after the functions typically performed by a mutual fund board. However several of its functions are tailored to the unique characteristics of CFE and the Funds and the relationships they bear to CSOM, its students, and the University of Minnesota. The advisory board has established five committees: governance; investment; marketing; finance, budget, and operations; and internships/placement. The Governance Committee presently has set the maximum number of Board members at 15.

Mentors

The CFE has a mentor program in which each student is partnered with a money management professional who counsels the student, evaluates his or her investment proposals, and provides helpful feedback. The mentors, serving as investment oversight committees for the funds, meet at the end of each semester to evaluate student investment recommendations. Committee approval is required before new securities can be purchased in either fund. Many of the mentors are alumni of the CFE program and/or graduates of the Carlson School of Management and work as analysts and portfolio managers for investment firms both in and outside of the Twin Cities.

Students

The CFE is open to all full-time MBA students and selected undergraduate seniors interested in the investment industry. Class size has varied from eleven to thirty students. MBA students apply for membership in the CFE during the "A" term of the second semester of their first year, join the CFE during the "B" term when a transition from the graduating class to the new class occurs, and manage the portfolio beginning in May and continuing through the second year of the MBA program. Undergraduates follow a similar time line. Monthly portfolio strategy meetings are held throughout the summer.

Alumni

Over the ten years of the CFE's operation, over 200 students have completed the program. These graduates are employed by investment firms and corporations around the country. Many CFE alumni continue to be actively involved in the program as mentors, advisory board members, and donors.

Staff

The Carlson Funds Enterprise is overseen by a staff that includes a professional advisor for each fund, a program coordinator, and an academic advisor.

Summary Consolidated Financial Data

The summary consolidated financial data shown below should be read together with "Management's Discussion & Analysis of Financial Condition" included elsewhere in this prospectus. The summary consolidated statements of operations data for the previous five fiscal years ended June 30 have been derived from unaudited financial statements. Fiscal 2008 data is as of December 31, 2007.

6 Mos. Fiscal Year ended June 30 (In thousands, except participants and enrollment) 12/31/07						
	2003	2004	2005	2006	2007	2008
Fund balances						
Carlson Growth Fund	$3,653	$4,862	$5,775	$8,591	$10,511	$10,804
Carlson Fixed Income Fund	$11,148	$11,131	$11,635	$11,626	$14,222	$15,022
TOTAL	**$14,801**	**$15,993**	**$17,410**	**$20,217**	**$24,733**	**$25,826**
Administrative fees						
Carlson Growth Fund	$15	$32	$49	$75	$92	$56
Carlson Fixed Income Fund	$18	$60	$57	$58	$60	$37
TOTAL	**$33**	**$92**	**$106**	**$133**	**$152**	**$93**
Number of participants						
Carlson Growth Fund	5	5	6	8	8	8
Carlson Fixed Income Fund	6	6	6	6	7	7
Student enrollment						
Full-time MBA	11	19	14	18	17	17
Part-time MBA	0	1	1	2	3	2
Undergraduate	0	1	3	5	5	11
TOTAL	**11**	**21**	**18**	**25**	**25**	**30**

Risk Factors

In a traditional offering statement, investors would be advised of a number of risk factors which could negatively affect expected performance. However, this opportunity to support the Carlson Funds Enterprise presents benefits rather than risks. Our goal, with the help of your support, is to exceed expectations as follows:

Investing in the CFE will help make possible a continued supply of well-trained financial analysts to the Twin Cities business community and beyond. The CFE has traditionally supplied many of the financial analysts hired by Twin Cities financial services firms and Fortune 500 corporate treasury departments. In addition, firms outside of the Twin Cities are seeking our graduates, which will help build the national and international reputation of the CFE and the Carlson School of Management. On average, about half the members of each graduating class accept positions in the financial services industry, while the other half pursue careers in corporate finance.

Investing in the CFE will help the CFE to continue to distinguish itself as one of the country's leading student-run investment operations. The CFE is among the best student-managed investment fund programs of any educational institution. To provide the best quality experience to our students and to better serve our participants, the CFE needs to continually invest in its infrastructure, including additional lab space, investment accounting and portfolio management systems, and on-line data services. An investment in the CFE will allow the program to serve more students, to provide employers with well-trained graduates, and to accept new participants.

Investing in the CFE will provide an endowment to ensure the sound future of the program. Unlike the risks associated with traditional investing, investing in the CFE will help to assure that future financial professionals will benefit from the CFE's experiential learning program. Graduates will continue to "hit the ground running" as a result of their CFE participation.

Use of Proceeds

The CFE hopes to raise $7 million in this offering. We intend to use these funds to expand and remodel the Financial Markets Lab, to fund a CFE fellowship program, to invest in investment management and accounting systems, and to provide an endowment at the University of Minnesota Foundation to cover the annual operating deficit of the Carlson Funds Enterprise.

Management estimates that the proceeds from this offering will be used as follows:

Financial Markets Lab expansion/remodel	$2,000,000
Funding CFE fellowship program	$1,000,000
Investment management and accounting systems	$500,000
U of MN Foundation endowment	$3,500,000

Management's Discussion & Analysis of Financial Condition

The charts that follow show the operating results of the Carlson Funds Enterprise for the previous five fiscal years and estimated results for fiscal year 2008.

Carlson Funds Enterprise (Fiscal Year Ended June 30)						
	2003A	2004A	2005A	2006A	2007A	2008E
REVENUE						
Administrative Fees						
CGF	$16,412	$32,000	$48,812	$75,386	$92,305	$110,000
CFIF	$0	$60,430	$56,868	$58,040	$59,663	$70,000
TOTAL	$16,412	$92,430	$105,680	$133,426	$151,968	$180,000
Other Revenue/Gifts	$139,230	$89,000	$117,668	$116,198	$59,280	$40,000
TOTAL REVENUE	**$155,642**	**$181,430**	**$223,348**	**$249,624**	**$211,248**	**$220,000**
EXPENSES						
Salaries & Fringe Benefits	$190,503	$258,230	$283,581	$260,617	$233,767	$241,949
General Operating Expenses	$61,227	$90,450	$90,499	$98,102	$105,550	$108,100
TOTAL EXPENSE	**$251,730**	**$348,680**	**$374,080**	**$358,719**	**$339,317**	**$350,049**
Office of Dean Funding	$96,088	$167,250	$150,732	$109,095	$128,069	$130,049

Since fiscal 2003, the CFE has grown at a measured pace, serving more students and enriching the learning experience, while controlling costs. The introduction of the fixed income fund in 2003, an increase in the administrative fee charged on the growth fund beginning on January 1, 2004, excellent investment performance by the growth fund, and new participants to the funds are the major factors affecting funds available to the CFE. At the same time, revenue from gifts has declined significantly as several "one-time" gifts have not recurred and multi-year pledges have been fulfilled.

Expenses have been relatively flat since fiscal 2004. The increase from 2003 to 2004 in salaries and fringe benefits was due to the launch of the fixed income fund and the hiring of a professional advisor for the fund. The majority of general operating expenses consist of fees paid for critical on-line market data services used by CFE students. In order to provide the most meaningful experience to our students, the CFE has subscriptions to Bloomberg and FactSet, data services used in most investment management firms. In addition, a significant corporate gift in 2004 allowed the CFE to establish a travel program for students to visit with management as part of the due diligence process used in researching new stock and bond ideas. The ability to travel and visit management has become a key differentiator for the CFE program compared with other university student investment programs. Travel expenses are included in general operating expenses.

From fiscal 2004 to fiscal 2006, funding from the Office of the Dean has been reduced; however, beginning in fiscal 2007, operating expenses have started to increase (particularly technology costs). Management estimates that the CFE will need to rely on Office of the Dean funding in the amount of $125,000–150,000 annually for the foreseeable future. In order to reduce this funding need, to improve the quality of the program, and to deliver the best experience for our students, the CFE is undertaking this offering.

Management

Name	Age	Position
Tim Nantell	62	Founder, Academic Director
Joe Barsky	58	Program Director, CGF Professional Advisor
Jeannette Parr	47	CFIF Professional Advisor
Emily Dombeck	29	Program Coordinator

Tim Nantell, PhD, founded the Carlson Funds Enterprise in 1998. He has been the Academic Director of the CFE since its founding. He is a Professor of Finance and has served on the faculty of the Carlson School of Management for 27 years. He holds an MBA and doctorate from the University of Wisconsin.

Joe Barsky, CFA, is the Program Director for the CFE and the professional advisor to the Carlson School Growth Fund. He joined the CFE in 2003 after spending 24 years with Ameriprise Financial as an equity analyst and portfolio manager. He has over 30 years of experience in the securities industry and holds an MBA from the University of Michigan.

Jeannette Parr, CFA, is the professional advisor to the Carlson School Fixed Income Fund. Prior to joining the CFE in 2006, she worked for more than 17 years in the investment industry, the last 10 of which were with Ameriprise Financial as a fixed income portfolio manager. She holds an MBA from the Carlson School of Management.

Emily Dombeck has been the program coordinator for the CFE since 2005. She is also currently a student at the University of Minnesota, pursuing a bachelor's degree in biology.

Organization

The organizational structure of the CFE is depicted below:

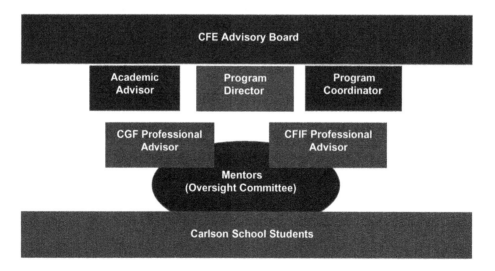

Current members of the CFE Advisory Board and mentors for both the growth fund and fixed income fund are shown below. Many are alumni of the University of Minnesota, the Carlson School of Management, and the CFE program.

The CFE Advisory Board is comprised of:

Matt Dudley, '00 MBA	The Leuthold Group
William Dudley, '55 BSB	Ameriprise Financial (retired)
Marilyn Froelich, '77 MBA	Advantus Capital Management
Lorraine Hart	RiverSource Investments (retired)
Donald Heltner, '74 MBA	State Farm Insurance
Mark Jordahl, '94 MBA	FAF Advisors
Jay Kiedrowski, '71 BME, '73 MPA	U of Minnesota Humphrey Institute
Robert Peterson	Piper Jaffray & Co.
John Sabre, '79 BSB	Mount Yale Capital Group
Debbie Sit, '82 BA	Sit Investment Associates
Russell Swansen, '82 MBA	Thrivent Financial for Lutherans
Matt Thompson, '85 JD	Faegre & Benson
William Westhoff, '74 MBA	Lakeview Investment Advisors

Mentors for the Carlson Growth Fund are listed below:

Wendy Clements, '96 MBA	RBC Capital Markets
Michael Cox, '03 MBA	Piper Jaffray
Patrick Donohue	Northland Securities
Phil Dobrzynski, '99 MBA	Riverbridge Partners
Peter Ginsberg	SurModics, Inc.
Eric Hewitt, '00 MBA	Alliance Bernstein
Jon Horick, '97 MBA	Northland Directions Equity Group
Dean Junkans	Wells Fargo Investment Management
Paul Kaump, '97 MBA	Northland Securities
Michael Lee, '94 MBA	Voyageur Asset Management
Tom Mahowald	FAF Advisors
Rick Moulton, '92 BSB	Riverbridge Partners
Paul Roach, '98 MBA	Cornerstone Capital Management
Keith Tufte	Longview Wealth Management

Mentors for the Carlson Fixed Income Fund are listed below:

Mark Arnold	Piper Jaffray
Mark Book, '92 MBA	Sit Investment Associates
Mark Churchill, '02 BSB	Piper Jaffray
Vitali Datsenko	University of Minnesota
John Huber, '95 MBA	Voyageur Asset Management
Tim Masek, '86 MBA	Riversource Investments
Matt Bentley, '07 MBA	Galliard Capital Management
Tim Palmer	FAF Advisors
Thor Raarup	The St. Paul Travelers Co.
Chris Sebald, '89 MBA	Advantus Capital Management
Mark Simenstad, '83 MBA	Thrivent Financial
Chris Zinn, '98 MBA	U.S. Bancorp

Exhibit 5.9 Southern Illinois University Proposal for a Graduate Student Investment Fund

Graduate Student Investment Fund (GSIF) Proposal

Executive Summary

The purpose of the Graduate Saluki Investment Fund (GSIF) is to provide graduate students at Southern Illinois University Carbondale with the opportunity to better understand the financial markets through practical investment experience in managing a real portfolio. In addition to this opportunity, there are many other benefits to SIU of having a GSIF, which are discussed in greater detail in the attached proposal. We are requesting an initial mandate of $500,000 from the SIU Foundation, which we propose managing against a large cap S&P 500 benchmark using a Value-Tilted Strategy. The GSIF seeks to outperform the S&P 500 index through the various competitive advantages of its process and its graduate student members. The strategy's investment process benefits from the dedication, diverse backgrounds, and unique perspectives of the graduate students who participate in the GSIF.

Purpose

The purpose of the Graduate Student Investment Fund (GSIF) is to provide Southern Illinois University Carbondale (SIU) graduate students with:

• Real-world portfolio management and security analysis experience.
• A greater understanding of financial markets, economics, financial theory, and practice.
• Enriched teaching and learning opportunities.

Responsibly investing and managing money on behalf of a client is difficult to simulate. Therefore, the opportunity to manage a portion of the SIU Foundation portfolio will be an invaluable experience to the GSIF members. In addition to the above-mentioned benefits to the participating graduate students, the GSIF will have meaningful indirect benefits to Southern Illinois University, in general, and the College of Business, in particular. The GSIF can help enhance recruitment of MBA and Master of Accountancy students, career placement of College of Business graduate students, and fundraising efforts for SIU.

Investment Objective

The primary investment objective of GSIF is to outperform the S&P 500 benchmark over the long term. A secondary goal of the GSIF is to enhance each member's knowledge of investing by including every student in decision making and portfolio management. We believe this goal is best achieved by focusing on our primary objective.

Eligible Securities and Strategies

The Graduate Student Investment Fund will select securities for the portfolio from the constituents of the benchmark S&P 500 index. We believe this index provides a suitably large number of securities from which to select and will serve as a transparent benchmark for the Foundation.

The intent of the GSIF is to outperform the benchmark by identifying and investing in the benchmark securities that are undervalued and have the potential to appreciate over the long term. In accordance with our belief that markets are generally efficient, but opportunities exist to identify currently mispriced securities, we will employ fundamental research to identify those undervalued stocks. In addition, academic and practitioner research has shown that "value" stocks — those that have high book-to-market values — historically have displayed higher returns relative to lower book-to-market value stocks. As academics and practitioners, we aim to add value by utilizing this research in the practice of managing the portfolio. Our value-tilting strategy[1] will aim to hold the stocks we have selected with greater value characteristics (i.e., higher book-to-market value stocks, low price to earnings ratio) at higher weights than those we have selected with more growth-oriented characteristics.

Investment Decision Making and Policies

Investment decisions will be made based on fundamental analysis performed by GSIF members organized in sector teams. Sector teams are responsible for identifying securities that are currently undervalued based on a company's current situation and growth prospects. However, majority approval by the GSIF is required in order to add or remove any stock to the portfolio. Policies are written in detail to maintain a clear frame of reference for new and current members to help facilitate the continuity of the process from semester-to-semester and year-to-year. These policies can be adapted if needed by majority approval of the GSIF membership and approval of its faculty advisor.

Our Competitive Advantage

As graduate student portfolio managers, we stand firm in our commitment to provide multiple advantages over our professional counterparts. The members of the Graduate Student Investment Fund represent a diverse group of students who bring many different undergraduate degrees, work experiences, and cultural backgrounds to the team.

We believe that our status as students gives us the unique ability to identify consumer and technological trends that may be overlooked by more traditional managers. All eligible stocks are examined with an unbiased perspective and attention, without the potential conflicts or distractions of professional managers in investment firms. As a group, we are entirely committed to our sole client, the SIU Foundation. We offer a significant cost advantage for the Foundation compared to other active managers, with a fee structure similar to that of the undergraduate Saluki Student Investment Fund (SSIF): 20 basis points, plus a small performance fee.

Collectively, the founding members of the team boast many years of corporate and entrepreneurial experience across five undergraduate specialties, including accounting, finance, economics, mathematics, and entrepreneurship. The GSIF is also culturally diverse, with member representation from several different countries. The team includes three former members of undergraduate student investment funds, as well as SIU Professor of Finance Dr. Jason Greene, who serves as our current faculty advisor to the GSIF. This combination of experience and diversity will continue to reside in the program for the indefinite future. We believe that this blend of diversity and experience, particularly in the area of student investment funds, will provide the necessary decision-making skills required to manage the portfolio and correspond with the Foundation proficiently.

In addition, establishing the graduate investment fund provides a mutual benefit between the GSIF and the SSIF through direct interaction and exchange of perspectives. The GSIF will enhance the SSIF learning experience by sharing our knowledge and experience with the undergraduate students, as well as offering critical assessment of their analysis. Likewise, the

SSIF will benefit the GSIF through the same process and by sharing growing trends within various industries and keeping us abreast on Midcap equities, many of which are natural candidates to move into the S&P 500. As a result of the interactions between the undergraduate and the graduate funds, our decision-making and research capabilities will be expanded, adding value for our client.

Documentation, Review, and Reporting

For each trading strategy and/or stock selection approved for the GSIF portfolio, the responsible sector team is required to document their reasons for the recommendation. They must then maintain a written record of their work and research in GSIF archives. This will hold the members of the GSIF accountable and also provide records that can be later analyzed by future GSIF members, adding to the learning opportunity both now and in the future, and ensure continuity of our philosophy and process. The GSIF portfolio management team will conduct an annual review and convey the results to the SIU Foundation in a formal report at the end of the fiscal year. Copies of any records or reports will be made available to the SIU Foundation in a timely manner upon request.

Conclusion

Establishing the Graduate Student Investment Fund is an excellent opportunity for SIU, the College of Business, and its students. Students involved in managing a large cap portfolio on behalf of the foundation will gain practical experience in business and investment management, and further develop their business acumen and skills. Successful management and performance of the fund will also promote the image and mission of SIU, while benefiting the students involved and contributing to the Foundation's overall portfolio. As such, we believe that by responsibly adhering to the mandate provided by the Foundation, our fund will add value to the university. Therefore, we are requesting a $500,000 mandate to achieve these goals.

Thank you for your consideration and support.

Appendix

Summary of Investment Philosophy and Process

Philosophy

The GSIF chooses to implement the S&P 500 as a benchmark. We believe that this index provides a sufficient number of securities for purchase and will serve as a clear and transparent benchmark for our client, the SIU Foundation.

The GSIF believes that markets are generally efficient, but that opportunities exist for a fundamental active strategy to outperform a passive benchmark. We believe that stocks may be temporarily undervalued or overvalued, but that prices eventually adjust to reflect their underlying fundamental values. Therefore, undervalued stocks have the potential to appreciate over time and contribute to performance in excess of that of a passive benchmark. Our focus is oriented towards a firm's fundamentals, allowing us to accurately assess a stock's intrinsic value with a forward-looking mindset.

In addition, one anomaly that research has shown over time is the abnormal positive return of high book-to-market value stocks (also referred to as "value stocks") relative to low book-to-market value stocks (also referred to as "growth stocks"). As such, our fund seeks to be value-tilted, as we believe this can be a source of excess returns over the long term.

Admittedly, our strategy could expose the fund to active risk by holding many stocks with similar value/growth characteristics. However, by implementing other diversification measures and appropriate rebalancing, we believe that this risk can be mitigated and the potential for excess returns realized over the long term.

In order to accurately assess our fund's performance, as well as add the benefits of diversification, our fund will implement a sector-neutral strategy. By maintaining sectors in weights similar to the benchmark, the true stock-selecting ability of our fund will be transparent to us and our client. We believe this strategy is in keeping with the GSIF's primary objective, namely, to outperform by purchasing stocks which are presently undervalued, and not by over- or under-weighting certain sectors.

Our competitive advantage arises from our fund's diverse group of analysts. All of our members hold bachelor's degrees from various universities, representing a number of different majors. Some members also have years of work experience, further contributing to our understanding of the market. However, while our fund is comprised of many well-educated students and years of real-world experience, we are still able to maintain an unbiased perspective of the market and economy due to a lack of conflicting interests. Therefore, our primary motivations are to outperform the benchmark and gain knowledge of sound investment management, both of which have the potential to add value to our client's portfolio.

Philosophy Pillars

1. *S&P 500 Benchmark*: The GSIF will implement the S&P 500 as a benchmark. We believe this index provides sufficient securities and liquidity, and will serve as a transparent benchmark for the client.
2. *Market Efficiency*: The GSIF believes that markets are generally efficient, but that opportunities exist for a fundamental active strategy to outperform a passive benchmark (Fama, 1965; Fama, 1970; Fama, 1991).
3. *Value-Tilted*: The GSIF is value-oriented in nature. The fund will select stocks that we believe to be temporarily undervalued but that have the potential to appreciate in the long run. After selection, our optimization tool will weight our holdings in favor of stocks with value characteristics. Research has shown that over time, value stocks outperform growth stocks (Fama and French, 1992; Fama and French, 1996; Daniel and Titman, 1997; Fama and French, 2008).
4. *Sector-Neutrality and Diversification*: The GSIF will implement a sector-neutral strategy by maintaining our portfolio holdings similar to the benchmark. We believe this approach provides the most accurate performance evaluation, as well as added diversification benefits. In order to be well-diversified, our fund will aim to hold at least 30 securities (Statman, 1987).
5. *Unbiased Views*: The GSIF's competitive advantage arises from an unbiased student perspective of the market and overall economy. This perspective is formed from the broad knowledge set of our graduate students, who possess strong academic backgrounds and a variety of work experiences, both of which add value for our client.

Investment Process

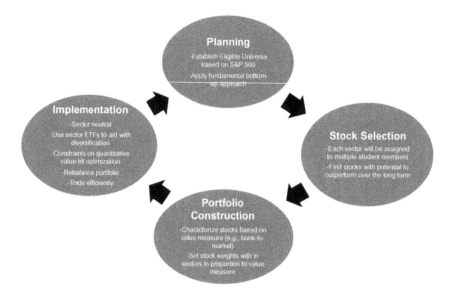

Policies

Eligible Universe

Constituents of the S&P 500 comprise the universe of eligible securities. The Graduate Student Investment Fund (GSIF) will not purchase any stock that is not a constituent of the S&P 500, as we believe this index provides a sufficient number of securities and will serve as a transparent benchmark for the Foundation. If any of the current holdings move out of the S&P 500, those stocks will be removed within one semester. This will ensure that the fund adheres to the specified mandate and fits into the Foundation's overall strategy and will allow for meaningful performance measurement.

Sector Weight Policy

The GSIF will employ a sector-neutral strategy. All sectors will generally maintain a weight within ± 2% of sector's weight in the benchmark S&P 500 index. The 2% limit is chosen in consideration of the tradeoffs between the benefits of risk reduction and transaction costs. If the sector weights of the portfolio fall out of this range, the portfolio will be rebalanced in a timely manner.

ETF Policy

The ETF policy is initiated to add liquidity to and diversify risk in the portfolio. Members can invest in any sector ETF to diversify within that sector or to temporarily gain or maintain exposure to that sector. Total sector ETFs should not exceed 30% of the total portfolio weight, with no weight constraints for each individual sector ETFs. ETF securities allow the GSIF to remain sector neutral by providing diversified holdings in sectors with few individual security holdings. Holding ETFs is not mandatory but optional for sectors that wish to enhance the diversification of the individual holdings within the sector. This policy becomes effective as GSIF completes the transition process that is described below.

Individual Security Weights Policy

As part of the investment strategy, the weight of an individual security, other than an ETF, should not exceed 7% of the total portfolio. This weight limit is intended to help mitigate firm-specific risk. The GSIF does not impose a minimum holding weight in order to maximize the effectiveness of our value tilting function. In accordance with the fund's value-tilted strategy, the target weights of each security within each sector will be determined by their relative value characteristics. Market values of stocks change over time, resulting in deviation from the stock's original target weight. The GSIF will rebalance the portfolio weights in a timely manner to maintain security weights at their target level, while considering the impact of transaction costs.

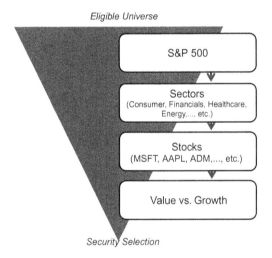

Cash Policy

The portfolio will aim to be fully invested, holding cash between 0.25% and 1.50%, as needed to cover transaction costs and the Foundation's need to withdraw cash at their discretion. Cash received from dividends will be reinvested during the rebalancing process. If the cash balance falls below 0.25% or rises above 1.50%, action will be taken to either raise cash or reduce the cash weight, respectively, during the rebalancing process.

Administrative & Organizational Structure Policy

Each person is assigned a primary responsibility for at least one sector and serves as an additional resource for other sectors as needed. Each sector will have at least one person with primary responsibility and at least one person as an additional resource. This administrative structure will provide a platform that encourages individual responsibility, while benefitting from overall team collaboration and accountability. Members are expected to attend the meetings and participate in presentations internal and external to the GSIF.

Value-Tilting Strategy

Members can choose any stock from the eligible universe, regardless of its value or growth characteristics. The goal is to choose stocks that research shows to be currently undervalued with the potential to appreciate over the long term regardless of "growth" or "value" classification. That is, "growth" stocks are allowable investments. The GSIF value-tilting strategy will tend to reduce growth stocks' weight and tilt the portfolio toward value stocks. However, the strategy is considered a large cap core strategy and could, at times, have more exposure to either growth or value stocks. As such, performance will be judged against the benchmark S&P 500 index.

Optimization Tool

The purpose of the optimization tool is to tilt the weightings of GSIF holdings toward value characteristics. As developed in the philosophy, research has shown that value stocks outperform growth stocks over the long term. After selecting the stocks from the eligible universe that members believe are currently undervalued in the market, the optimizer will determine the target weight of each stock in the portfolio. The weight will be determined as a function of the stock's value measure (e.g., book-to-market ratio) relative to the benchmark's stocks, subject to the investment constraints GSIF has implemented to manage risk and tracking error. The optimizer's objective to allocate more weight to value-characteristic stocks is supplemented by sector-neutral and maximum security weight policies to help mitigate tracking error. As the value measures of our holdings change relative to the benchmark over time, the portfolio will be rebalanced in a timely manner, while considering transaction costs.

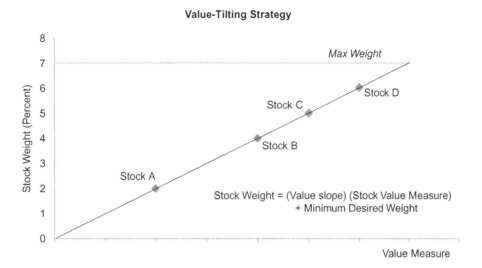

Value-Tilting Strategy

Stock Weight = (Value slope) (Stock Value Measure)
+ Minimum Desired Weight

Transition Process

Since GSIF is a new investment fund, the process of transitioning the investment will go through three phases. Though the GSIF will begin transitioning the portfolio immediately upon assets being placed under its responsibility, the estimated time during transition may take up to one year to complete.

Phase 1: All funds will be immediately invested to mimic the S&P 500 using sector ETFs. The intent is to begin with a portfolio that mimics a passive exposure to the benchmark. As such, each sector ETF weight will correspond with each S&P 500 sector weight.

S&P 500 Sector Weights

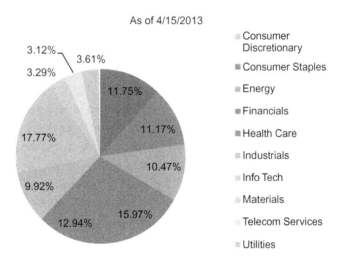

As of 4/15/2013

Phase 2: The passive ETF portfolio is transitioned to include individual stocks by implementing the GSIF investment process. All members will work simultaneously on one or more sectors, based on the team capabilities, to identify undervalued securities in accordance with the investment philosophy and process. The active investing process will start from the largest sector weight and progress to the smallest. As per the investment process, a small portion of the sector ETFs in each sector could be maintained in order to aid in diversification.

Phase 3: The portfolio exits the transition phase when every sector has been evaluated by the GSIF and individual security and ETF positions are held in accordance with the investment process's requirement that at least 70% of the portfolio be held in individual securities.

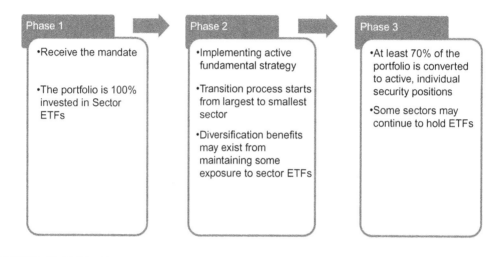

Phase 1
- Receive the mandate
- The portfolio is 100% invested in Sector ETFs

Phase 2
- Implementing active fundamental strategy
- Transition process starts from largest to smallest sector
- Diversification benefits may exist from maintaining some exposure to sector ETFs

Phase 3
- At least 70% of the portfolio is converted to active, individual security positions
- Some sectors may continue to hold ETFs

[1]See Appendix below for details concerning our value-tilting strategy.
[2]Policies are discussed in detail in the Policies section below.

Exhibit 5.9 shows a business development presentation by graduate students at Southern Illinois University who wanted to initiate a student-managed investment fund for graduate students. The proposal and presentation were made to the university endowment fund's investment committee, seeking a large cap equity mandate of $500,000. This business development presentation has a primary focus on the investment philosophy and process, since its objective is to convince the board of the endowment fund that the graduate students should be essentially hired to manage a portion of that fund. As such, the presentation addresses how the assets would be managed, including a plan for transitioning the assets of the foundation into a portfolio that is managed by a newly created organization. Recognizing that the investment committee must conduct a lot of business during its infrequent meetings, the presentation that accompanies the proposal is brief and concise, summarizing the key points. By summarizing the proposal's key points, the presentation facilitates a discussion about the proposal between the investment committee and the students. Such discussions between a client and investment manager are important in establishing a mutual understanding of the capabilities of the investment manager and the expectations of the client.

Summary of Key Points

- An internal report or presentation is an efficient and effective means for communicating important ideas and facilitating discussions within an organization.
- Internal reports and presentations are common within student-managed investment funds in support of security selection decisions.
- External presentations are used to communicate outside the organization and most often have a business development or client service objective.
- All presentations should be concise with clear points or takeaways summarized in the introduction and conclusion.

Exercises

1. Choose a current holding in your portfolio. Write an analyst report on the security. Be sure to clearly state a hold or sell recommendation.
2. Choose a security that is not currently held in your portfolio. Write an analyst report on the security. Be sure to clearly state a buy or pass recommendation.
3. Choose two competing companies in the same sector and industry from the S&P 500. Write an analyst report that makes the case to purchase (or sell) one stock over the other.
4. Develop and draft an outline for an internal stock selection presentation.
5. Develop and draft an outline for an internal portfolio construction presentation.
6. Develop and draft an outline for an external business development presentation under each of the following two scenarios. In each case, be sure to include sections that anticipate questions or concerns from the target audience.
   a. You are proposing the launch of a new student-managed investment fund.
   b. You are proposing an increase in the size of an existing student-managed investment fund.
7. Locate past internal and external presentations from your organization. Critique the presentations by noting the good aspects and those that are missing or need improvement. Be sure to articulate specifically how you would improve the presentation.

Performance Evaluation

Chapter Contents

Every investment manager must report his or her portfolio's performance. However, the obligation of an investment manager goes beyond simply reporting performance – the investment manager must understand performance and provide an explanation of it that is consistent with the manager's investment process. This understanding and explanation help both internally and externally. Internally, the investment manager can use the understanding of past performance to monitor performance and assure that the investment process is working as expected. Performance evaluation can help identify opportunities to enhance the investment process, increase returns, or mitigate risks. Externally, the investment manager

Trading and Money Management in a Student-Managed Portfolio.
DOI: http://dx.doi.org/10.1016/B978-0-12-374755-6.00006-6
© 2014 Elsevier Inc. All rights reserved.

can use performance evaluation to help explain how the investment process works to capitalize on the opportunities identified in the investment philosophy.

We distinguish between *performance reporting*, which usually emphasizes the percentage return on an investment, and *performance analysis*, which aims to provide an understanding of the performance. Performance reporting is an *accounting* exercise. Performance analysis is an *economic* exercise. In both cases, such reports help provide transparency both internally and externally as to the returns and risks of the investment strategy, as well as their sources.

This chapter begins by discussing the importance and methods of performance reporting standards. In a basic performance report, an investment manager should report annualized returns over specific time periods for the portfolio and, if applicable, the portfolio's benchmark. Beyond the basic report, the chapter discusses how performance evaluation reveals the story behind the annualized returns. We provide discussions of two general classes of performance evaluations: performance attribution and returns-based performance analysis. These methods complement each other in providing insights into the sources of returns and relative returns, as well as the risk exposures in the portfolio. We show numerous equations in order to provide the technical background of these methods before applying them in several examples. Finally, we discuss transaction cost analysis as an important element in understanding the overall performance of a portfolio.

Performance Calculation

There are two overarching goals in reporting performance: accuracy and consistency. Accuracy comes from using the right information and carefully applying the appropriate calculation methods. An investment manager achieves consistency in the performance report by developing a process and implementing it the same way through time. Performance reporting standards, such as GIPS™ (Global Investment Performance Standards) maintained by the CFA Institute, assist the investment manager in achieving both goals. We reprint the GIPS standards in Exhibit 6.1. Exhibit 6.2 contains a discussion by Ashland Partners and Advent Software on implementing GIPS-compliant performance measurement standards.

The calculation of portfolio performance seems to be quite straightforward. For a portfolio that has no cash flows and that holds securities for which market values are readily available, the calculation of the portfolio return over period t, r_t, is simply the percentage change from the beginning portfolio value, MV_{t-k}, to the ending portfolio value, MV_t, as given by:

$$r_{t-k,t} = \frac{MV_t - MV_{t-k}}{MV_{t-k}} \qquad (6.1)$$

Exhibit 6.1 Global Investment Performance Standards[1]

Global Investment Performance Standards

Revised Effective Date: 1 January 2006
Adoption Date: 4 March 2004
Effective Date: 1 June 2004
Retroactive Application: Not Required
Public Comment Period: August—November 2002
© 2008 CFA Institute

Guidance Statement on Calculation Methodology (Revised)

Introduction

Achieving comparability among investment management firms' performance presentations requires as much uniformity as possible in the methodology used to calculate portfolio and composite returns. The uniformity of the return calculation methodology is dependent on accurate and consistent input data, a critical component to effective compliance with the GIPS® standards. Although the GIPS standards allow flexibility in return calculation, the return must be calculated using a methodology that incorporates the time-weighted rate of return concept for all assets (except Private Equity assets). For information on calculating performance for these assets, see the separate Private Equity Provisions and Guidance.

The Standards require a time-weighted rate of return because it removes the effects of cash flows, which are generally client-driven. Therefore, a time-weighted rate of return best reflects the firm's ability to manage the assets according to a specified strategy or objective, and is the basis for the comparability of composite returns among firms on a global basis.

In this Guidance Statement, the term "return" is used rather than the more common term "performance" to emphasize the distinction between return and risk and to encourage the view of performance as a combination of risk and return. Risk measures are valuable tools for assessing the abilities of asset managers; however, this Guidance Statement focuses only on the return calculation.

Money- or dollar-weighted returns may add further value in understanding the impact to the client of the timing of external cash flows, but are less useful for return comparison and are therefore not covered by this Guidance Statement.

---

[1] Reprinted with the permission of the CFA Institute.

Guiding Principles
Valuation Principles
The following are guiding principles that firms must use when determining portfolio values as the basis for the return calculation:

- Portfolio valuations must be based on market values (not cost basis or book values).
- For periods prior to 1 January 2001, portfolios must be valued at least quarterly. For periods between 1 January 2001 and 1 January 2010, portfolios must be valued at least monthly. For periods beginning 1 January 2010, firms must value portfolios on the date of all large external cash flows.
- For periods beginning 1 January 2010, firms must value portfolios as of calendar month-end or the last business day of the month. Firms must use trade-date accounting for periods beginning 1 January 2005. (Note: for purposes of the Standards, trade-date accounting recognizes the transaction on the date of the purchase or sale. Recognizing the asset or liability within at least 3 days of the date the transaction is entered into satisfies this requirement.)
- Accrual accounting must be used for fixed-income securities and all other assets that accrue interest income. Market values of fixed-income securities must include accrued income.
- Accrual accounting should be used for dividends (as of the ex-dividend date).

Calculation Principles
The following are guiding principles that firms must use when calculating **portfolio** returns:

- Firms must calculate all returns after the deduction of the actual trading expenses incurred during the period. Estimated trading expenses are not permitted.
- Firms must calculate time-weighted total returns, including income as well as realized and unrealized gains and losses.
- The calculation method chosen must represent returns fairly, must not be misleading, and must be applied consistently.
- Firms must use time-weighted rates of return that adjust for external cash flows. External cash flows are defined as cash, securities, or assets that enter or exit a portfolio (capital additions or withdrawals) and are generally client-driven. Income earned on a portfolio's assets is not considered an external cash flow.
- The chosen calculation methodology must adjust for daily-weighted external cash flows for periods beginning 1 January 2005, at the latest. An example of this methodology is the Modified Dietz method.
- For periods beginning 1 January 2010, at the latest, firms must calculate performance for interim periods between all large external cash flows and geometrically link performance to calculate period returns. (Note: as such, at 1 January 2010, or before if appropriate, each firm must define, prospectively, on a composite-specific basis, what constitutes a large external cash flow.) For information on calculating a "true" time-weighted return (see below).
- External cash flows must be treated in a consistent manner with the firm's documented, composite-specific policy.
- Firms must calculate portfolio returns at least on a monthly basis. For periods prior to 2001, firms may calculate portfolio returns on a quarterly basis.
- Periodic returns must be geometrically linked.

Calculation Principles

The following are guiding principles that firms must use when calculating **composite** returns:

- Composite returns must be calculated by asset weighting the individual portfolio returns using beginning-of-period values or a method that reflects both beginning-of-period values and external cash flows.
- The aggregate return method, which combines all the composite assets and cash flows to calculate composite performance as if the composite were one portfolio, is acceptable as an asset-weighted approach.
- For periods prior to 1 January 2010, firms must calculate composite returns by asset weighting the individual portfolio returns at least quarterly. For periods beginning 1 January 2010, composite returns must be calculated by asset weighting the individual portfolio returns at least monthly.
- Periodic returns must be geometrically linked.

Cash Flow Principles

The following are guiding principles that firms must consider when defining their Cash Flow policies:

- An **external cash flow** is a flow of cash, securities, or assets that enter or exit a portfolio, which are generally client driven. When calculating approximated rates of return, where the calculation methodology requires an adjustment for the daily-weighting of cash flows, the formula reflects a weight for each external cash flow. The cash flow weight is determined by the amount of time the cash flow is held in the portfolio.
- When calculating a more accurate time-weighted return, a **large external cash flow** must be defined by each firm for each composite to determine when the portfolios in that composite are to be revalued for performance calculations. It is the level at which a client-initiated external flow of cash and or securities into or out of a portfolio may distort performance if the portfolio is not revalued. Firms must define the amount in terms of the value of the cash/asset flow, or in terms of a percentage of portfolio or composite assets.
- The large external cash flow (described above) determines when a portfolio is to be revalued for performance calculations. This is differentiated from a **significant cash flow**, which occurs in situations where cash flows disrupt the implementation of the investment strategy. Please see the Guidance Statement on the Treatment of Significant Cash Flows, which details the procedures and criteria that firms must adhere to and offers additional options for dealing with the impact of significant cash flows on portfolios.

Time-Weighted Rate of Return

Valuing the portfolio and calculating interim returns each time there is an external cash flow ought to result in the most accurate method to calculate the time-weighted rates of return, referred to as the "true" Time-Weighted Rate of Return Method. A formula for calculating a true time-weighted portfolio return whenever cash flows occur is

$$R_i = \frac{(EMV_i - BMV_i)}{BMV_i}$$

where EMV_i is the market value of the portfolio at the end of sub-period i, excluding any cash flows in the period, but including accrued income for the period. BMV_i is the market value at the end of the previous sub-period (i.e., the beginning of the current sub-period), plus any cash flows at the end of the previous sub-period, where an inflow is positive and an outflow is negative, and including accrued income up to the end of the previous period. The cash inflow is included in the BMV (previous period EMV + positive cash inflow) of the sub-period when the cash inflow is available for investment at the start of the sub-period; a cash outflow is reflected in the BMV (previous period EMV + negative cash outflow) of the sub-period when the cash outflow is no longer available for investment at the start of the sub-period.

The sub-period returns are then geometrically linked to calculate the period's return according to the following formula:

$$R_{TR} = ((1 + R_1) \times (1 + R_2) \ldots (1 + R_n)) - 1$$

where *RTR* is the period's total return and $R_1, R_2, \ldots, R_n$ are the sub-period returns for sub-period 1 through *n*, respectively.

Approximation of Time-Weighted Rate of Return

As mentioned in the Introduction, the GIPS standards require firms to calculate returns using a methodology that incorporates the time-weighted rate of return concept (except for Private Equity assets). The Standards allow flexibility in choosing the calculation methodology, which means that firms may use alternative formulas, provided the calculation method chosen represents returns fairly, is not misleading, and is applied consistently.

Calculating a true time-weighted rate of return is not an easy task and may be cost intensive. For these reasons, firms may use an approximation method to calculate the total return of the individual portfolios for the periods and sub-periods. The most common approximation methods combine specific rate of return methodologies (such as the original Dietz method, the Modified Dietz method, the original Internal Rate of Return (IRR) method, and the Modified IRR method) for sub-periods and incorporate the time-weighted rate of return concept by geometrically linking the sub-period returns.

Just as the GIPS standards transition to more frequent valuations, the Standards also transition to more precise calculation methodologies. Therefore, the GIPS standards require firms to calculate approximated time-weighted rates of return that adjust for daily-weighted cash flows by 1 January 2005 (e.g., Modified Dietz method) and will require the calculation of a more accurate time-weighted rate of return with valuations occurring at each large external cash flow as well as calendar month-end or the last business day of the month for periods beginning 1 January 2010.

This Guidance Statement does not contain details on the different formulas for calculating approximate time-weighted rates of return.

Composite Return Calculation

Provision 2.A.3 requires that composite returns must be calculated by asset weighting the individual portfolio returns using beginning-of-period values or a method that reflects both beginning-of-period values and external cash flows.

The intention is to show a composite return that reflects the overall return of the set of the portfolios included in the composite.

To calculate composite returns, firms may use alternative formulas so long as the calculation method chosen represents returns fairly, is not misleading, and is applied consistently.

According to the *Beginning Market Value-Weighted Method* the composite return, R_{BMV}, can be calculated using the formula:

$$R_{BMV} = \frac{\sum_{i=1}^{n}(BMV_i \times R_i)}{BMV_{TOTAL}}$$

where BMV_i is the beginning market value (at the start of the period) for a portfolio, R_i is the rate of return for portfolio i, and BMV_{TOTAL} is the total market value at the beginning of the period for all the portfolios in the composite.

The *Beginning Market Value Plus Cash Flow-Weighted Method* represents a refinement to the asset-weighted approach. Consider the case in which one of two portfolios in a composite doubles in market value as the result of a contribution on the third day of a performance period. Under the asset-weighted approach, this portfolio will be weighted in the composite based solely on its beginning market value (i.e., not including the contribution). The beginning market value and cash flow-weighted method resolves this problem by including the effect of cash flows in the weighting calculation as well as in the market values. Assuming that cash flows occur at the end of the day, the weighting factor for each cash flow is calculated as:

$$W_{i,j} = \frac{(CD - D_{i,j})}{CD}$$

where CD is the total number of calendar days in the period and $D_{i,j}$ is the number of calendar days since the beginning of the period in which cash flow j occurred in portfolio i.

The beginning market value plus cash flow-weighted composite return, R_{BMV+CF}, can be calculated as follows:

$$R_{BMV+CF} = \frac{\sum_{i=1}^{n}\left\{\left(\left(BMV_i + \left(\sum_{j=1}^{m} CF_{i,j} \times W_{i,j}\right)\right) \times R_i\right)\right\}}{\sum_{i=1}^{n}\left(BMV_i + \left(\sum_{j=1}^{m} CF_{i,j} \times W_{i,j}\right)\right)}$$

where $CF_{i,j}$ is the cash flow j within the period for portfolio i (contributions to the portfolio are positive flows, and withdrawals or distributions are negative flows) and R_i is the return for portfolio i.

The *Aggregate Return Method* combines all the composite assets and cash flows before any calculations occur to calculate returns as if the composite were one portfolio. The method is also acceptable as an asset-weighted approach.

Geometric Linking of the Periodic Composite Returns

To calculate the composite return over more than one (sub-)period, the composite return over the total period is calculated by geometrically linking the individual composite sub-period returns using the following formula:

$$R_{CT} = ((1 + R_{C1}) \times (1 + R_{c2}) \ldots (1 + R_{Cn})) - 1$$

where R_{CT} is the composite return over the total period and RC_1, RC_2, and RC_n are the individual composite returns for the sub-periods 1, 2, and n, respectively.

Additional Considerations

Changes to the Methodology—Where appropriate, in the interest of fair representation and full disclosure, firms should disclose when a change in a calculation methodology or valuation source results in a material impact on the composite return.

Third-Party Performance Measurement—Firms may use portfolio returns calculated by a third-party performance measurer as long as the methodology adheres to the requirements of the GIPS standards.

Different Valuation and/or Calculation Method—Firms are permitted to include portfolios with different valuation and/or calculation methodologies within the same composite (as long as the methodologies adhere to the requirements of the GIPS standards). Firms must be consistent in the methodology used for a portfolio (e.g., firms cannot change the methodology for a portfolio from month-to-month).

Month End Valuations—Firms must be consistent in defining the (monthly) valuation period. The valuation period must end on the same day as the reporting period. In other words, firms must value the portfolio/composite on the last day of the reporting period (or the nearest business day). Aggregating portfolios with different ending valuation dates in the same composite is not permitted after 1 January 2006.

Trading Expenses—Returns must be calculated after the deduction of all trading expenses. Trading expenses are the costs of buying or selling a security, and include brokerage commissions and any other regulatory fee, duty, etc. associated with an individual transaction.

Trade Date Accounting—Firms must use trade-date accounting for periods beginning 1 January 2005. Trade-date accounting recognizes an asset or liability on the date the transaction is entered into. Recognizing the asset or liability within at least 3 days of the date the transaction is entered into satisfies the trade-date accounting requirement. As a result, the account will recognize any change between the price of the transaction and the current market value.

Taxes—Firms must disclose relevant details of the treatment of withholding tax on dividends, interest income, and capital gains. Returns should be calculated net of non-reclaimable withholding taxes on dividends, interest, and capital gains. Reclaimable withholding taxes should be accrued.

Grossing-Up or Netting-Down of Investment Management Fees—Firms are allowed to include portfolios with different grossing-up methodologies within the same composite. Firms must be consistent in the methodology used for a portfolio (e.g., firms cannot change the methodology for a portfolio from month-to-month). Please see the guidance on Fees for the GIPS standards.

Large Cash Flows—The firm must have an established policy on defining and adjusting for large cash flows and apply this policy consistently. Actual valuation at the time of any large external cash flow is required for periods beginning 1 January 2010.

Disclosures—Firms must disclose that additional information regarding policies for calculating and reporting returns is available upon request. Generally, the firm's policies and procedures on calculating and reporting returns could serve as the basis for this information.

Effective Date

This Guidance Statement was originally effective 1 June 2004 and was revised to reflect the changes to the GIPS standards effective as of 1 January 2006.

Firms are encouraged, but not required, to apply this guidance prior to the original Effective Date of 1 June 2004; however, the original guidance must be applied to all presentations that include performance for periods on and after that date.

The revisions made to this guidance (effective 1 January 2006) must be applied to all presentations that include performance for periods after 31 December 2005.

Key GIPS Provisions Specifically Applicable to Calculation Methodology

1.A.2 Portfolio valuations must be based on market values (not cost basis or book values).

1.A.3 For periods prior to 1 January 2001, portfolios must be valued at least quarterly. For periods between 1 January 2001 and 1 January 2010, portfolios must be valued at least monthly. For periods beginning 1 January 2010, firms must value portfolios on the date of all large external cash flows.

1.A.4 For periods beginning 1 January 2010, firms must value portfolios as of the calendar month-end or the last business day of the month.

1.A.5 For periods beginning 1 January 2005, firms must use trade date accounting.

1.A.6 Accrual accounting must be used for fixed-income securities and all other assets that accrue interest income. Market values of fixed-income securities must include accrued income.

1.A.7 For periods beginning 1 January 2006, composites must have consistent beginning and ending annual valuation dates. Unless the composite is reported on a non-calendar fiscal year, the beginning and ending valuation dates must be at calendar year-end (or on the last business day of the year).

2.A Calculation Methodology—Requirements

2.A.1 Total return, including realized and unrealized gains and losses plus income, must be used.

2.A.2 Time-weighted rates of return that adjust for external cash flows must be used. Periodic returns must be geometrically linked. External cash flows must be treated in a consistent manner with the firm's documented, composite-specific policy. At a minimum:

    a. For periods beginning 1 January 2005, firms must use approximated rates of return that adjust for daily-weighted external cash flows.

    b. For periods beginning 1 January 2010, firms must value portfolios on the date of all large external cash flows.

2.A.3 Composite returns must be calculated by asset weighting the individual portfolio returns using beginning-of-period values or a method that reflects both beginning-of-period values and external cash flows.

2.A.4 Returns from cash and cash equivalents held in portfolios must be included in total return calculations.

2.A.5 All returns must be calculated after the deduction of the actual trading expenses incurred during the period. Estimated trading expenses are not permitted.

2.A.6 For periods beginning 1 January 2006, firms must calculate composite returns by asset weighting the individual portfolio returns at least quarterly. For periods beginning 1 January 2010, composite returns must be calculated by asset weighting the individual portfolio returns at least monthly.

2.A.7 If the actual direct trading expenses cannot be identified and segregated from a bundled fee:

    a. when calculating gross-of-fees returns, returns must be reduced by the entire bundled fee or the portion of the bundled fee that includes the direct trading expenses. The use of estimated trading expenses is not permitted.

b. when calculating net-of-fees returns, returns must be reduced by the entire bundled fee or the portion of the bundled fee that includes the direct trading expenses and the investment management fee. The use of estimated trading expenses is not permitted.

2.B Calculation Methodology—Recommendations

2.B.1 Returns should be calculated net of non-reclaimable withholding taxes on dividends, interest, and capital gains. Reclaimable withholding taxes should be accrued.

2.B.2 Firms should calculate composite returns by asset weighting the member portfolios at least monthly.

2.B.3 Firms should value portfolios on the date of all large external cash flows.

Applications:

1. Does the firm violate the GIPS standards by reporting money-weighted rates of return to an existing client for their portfolio (which contains no private equity assets)?

No, the Standards would not be violated if the firm reported money-weighted rates of return to an existing client for their portfolio. The Standards are primarily based on the concept of presenting the firm's composite performance to a prospective client rather than presenting individual portfolio returns to an existing client. The IRR (or money-weighted return) represents the performance of the specific client's fund holdings (i.e., influenced by the client's timing and amount of cash flows) and measures the performance of the fund rather than the performance of the fund manager. Money-weighted returns may add further value in understanding the impact to the client of the timing of external cash flows, but are less useful for comparison purposes.

IRRs are only required in the GIPS standards when calculating performance for private equity assets where the investment firm controls the cash flows.

2. The GIPS standards currently state that firms are required to use trade-date accounting as of 1 January 2005. How should trade date be defined?

For the purposes of the GIPS standards, trade-date accounting is defined as "recognizing the asset or liability within at least 3 days of the date the transaction is entered into." Settlement-date accounting is defined as "recognizing the asset or liability on the date in which the exchange of cash, securities, and paperwork involved in a transaction is completed." When using settlement-date accounting, any movement in value between the trade date or booking date and the settlement date will not have an impact on performance return until settlement date; whereas for trade-date accounting, the change in market value will be reflected for each valuation between trade date and settlement date. If the trade and settlement dates straddle a performance measurement period-end date, then performance return comparisons between portfolios that use settlement-date accounting and those that use trade-date accounting may not be valid. The same problem occurs when comparing settlement-date portfolios and benchmarks. The principle behind requiring trade-date accounting is to ensure there is not a significant lag between trade execution and reflecting the trade in the performance of a portfolio. For the purposes of compliance with the GIPS standards, portfolios are considered to satisfy the trade-date accounting requirement provided that transactions are recorded and recognized consistently and within normal market practice—typically, a period between trade date and up to three days after trade date (T + 3). After 1 January 2005, all firms must recognize transactions on trade date as defined herein.

3. Given the following information, calculate the rate of return for this portfolio for January, February, March, and the first quarter of 2000, using a true time-weighted rate of return:

Date	Market Value (€)	Cash Flow (€)	Market Value Post Cash Flow (€)
12/31/99	500,000		
1/31/00	509,000		
2/19/00	513,000	+50,000	563,000
2/28/00	575,000		
3/12/00	585,000	−20,000	565,000
3/31/00	570,000		

SOLUTION:

January

$$R = \frac{(509,000 - 500,000)}{500,000} = 1.80\%$$

February
  1/31/00−2/19/00

$$R = \frac{(513,000 - 509,000)}{509,000} = 0.79\%$$

  2/19/00−2/28/00

$$R = \frac{(575,000 - 563,000)}{563,000} = 2.13\%$$

  1/31/00−2/28/00
March
  2/28/00−3/12/00

$$R = \frac{(570,000 - 565,000)}{565,000} = 0.88\%$$

$$R_{FEB} = ((1 + 0.008) \times (1 + 0.021)) - 1 = 2.92\%$$

  3/12/00−3/31/00

$$R = \frac{(585,000 - 575,000)}{575,000} = 1.74\%$$

  2/28/00−3/31/00

$$R_{Mor} = ((1 + 0.017) \times (1 + 0.009)) - 1 = 2.62\%$$

Quarter 1

$$R_{QT1} = ((1 + 0.018) \times (1 + 0.029) \times (1 + 0.026)) - 1 = 7.48\%$$

Exhibit 6.2 Best Practices in Performance Measurement and Reporting: Understanding the Global Investment Performance Standards

A Practical Guide to Implementing GIPS Standards for Asset Managers

Advent Software, Inc. and Ashland Partners & Company LLP

Table of Contents

Foreword
If you are thinking about becoming GIPS compliant or need to fine-tune your existing process, this document will help you understand the steps involved. It is not a substitute for the Standards themselves. It is designed to help you understand the value of compliance, what's needed to achieve it, pitfalls to avoid, and how to have greater assurance that your performance reporting is indeed GIPS compliant.

Overview
Performance is an investment manager's calling card. It is what keeps clients and wins new ones. The ability to promote your firm's performance is a competitive necessity. Equally essential, however, is that clients and prospects can trust the integrity and fairness of your performance claims.

That is why the CFA Institute (the body that confers the Chartered Financial Analyst® certification) implemented the Global Investment Performance Standards or GIPS®. Based on the underlying principle of "full disclosure and fair representation," GIPS is just what the name implies—a worldwide set of standards for measuring, calculating, and presenting aggregate gain and loss percentages in discretionary, managed investment accounts. While compliance with the GIPS standards is voluntary, institutional investors usually require their portfolio managers to be in compliance with the Standards and often even go a step further and require verification of compliance by an independent party with GIPS expertise.

Advantages of Compliance

There are three major advantages to complying with GIPS and getting third-party verification. One is the additional credibility the claim of compliance brings to performance numbers in sales presentations, service negotiations, advertising, media relations, and marketing literature. This added credibility can help reinforce your existing client relationships and open doors to consultants and more potential clients. A second advantage is that compliance provides a framework that helps strengthen a firm's internal control structure. Processes run smoother and portfolios are managed more cohesively as a result of established policies and procedures around the calculation and presentation of performance. The third advantage is to avoid running afoul of the SEC. Claiming compliance without actually being in compliance is considered misleading advertising by the SEC; a qualified third-party verifier can assist firms in keeping up with the requirements of the Standards and avoid a fraudulent claim of compliance.

Of course, realizing these advantages comes with a price. Adoption of the GIPS standards means yet another set of demands on managers. Firms need to learn the GIPS standards, implement new processes and controls, and understand the intricacies of creating portfolio composites. This initiative requires an investment of time, labor, resources, and commitment. The price of compliance, however, is far outweighed by the potential costs of non-compliance: fewer growth opportunities, damage to your firm's reputation by not keeping up with industry best practices, and ultimately, lost business.

> *"It takes 20 years to build a reputation and five minutes to ruin it. If you think about that, you'll do things differently." Warren Buffett*

This communication is provided by Advent Software, Inc. for informational purposes only and should not be construed as, and does not constitute, legal advice on any matter whatsoever discussed herein.

The Evolution of Performance Reporting Standards

GIPS has its origins in the Financial Analysts Federation's (FAF) Performance Presentation Standards, first published in 1987. In 1990, the FAF and the Institute of Chartered Financial Analysts joined and eventually merged under the umbrella of the Association for Investment Management and Research (AIMR®). The standards developed by the FAF became the AIMR Performance Presentation Standards (AIMR-PPS) and enjoyed widespread acceptance in North America. During this same period, however, global investing was on the rise, and many countries followed different performance measurement guidelines. The globalization of financial markets called for a global standard; thus, the "global" in GIPS—Global Investment Performance Standards.

AIMR initiated the development of a global standard in 1995 and, in 1999, formally adopted GIPS. AIMR's name was subsequently changed to the CFA Institute and GIPS replaced the AIMR-PPS. Subject to continual reevaluation and modification, the most recent version of the GIPS standards was adopted in January 2010.

While the CFA Institute initiated GIPS and funded its development, GIPS is governed by an executive committee made up of Institute officials as well as representatives from investment and accounting firms and public investors around the world. The GIPS Executive Committee is responsible for maintaining the Standards, with global participation and input from volunteer committee members. As of 2010, 32 countries have adopted the GIPS standards or have had their local performance reporting standards endorsed by the GIPS Executive Committee.

GIPS in a Nutshell: Creating and Managing Composites

The key provision of GIPS is the requirement to include all of a firm's fee-paying, discretionary accounts in meaningful composites. Creating composites is the crucial first step towards GIPS compliance. Firms that are contemplating GIPS compliance will need to set up composites and have a system in place for managing them well in advance of actually claiming compliance.

Composites are aggregates of portfolios that share common investment objectives or strategies. The composite return is the asset-weighted average of the returns of all the portfolios in the composite. The goal of composites is to ensure "apples to apples" performance comparability from one firm to another and prevent cherry picking of only a manager's best performing accounts. As stated in the Standards document:

> *"The GIPS standards require firms to include all actual fee-paying, discretionary portfolios in composites defined according to similar strategy and/or investment objective and require firms to initially show GIPS-compliant history for a minimum of five (5) years or since inception of the firm or composite if in existence less than 5 years. After presenting at least 5 years of compliant history, the firm must add annual performance each year going forward up to ten (10) years, at a minimum."*

While non-fee paying discretionary accounts may also be included in composites, the Standards specifically exclude non-discretionary portfolios. A broad definition of a non-discretionary portfolio would be any account that contains investment guidelines significantly restricting the ability to manage the assets according to an appropriate composite strategy. The returns on such portfolios are more reflective of the client's decisions rather than an investment manager's decisions. Even certain accounts that meet the legal definition of discretionary may be deemed non-discretionary for GIPS purposes and exempted from composites if client restrictions (e.g., no "sin stocks") or liquidity requirements limit the manager's discretion.

Constructing and maintaining composites is perhaps the greatest challenge—and the one that consumes the most time and resources—in GIPS compliance. Managers need to define composites, understand their nuances, select portfolios correctly, and deal with portfolios that do not fit neatly into composites—avoiding too many overly narrow composites or too few overly broad, meaningless composites.

Composites are difficult if not impossible to piece together in retrospect, which is why they need to be well established before you start claiming GIPS-compliant performance. Moreover, composite creation is not a one-time event. Portfolios fluctuate as the values of holdings change, issues are traded, accounts are opened or closed, or client mandates change. Composites must be monitored and managed continuously. Portfolios that no longer meet the defined criteria must be removed to maintain the integrity of performance calculations. Before your firm can claim compliance, you will need to demonstrate a track record of effective composite management. (For a more detailed discussion of composites, see Advent's white paper, "Best Practices in Composite Management.")

Other Key Provisions

In addition to composite construction, GIPS has a number of other provisions to address key investment performance issues. Chief among them:

> **Written Policies and Procedures for Firm-wide Compliance**. The first requirement of GIPS is a written definition of the "distinct business entity" representing itself, be it an investment firm or, for example, the investment subsidiary or division of a larger financial institution. Further documentation of policies and procedures relevant to complying with the Standards is also a fundamental requirement, and a checklist is provided later in this report.
>
> **Data Integrity.** Firms must capture and maintain all data needed to support performance claims. At the very least, such data includes transaction details and valuations, as well as support for composite membership changes and the timing of such changes.

Tips and Tricks for Building and Managing Composites

Avoid having too many composites by focusing on the firm's primary mandates. If there are a lot of unique accounts left over without a composite, you can create single account composites or expand on your firm's definition of discretion:

- Is it because the accounts have a lot of low cost basis stock that makes them unrepresentative?
- Are there limits on duration that constrain the portfolio manager's ability to implement the firm's strategy?
- Sin-stock restrictions?
- Frequent communications from clients regarding cash flow/liquidity needs?

All these and more are good examples of accounts that could be the beginning of a future firm strategy (for example, a Socially Responsible Composite or a Limited Duration Composite) or accounts that could be deemed non-discretionary for GIPS purposes, even if they have a fully discretionary contract. What this means is that they don't have to go in a composite, because the performance reflects the client's directives as much as it does the manager's performance.

These are also good examples of the flexibility the Standards provide individual firms, because the decision is not limited to either including accounts in a composite or excluding the account because a few of the assets are restricted. A firm could also carve out non-discretionary or restricted assets, allowing the remaining account assets to be included in a composite.

If newly created composites have high dispersion, track down the accounts in the composite that are performance outliers and determine if there is an underlying client directive contributing to the difference. Upon reviewing the accounts, a portfolio manager might realize that two or three accounts in the composite might be better off in their own composite because, for example, they are more concentrated than the other portfolios or because they have concentrations in different sectors due to their clients' age/risk tolerances.

Uniform Calculation Methodology. The Standards mandate specific calculation methodologies to be used for both portfolios and composites to assure uniformity among compliant firms.

Disclosures. The presentation of performance results must be accompanied by mandated disclosures, some required for all firms and some specific to the firm's circumstances. A list of required and recommended disclosures can be found in the Standards in sections 4A and B.

Presentation and Reporting. In addition to disclosures, sections 5A and B of the Standards spell out other types of information that must accompany the presentation of performance results. The key reporting requirement is the five- and ten-year or since-inception annual performance history. The Standards also contain additional guidance for specific asset types, such as real estate and private equity provisions in sections 6 and 7, and specific presentation types, such as advertisements versus one-on-one presentations.

Why Comply?

Compliance with the GIPS standards has become a virtual requirement in North America in order to stay competitive. The Standards are recognized as an industry best practice. Because the SEC requires firms that claim compliance to adhere to the requirements of the Standards on a firm-wide basis, firms that choose to comply without putting forth the necessary due diligence do so at great risk.

Credibility. GIPS compliance signals that you are committed to competing on a level playing field, that your performance reporting utilizes industry best practices and that product-to-product comparisons with other firms are valid.

Improved Client Confidence. Client trust is arguably an investment firm's most valuable asset. GIPS compliance reinforces that trust.

Marketing Support. Particularly if a firm has a record of outperforming key indices or industry averages, GIPS adds credibility to their success story. The greater the performance claimed, the more advantageous it is to support that claim with GIPS compliance.

More common than firms choosing not to comply with GIPS are firms that have every intention of complying, but face challenges in doing so. They may experience time and resource constraints or difficulty in interpreting the Standards correctly, especially in the areas of composites and calculations. How do you validate your firm's reporting process and procedures? Start by understanding these 12 steps to GIPS compliance and determining whether or not your firm is following them.

Twelve Steps to GIPS Compliance

An effective compliance program has completed these steps:

1. Management support. Management must make a commitment of time and resources to bring the firm into compliance.
2. Know the Standards. Assign individuals or teams to review and familiarize themselves with the Standards and to complete each subsequent step.
3. Define the firm. The definition should accurately reflect how the entity is held out to the public and will determine the scope of firm-wide assets under management.
4. Define investment discretion. The Standards use the term "discretion" more broadly than just whether or not a manager can place trades for a client. Defining investment

discretion is an important step in determining whether or not accounts must be included in a composite.

5. Identify all accounts under management within the defined firm over the past five years, or since firm inception if less than five years. This should include all discretionary and non-discretionary accounts, including terminated relationships.
6. Determine if your firm has the appropriate books and records to support historical discretionary account performance.
7. Separate the list of accounts into groups based on discretionary status, investment mandate, and/or other criteria. These groups will be the foundation for your composites.
8. List and define the composites that will be constructed and establish a process for composite management.
9. Document your firm's policies and procedures for establishing and maintaining compliance with the Standards. (See the Policy and Procedure checklist later.)
10. Document reasons for composite membership changes throughout each account's history and reasons for non-discretionary status, if applicable.
11. Calculate composite performance and required annual statistics.
12. Develop fully compliant marketing materials.

Don't Just Comply—Verify

The GIPS standards strongly recommend (but do not require) that firms claiming compliance verify that their policies, procedures, and composite construction methodology adhere to the Standards. That means firms need to bring in an independent firm to check their work. In practice, most firms prefer bringing in the verification firm early on for objective guidance on the process. Working with a verifier to see potential problem areas is invaluable to large and small investment firms alike. Verification services are offered by accounting firms and firms focused primarily or exclusively on GIPS consulting and verification.

Effective verification generally follows three phases:

1. **Preverification.** The verifier reviews your performance policies and procedures, if any, firm brochures, and performance presentations. This provides the verifier with an understanding of your firm and establishes the framework for a gap analysis wherever existing policies do not meet GIPS requirements. The verifier can advise you on areas to round out your written policies and procedures and refine your composite definitions and presentation disclosures.

Common Obstacles to Becoming GIPS Compliant

1. Lack of a complete commitment of the necessary resources to attain compliance from top management. This can result from underestimating how much time, labor and other resources will be needed.
2. Lack of books and records to support performance and composite membership (client contracts and investment guidelines, custodial statements, etc.).
3. Survivorship bias in the composites: terminated accounts have been removed for historical periods as well.
4. Lack of historical records to support assets under management. This is particularly problematic when building composites from scratch; you need to ensure all historical, discretionary, fee-paying accounts are in at least one composite.

5. Performance calculation issues:
   a. Monthly portfolio valuations required beginning 1/1/01; quarterly valuations required prior to 1/1/01
   b. Trade date accounting beginning 1/1/05
   c. Interest accrual on fixed income for all periods
   d. Daily weighting of cash flows beginning 1/1/05
   e. Unique fee issues, such as not knowing fees charged on wrap accounts or not booking all fees to the accounting system.
6. Composite policies that have been inconsistently applied historically, or policies applied historically were not documented.
7. Books and records issues surrounding a portable performance track record.
8. Lack of clear understanding regarding "investment discretion" for GIPS purposes, and/or lack of conceptual direction for meaningful composites.
9. Operational challenges when creating composites that include carve-outs, wrap accounts or other account types with difficult valuation or data integration issues.

If any of these obstacles might apply at your firm, contact a GIPS verifier/consultant to discuss possible solutions.

2. **Verification**. The verifier reviews the same documentation as in a preverification, with expectation that any areas of non-compliance have been corrected. The verification process also tests supporting documentation on a sample basis. This engagement will result in either a management letter outlining areas of non-compliance or the issuance of an opinion letter stating that your firm has complied with all the composite construction requirements of the GIPS standards on a firm-wide basis, and that your firm's processes and procedures are designed to calculate and present performance results in compliance with the GIPS standards.

3. **Performance Examination.** A drill-down into one or more specific composite's performance track record to affirm whether the underlying valuations, calculation methodologies, and transaction records for the composite in question adhere to GIPS requirements.

Options for Implementing a GIPS Compliance Program

Implementing and maintaining GIPS compliance requires time, resources, and expertise. The question for most firms is: how much dedicated GIPS expertise can you afford to have on staff? It may make sense for the largest firms to hire or train several specialists in GIPS compliance. It's a bigger challenge for smaller firms, where portfolio managers, traders, and operations staff are already wearing multiple hats, and chief compliance officers have their hands full with everyday SEC compliance. Whether or not one or more GIPS specialists are hired or trained, the creation of a GIPS Committee that includes members from each of the firm's key departments (e.g., compliance, operations, portfolio management, trading, performance measurement, IT and marketing) can greatly enhance the efficiency and effectiveness of the process of becoming compliant.

Regardless of internal resources, if you plan to have your compliance verified, you should engage a verifier early on, because the costs of preverification services are usually nominal if such services are provided in conjunction with a verification, and experienced verifiers are a natural resource for an informed GIPS consultant. Specialized GIPS consultants bring to the process the experience of working with other firms facing similar firm-specific challenges and solutions.

While maintaining independence is critical for any consultant also providing independent verification, such firms can provide suggestions on how to implement a GIPS compliance project. They can assess books and records and data integrity challenges and prevent ineffective fundamental decisions around composite building.

For firms further along with process, GIPS consultants can suggest necessary adjustments to ensure GIPS-compliant GIPS requirements and interpretations, something many firms simply do not have time for on their own. Working performance measurement and reporting practices on an ongoing basis and take on the responsibility of staying current with and communicating changing GIPS requirements and interpretations, something many firms simply do not have time for on their own. Working with GIPS experts can help keep overhead and training costs down, while providing greater assurance that you are getting the right answers and guidance in establishing and maintaining your program.

GIPS Policy and Procedures Checklist

At a minimum, a firm's policies and procedures should address:

- ✓ Firm definition.
- ✓ Definition of discretion.
- ✓ Definitions for each composite.
- ✓ Policy regarding timing of inclusion/exclusion of new/closed account in a composite and accounts with changes in investment mandates.
- ✓ Policy with regard to minimum account size requirements, if any.
- ✓ Method for computing time-weighted rates of returns, gross/net.
- ✓ Policy with regard to treatment of significant cash flows.
- ✓ Method for computing composite returns.
- ✓ Treatment of special issues relevant to the firm's performance: portability, carve-outs, SMAs, pricing sources, and foreign exchange rates.

The Role of Technology

By now, of course, most investment firms' "books and records" are virtually all electronic. Given that data integrity is one of the key requirements of GIPS, technology has an important role to play in GIPS compliance.

Today's most advanced portfolio management, accounting, and reporting systems offer a high level of flexibility in the ways data can be organized and managed. They allow quick access to portfolio information for verification and portfolio examination purposes. With the latest technology, they can even automate composite creation and management based on user-defined rules and criteria—making one of the main hurdles in GIPS compliance far more manageable.

Using the most up-to-date technology also helps ensure the accuracy and consistency of data used for performance measurement and reporting. Customized reporting capabilities enable firms to create and generate performance reports in accordance with GIPS. And, in the event of an SEC inquiry, the right answers are readily available.

Generally, the right technology can help ease the administrative burden of compliance while bringing greater speed, efficiency, and accuracy to the process—ultimately enabling managers to sleep at night with greater confidence that their performance reporting is GIPS compliant.

Clearly, adhering to the GIPS standards is in the best interest of any investment firm that wants to compete effectively and fairly. It helps you build a framework for implementing industry best practices, while providing you with an effective marketing tool and a competitive advantage. Most significantly, it helps engender trust on the part of clients and prospects. All these advantages are further reinforced and strengthened by expert third-party verification.

The issue for most firms is not whether to comply with GIPS, but how to accomplish it successfully. Whether that means adding GIPS experts to staff or turning to outside professionals will depend largely on the firm's size, available resources, and overall business strategy. Either way, given the importance of GIPS compliance from both the regulatory and marketing perspectives, independent verification by qualified GIPS experts is an additional key consideration. There is simply no substitute for focused, in-depth knowledge of the GIPS standards and how they have been applied historically. The value of that expertise will be realized in the form of one or more confidence in a regulatory examination, a more efficient compliance process, and more new business won.

Resources
  GIPS: www.gipsstandards.org
  CFA Institute: www.cfainstitute.org
  Ashland Partners: www.ashlandpartners.com

About Advent Software, Inc.
Advent Software, Inc., a global firm, has provided trusted solutions to the world's leading financial professionals since 1983. Firms in more than 60 countries rely on Advent technology to run their mission-critical operations. Advent's quality software, data, services, and tools enable financial professionals to improve service and communication to their clients, allowing them to grow their business while controlling costs. Advent is the only financial services software company to be awarded the Service Capability and Performance certification for its service and support organizations.

About Ashland Partners
Ashland Partners is the leading CPA firm providing GIPS compliance and verification services to the investment management community. With strategic offices around the world and focused professionals, Ashland delivers innovative compliance solutions through effective one-on-one relationships with their clients.

ADVENT SOFTWARE, INC.

A challenge in performance calculations arises when the market values are not readily available. For U.S. publicly traded equity securities, market values are usually readily available in the form of the daily closing price. Likewise, any other security or commodity that is actively traded has its market value readily available in the form of its market-determined price. Since market prices are unavailable for illiquid securities, such as equity or debt securities, that are not regularly traded on a daily basis, the fair market value of those securities must be determined using a "fair value" method. Fair value methods generally utilize the observed market value of related securities to impute the values of illiquid securities. For example, the current fair value of a plot of land is generally not its last sale price, since real estate trades very infrequently and the sale price might have been the result of a transaction that occurred years or decades ago. The value of land can be imputed by observing the recent sale prices of land with similar characteristics and in a similar location, adjusting for acreage. Likewise, the imputed fair value of illiquid securities relies on the observed market prices of related securities. Investment firms who hold such securities typically utilize third party vendors who specialize in fair value analysis. Having a third party calculate the fair value also helps avoid the moral hazard problem of having the investment manager determine the value of something that affects the manager's reported performance.

Another complexity in portfolio return calculations arises when there are cash flows in the form of cash withdrawals from the account or cash deposits to the account. The return calculation must account for the cash flow by splitting the return calculation into two periods and linking those periods' returns. Specifically, consider a month in which there is a significant cash flow of CF_{t-k} in the middle of the month. Let time t denote the last day of the month and assume that the cash flow arrives k days before the end of the month, where $k < 21$. Finally, we consider a month that has 21 days, since the average number of trading days in a month is 21. In this way, there are three relevant dates: $t - 21$, $t - k$, and t.

As in Equation 6.1, the beginning market value for our calculation is MV_{t-21}. The market value of those same assets at time $t - k$ is reflected in the pre-flow market value or MV_{t-k}^{pre}. Note that the pre-flow market value at time $t - k$ ignores the cash flow that comes in during that same day. Using the pre-flow market value and the value at the beginning of the month, we calculate the return over the first period within the month as:

$$r_{t-21,t-k} = \frac{MV_{t-k}^{pre} - MV_{t-21}}{MV_{t-21}} \tag{6.2}$$

We now calculate the post-flow value of the assets by adding the cash flow at time $t - k$. The post-flow market value of the portfolio at time $t - k$ is:

$$MV_{t-k}^{post} = MV_{t-k}^{pre} + CF_{t-k} \tag{6.3}$$

The post-flow assets are a part of the portfolio from this point on, so the performance for the second period within the month utilizes this post-flow market value as its beginning value. The portfolio return from time $t - k$ to time t is calculated as:

$$r_{t-k,t} = \frac{MV_t - MV_{t-k}^{post}}{MV_{t-k}^{post}} \tag{6.4}$$

Note that we omit the superscript (pre or post) for periods in which there is no flow, since the market values are unambiguous in these periods. The final step is to link the two periods' returns to calculate the entire month's returns, as given by:

$$r_{t-21,t} = (1 + r_{t-21,t-k}) \times (1 + r_{t-k,t}) - 1 \tag{6.5}$$

In summary, the first period's return is calculated using the pre-flow value of the portfolio as the ending market value. The second period's return then uses the post-flow market value of the assets as the beginning market value. The full month's return is calculated by compounding the two periods' returns.

A further complication in the calculation of performance arises from cash flows relating to the initiation of the performance calculation. This issue becomes especially important for strategies that are benchmarked to a particular non-cash index. Any cash into a fund must be invested in the underlying portfolio securities. This process, known as a transition, results in direct transaction costs and indirect performance gains or losses as the cash is being traded for the portfolio's underlying securities. For example, suppose a portfolio is benchmarked to the S&P 500 Index and holds a large number of S&P 500 stocks. On the day the cash flow arrives, the cash effectively earns 0% until it is "equitized" (i.e., converted to stock). The portfolio manager must trade the cash for the portfolio stocks, which results in transaction costs. As a result, the portfolio performance will look relatively low compared to the S&P 500 on this day, since the cash earns nothing until converted to stock and the transaction costs lower the account value. Note that this negative relative performance has nothing to do with the portfolio manager's strategy or ability. Rather, the relative performance is due to the cash flow. Therefore, most investment managers and clients set a performance date that is subsequent to the cash flow date.

To illustrate how the performance calculation can be done in the presence of a large cash flow, consider the example shown in Exhibit 6.3. In this example, a portfolio is benchmarked to the S&P 500 Index. It has a market value of approximately $700,000 when a cash inflow of $300,000 occurs at the beginning of the day on November 7, 2012. The portfolio manager has agreed with the client that performance begins as of the same-day market close if the cash flow arrives before 3 PM New York time or as of the next-day market close if the cash flow arrives after 3 PM New York time. The 3 PM cutoff is to allow the investment manager time to determine and submit an order to convert the cash to the strategy's weights prior to the close of the market that day. Furthermore, the agreement sets forth that the manager will attempt to equitize the cash with "market on close" orders.

Exhibit 6.3 Example of a Monthly Performance Calculation When a Large Cash Flow Occurs during the Month

A cash flow of $300,000 arrives at the beginning of the day on November 7, 2012. Performance begins as of Market Close on November 7, 2012. The cash flow is equitized (i.e., converted to equity securities through transactions) using "Market on Close" on November 7, 2012. No other cash flows during the month of November. The calculation requires that the market values be calculated at the end of the previous month (October 31, 2012), on the day of the cash flow, and at the end of the current month (November 30, 2012). Note that the market value of the portfolio on the day of the cash flow is calculated both Pre-Flow and Post-Flow. The Pre-Flow market value reflects only the value of the securities and cash that were held prior to the cash flow. The Post-Flow market value reflects the value of all securities, including those that were purchased as a result of the cash flow.

Security	October 31, 2012			November 6, 2012			November 7, 2012 (Pre-Flow)		
	Shares Held	Price at Close	Market Value at Close	Shares Held	Price at Close	Market Value at Close	Shares Held	Price at Close	Market Value at Close
A	800	35.99	28,792.00	800	38.28	30,624.00	800	37.58	30,064.00
AEE	1,200	32.88	39,456.00	1,200	32.10	38,520.00	1,200	31.39	37,668.00
APC	600	68.81	41,286.00	600	73.07	43,842.00	600	70.41	42,246.00
BF/B	500	64.06	32,030.00	500	64.60	32,300.00	500	64.40	32,200.00
BMS	800	33.05	26,440.00	800	33.79	27,032.00	800	33.55	26,840.00
FLR	600	55.85	33,510.00	600	54.49	32,694.00	600	53.23	31,938.00
FOSL	400	87.10	34,840.00	400	84.24	33,696.00	400	83.93	33,572.08
FSLR	1,400	24.30	34,020.00	1,400	24.79	34,707.82	1,400	23.67	33,142.48
GWW	200	201.41	40,282.00	200	203.08	40,616.00	200	198.44	39,688.00
JBL	2,000	17.34	34,680.00	2,000	18.48	36,960.00	2,000	17.85	35,700.00
L	800	42.28	33,824.00	800	42.33	33,864.00	800	41.20	32,960.00
MAC	700	57.00	39,900.00	700	57.36	40,152.00	700	56.69	39,683.00
MCK	400	93.31	37,324.00	400	93.48	37,392.00	400	94.69	37,876.00
MDLZ	1,500	26.55	39,825.00	1,500	26.49	39,735.00	1,500	26.25	39,375.00
MMC	1,000	34.03	34,030.00	1,000	34.92	34,920.00	1,000	34.50	34,500.00
NTAP	600	26.91	16,146.00	600	28.14	16,884.00	600	27.73	16,638.00
NVDA	3,100	11.98	37,122.50	3,100	13.01	40,331.00	3,100	12.61	39,090.38
OXY	500	78.96	39,480.00	500	79.58	39,790.00	500	77.45	38,725.00

(Continued)

(Continued)

Security	October 31, 2012			November 6, 2012			November 7, 2012 (Pre-Flow)		
	Shares Held	Price at Close	Market Value at Close	Shares Held	Price at Close	Market Value at Close	Shares Held	Price at Close	Market Value at Close
PETM	500	66.39	33,195.00	500	67.25	33,625.00	500	66.64	33,320.00
T	500	34.59	17,295.00	500	34.80	17,400.00	500	33.64	16,819.10
WYNN	200	121.06	24,212.00	200	112.21	22,442.00	200	111.03	22,206.00
Cash			5,823.43			6,043.62			6,043.84
Portfolio Market Value			$703,512.93			$713,570.44			$700,294.88

Security	November 7, 2012 (Post-Flow)			November 30, 2012			Trades on November 7, 2012			
	Shares Held	Price at Close	Market Value at Close	Shares Held	Price at Close	Market Value at Close	Shares Held	Trade Price	Market Value at Close	Comm.
A	1,100	37.58	41,338.00	1,100	38.29	42,119.00	300	37.58	11,274.00	8.95
AEE	1,700	31.39	53,363.00	1,700	29.97	50,949.00	500	31.39	15,695.00	8.95
APC	900	70.41	63,369.00	900	73.19	65,871.00	300	70.41	21,123.00	8.95
BF/B	700	64.4	45,080.00	700	70.18	49,126.00	200	64.40	12,880.00	8.95
BMS	1,100	33.55	36,905.00	1,100	33.60	36,960.00	300	33.55	10,065.00	8.95
FLR	800	53.23	42,584.00	800	53.08	42,464.00	200	53.23	10,646.00	8.95
FOSL	600	83.9302	50,358.12	600	86.44	51,864.00	200	83.93	16,786.00	8.95
FSLR	2,000	23.6732	47,346.40	2,000	26.99	53,980.00	600	23.67	14,202.00	8.95
GWW	300	198.44	59,532.00	300	194.02	58,206.00	100	198.44	19,844.00	8.95
JBL	2,900	17.85	51,765.00	2,900	19.00	55,100.00	900	17.85	16,065.00	8.95
L	1,100	41.2	45,320.00	1,100	40.88	44,968.00	300	41.20	12,360.00	8.95
MAC	1,000	56.69	56,690.00	1,000	56.50	56,500.00	300	56.69	17,007.00	8.95
MCK	600	94.69	56,814.00	600	94.47	56,682.00	200	94.69	18,938.00	8.95
MDLZ	2,100	26.25	55,125.00	2,100	25.89	54,369.00	600	26.25	15,750.00	8.95
MMC	1,400	34.5	48,300.00	1,400	35.22	49,308.00	400	34.50	13,800.00	8.95
NTAP	900	27.73	24,957.00	900	31.71	28,539.00	300	27.73	8,319.00	8.95

Security	November 7, 2012 (Post-Flow)			November 30, 2012			Trades on November 7, 2012			
	Shares Held	Price at Close	Market Value at Close	Shares Held	Price at Close	Market Value at Close	Shares Held	Trade Price	Market Value at Close	Comm.
NVDA	4,400	12.6098	55,483.12	4,400	11.97	52,668.00	1,300	12.61	16,393.00	8.95
OXY	700	77.45	54,215.00	700	75.21	52,647.00	200	77.45	15,490.00	8.95
PETM	700	66.64	46,648.00	700	70.66	49,462.00	200	66.64	13,328.00	8.95
T	700	33.6382	23,546.74	700	34.13	23,891.00	200	33.64	6,728.00	8.95
WYNN	300	111.03	33,309.00	300	112.40	33,720.00	100	111.03	11,103.00	8.95
Cash			8,059.89			9,974.00				
Portfolio Market Value			**$1,000,108.27**			**$1,019,367.00**			**$297,796.00**	**$187.95**

Cash at Close on 11/7/2012 = Cash at Close on 11/6/2012 + Interest on on 11/7/2012 + Cash Inflow – Cost of Security Purchases – Cost of Commissions

$5,011.67	= $6,043.62	+ $0.12	+ $300,000.00 – $297,796.00	– $187.95

Return from October 31, 2012 to November 7, 2012 (Pre-Flow):

$$r_1 = \frac{700{,}294.88 - 703{,}512.93}{703{,}512.93} = -0.4574\%$$

Return from November 7, 2012 (Post-Flow) to November 30, 2012:

$$r_2 = \frac{\$1{,}019{,}367.00 - \$1{,}000{,}108.27}{\$1{,}000{,}108.27} = +1.9257\%$$

Return for month of November 2012:

$$r_{November} = (1 - 0.004574) \times (1 + .019257) - 1 = 1.46\%$$

The exhibit shows the market value of the portfolio's holdings on the four dates in 2012: October 31, November 6, November 7, and November 30. Notice that November 7, 2012, is shown with both pre-flow and post-flow values. Furthermore, the post-flow values reflect the portfolio after the cash has been equitized. In this case, the commissions on the trades to convert the cash to portfolio holdings are not counted against the investment manager, since the post-flow market values are determined after the equitizing transactions have taken place. Had the cash flow remained as cash until after the performance date, any transaction costs would be counted in the manager's performance. Following Equation 6.2, we calculate the performance between October 31 and November 7 (using the pre-flow market values) to be -0.46%. Similarly, the post-flow market values are used according to equation 6.3 and 6.4 to calculate the performance from November 7 through November 30 to be 1.93%. These returns are compounded according to Equation 6.5 to determine the strategy's performance 1.46% for the entire month of November. We include as an end-of-chapter exercise the calculation of the portfolio's performance in this example if there had not been a cash flow during the month. In this case, the difference in the return is less than 10 basis points and is due to the fact that the trades are executed in round lots, which causes the security weightings to differ slightly after the cash flow occurs.

The importance of the timing and performance date of the cash flow can be seen in this example. Had the $300,000 cash flow been included at the end of the day on November 6 (i.e., the beginning of the day on November 7), the return would have appeared to have been higher. Indeed, using pre-flow market values on November 6, we would calculate a return of 1.43% from October 31 to November 6. Adding the $300,000 cash flow to get the post-flow value for November 6, we calculate the return from November 6 to November 30 to be 0.57%, resulting in a compound return of 2.01% for the entire month. The higher return occurs because the market and portfolio stocks experience a negative return of almost 2% on November 7. The zero return to cash on this down day increases the measured return.

It might appear that the 2.01% is the more accurate measure of the performance of the client's overall portfolio, since the cash is, after all, in the account for the entire day on November 7. However, the important point here is that the performance that we are calculating is that of the investment manager's strategy, not the client's overall performance. Since the investment manager's strategy is only implemented after the market on close order, the calculation presented in the exhibit is the more accurate measure of the investment manager's return. We should not give the manager credit for having cash during the day on November 7 when the market moves down, just as we should not penalize the manager in a situation in which the market moves up while a cash flow is pending. Our purpose is not to present these calculations as acceptable alternatives that are at the *ex post* discretion of the manager. Rather, we highlight the difference in these calculations to emphasize the importance of the *ex ante* agreement between the investment manager and the client as to the starting date of performance on significant cash flows and how cash flows are treated. Finally, we note that small cash flows are deemed insignificant and are usually handled without explicitly considering the transaction costs. In this example, had the cash flow been $3000, the impact of using November 6 versus November 7 on the performance calculation would have been negligible. Likewise, had the cash flow been $30,000, the difference in the treatments of the cash flow might result in a performance difference of only a basis point or so.

As illustrated in the example, the determination of the performance date can be particularly important for investment managers and student-managed investment funds at the start-up stage, since the calculated performance, and especially the relative performance of the fund against a specific benchmark, can be greatly affected. No single performance date is considered correct, though the market close date described above is quite common. It is critical that the investment manager and the client or portfolio beneficiary understand and agree on the performance date and the portfolio transition prior to the funding of the account. Having the transition plan and performance date that are clearly articulated in the investment management agreement helps assure that the parties share a mutual understanding of an issue that could have a significant impact on the portfolio's reported performance.

Performance Reporting

Whether the ultimate goal is to preserve capital or to earn a high growth rate, the percentage return on a portfolio is the ultimate goal of investment management and the portfolio performance report is the ultimate scorecard. Performance reports allow an investor to monitor the portfolio's progress. As such, performance reports should be made on a regular basis. It is common for investment managers to issue formal performance reports on a quarterly basis, though monthly reports or updates are also common.

Exhibit 6.4 shows a quarterly performance summary from Southern Illinois University's student-managed investment fund. This summary contains several items that are standard in most investment management firms' reports to clients. First, note that there are multiple periods reported. Each period ends on the "as of" date of the report, which is June 30, 2013, in this case. It is common practice to report the most recent quarter, year-to-date (YTD), and 1-year periods as the actual percentage return on the portfolio over those horizons. For reports that are made on months that are not quarter-ends (e.g., January, February, April, etc.), the 1-month and/or quarter-to-date returns are also commonly reported. The returns over 3-month and 6-month periods are reported by some managers. We caution against reporting too many short-term periods, as this might suggest that the investment manager puts too much emphasis on short-term returns. Beyond one year, it is most common to report 3-, 5-, and 10-year returns. Beyond 10 years, multiples of 5 years are also common.

Exhibit 6.4 Quarterly Performance Summary from Southern Illinois University's Saluki Student Investment Fund

Saluki Student Investment Fund
SIU Foundation Portfolio

Performance Summary
As of June 30, 2013

	Quarter	Calendar YTD	1-Year	3-Year	5-Year	7-Year	10-Year	Since Inception
SSIF	1.24%	15.15%	25.31%	22.34%	10.01%	9.67%	11.81%	6.97%
S&P 400 Benchmark*	1.00%	14.59%	25.18%	19.45%	8.91%	7.72%	10.74%	8.48%
Difference	*0.24%*	*0.56%*	*0.12%*	*2.89%*	*1.10%*	*1.95%*	*1.06%*	*-1.51%*
Tracking Error**			1.75%	2.42%	4.36%	4.37%	4.86%	5.74%
Information Ratio***			0.07	1.20	0.25	0.45	0.22	-0.26
Months > Benchmark			42%	56%	55%	52%	52%	49%

Periods greater than one year are annualized. Inception date is June 1, 2000.
* Performance of the benchmark is reported for the S&P Midcap 400 Total Return Index (Source: Bloomberg SPTRMDCP Index)
** Tracking error is annualized and based on monthly return differences relative to the benchmark.
*** Information ratio is the ratio of the annualized relative return divided by the tracking error.
SIU Foundation portfolio value as of June 30, 2013: $1,203,239.08.

The 7-year horizon is also often used, especially for a strategy that has existed for more than 7 years, but less than 10 years. Finally, the "Since Inception" (also sometimes referred to as inception-to-date, or ITD) period reflects the performance of the portfolio or strategy since it began its most recent continuous run.

In words, the performance summary in Exhibit 6.4 shows that the SSIF portfolio has a return of 1.24% for the 3-month period ending June 30, 2013, compared to the benchmark's return of 1.00% over the same period. That is, the portfolio outperformed the benchmark by 0.24% in the second quarter of 2013. Likewise, the portfolio outperformed the benchmark by 56 basis points for the first six months of 2013. The average annualized return on the portfolio over the three years ending June 30, 2013, is 22.34%, which is 2.89% higher than the benchmark S&P Midcap 400 Index's 19.45% average annualized return over the same period.

The SSIF's performance summary notes that "periods greater than one year are annualized." Reporting annualized time-weighted average returns is standard practice. It is also best practice to use geometric (i.e., compounded) average returns, which are typically calculated from monthly returns. Specifically, if a strategy has a monthly return of r_t in month t within a period of T months, where $T > 12$, the annualized average return is calculated as:

$$\bar{r}_a = \left(\prod_{t=1}^{T}(1+r_t) \right)^{12/T} - 1 \tag{6.6}$$

The annualized average puts the average return on a "per year" basis, making each period easy to compare the others. It is not good practice to annualize returns for periods less than one year. That is, monthly or quarterly returns should be reported without an adjustment.

The performance summary in Exhibit 6.4 reports the benchmark returns over the same periods as the portfolio or strategy. The benchmark returns are particularly important for strategies that have an explicit benchmark. For those that do not have a formal benchmark, the performance of one or more indexes of similar asset classes may be reported for informal benchmarking purposes. The benchmark returns are calculated using the same method as is used to calculate the portfolio returns. With compound (i.e., geometric average) returns, the order of operation matters. Note that the compound returns are first calculated for the portfolio and the benchmark in Exhibit 6.4. The average relative return is reported as the "Difference" in the row below the SSIF and S&P 400 Benchmark returns. It is incorrect to calculate an average annualized relative return by using compounding monthly relative returns. We illustrate this in two exercises at the end of this chapter. In short, the relative return calculation should be the last calculation, and it is simply the difference between the portfolio return and the benchmark return over that horizon.

The last three rows of data in the performance summary in Exhibit 6.4 report the tracking error, information ratio, and months greater than the benchmark. Recall from Chapter 4 that the information ratio is the average relative return divided by the tracking error. In some sense, the information ratio is redundant in this report, since it can be calculated from the numbers already present in the report. However, it is convenient to have important performance measures calculated in the report. The "months greater than the benchmark" is commonly referred to as the batting average of a strategy. The baseball-inspired statistic counts a month in which the portfolio beats the benchmark as a "hit." While the batting average does not provide information about the magnitude of the relative return (just as a "hit" does not indicate how many bases the batter achieves), it does provide an indication of how consistently the strategy beats the benchmark. A batting average less than 0.500 might still result in a positive average relative return if the amount by which the strategy beats the benchmark in "hit" months exceeds the amount by which it lags the benchmark in other months.[2]

---

[2] Baseball fans might think of the average relative return as akin to the slugging percentage. In baseball, the batting average and slugging percentage are different, but related to one another. Similarly, in investment management, the batting average and average relative return are related, but the average relative return is almost always the more relevant statistic.

The statistics in the last three rows of Exhibit 6.4 are not compulsory items in all performance summaries, though they may be relevant for both the investment manager and its client. Tracking error may be of concern for strategy that has a specific benchmark, especially if tracking error is an integral part of the strategy. Indeed, the tracking error might be as important as the average relative return for a strategy that is mandated to track a specific benchmark. For example, an index fund that claims to track the S&P 500 might have an average relative return close to zero, but would only be deemed a good substitute for the index if its tracking error is low. Additionally, if tracking error minimization or information ratio maximization are objectives of the investment process, as they are for the SSIF, they are relevant statistics for any performance summary.

As with the presentations discussed in the previous chapter, it is important that performance reports and summaries be presented in a clear and consistent manner. Frequent changes to the format of information that is presented can be confusing, especially to those who only see the performance once each quarter. Think of the layout of the report in terms of the layout of a grocery store. Customers of a grocery store appreciate consistency in the layout so that they can readily find the items they need. When the customer only needs a gallon of milk and loaf of bread, the consistent layout allows the customer to quickly and efficiently find those items. The customers are happy to shop at the grocery store, knowing that they can get in and out of the store quickly with the items they need. Likewise, such consistency in an investment manager's performance summary allows clients to become familiar with the location of information that is important to them. In return, such familiarity and ease of access help build confidence in the quality of the information and perhaps even in the manager. This is especially important in a student-managed investment fund, since the turnover in personnel means that the same people will not be present to answer to the client year after year. Furthermore, graduates of the program would be able to view a performance report years later and be familiar with the content of the report.

Supplemental performance reports can also provide useful information to an investment manager's internal and external constituents. A common supplemental report is a history of period-by-period (such as monthly or annual) returns for a strategy. Such reports might be used internally or externally to conduct performance analysis as describe later in this chapter. Additionally, these reports provide information about the historical distribution of returns from an investment strategy. For example, Exhibit 6.5 shows the annual returns for the student-managed investment fund from Exhibit 6.4. In this case, the report shows both calendar-year returns and fiscal-year returns for the SSIF's client, the SIU Foundation. It is easy to verify that the geometric average of the calendar-year returns is equal to the annualized since inception returns in Exhibit 6.4 using a total of 157 months from the inception to the "as of" date of the report. So, it might seem that this supplemental report adds little information. However, this report shows that the strategy generally rises and falls with the benchmark index. Indeed, the portfolio and the benchmark had their best years in

Exhibit 6.5 Supplemental Year-By-Year Historical Performance Report from Southern Illinois University's Saluki Student Investment Fund

As of June 30, 2013

Fiscal Year	2001	2002	2003	2004	2005	2006	2007	2008	2009	2010	2011	2012	2013
SSIF	-2.62%	-13.03%	-4.01%	18.75%	19.31%	12.95%	24.99%	-5.28%	-29.40%	24.67%	48.10%	-1.34%	25.31%
S&P 400 Benchmark*	8.87%	-4.72%	-0.71%	27.99%	14.03%	12.98%	18.51%	-7.34%	-28.02%	24.93%	39.38%	-2.33%	25.18%
Difference	-11.50%	-8.31%	-3.29%	-9.23%	5.29%	-0.03%	6.49%	2.05%	-1.38%	-0.26%	8.72%	0.99%	0.12%

Calendar Year	2000**	2001	2002	2003	2004	2005	2006	2007	2008	2009	2010	2011	2012	2013***
SSIF	-2.88%	-10.12%	-19.13%	34.14%	13.69%	13.97%	13.64%	9.93%	-34.43%	30.84%	32.59%	3.40%	16.25%	15.15%
S&P 400 Benchmark*	9.41%	-0.60%	-14.51%	35.62%	16.48%	12.56%	10.32%	7.98%	-36.23%	37.38%	26.64%	-1.73%	17.88%	14.59%
Difference	-12.30%	-9.52%	-4.62%	-1.48%	-2.79%	1.42%	3.32%	1.95%	1.80%	-6.54%	5.94%	5.13%	-1.63%	0.56%

Fiscal Year ends on June 30 of the given year.

* Performance of the benchmark is reported for the S&P Midcap 400 Total Return Index (Source: Bloomberg SPTRMDCP Index)

** Partial year. Performance begins June 1, 2000.

*** Partial year.

2003, 2009, and 2010 and had their worst years in 2002 and 2008. Furthermore, the variability of the relative returns is shown, with the portfolio having returns 1230 basis points below the benchmark in its first partial year and 594 basis points above the benchmark in 2010. Moreover, the story of how the SSIF lagged the benchmark by an average of 151 basis points per year since inception (from Exhibit 6.4) is clearer, showing that most of the negative relative performance occurred in its first few years, while the portfolio underperformed the benchmark in only three of the last ten calendar years. Such supplemental reports can help provide context to the performance summary information.

In conclusion, performance reports should be consistent. The report should provide information that is consistent with the strategy or mandate. As such, the report should include not only the average annualized returns of the portfolio, but also the returns of relevant benchmarks and statistics, such as standard deviation or tracking error, that are meaningful to the investment process. The report should also be consistent through time, allowing the consumer of such reports to become familiar with the layout and content so that information is readily accessible.

Performance Analysis

Performance analysis is an attempt to provide an understanding of the sources of risk and returns to an investment strategy. In short, the goal of performance analysis is to explain a strategy's performance. Such an explanation can be beneficial both internally to an investment organization and externally to the organization's current and prospective clients because it has the potential to provide insight into the investment philosophy and process of the organization. To do so, the performance analysis should be constructed in a way that is consistent with the investment philosophy and process. In other words, performance analysis should be constructed to measure the contributions from the opportunities identified in the investment philosophy and the objectives defined in the investment process.

We discuss the two primary forms of performance analysis: holdings-based performance attribution and returns-based performance analysis. Performance attribution breaks performance into components based on security-specific characteristics, such as sector or size. Attribution analysis relies on portfolio weights and the underlying security returns over a specific period. Returns-based analysis utilizes portfolio-level returns to estimate their statistical relationship to economic or market factors. Each form has its strengths and each type of analysis can complement the other.

Performance Attribution

The goal of performance attribution is to identify the sources of a portfolio's relative returns compared to a benchmark. We build on the analysis in Chapter 4 discussing the sources of portfolio returns and utilize similar terminology and notation relating to portfolio weights and returns, benchmark weights and returns, active weights, and relative returns. We focus on performance attribution methods of performance that are attributed (pun intended) to Brinson and are commonly referred to as "Brinson Attribution."[3] The general attribution method is widely accepted, but its implementation can differ in subtle ways. We attempt to point out where there are commonly seen variations in practice.

Performance attribution is generally inspired by the notion that an active portfolio manager can beat a benchmark in at least one of two ways: (1) the manager can allocate investments toward outperforming factors, characteristics, or sectors; or (2) the manager can select individual securities that outperform. The first method is attributed to an *allocation effect*, also referred to as *sector allocation*. The second method is attributed to a *security selection effect*, or simply *security selection*. The goal of performance attribution is to decompose relative performance into these two main categories to determine each category's contribution to the portfolio's total relative return.

Recall from Chapter 4 that a portfolio's relative return is calculated by subtracting the benchmark return. We restate Equation 4.8, but drop the time subscript for ease of exposition in this chapter, so that the portfolio's relative return is:

$$r_p - r_b = \sum_{i=1}^{N} w_i^p \times r_i - \sum_{i=1}^{N} w_i^b \times r_i = \sum_{i=1}^{N} (w_i^p - w_i^b) \times r_{i,t} \qquad (6.7)$$

Our goal is to determine and identify the sources of the relative returns. To do so, consider grouping securities by characteristic *s*, which we generically refer to as a *sector*. The sector might be a proper sector (e.g., financials, industrials, etc.), an asset class (e.g., stocks, bonds, etc.), or a characteristic (firm size, duration or term, etc.). We begin with a restatement of Equation 4.11, but we drop the time subscript for ease of exposition. We let *i* enumerate securities and *s* enumerate sectors. Each security *i* has a portfolio weight of w_i^p and there are N_s securities in sector *s* in the market. The portfolio's overall exposure to this sector is the sum of all portfolio weights for securities that belong to sector *s*, as given by:

$$w_s^p = \sum_{i=1}^{N_s} w_i^p \qquad (6.8)$$

---

[3] See Brinson, G. P., and N. Fachler, *Measuring Non-US Equity Portfolio Performance*, *Journal of Portfolio Management*, Spring 1985, pp. 73–76; Brinson, G. P., L. R. Hood, and G. L. Beebower, *Determinants of Portfolio Performance*, *Financial Analysts Journal*, July-August 1986, pp. 39–44; and Brinson, G. P., B. D. Singer, and G. L. Beebower, *Determinants of Portfolio Performance II: An Update*, *Financial Analysts Journal*, May-Jun 1991, pp. 40–48.

Note that N_s refers to the number of sector s securities in the entire market, not just the number of such securities in the portfolio. Any sector s securities that exist in the market but not in the portfolio have a portfolio weight of zero. We denote the number of sectors in the market as S. Of course, the weight in all sectors must sum to one, as given by:

$$1 = \sum_{i=s}^{S} w_s^p \tag{6.9}$$

Portfolio p experiences a return to sector s over a given time period of:

$$r_s^p = \frac{1}{w_s^p} \sum_{i=1}^{N_s} w_i^p r_i \tag{6.10}$$

Note that we divide the weighted sum of the returns by the total portfolio weight in sector s in order to get a proper weighted average of all sector s securities' returns within the portfolio. In essence, we are treating each sector as its own sub-portfolio.

Since the benchmark is simply another portfolio, we can express the same quantities from equations 6.8 and 6.10 for the benchmark. Specifically, the benchmark's weight in sector s is:

$$w_s^b = \sum_{i=1}^{N_s} w_i^b \tag{6.11}$$

and the benchmark's return in sector s is:

$$r_s^b = \frac{1}{w_s^b} \sum_{i=1}^{N_s} w_i^b r_i \tag{6.12}$$

The difference between the sector weights in equations 6.7 and 6.10 contribute to the allocation effect, since the weights represent allocations to sectors. Specifically, the contribution to the portfolio's relative return that is due to an allocation to sector s is given by:

$$r_s^{Alloc} = (w_s^p - w_s^b) \times r_s^b \tag{6.13}$$

Note that we use the return to the sector for the benchmark (not the portfolio) in this calculation, since the purpose is to isolate the impact of the portfolio active sector weight, not its security selection within the sector. In essence, this calculation would explain all of the portfolio's relative return if the investment manager simply invests proportionally in all of the benchmark's stocks, but alters the weights allocated to each sector.

An alternative calculation of the sector allocation effect is to use the sector's relative return compared to the overall benchmark, as given by:

$$r_s^{Alloc(relative)} = (w_s^p - w_s^b) \times (r_s^b - r_b) \tag{6.14}$$

To determine the total sector allocation contribution from all sectors, we sum across all sectors' allocation effects, as given by:

$$r^{Alloc} = \sum_{s=1}^{S} w_s^p r_s^{Alloc} = \sum_{s=1}^{S} w_s^p r_s^{Alloc(relative)} \tag{6.15}$$

Note that the total portfolio sector allocation contribution is the same regardless of whether the specification in Equation 6.13 or 6.14 is used. As we discuss in the example below, the decision of whether to use sector returns as in Equation 6.13 or sector relative returns as in Equation 6.14 usually depends on the objective of the portfolio and the desired meaning of the performance attribution.

The attribution of portfolio returns to stock selection derives from the returns to the portfolio's sector securities compared to returns of the benchmark's sector securities. As with sector allocation, the goal is to isolate the security selection skill from the asset allocation skill. Using the same approach as above, we first consider the situation in which there is no active weight to the sector and only consider the return of the portfolio's sector securities relative to the return of the benchmark's sector securities. As such, this "pure security selection effect" for sector s is given by:

$$r_s^{PureSelect} = w_s^b \times (r_s^p - r_s^b) \tag{6.16}$$

Unfortunately, there is a third effect that arises that is not so easily classified. In general, an investment manager can have both an active weight to the sector and a sector portfolio return that differs from the sector benchmark return. For example, an investment manager might overweight a sector that generally does poorly, but for which the manager's security selection is so good that the portfolio's sector does well. This effect is usually referred to as an *interaction effect*, since the sector allocation effect from relative sector weights and the security selection effect from relative sector returns interact with one another. The interaction effect is given by:

$$r_s^{Interact} = (w_s^p - w_s^b) \times (r_s^p - r_s^b) \tag{6.17}$$

It is common to "count" the interaction effect as part of security selection, though in some investment processes, it could be more appropriate to count it with the sector allocation. We add the pure selection effect in Equation 6.16 with the interaction effect in Equation 6.17 to obtain the total security selection effect, which we will hereafter refer to as the security selection effect. Note that the security selection effect reduces to simply using the portfolio's sector weight multiplied by the difference between the portfolio's and benchmark's sector return, as given by:

$$r_s^{Select} = w_s^p \times (r_s^p - r_s^b) \tag{6.18}$$

From here forward, we will use Equation 6.18 when referring to security selection and, as is quite common in practice, largely ignore the interaction effect as a separate part of performance attribution.

Adding the sector allocation in Equation 6.13 to the security selection in Equation 6.18, we have the sector's contribution to the portfolio's total relative return, as given by:

$$r_s^{Contribution} = r_s^{Alloc} + r_s^{Select} \tag{6.19}$$

As with the sector allocation effect, the total contribution to the portfolio's relative return is the sum of each sector's security selection, or:

$$r^{Select} = \sum_{s=1}^{S} r_s^{Select} \tag{6.20}$$

Together, the relative return of a portfolio is the sum of the allocation and the security selection components, or:

$$r_p - r_b = r^{Alloc} + r^{Select} \tag{6.21}$$

Performance Attribution Examples

Consider Example A in Exhibit 6.6. The table shows all of the inputs and resulting calculations for performance attribution. The beginning-of-period weight in each sector appears in columns (A) and (B) for the portfolio and the benchmark, respectively. The benchmark and the portfolio have positions in Treasury bonds, corporate bonds, and stocks. The portfolio's 20% weight in Treasury bonds results in an underweight of 5% compared to the benchmark's 25% weight in that sector. The portfolio has 10% underweight in stocks and a 5% overweight in corporate bonds. Finally, the portfolio has a 10% weight in cash, a "sector" in which the benchmark has no position, resulting in a 10% overweight to cash. These overweights and underweights are shown in column (C).

The sector returns for the portfolio and benchmark are shown in columns (D) and (E), respectively. Column (F) shows the out- or underperformance of the portfolio's sector

Exhibit 6.6 Example of Return and Relative Return Contributions in Performance Attribution Calculations

Example A

	Sector Weights			Returns			Return Contributions		
	(A) Port.	(B) Bench.	(C) +/–	(D) Port.	(E) Bench.	(F) +/–	Sector Allocation	Security Selection	Total
Cash	10.00%	0.00%	10.00%	0.00%	0.00%	0.00%	0.00%	0.00%	0.00%
Treasury Bonds	20.00%	25.00%	–5.00%	4.00%	4.00%	0.00%	–0.20%	0.00%	–0.20%
Corporate Bonds	30.00%	25.00%	5.00%	16.00%	12.00%	4.00%	0.60%	1.20%	1.80%
Stocks	40.00%	50.00%	–10.00%	26.00%	30.00%	–4.00%	–3.00%	–1.60%	–4.60%
Total	100.00%	100.00%	0.00%	16.00%	19.00%	–3.00%	–2.60%	–0.40%	–3.00%

Return Attribution

$$\text{Sector Allocation} = C \times E$$

$$\text{Stock Selection} = A \times F$$

Example B

	Sector Weights			Relative Returns			Relative Return Contributions		
	(A) Port.	(B) Bench.	(C) +/–	(G) Port.	(H) Bench.	(I) +/–	Sector Allocation	Security Selection	Sector Total
Cash	10.00%	0.00%	10.00%	–19.00%	–19.00%	0.00%	–1.90%	0.00%	–1.90%
Treasury Bonds	20.00%	25.00%	–5.00%	–15.00%	–15.00%	0.00%	0.75%	0.00%	0.75%
Corporate Bonds	30.00%	25.00%	5.00%	–3.00%	–7.00%	4.00%	–0.35%	1.20%	0.85%
Stocks	40.00%	50.00%	–10.00%	7.00%	11.00%	–4.00%	–1.10%	–1.60%	–2.70%
Total	100.00%	100.00%	0.00%	–3.00%	0.00%	–3.00%	–2.60%	–0.40%	–3.00%

Relative Return Attribution

$$\text{Sector Allocation} = C \times H$$

$$\text{Stock Selection} = A \times F$$

securities relative to the benchmark's sector securities. For example, the portfolio's positions in corporate bonds average a return of 16% this period, compared to only 12% for the benchmark in the corporate bond sector—an outperformance of 4%. The portfolio's positions in stocks underperformed the benchmark's position in stocks by 4% over this period. The total row at the bottom of the table shows portfolio and benchmark returns, as well as the total relative return of the portfolio compared to the benchmark. During this period, the portfolio's return of 16.00% lags the benchmark return of 19.00% by 3.00%. In other words, the portfolio's relative return is negative 3.00%. The right-most three columns of the table attribute this performance to each sector, and to sector allocation and stock selection components within each sector and in total.

The sector allocation contributions result from the combination of the investment manager's sector over-/underweight choices and the market's sector performance. The product of these two components, as in Equation 6.13, is shown in the Sector Allocation Return Contribution column. The portfolio's 10% overweight to cash contributes nothing to the portfolio's return, since cash has a zero return during this period. The 5% underweight to Treasury bonds contributes −20 basis points to the portfolio's return, since Treasury bonds have a 4% return. Likewise, the 10% underweight and 30% benchmark return in stocks results in a −300 basis point contribution.

The portfolio's exposure of 30% to its corporate bond outperformance of 4% compared with the benchmark's corporate bond performance results in a 120 basis point security selection contribution to the portfolio's total relative return. Conversely, the portfolio's 40% weight in stocks combines with the 4% underperformance of its stocks compared to the benchmark's stocks, resulting in a security selection contribution of −160 basis points for that sector. For the stocks sector, the sector allocation and security selection contributions combine to decrease the portfolio's relative return by 460 basis points. The contribution from the Treasury bonds sector reduces the portfolio's relative return by another 20 basis points, while the corporate bond's total contribution adds 180 basis points to the portfolio's relative return. Note that the sector total relative returns sum up to the portfolio's total relative return of −300 basis points. In summary, we have used performance attribution to explain the sources of the portfolio's 300 basis points of underperformance relative to the benchmark. Most of the negative relative performance originates in the stocks sector, with both an underweight (or underallocation) to stocks during that sector's high return and an underperformance of the portfolio's securities within that sector. According to this attribution model, corporate bonds contributed positively from both allocation and security selection impacts, while cash contributed nothing.

The careful reader might notice that we attributed a zero contribution to the cash sector in Example A, even though a 10% overweight on cash exists when cash earns zero and all other sectors earn a positive return. The model in Example A attributes a positive allocation contribution of 60 basis points to corporate bonds, even though corporate bonds have a 12% sector return while the benchmark's return overall is 19%. Likewise, Example A attributes a negative impact to sector allocation in Treasury bonds, even though the investment manager underweighted this sector at a time when its return is below that of the benchmark. While the attribution model in Example A provides an accurate measure of the total relative return, it treats asset allocation in terms of absolute returns, as if the benchmark for a sector return is zero. For this reason, we have labeled this method "Return Attribution." If the investment manager's mandate is to beat this specific benchmark, then it we might prefer an attribution method that is focuses more on relative returns when assessing asset allocation skill, such as the method in Equation 6.14.

Example B in Exhibit 6.6 illustrates Relative Return Attribution utilizing the same portfolio and benchmark as in Example A. The difference appears in the use of sector relative returns for the portfolio and the benchmark, which are shown in columns (G) and (H), respectively. The relative return in each sector (for both the portfolio and the benchmark) is calculated by subtracting the benchmark's total return from the sector's return. Since the same quantity is subtracted from both the portfolio and the benchmark sector return, the sector difference in column (I) is identical to the difference in column (F) in Example A. For this reason, the security selection contributions remain unchanged in Example B compared with Example A.

The relative return sector allocation in Example B identifies positive contributions when sectors that outperform the benchmark are overweighted or sectors that underperform the benchmark are underweighted. Specifically, underweight to the Treasury bonds sector results in a positive sector allocation contribution because Treasury bonds underperform the benchmark by 15%. The interpretation is that the decision by the investment manager to underweight Treasury bonds was accretive to (i.e., benefitted) the portfolio, since the other sectors, on average, had higher returns. The negative sector allocation contribution of 190 basis points for the cash sector reflects the fact that the investment manager held a position in a sector that substantially underperformed the benchmark. Likewise, the overweight in the corporate bonds sector reduces the portfolio's overall relative return by 35 basis points because the corporate bonds sector underperforms the benchmark. Finally, the stocks sector allocation contribution is −110 basis points. Any decision to underweight one sector is necessarily a decision to overweight another sector. The relative return attribution method assigns the sector allocation to both decisions, reflecting the impact of an over- or under-weight in the context of that sector's return compared to the overall benchmark return.

Both methods reflected in the two examples in Exhibit 6.6 are common in practice. Student-managed investment funds should choose the method that best fits the objective of the investment strategy or investment process. To the extent that the portfolio is benchmarked to a specific index, the relative return contributions might be more meaningful.

Performance Attribution Commentary and Interpretation

Performance analysis utilizes performance attribution to provide insights into the performance and behavior of the investment process. This means that performance attribution should not be simply a quantitative exercise of calculating the contributions of sector allocation and security selection. Rather, performance attribution requires thoughtful consideration in designing the performance attribution and care in interpreting the results. As with all other aspects of investment management, the investment philosophy and process should be employed in conducting performance attribution. Specifically, the performance attribution should be designed to identify the sources of performance that the investment philosophy indicates exists and the objectives that the investment process seeks to achieve.

Sectors should be defined in a way that matches the investment process objectives or methods. Sectors can be defined along any dimension by which assets can be classified. For equity strategies, sectors might be defined in terms of capitalization range (e.g., micro cap, small cap, mid cap, etc.), industry groups (e.g., computer and office equipment, household appliances, aircraft, life insurance, etc.), sectors (e.g., Materials, Utilities, Information Technology, etc.), geographic regions (e.g., Asia, Europe, North America, etc. or Midwest, Northeast, Southeast, etc.), style (growth, value, distressed, etc.), economic status (frontier, emerging, developed, etc.), or any other relevant scheme. For fixed income strategies, sectors might be defined in terms of term or duration (e.g., ultra-short, short, medium, long), credit quality (e.g., AAA, BAA, BBB, etc.), issuer characteristic (municipal, Treasury, corporate, etc.), geography (e.g., Asia, Europe, North America, etc. or Midwest, Northeast, Southeast, etc.), or, again, any other relevant scheme. While some classification schemes are more common than others, the key consideration should be whether the classification scheme is relevant to the investment strategy. For example, if an investment philosophy identifies opportunities in predicting which broad asset classes (e.g., stocks, bonds, etc.) will be "in favor" over a given time period, then the performance attribution should define sectors accordingly, perhaps similar to the broad asset class sector definitions in Exhibit 6.6. The success of the associated investment process could be measured by the total contribution from sector allocation, since successfully picking the outperforming asset class should result in positive sector allocation contributions. Furthermore, we might expect the security selection component to be small in magnitude, unless security selection is also an integral part of the investment philosophy and process.

Southern Illinois University's Saluki Student Investment Fund utilizes a fundamental, bottom-up investment process and is benchmarked by mandate to the S&P Midcap 400 Index. A key element of the SSIF's investment philosophy is that student members' focused company research and application of fundamental valuation techniques help them identify stocks that have the potential to outperform the market. Furthermore, the SSIF's investment process is executed by members who are organized into teams according to GICS sectors. Each sector team is responsible for using fundamental analysis to pick the best stocks (i.e., those with the most potential to outperform) from within their sector. To this end, the SSIF has a "sector neutral" policy in which it maintains it sector weights within a narrow range of the benchmark's sector weights. This background motivates the SSIF's use of performance attribution in which it defines sectors according to the GICS sector classifications. Furthermore, the SSIF's success in implementing its investment process can be judged along several dimensions. First, if the sector neutral policy is successful, not only should the total sector allocation relative return contribution be zero, each sector's allocation contribution should be zero. Second, if the SSIF members successfully pick stocks that outperform, the portfolio should have a positive relative return that is due to a positive total security selection contribution. In sum, the contribution from security selection should explain all of the portfolio's relative return in a given period and over time. Furthermore, the security selection within each sector can be used to determine which sector teams have been the most successful.

The SSIF's quarterly performance attribution report appears in Exhibit 6.7 in graphical form. Consistent with the investment philosophy and process described above, the relative return contribution from sector allocation in each quarter is nearly zero, both in total and within sectors. This indicates that the SSIF's sector neutral policy appears to be implemented consistently through time. In contrast, the security selection contributions are relatively large in magnitude, indicating that the SSIF is making active security selection decisions. In some cases, the outcomes of these security selection decisions have not added to the relative return of the portfolio. For example, the SSIF's chosen stocks in the Consumer Discretionary sector underperformed the benchmark significantly in the second and third quarters of FY 2013. On the other hand, the security selection contribution from the Financials sector is consistently positive in all four quarters of the fiscal year. Most other sectors have mixed results throughout the year, while the Information Technology sector has positive security selection contributions in three of the four quarters that appear to outweigh the negative contribution in the fourth quarter.

Exhibit 6.8 shows the detailed calculations behind the graphs in Exhibit 6.7. We provide these details to illustrate several issues that arise when doing performance attribution. As we emphasized in the discussion of Exhibit 6.6, the sector allocation contributions can be calculated using either returns or relative returns. Columns (D) and (E) in Exhibit 6.8 report the portfolio and benchmark returns that are used to calculate the return contributions. Columns (G) and (H) report the relative returns that are used for the relative return contributions. As in the example in Exhibit 6.6, the sector allocations are different, depending on whether returns or relative returns are used, while security selection contributions are the same, regardless. The SSIF uses the relative return contributions, since its mandates is performance relative to the S&P Midcap 400 Index. By using relative returns, the impact of maintaining a cash balance becomes clearer, since the benchmark holds no cash. The impact from cash is especially large in Q3 of FY 2013, when the benchmark returns more than 13%. The cash position of 1.26% has a measurable negative impact on the relative returns of the portfolio, contributing 17 basis points of underperformance in that quarter. In contrast, an overweight of close to 1% to the Health

Exhibit 6.7 Performance Attribution Report from SIU's Saluki Student Investment Fund for Fiscal Year Ending June 30, 2013

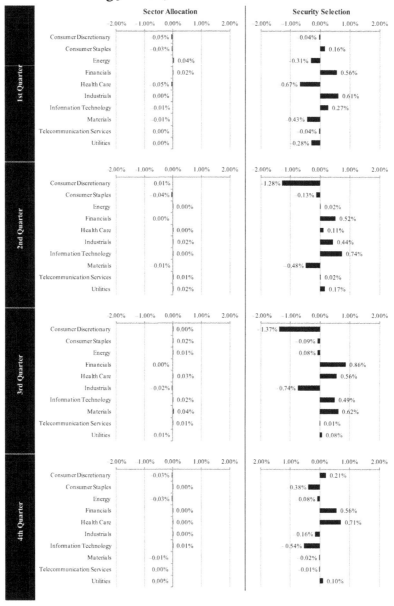

Exhibit 6.8 Example of Quarterly Performance Attribution Calculations

FY 2013 Q1

	Sector Weights			Returns			Relative Returns			Return Contributions			Relative Return Contributions		
	(A) Port.	(B) Bench.	(C) +/-	(D) Port.	(E) Bench.	(F) +/-	(G) Port.	(H) Bench.	(I) +/-	Sector Allocation	Security Selection	Total	Sector Allocation	Security Selection	Total
Cash	1.18%	0.00%	1.18%	0.00%	0.00%	0.00%	-5.46%	-5.46%	0.00%	0.00%	0.00%	0.00%	-0.06%	0.00%	-0.06%
Consumer Discretionary	11.90%	13.41%	-1.51%	8.11%	8.46%	-0.35%	2.65%	3.00%	-0.35%	-0.13%	-0.04%	-0.17%	-0.05%	-0.04%	-0.09%
Consumer Staples	4.00%	3.54%	0.46%	2.73%	-1.29%	4.02%	-2.73%	-6.76%	4.02%	-0.01%	0.16%	0.16%	-0.03%	0.16%	0.13%
Energy	6.20%	5.37%	0.83%	5.67%	10.65%	-4.98%	0.21%	5.18%	-4.98%	0.09%	-0.31%	-0.22%	0.04%	-0.31%	-0.27%
Financials	21.47%	22.30%	-0.83%	5.56%	2.95%	2.61%	0.10%	-2.51%	2.61%	-0.02%	0.56%	0.54%	0.02%	0.56%	0.58%
Health Care	10.04%	11.03%	-0.99%	3.45%	10.15%	-6.70%	-2.01%	4.69%	-6.70%	-0.10%	-0.67%	-0.77%	-0.05%	-0.67%	-0.72%
Industrials	17.28%	16.21%	1.07%	8.58%	5.05%	3.53%	3.12%	-0.41%	3.53%	0.05%	0.61%	0.66%	0.00%	0.61%	0.61%
Information Technology	15.81%	15.54%	0.27%	5.03%	3.33%	1.70%	-0.43%	-2.14%	1.70%	0.01%	0.27%	0.28%	-0.01%	0.27%	0.26%
Materials	6.28%	6.88%	-0.60%	0.17%	7.04%	-6.87%	-5.29%	1.58%	-6.87%	-0.04%	-0.43%	-0.47%	-0.01%	-0.43%	-0.44%
Telecommunication Services	0.53%	0.53%	0.00%	1.60%	8.26%	-6.66%	-3.86%	2.80%	-6.66%	0.00%	-0.04%	-0.04%	0.00%	-0.04%	-0.04%
Utilities	5.31%	5.18%	0.13%	-2.26%	3.08%	-5.34%	-7.72%	-2.38%	-5.34%	0.00%	-0.28%	-0.28%	0.00%	-0.28%	-0.29%
Total	100.00%	100.00%	0.00%	5.14%	5.46%	-0.32%	-0.32%	0.00%	-0.32%	-0.15%	-0.17%	-0.32%	-0.15%	-0.17%	-0.32%
Actual Returns				5.02%	5.44%	-0.42%				Actual - Total:		-0.10%	Actual - Total:		-0.10%

FY 2013 Q2

	Sector Weights			Returns			Relative Returns			Return Contributions			Contribution to Relative Return		
	(A) Port.	(B) Bench.	(C) +/-	(D) Port.	(E) Bench.	(F) +/-	(G) Port.	(H) Bench.	(I) +/-	Sector Allocation	Security Selection	Total	Sector Allocation	Security Selection	Total
Cash	0.58%	0.00%	0.58%	0.00%	0.00%	0.00%	-3.58%	-3.58%	0.00%	0.00%	0.00%	0.00%	-0.02%	0.00%	0.00%
Consumer Discretionary	14.56%	13.92%	0.64%	-7.10%	1.69%	-8.79%	-10.68%	-1.89%	-8.79%	0.01%	-1.28%	-1.27%	-0.01%	-1.28%	-1.27%
Consumer Staples	2.87%	3.29%	-0.42%	8.95%	13.50%	-4.55%	5.37%	9.92%	-4.55%	-0.06%	-0.13%	-0.19%	-0.04%	-0.13%	-0.19%
Energy	6.00%	5.88%	0.12%	4.10%	3.81%	0.29%	0.52%	0.23%	0.29%	0.00%	0.02%	0.02%	0.00%	0.02%	0.02%
Financials	22.33%	22.14%	0.19%	4.19%	1.88%	2.31%	0.61%	-1.70%	2.31%	0.00%	0.52%	0.52%	0.00%	0.52%	0.52%
Health Care	10.35%	10.41%	-0.06%	-0.41%	-1.52%	1.11%	-3.99%	-5.10%	1.11%	0.00%	0.11%	0.12%	0.00%	0.11%	0.12%
Industrials	16.58%	16.21%	0.37%	12.85%	10.22%	2.63%	9.27%	6.64%	2.63%	0.04%	0.44%	0.47%	0.02%	0.44%	0.47%
Information Technology	15.12%	15.52%	-0.40%	7.29%	2.41%	4.88%	3.71%	-1.17%	4.88%	-0.01%	0.74%	0.73%	0.00%	0.74%	0.73%
Materials	6.46%	6.96%	-0.50%	-0.95%	6.52%	-7.47%	-4.53%	2.94%	-7.47%	-0.03%	-0.48%	-0.51%	-0.01%	-0.48%	-0.51%
Telecommunication Services	0.51%	0.56%	-0.05%	-2.30%	-6.57%	4.27%	-5.88%	-10.15%	4.27%	0.00%	0.02%	0.03%	0.01%	0.02%	0.03%
Utilities	4.64%	5.10%	-0.46%	2.99%	-0.58%	3.57%	-0.59%	-4.16%	3.57%	0.00%	0.17%	0.17%	0.02%	0.17%	0.17%
Total	100.00%	100.00%	0.00%	3.66%	3.58%	0.08%	0.08%	0.00%	0.08%	-0.04%	0.12%	0.08%	-0.04%	0.12%	0.08%
Actual Returns				3.62%	3.61%	0.01%				Actual - Total:		-0.07%	Actual - Total:		-0.07%

FY 2013 Q3

	Sector Weights			Returns			Relative Returns			Return Contributions			Relative Return Contributions		
	(A) Port.	(B) Bench.	(C) +/-	(D) Port.	(E) Bench.	(F) +/-	(G) Port.	(H) Bench.	(I) +/-	Sector Allocation	Security Selection	Total	Sector Allocation	Security Selection	Total
Cash	1.26%	0.00%	1.26%	0.00%	0.00%	0.00%	-13.47%	-13.47%	0.00%	0.00%	0.00%	0.00%	-0.17%	0.00%	-0.17%
Consumer Discretionary	13.11%	13.30%	-0.19%	2.32%	12.79%	-10.47%	-11.15%	-0.68%	-10.47%	-0.02%	-1.37%	-1.40%	0.00%	-1.37%	-1.37%
Consumer Staples	4.01%	3.82%	0.19%	19.60%	21.78%	-2.18%	6.13%	8.32%	-2.18%	0.04%	-0.09%	-0.05%	0.02%	-0.09%	-0.07%
Energy	5.72%	6.08%	-0.36%	10.10%	11.51%	-1.41%	-3.37%	-1.96%	-1.41%	-0.04%	-0.08%	-0.12%	0.01%	-0.08%	-0.07%
Financials	21.90%	21.93%	-0.03%	17.38%	13.45%	3.93%	3.91%	-0.01%	3.93%	0.00%	0.86%	0.86%	0.00%	0.86%	0.86%
Health Care	10.31%	9.39%	0.92%	21.82%	16.36%	5.46%	8.35%	2.89%	5.46%	0.15%	0.56%	0.71%	0.03%	0.56%	0.59%
Industrials	16.77%	17.34%	-0.57%	13.12%	17.56%	-4.44%	-0.35%	4.09%	-4.44%	-0.10%	-0.74%	-0.84%	-0.02%	-0.74%	-0.77%
Information Technology	15.13%	15.51%	-0.38%	11.73%	8.47%	3.26%	-1.74%	-5.00%	3.26%	-0.03%	0.49%	0.46%	0.02%	0.49%	0.51%
Materials	6.66%	7.22%	-0.56%	16.03%	6.77%	9.26%	2.56%	-6.69%	9.26%	-0.04%	0.62%	0.58%	0.04%	0.62%	0.65%
Telecommunication Services	0.48%	0.51%	-0.03%	-1.10%	-2.24%	1.14%	-14.57%	-15.71%	1.14%	0.00%	0.01%	0.01%	0.01%	0.01%	0.01%
Utilities	4.65%	4.90%	-0.25%	20.23%	18.61%	1.62%	6.76%	5.14%	1.62%	-0.05%	0.08%	0.03%	-0.01%	0.08%	0.06%
Total	100.00%	100.00%	0.00%	13.70%	13.47%	0.23%	0.23%	0.00%	0.23%	-0.09%	0.33%	0.23%	-0.09%	0.33%	0.23%
Actual Returns				13.74%	13.45%	0.29%				Actual - Total:		0.05%	Actual - Total:		0.05%

FY 2013 Q4

	Sector Weights			Returns			Relative Returns			Return Contributions			Relative Return Contributions		
	(A) Port.	(B) Bench.	(C) +/-	(D) Port.	(E) Bench.	(F) +/-	(G) Port.	(H) Bench.	(I) +/-	Sector Allocation	Security Selection	Total	Sector Allocation	Security Selection	Total
Cash	0.57%	0.00%	0.57%	0.00%	0.00%	0.00%	-0.96%	-0.96%	0.00%	0.00%	0.00%	0.00%	-0.01%	0.00%	-0.01%
Consumer Discretionary	11.56%	12.48%	-0.92%	6.24%	4.45%	1.79%	5.28%	3.49%	1.79%	-0.04%	0.21%	0.17%	-0.03%	0.21%	0.18%
Consumer Staples	3.74%	3.68%	0.06%	-4.74%	5.40%	-10.14%	-5.70%	4.44%	-10.14%	0.00%	-0.38%	-0.38%	0.00%	-0.38%	-0.38%
Energy	6.42%	5.99%	0.43%	-6.30%	-4.98%	-1.32%	-7.26%	-5.95%	-1.32%	-0.02%	-0.08%	-0.11%	-0.03%	-0.08%	-0.11%
Financials	22.97%	23.30%	-0.33%	3.34%	0.91%	2.43%	2.38%	-0.05%	2.43%	0.00%	0.56%	0.56%	0.00%	0.56%	0.56%
Health Care	9.69%	9.65%	0.04%	15.01%	7.68%	7.33%	14.05%	6.72%	7.33%	0.00%	0.71%	0.71%	0.00%	0.71%	0.71%
Industrials	17.25%	17.45%	-0.20%	-2.31%	-1.40%	-0.91%	-3.27%	-2.36%	-0.91%	0.00%	-0.16%	-0.15%	0.00%	-0.16%	-0.15%
Information Technology	14.86%	15.13%	-0.27%	-4.63%	-1.02%	-3.61%	-5.59%	-1.98%	-3.61%	0.00%	-0.54%	-0.53%	0.01%	-0.54%	-0.53%
Materials	7.11%	6.78%	0.33%	-2.30%	-1.95%	-0.35%	-3.26%	-2.91%	-0.35%	-0.01%	-0.02%	-0.03%	-0.01%	-0.02%	-0.03%
Telecommunication Services	0.42%	0.44%	-0.02%	11.71%	13.83%	-2.12%	10.75%	12.87%	-2.12%	0.00%	-0.01%	-0.01%	0.00%	-0.01%	-0.01%
Utilities	5.41%	5.11%	0.30%	2.38%	0.47%	1.91%	1.42%	-0.50%	1.91%	0.00%	0.10%	0.10%	0.00%	0.10%	0.10%
Total	100.00%	100.00%	0.00%	1.29%	0.96%	0.33%	0.33%	0.00%	0.33%	-0.06%	0.39%	0.33%	-0.06%	0.39%	0.33%
Actual Returns				1.24%	1.00%	0.24%				Actual - Total:		-0.09%	Actual - Total:		-0.09%

Care sector contributes only 3 basis points to the relative return, since the Healthcare sector's return is only a few percentage points higher than the benchmark in Q3. Had the SSIF used returns (rather than relative returns) in its attribution method, the impact of allocations to cash would have appeared to have been zero and the contribution from a slight overweight to Health Care would have appeared to have been a significant contributor. In short, for the SSIF's investment process, the attribution method employing relative returns is more meaningful. While we present the use of returns or relative returns as a choice, we note that this choice should be made *ex ante* as a matter of policy, not *ex post* as a way to choose numbers that "look better."

In summary, performance attribution reports can be used externally to give clients or constituents insight into how the investment process works. Oftentimes, performance attribution is the integral part of performance "commentary," which tells the story of the investment manager's performance over a specific time horizon, such as a quarter or year. Such transparency is essential in helping clients to have confidence in their hired managers' ability. Furthermore, performance analysis allows clients to understand the sources of performance for each manager so that they can make informed decisions about how they allocate their assets among their hired managers to maximize their portfolio's objectives. Internally, the performance attribution can be used to extract lessons about "what worked" and "what didn't work" as the investment manager implemented the investment process. For a student-managed investment fund, such analysis can meaningfully enhance the educational value of the experience by identifying sources of out- and underperformance and comparing those sources to expected outcomes. In an investment firm, the information in the performance attribution might be used to assign bonuses, allocated resources to remedy "problem" areas, or identify aspects of the investment process that need to be enhanced. For these reasons, performance attribution is a standard tool in performance analysis for nearly every investment manager.

Performance Attribution Complexities

There are several complexities that arise when calculating performance attribution. The impact of these complexities can be quite small in most cases or surprisingly large in others. We address them here and emphasize that the purpose in our presentation of performance attribution is to provide an estimate of the sources of relative performance instead of a perfect accounting of them.

Trading and Rebalancing Effects

Equations 6.7 through 6.21 are mathematical relationships that hold exactly when there is no rebalancing of the portfolio during the period of measurement. That is, traditional performance attribution assumes no rebalancing during the period over which the attribution is calculated. If there is rebalancing, then the beginning-of-period weights generally will not reflect the exposure to a given sector throughout the entire period. Therefore, the calculation of sector allocation and selection contributions will not add up to the actual portfolio's relative return. Indeed, if there is rebalancing within the portfolio during the period of measurement, the total portfolio return in the attribution model will generally not equal the actual portfolio return for the period, since the portfolio performance will not simply be the sum of the product of the portfolio's beginning sector weights and sector returns. This issue is illustrated in Exhibit 6.8, which shows the full calculations behind Exhibit 6.7's quarterly performance attribution for the SSIF. The SSIF portfolio's actual return for the FY 2013 Q4 is 1.24%, which is 0.24% above the benchmark's 1.00% return for the quarter. However, the total portfolio returns in column (D) are 1.29% while the benchmark's total return is 0.96%. That is, the actual portfolio return does not equal the product of the beginning-of-period sector weights and sector returns. The same inconsistency exists between the benchmark's total and actual returns.

While it seems especially odd that a passive benchmark would experience rebalancing, we note that there are usually numerous additions and deletions to most indexes throughout a year. Importantly, when a name is deleted from an index, such as the S&P Midcap 400 Index, it is not necessarily replaced with a company from the same sector. For example, in April 2013, a stock in the Health Care sector was replaced in the S&P 400 with a stock in the Materials sector.[4] An actively managed portfolio is even more likely to experience trading or rebalancing, causing the total return calculation to be different from the actual portfolio return. Indeed, the difference between the portfolio's calculated total return and actual return for each quarter is larger than the difference for the benchmark in Exhibit 6.8. However, we note that the difference is relatively small compared to the actual return and can be either positive or negative. For example, the SSIF portfolio's calculated total return is 4 basis points lower than the actual portfolio return of 13.74% in FY 2013 Q3, while the calculated total return is 4 basis points higher than the actual return of 3.62% in FY 2013 Q2.

A solution to this issue is to calculate attribution during periods between portfolio (and benchmark) trades and rebalancing. These periods could then be linked together for the period of interest. Depending on the significance of such trades, this might not result in significantly more precise attribution calculations, as discussed in the next section. Alternatively, some widely available commercial attribution methods utilize average weights rather than beginning-of-period weights.

---

[4] In the first half of 2013, there were 12 days in which a stock was added and a stock was deleted from the S&P 400, and the stocks generally were not from the same sector.

Attribution over Multiple Periods

It is often desirable to perform performance attribution over longer time horizons, such as a year. Exhibit 6.9 continues the SSIF example and shows the SSIF's performance attribution for the entire FY 2013 in both graphical and tabular form. The issues that arise when doing attribution calculations over multiple time periods are closely related to the issue of trading and rebalancing discussed above. Specifically, the longer the time horizon, the less likely it is that the implicit "no rebalancing" assumption holds. Therefore, the longer the time horizon, the worse the standard attribution method works.

Since the simple approach of using beginning-of-period weights and full-horizon returns might result in larger deviations from the actual relative return as the time horizon increases, alternative methods should be considered. For example, the use of average weights might result in better estimates of the attribution impacts. Alternatively, another feasible and computationally convenient solution is to sum each sub-period's relative return contributions to arrive at the relative return contributions for the entire period. While this arithmetic approach seems inconsistent with the principle of compounding returns, its use is

Exhibit 6.9 Example of Quarterly Performance Attribution Calculations for Fiscal Year Ending June 30, 2013

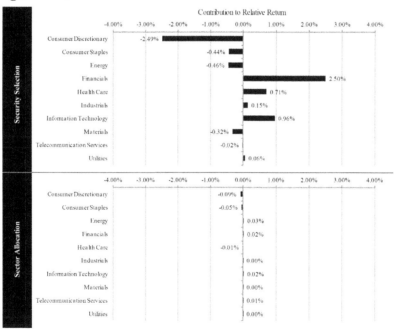

Sector	Full Year Sector Allocation	Full Year Security Selection	Full Year Total
Cash	-0.26%	0.00%	-0.26%
Consumer Discretionary	-0.09%	-2.49%	-2.58%
Consumer Staples	-0.05%	-0.44%	-0.49%
Energy	0.03%	-0.46%	-0.43%
Financials	0.02%	2.50%	2.51%
Health Care	-0.01%	0.71%	0.70%
Industrials	0.00%	0.15%	0.15%
Information Technology	0.02%	0.96%	0.99%
Materials	0.00%	-0.32%	-0.32%
Telecommunication Services	0.01%	-0.02%	-0.01%
Utilities	0.00%	0.06%	0.06%
Total	-0.34%	0.66%	0.32%
Actual Relative Return			0.12%
Unexplained by Attribution Model			-0.20%

also quite common. Again, we emphasize that performance attribution's purpose is not to account for performance, but to estimate economically meaningful sources of out- and underperformance. Exhibit 6.10 shows all three approaches applied to the SSIF portfolio example used throughout this chapter. The sum of quarterly contributions method appears to result in the smallest total deviation from the actual portfolio relative return. More importantly, the results are strikingly consistent across methods for this portfolio during this period, though the method using beginning-of-period weights appears to be somewhat less consistent with the other two methods. Other arithmetic linking or cumulating methods exist, often with the goal of approximating a geometric approach.

Geometric Attribution vs. Arithmetic Attribution

We have presented the arithmetic approach to performance attribution, which is generally favored in the United States. In short, the arithmetic approach treats relative returns and contributions arithmetically. The alternative geometric approach, which is more common in Europe, considers relative returns to be compounded with the benchmark to achieve the total portfolio return. Though both approaches are accurate over a single time period in which there is no rebalancing, the geometric method has the virtue of having a consistently applied and mathematically accurate method of aggregating (and compounding) over multiple periods. Still, the geometric approach is sometimes sacrificed in favor computational convenience and transparency of calculation.

Exhibit 6.10 Example of Quarterly Performance Attribution Calculations

| | FY 2013 Attribution Inputs | | | | | | | | |
| | Beginning Weights | | | Average Weights | | | Returns | | |
	(A1) Port.	(B1) Bench.	(C1) +/-	(A2) Port.	(B2) Bench.	(C2) +/-	(D) Port.	(E) Bench.	(F) +/-
Cash	1.19%	0.00%	1.19%	0.89%	0.00%	0.89%	0.00%	0.00%	0.00%
Consumer Discretionary	11.90%	13.41%	-1.51%	13.28%	13.41%	-0.13%	9.17%	29.93%	-20.76%
Consumer Staples	4.00%	3.54%	0.46%	3.52%	3.74%	-0.22%	27.51%	43.80%	-16.29%
Energy	6.20%	5.37%	0.83%	5.91%	5.69%	0.22%	13.48%	21.69%	-8.21%
Financials	21.47%	22.30%	-0.83%	22.50%	22.59%	-0.09%	33.40%	20.07%	13.33%
Health Care	10.04%	11.03%	-0.99%	9.91%	9.93%	-0.02%	44.33%	35.93%	8.40%
Industrials	17.28%	16.21%	1.07%	16.79%	16.75%	0.04%	35.41%	34.21%	1.20%
Information Technology	15.81%	15.54%	0.27%	15.02%	15.39%	-0.37%	20.09%	13.61%	6.48%
Materials	6.28%	6.88%	-0.60%	6.72%	6.95%	-0.23%	12.48%	19.37%	-6.89%
Telecommunication Services	0.53%	0.53%	0.00%	0.48%	0.51%	-0.03%	9.66%	12.56%	-2.90%
Utilities	5.31%	5.18%	0.13%	4.98%	5.05%	-0.07%	23.91%	22.12%	1.79%
Total	100.01%	100.00%	0.01%	100.00%	100.00%	0.00%	26.05%	25.38%	0.67%
Actual Returns							25.31%	25.18%	0.12%

| | FY 2013 Relative Return Contributions | | | | | | | | |
| | Using Beginning Weights | | | Using Average Weights | | | Sum of Quarterly Contributions | | |
	Sector Allocation	Security Selection	Total	Sector Allocation	Security Selection	Total	Sector Allocation	Security Selection	Total
Cash	-0.30%	0.00%	-0.30%	-0.23%	0.00%	-0.23%	-0.03%	0.00%	-0.03%
Consumer Discretionary	-0.07%	-2.47%	-2.54%	-0.01%	-2.76%	-2.76%	-0.20%	-2.49%	-2.68%
Consumer Staples	0.08%	-0.65%	-0.57%	-0.04%	-0.57%	-0.61%	0.00%	-0.44%	-0.44%
Energy	-0.03%	-0.51%	-0.54%	-0.01%	-0.49%	-0.49%	0.02%	-0.46%	-0.43%
Financials	0.04%	2.86%	2.91%	0.00%	3.00%	3.00%	-0.03%	2.50%	2.46%
Health Care	-0.10%	0.84%	0.74%	0.00%	0.83%	0.83%	0.06%	0.71%	0.77%
Industrials	0.09%	0.21%	0.30%	0.00%	0.20%	0.21%	-0.02%	0.15%	0.13%
Information Technology	-0.03%	1.02%	0.99%	0.04%	0.97%	1.02%	-0.01%	0.96%	0.95%
Materials	0.04%	-0.43%	-0.40%	0.01%	-0.46%	-0.45%	-0.10%	-0.32%	-0.43%
Telecommunication Services	0.00%	-0.02%	-0.02%	0.00%	-0.01%	-0.01%	0.00%	-0.02%	-0.01%
Utilities	0.00%	0.09%	0.09%	0.00%	0.09%	0.09%	-0.03%	0.06%	0.04%
Total	-0.28%	0.95%	0.67%	-0.21%	0.80%	0.59%	-0.34%	0.66%	0.32%
		Total - Actual:	0.55%		Total - Actual:	0.47%		Total - Actual:	0.20%

Returns-Based Performance Analysis

Returns-based analysis is a popular method to accomplish the goal of identifying the sources of a portfolio's risk and explaining the portfolio's performance. Unlike performance attribution, returns-based analysis does not require detailed knowledge of the portfolio's holdings and weights. Rather, returns-based analysis only uses the observed returns of a portfolio combined with the returns of other market factors, such as market returns, returns to characteristic-based portfolios, or changes in economic variables. By employing factor models to estimate the sensitivity of a portfolio's returns or relative returns to the factor returns, the analysis provides an understanding of the determinants of a portfolio's performance.

The underlying premise of returns-based analysis is that factor exposures are under the control of the investment manager, but factor returns are not. For example, a portfolio manager might hold a portfolio of large cap, growth-oriented stocks. It is reasonable to expect the value of such a portfolio to rise and fall with the market, but to also do better than the market when large stocks and growth-oriented stocks do relatively well. The question of interest would be whether the portfolio's returns are attributable to these factors or whether the portfolio's performance exceeds those factor returns as a result of security selection skill. Thinking of the performance attribution analysis from the discussion above, we aim to allocate relative returns to large and growth-oriented "sectors" in order to discern the security selection component of the portfolio's returns. Unlike performance attribution, we rely on portfolio returns to infer or estimate exposures to factors rather than assigning factor exposures based on portfolio weights.

Multifactor performance analysis has two objectives: (1) explain the variance of portfolio returns or relative returns, and (2) explain the average portfolio returns or relative returns. The first objective is motivated by the observation that portfolio returns are sensitive to certain factors in the market or the economy. These factors have been found to be associated with period-to-period asset returns, but may or may not be associated with long-term average returns. Such factors include the level of or changes in an economic variable (e.g., inflation, interest rates, unemployment, GDP, etc.) or an index or portfolio (e.g., a portfolio formed on the basis of size, style, price-momentum, etc.). The second objective is motivated by the observation that some factors, usually labeled as "risk factors," have historically had risk premia associated with them. That is, some factors appear to explain assets' long-term average returns. The most popular such factors for equity portfolios are market returns, size, and growth/value style, which were popularized in research by Fama and French in the 1990s.[5]

Single Factor Model

We begin with a discussion of a single factor model in order to establish some intuition that carries over to multifactor models. Consider a single factor, F, that influences a portfolio's return. This factor has a return of $R_{F,t}$ in period t.[6] The portfolio's return in period t can be written as a function of the factor's return during the same period, as given by:

$$R_{p,t} = \alpha + \beta_F R_{F,t} + e_t \qquad (6.20)$$

---

[5] See Fama, E. F., and K. R. French, 1993. Common risk factors in stocks and bonds, *Journal of Financial Economics* 33, pp. 3–53; and Fama, E. F., and K. R. French, 1996. *Multifactor Explanations of Asset Pricing Anomalies, Journal of Finance* 51, pp. 55–84.

[6] Since portfolio returns analysis typically employs excess returns (i.e., returns net of the risk-free rate), we adopt the convention of capitalizing the returns variable to emphasize that it is an excess return; however, we will refer to excess returns throughout this chapter simply as "returns."

The sensitivity of the portfolio returns to the factor returns is reflected in the "beta" parameter β_F. The beta reflects the covariance (and correlation) between the portfolio returns and the factor returns. Specifically:

$$\beta_F = \frac{Cov(R_{p,t}, R_{F,t})}{\sigma_F^2} = \rho_{p,F}\frac{\sigma_p}{\sigma_F} \tag{6.21}$$

where σ_F is the standard deviation of the returns to factor F and $\rho_{p,F}$ is the correlation between returns to factor F and the portfolio returns. Since we generally do not believe that the factor is fully responsible for the exact return of the portfolio in each period, Equation 6.20 allows for the portfolio to have a constant (or average) return component, α, that applies over all periods. Likewise, an "error" term, e_t, accounts for any portfolio returns in a given period t that are not related to the factor or reflected in the constant α. Equation 6.20 is also considered to be a regression equation in which the dependent variable is the series of portfolio returns and the single independent variable is the series of factor returns. As discussed below, a regression is used to estimate the parameters α and β_F, since they are not directly observable.

The single factor model is illustrated in Exhibit 6.11, where $\alpha = 3\%$ and $\beta_F = 1.0$. As shown in the graph, the portfolio's return is determined by the realization of the factor return and the error term. For example, one period's return is highlighted in the lower-left quadrant of the graph when the factor's return is -10% and the error term is $+5\%$, to give a resulting portfolio return of $-2\% = 3\% + 1 \times (-10\%) + 5\%$. Likewise, the portfolio return of 6% highlighted in the upper-right quadrant results from a factor return realization of 7% and an error term of -3% in that period.

Average Returns in the Single Factor Model

The single factor model allows us to derive the relationship between the average portfolio return and average factor return by taking the mathematical average of each side of Equation 6.20. Since the average of a sum is the sum of the averages, then:

$$\begin{aligned} Avg(R_{p,t}) &= Avg(\alpha + \beta_F R_{F,t} + e_t) \\ &= Avg(\alpha) + Avg(\beta_F R_{F,t}) + Avg(e_t) \end{aligned} \tag{6.22}$$

Note that α is a constant and the average of the error term is zero, so we can write the average portfolio return, $\overline{R}_p$, in terms of the single factor model parameters and the average factor return, $\overline{R}_F$, as given by:

$$\overline{R}_p = \alpha + \beta_F \overline{R}_F \tag{6.23}$$

Exhibit 6.11 Example of a Single Factor Model

Single factor model:

$$R_{p,t} = \alpha + \beta_F R_{F,t} + e_t$$

$$\alpha = 3\%$$

$$\beta_F = 1.0$$

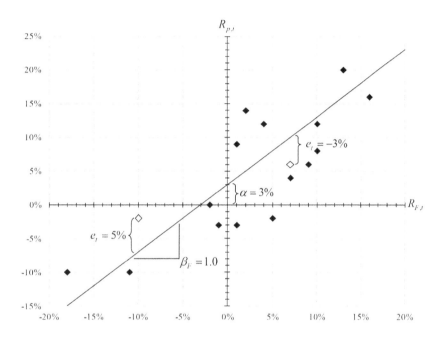

Equation 6.23 provides the primary method by which returns-based analysis is used to assess performance or to attribute performance to a factor. Specifically, we employ a univariate (i.e., single factor) linear regression model using the portfolio returns as the dependent (left-hand side) variable and the factor returns as the independent variable model to estimate the slope (β_F) and intercept (α). Rather than using portfolio and factor returns, it is common to use excess returns (i.e., returns net of the risk-free rate) for both the portfolio and the factor, when estimating the regression model. The association between the portfolio and factor returns, as estimated by β_F, control for the contribution of the factor to the portfolio's average returns. The average return that is not attributed to the factor appears in the estimated parameter α.

When the "market portfolio" or a proxy index is used as the factor in this model, it is common to interpret the alpha as an "abnormal return."[7] More specifically, a positive abnormal return is interpreted to mean that the portfolio outperformed the "fair" return for its given level of exposure to the non-diversifiable risk associated with the proxy index. It is inferred, therefore, that an investment manager with a significantly positive alpha possesses skill and that the application of the investment process creates value over and above what is available on average in the market. We note that this interpretation applies to the time period over which the portfolio and market returns are measured. As such, any such observations or statements about skill or value are inherently *ex post* in nature. To the extent that an investor believes that skill or value in an investment process persists through time, the investor may believe such analysis to be a valuable ex ante tool.

Analysis of Portfolio Risk in the Single Factor Model

We can also utilize the single index model to reveal insights about the risk exposures in the portfolio. To do so, we decompose the variance of the portfolio's returns by taking the variance of both sides of Equation 6.20, so that:

$$Var(R_{p,t}) = Var(\alpha + \beta_F R_{F,t} + e_t)$$
$$= Var(\alpha) + Var(\beta_F R_{F,t}) + Var(e_t) \tag{6.24}$$

We have omitted the covariance term between the factor returns and the error term, since the error term and factor returns are assumed to be uncorrelated. Since α is a constant, its variance is zero. If we define the variance of the factor returns as σ_F^2 and the variance of the error term as σ_e^2, then the portfolio variance, σ_p^2, is given by:

$$\sigma_p^2 = \beta_F^2 \sigma_F^2 + \sigma_e^2 \tag{6.25}$$

The portfolio's risk is comprised of two sources: (1) a source due to the risk of the factor and (2) a source due to the error term. If the factor is the market portfolio or its proxy index, we interpret the first term on the right-hand side of Equation 6.25 to be the systematic risk of the portfolio that is due to the variance of the index. The second term represents the diversifiable (i.e., unsystematic or idiosyncratic) risk of the portfolio. The variance of the error term is known as the residual variance in the context of a regression.

---

[7] This interpretation is rooted in the Capital asset pricing Model of Sharpe, Black, and Mossin (c.f., Sharpe, W. F., 1964, Capital asset prices: A theory of market equilibrium under conditions of risk, *Journal of Finance* 19, pp. 425–442; Lintner, J., 1965, The valuation of risk assets and the selection of risk investments in stock portfolios and capital budgets, *Review of Economics and Statistics* 47, pp. 13–37; and Mossin, J., 1966, Equilibrium in a capital asset market, *Econometrica* 34, pp. 768–783). The CAPM's "normal" return is based on an asset's equilibrium risk premium that is a function of only the beta of the asset with the market portfolio and the market risk premium.

When evaluating performance using the portfolio's benchmark as the single factor, an alternative definition of the tracking error is the square root of the residual variance from the regression model.

Dividing both sides of Equation 6.25 by the portfolio variance, we see that:

$$\frac{\beta_F^2 \sigma_F^2}{\sigma_p^2} + \frac{\sigma_e^2}{\sigma_p^2} = 1 \tag{6.26}$$

Equation 6.26 states the sources of portfolio risk as proportions that sum to 100%. Note that the first term on the left-hand side of equation 6.26 is the regression R-squared. That is, R-squared measures what proportion of the portfolio's variation is explained by (i.e., due to) the variation in the model's independent variables—the single factor, in this case. When the market portfolio or proxy index is used as the model's single factor, then the R-squared indicates what proportion of the portfolio's risk is explained by market risk. A more diversified portfolio has a higher R-squared, while a less diversified portfolio has a lower R-squared.

We have been quite abstract heretofore in our discussion of the single factor model in usually referring to the factor only generically. In practice, the portfolio's benchmark is commonly used as the single factor in such a model. As indicated above, the parameters of the single factor model have a convenient interpretation when the portfolio's benchmark is used. The portfolio's beta measures the sensitivity or risk exposure of the portfolio to the benchmark, while the alpha measures the average return of the portfolio over and above what a passive investor would earn by holding the same exposure to the benchmark. In this way, the single factor model provides a concise measure of the ability of the investment manager to beat the benchmark. From the viewpoint of the investor, the alpha represents the reward for taking "active risk," rather than remaining with a passive exposure to the benchmark. Indeed, the active risk is even measured in the model's residual variance or its square root, σ_e. As discussed below, these measures are used to calculate a portfolio's information ratio.

Multifactor Models

Multifactor model analysis employs the single factor model's general approach to portfolio performance analysis by associating portfolio returns with factor returns. In short, the interpretation that is applied to the results remains similar to what we applied to the single factor model, except that we can attribute average returns and risk to more sources. As with the single factor, we begin with a generic definition of the model in which we have N factors $F1, F2, F3, \ldots, FN$, with factor returns $R_{F1,t}, R_{F2,t}, R_{F3,t}, \ldots, R_{FN,t}$ at time t. We estimate the parameters of the regression model:

$$R_{p,t} = \alpha + \beta_1 R_{F1,t} + \beta_2 R_{F2,t} + \beta_3 R_{F3,t} + \cdots + \beta_N R_{FN,t} + e_t \tag{6.27}$$

The factor betas reflect the sensitivity or exposure of the portfolio returns to the factor. If portfolio returns are positively correlated with a factor's returns, the beta for that factor will be positive. If the portfolio returns have a negative covariance with a factor's returns, the beta for that factor will be negative. Note that the alpha and the error term are different in Equation 6.27 compared the same terms in Equation 6.20, but the meaning of these terms remains the same. Alpha is the average return in excess of the average return that is explained by the model's factors. The error term has a zero average, but captures any period-to-period variation in returns that are not accounted for by the factor return variation. As such, the decomposition of the portfolio's average return and variance of returns is analogous to the decompositions using the single factor. Specifically, the average return of the portfolio is given by:

$$\overline{R}_p = \alpha + \beta_1 \overline{R}_{F1} + \beta_2 \overline{R}_{F2} + \beta_3 \overline{R}_{F3} + \cdots + \beta_N \overline{R}_{FN} \qquad (6.28)$$

Because factor returns can be correlated to one another, the variance of portfolio returns is not quite as straightforward as it is for the single factor model. Rather, instead of attributing the variance of portfolio returns to each factor individually (which is possible, but beyond the scope of this discussion), we separate the portfolio variance again into the variance explained by the model and the unexplained or idiosyncratic variance, as given by:

$$\sigma_p^2 = Var(\beta_1 R_{F1,t} + \beta_2 R_{F2,t} + \beta_3 R_{F3,t} + \cdots + \beta_N R_{FN,t}) + \sigma_e^2 \qquad (6.29)$$

In this case, the multivariate regression's R-squared reports the proportion of the portfolio's return variance that is explained by the multiple factors.

Fama-French 3-Factor Model

The Fama-French 3-Factor Model is one of the most popular multifactor models for analysis of equity portfolio returns. As its name suggests, the model utilizes three factors: a market factor, a size factor, and a style (growth vs. value) factor. These three have been shown in research to not only explain the variation in asset returns, but to also be associated with stocks' long-term returns. The equity market factor is the excess return on the market index, r, which is usually calculated from a capitalization-weighted index of all listed securities in the United States. Exposure to this market factor reflects a portfolio's systematic risk. In other words, this factor captures the impact of market-wide movements on the portfolio's returns.

To capture the size and style factors, Fama and French create "characteristic" portfolios based on size and style and calculate the returns to the factors based on the difference in the return on one portfolio compared to another. Specifically, the size factor is calculated as the return to a portfolio of small stocks minus the return to a portfolio of big stocks. This

"Small Minus Big" return is labeled as the SMB factor. Likewise, Fama and French create the style factor based on the book-to-market ratio, which is used to identify stocks as "growth" or "value" stocks. Stocks with low book values relative to their market values (i.e., low book-to-market) are considered growth-oriented firms. Recall from our valuation discussion in Chapter 3 that a high growth rate raises the market value of the firm, and hence would cause the book value of the firm's assets to be low compared to its market value. Conversely, "value stocks" have relatively high book-to-market ratios. The style factor is calculated as the return to a portfolio of high book-to-market (i.e., value) stocks minus low book-to-market (i.e., growth) stocks. This "High Minus Low" factor is labeled as the HML factor.

The Fama-French 3-Factor regression model is specified as:

$$R_{p,t} = \alpha + \beta_M R_{M,t} + \beta_{SMB} R_{SMB,t} + \beta_{HML} R_{HML,t} + e_t \tag{6.30}$$

The Fama-French model's parameters provide important insights into a portfolio's risk exposures. Since the market factor is positive when the overall stock market rises, a positive beta on the market factor would be expected for most long-oriented equity portfolios. Portfolios that hold stocks with high systematic risk exposure would be expected to have higher betas. The SMB factor returns are positive when small stocks outperform large stocks. Portfolios that place heavier weight on the smaller capitalization stocks in the market would likely have a positive exposure to the SMB factor (i.e., $\beta_{SMB} > 0$), while portfolios that have a tilt toward large cap stocks would be expected to have a negative SMB beta. The HML factor is generally positive when value stocks outperform growth stocks and negative when growth stocks outperform value stocks. In this way, a positive HML beta reflects an exposure to value stocks. Portfolios that hold more weight on growth-oriented stocks than value-oriented stocks would likely have a negative exposure to the HML factor (i.e., $\beta_{SMB} > 0$). Portfolios that have no tilt toward growth or value are sometimes referred to as style-neutral or core.

Style Analysis Using a Multifactor Returns Model

Exhibit 6.12 shows a style analysis of a selection S&P and Russell indexes from Exhibit 4.1. These indexes are among the most popular U.S. equity benchmarks for institutional equity portfolios. Similar style analysis is common in the industry, though the method varies slightly from vendor to vendor. In this case, we place the indexes in position on a 3×3 style grid according to estimated exposures to the Fama-French SMB and HML factors using the index returns over a ten-year period ending in June 2013. As described above, the "core" indexes, such as the S&P 500 Index and Russell Midcap Index include stocks based only on capitalization criteria and hold both growth- and value-oriented stocks. The associated "Growth" and "Value" indexes assign stocks from the core index into

Exhibit 6.12 Style Analysis Using Multifactor Returns Analysis

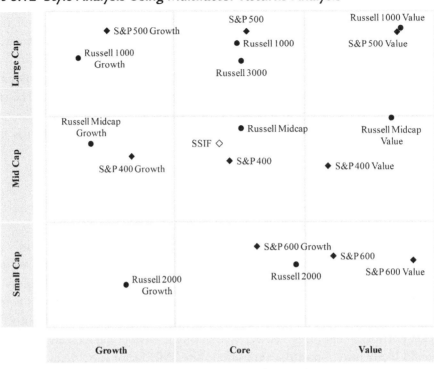

Source: Index returns are from Bloomberg. Fama-French 3-Factor Model factor data are from Kenneth French's data library.

growth or value groups based on various criteria, not simply the book-to-market ratio that is used in the HML factor.

Note that the Fama-French factors separate these indexes quite well on both the growth/value and the capitalization dimensions. The S&P 500 and Russell 1000 large cap indexes appear to have the most exposure to large cap stocks, which is reflected in the most negative exposure to the SMB factor. The exposure of the midcap S&P 400 and Russell Midcap indexes is in the middle, though the exposure to the SMB is actually negative for these indexes. The Russell Midcap index, made up of the 800 stocks from the Russell 1000 index with the lowest capitalizations, appears a bit more tilted toward large cap stocks than does the S&P 400, which has no overlap with its large cap S&P 500 counterpart. Interestingly, the S&P 600 Growth index has no meaningful exposure to the HML factor, though its exposure is less than that of the core S&P 600 index, indicating that it holds "growthier" stocks than the core index. The Russell 3000 index, which is a combination of the Russell 1000 (large cap) and Russell 2000 (small cap) indexes, shows up as having an exposure more similar to large cap indexes. While this might seem odd, it reflects the fact that the Russell 3000 is a capitalization-weighted index, and as such, it places most of its weight on the large cap stocks.

One motivation behind the use of style analysis is to recognize that some factors or styles appear to come into and out of favor in the market, creating short-lived market trends. A portfolio that is tilted toward a particular style, therefore, will be subject to such market trends. These trends are illustrated in the Callan Periodic Table of Investment Returns in Exhibit 6.13, published regularly by the investment consulting firm Callan Associates, Inc. The periodic table shows the ranked performance of various asset classes and styles in each year. For example, the Russell 2000 Value index was the top performing index in 2000 and 2001, but was among the worst in 2007. Therefore, a portfolio that plotted in the small cap value style quadrant would have been expected to perform relatively well in 2000 and 2001 and relatively poorly in 2007, compared to portfolios that plotted in other quadrants of the style box. Notice the rather long-lived trend in which large cap growth generally outperformed other styles from 1994 through 1998, but generally underperformed all other equity styles from 2001 through 2006. The multifactor analysis that we discuss below quantifies these effects and attributes performance to such factor exposures.

Exhibit 6.13 The Callan Periodic Table of Investment Returns'

The Callan Periodic Table of Investment Returns

Annual Returns for Key Indices (1993–2012) Ranked in Order of Performance

● S&P 500 measures the performance of large capitalization U.S. stocks. The S&P 500 is a market-value-weighted index of 500 stocks that are traded on the NYSE, AMEX, and NASDAQ. The weightings make each company's influence on the Index performance directly proportional to that company's market value.

● S&P 500 Growth and ● S&P 500 Value measure the performance of the growth and value styles of investing in large cap U.S. stocks. The indices are constructed by dividing the market capitalization of the S&P 500 Index into Growth and Value indices, using style 'factors' to make the assignment. The Value Index contains those S&P 500 securities with a greater-than-average value orientation, while the Growth Index contains those securities with a greater-than-average growth orientation. The indices are market-capitalization-weighted. The constituent securities are not mutually exclusive.

● Russell 2000 measures the performance of small capitalization U.S. stocks. The Russell 2000 is a market-value-weighted index of the 2,000 smallest stocks in the broad-market Russell 3000 Index. These securities are traded on the NYSE, AMEX, and NASDAQ.

● Russell 2000 Value and ● Russell 2000 Growth measure the performance of the growth and value styles of investing in small cap U.S. stocks. The indices are constructed by dividing the market capitalization of the Russell 2000 Index into Growth and Value indices, using style 'factors' to make the assignment. The Value Index contains those Russell 2000 securities with a greater-than-average value orientation, while the Growth Index contains those securities with a greater-than-average growth orientation. Securities in the Value Index generally have lower price-to-book and price-earnings ratios than those in the Growth Index. The indices are market-capitalization-weighted. The constituent securities are not mutually exclusive.

● MSCI EAFE is a Morgan Stanley Capital International index that is designed to measure the performance of the developed stock markets of Europe, Australasia, and the Far East.

● MSCI Emerging Markets is a Morgan Stanley Capital International Index that is designed to measure the performance of equity markets in 21 emerging countries around the world.

● Barclays Aggregate Bond Index (formerly the Lehman Brothers Aggregate Bond Index) includes U.S. government, corporate, and mortgage-backed securities with maturities of at least one year.

Callan   Knowledge. Experience. Integrity.

© 2013 Callan Associates Inc.

The Callan Periodic Table of Investment Returns 1993–2012

The Callan Periodic Table of Investment Returns conveys that the *case for diversification* across asset classes (stocks vs. bonds), investment styles (growth vs. value), capitalizations (large vs. small), and equity markets (U.S. vs. international) is strong.

While past performance is no indication of the future, consider the following observations:

a. The Table highlights the uncertainty inherent in all capital markets. Rankings change every year. Also noteworthy is the difference between absolute and relative performance. For example, witness the variability of returns for large cap growth, when it ranked second from last for the six years from 2001 to 2006, or the variability in the ranking for fixed income over the last 10 years while returns remained bound in a relatively narrow range.

b. Stock markets around the world rebounded smartly in 2012 after suffering through incredible volatility in 2011. Global economic growth remained subdued and policy uncertainty persisted in Europe and the U.S., unnerving investors. Nonetheless, equity markets broadly outperformed long-term averages and notched solid gains in the 15% to 20% range. The U.S. stock market generated 16%, with much of the gain recorded in a strong third quarter, and the **developed markets overseas** did even better (+17.32%). **Emerging markets** notched the highest return (+18.63%) among all asset classes displayed in the table during 2012, after suffering the worst loss in 2011 (-18.17%). After underperforming in four of the previous five years, **large cap value** (+17.68%) led the way in the U.S. large cap market, outperforming **growth** (+14.61%) by 3.07%.

c. Reverting to long-term trends, **small cap** (+16.35%) beat large cap (+16.00%) stocks in 2012, the 11th time in the past 14 years. **Small cap value** (+18.05%) bested **small cap growth** (+14.59%) for the first time in four years.

d. **Fixed income** (+4.21%) generated the lowest return among asset classes in 2012 after leading the pack in 2011. While muted, fixed income gains surprised on the upside, just as in 2010 and 2011. At the start of the 2012, yields remained exceptionally low (2.24% for the Barclays Aggregate). Economic growth was expected to lead to inevitably higher interest rates, and therefore weak performance for fixed income. However, investor confidence in the economic recovery wavered during the first half of 2012. Interest rates declined into the third quarter, with the yield on the Aggregate falling to 1.56% at the end of September, driving up bond prices and total returns. Yields backed up modestly in the fourth quarter, tempering total return for the year. The stage remains set for weak bond market performance should interest rates begin to rise.

e. The Table illustrates several sharply distinct periods for the capital markets over the past 20 years. First, note the unique experience of the 1995–1999 period, when large cap growth significantly outperformed other asset classes and the U.S. stock market in general enjoyed one of its strongest five-year runs.

f. The subsequent three years (2000–2002) saw consecutive declines in large cap stocks for the first time since 1929–1932. The S&P 500 suffered its largest loss since 1974, declining 40% from its peak in March 2000 through the end of 2002.

g. Stocks recorded five years of gains from 2003–2007, led by particularly strong growth in emerging markets. Then the bottom fell out in 2008, and the U.S. stock market sustained its worst drubbing since the 1930s. Large cap stocks suffered the second-worst annual decline (-37.00%) since 1926.

This analysis assumes that market indices are reasonable representations of the asset classes and depict the returns an investor could expect from exposure to these styles of investment. In fact, investment manager performance relative to the different asset class indices has varied widely across the asset classes during the past 20 years.

www.callan.com. *Source: Callan Associates, Inc.*

Example of Returns-Based Attribution Using the Fama-French 3-Factor Model

Exhibit 6.14 illustrates the regression analysis of portfolio returns using various mutual funds. Specifically, the exhibit summarizes the regression results for both a single factor model and the Fama-French 3-Factor model applied to monthly returns over a ten-year period. The exhibit also reports the average returns to the factors and the funds. Consider first the Fama-French 3-Factor Model (FF 3-Factor) for the Technology Fund. Exhibit 6.15 also shows the regression results from using Excel's Data Analysis Toolpak for this fund. The Technology Fund's Market beta is 1.49, indicating that the portfolio has relatively high market risk. Indeed, when the market goes up by 10%, this portfolio goes up by 14.9%, on average. The Technology Fund has an SMB beta of 0.35. The positive exposure to the SMB factor indicates that the Technology Fund is generally more heavily weighted toward smaller capitalization stocks. The negative HML beta indicates that the fund holds growth-oriented stocks. It is not surprising that a technology fund would hold riskier, smaller, and more growth-oriented stocks relative to the overall market.

Exhibit 6.14 Regression Estimates Using the Single Factor and Fama-French 3-Factor Models

Fund	Model	Beta Estimates				R-squared	P-Values			
		Alpha	Market	SMB	HML		Alpha	Market	SMB	HML
Technology Fund	Single-Factor	0.0011	1.90			0.71	0.83	<0.01		
	FF 3-Factor	0.0033	1.49	0.35	-1.01	0.88	0.33	<0.01	<0.01	<0.01
Growth Fund	Single-Factor	-0.0072	1.42			0.74	0.04	<0.01		
	FF 3-Factor	-0.0054	1.27	0.02	-0.45	0.79	0.11	<0.01	0.82	<0.01
Value Fund	Single-Factor	0.0035	0.77			0.54	0.25	<0.01		
	FF 3-Factor	0.0001	0.92	0.17	0.59	0.70	0.98	<0.01	0.01	<0.01
Large Cap 500 Index Fund	Single-Factor	-0.0013	0.92			0.95	0.15	<0.01		
	FF 3-Factor	-0.0003	0.97	-0.19	0.02	0.99	0.53	<0.01	<0.01	0.14
Total Market Index Fund	Single-Factor	-0.0004	0.97			1.00	0.07	<0.01		
	FF 3-Factor	-0.0003	0.98	-0.02	0.01	1.00	0.13	<0.01	<0.01	0.22

Factor	Average Factor Returns
Market	-0.18%
SMB	0.52%
HML	0.47%

Fund	Average Fund Returns
Technology Fund	-0.23%
Growth Fund	-0.98%
Value Fund	0.21%
Large Cap 500 Index Fund	-0.29%
Total Market Index Fund	-0.22%

Source: Fund returns are from the CRSP Survivorship-Free Mutual Fund Database. Fama-French 3-Factor Model factor data are from Kenneth French's data library.

If a portfolio has a significant (positive or negative) beta on one of the factors, then that factor helps explain the variation in the portfolio's returns.[8] Furthermore, the average return of the portfolio can be attributed to that factor. Over a given time period, the average return of the portfolio that is attributed to the factor is the product of the portfolio's factor beta and the average return on the factor. For example, the Technology Fund has an SMB beta of 0.35 in the Fama-French 3-Factor model during a period in which the average monthly return on the SMB factor is 0.52%. That is, the average monthly return on the portfolio of small capitalization stocks exceeds that of the large capitalization stocks by 0.52% over this

---

[8] Statistical significance is indicated by the parameter's "p-value." Recall that a p-value (i.e., a probability of observing a parameter at least as extreme by random chance, if the true parameter is zero) of 0.05 (or sometimes 0.10) or less is commonly considered statistically significant. Parameters with p-values of 0.05 (or sometimes 0.10) or more are usually considered to be statistically indistinguishable from zero.

Exhibit 6.15 Regression Estimates for a Technology Fund Using the Fama-French 3-Factor Models

	A	B	C	D	E	F	G	H	I
1	SUMMARY OUTPUT								
2									
3	*Regression Statistics*								
4	Multiple R	0.9407							
5	R Square	0.8848							
6	Adjusted R Square	0.8818							
7	Standard Error	0.0359							
8	Observations	120							
9									
10	ANOVA								
11		*df*	*SS*	*MS*	*F*	*Significance F*			
12	Regression	3	1.1465	0.3822	297.0573	0.0000			
13	Residual	116	0.1492	0.0013					
14	Total	119	1.2957						
15									
16		*Coefficients*	*Standard Error*	*t Stat*	*P-value*	*Lower 95%*	*Upper 95%*	*Lower 95.0%*	*Upper 95.0%*
17	Intercept	0.0033	0.0034	0.9821	0.3281	-0.0034	0.0100	-0.0034	0.0100
18	Market	1.4874	0.0775	19.1916	0.0000	1.3339	1.6409	1.3339	1.6409
19	SMB	0.3539	0.0901	3.9290	0.0001	0.1755	0.5323	0.1755	0.5323
20	HML	-1.0142	0.1034	-9.8052	0.0000	-1.2191	-0.8093	-1.2191	-0.8093
21									

Source: Technology Fund returns are from the CRSP Survivorship-Free Mutual Fund Database. Fama-French 3-Factor Model factor data are from Kenneth French's data library.

period. Therefore, an exposure of 0.35 to the SMB factor increases the Technology Fund's average monthly return by 18 basis points ($0.18\% = 0.35 \times 0.52\%$) over this period. Likewise, the Market and HML factors contribute -27 basis points and -48 basis points, respectively. Together, the Technology Fund's factor exposures contribute -56 basis points ($-0.56\% = -0.27\% + 0.18\% - 0.47\%$). In other words, an investor who has a passive exposure to the same risk factors averages a -56 basis points return per month over this period, while the actively managed portfolio with the same factor exposures averages a -23 basis points return, resulting in an alpha of $+33$ basis points.

We note that the alpha of 33 basis points for the Technology Fund is not statistically significant, since its p-value is 0.33. The p-value indicates that the chance of observing an alpha as high as 0.0033 or higher by random chance is 33% if the true alpha is zero. Since 33% is quite a bit higher than the typical cutoff level of 5% (or the more lenient 10%), the alpha for the Technology Fund would be labeled as statistically insignificantly different from zero and the conclusion would be that its alpha is indistinguishable from zero, in a statistical sense. The only fund with a statistically significant alpha in Exhibit 6.14 is the Growth Fund. In this case, the Growth Fund has a statistically significant negative estimated alpha. Interpreting the positive alpha as skill, it appears that we cannot be statistically confident that any of the funds in the exhibit have skill and it appears that the Growth Fund's monthly average underperformance of 72 basis points is statistically significant at the 5% level.

As discussed above, the R-squared indicates how much variation in the portfolio returns is explained by the variation of the model's factor returns. Not surprisingly, the two passive index funds (Large Cap 500 Index Fund and Total Market Index Fund) have the highest

R-squareds of the group, with nearly all of the variation in their returns being explained by the variation in factor returns. Both funds are very well diversified. The Total Market Index Fund appears to resemble the Market factor quite well. Indeed, the Market factor in the single factor model explained nearly all of the variation in that fund's returns, even without the two other Fama-French factors. In contrast, the Large Cap 500 Index Fund, which is intended to mimic the S&P 500 index, has a significant negative exposure to the SMB factor due to its tilt toward large cap stocks. Likewise, the 3-Factor model adds significant explanatory power beyond the single factor model for the Value Fund. The significantly positive estimated regression coefficients on the SMB and HML factors allow us to infer that the Value Fund holds smaller, value-oriented stocks. In contrast, the Growth Fund appears to have no size bias but holds growth-oriented firms in its portfolio.

Consider again the case of the Technology Fund. Recall that -56 basis points of the fund's return are attributed to the Market, SMB, and HML factors. In one sense, the -56 basis points return represents a sort of benchmark return based on the risk factors to which the fund is exposed. The alpha of 0.0033 indicates that the fund outperforms this "benchmark" by 33 basis points over this period. However, it is important to recognize that the factor exposure "benchmark" is an *imputed* benchmark, not necessarily one that was mandated by the manager. The portfolio may have an explicit benchmark against which its performance is measured. In such a case, it might be inappropriate to measure out- or underperformance of the portfolio with the multifactor model's alpha. However, this does not mean that the multifactor model is of no use. Rather, it might be more appropriate in such a case to use the portfolio's relative returns as the regression's left-hand side variable. That is, we can employ the multifactor model to analyze the portfolio's relative returns.

Recall the Saluki Student Investment Fund's performance summary from Exhibit 6.4. The report showed that, as of June 30, 2013, the SSIF outperformed its benchmark by 2.89% per year over the 3-year period and 1.06% per year over the 10-year period. The performance summary also shows that the SSIF portfolio has underperformed its S&P 400 benchmark by 1.51% per year since its inception. We apply the Fama-French 3-Factor Model to the monthly returns of the SSIF portfolio and its benchmark to identify the sources of the SSIF's performance over these three periods. We also apply the multifactor model to the SSIF portfolio's relative returns, as shown in Exhibit 6.16. For the 3-year period, the SSIF portfolio had a Market beta of 1.04, which is very close to the benchmark's Market beta of 1.02. Likewise, the SSIF portfolio has an exposure to smaller stocks, as reflected in the SMB beta of 0.38. Of course, the SSIF portfolio has a mid cap mandate. Accordingly, its benchmark also has an exposure to smaller stocks, with an SMB beta of 0.41. Finally, both the SSIF portfolio and benchmark index have HML betas that are statistically indistinguishable from zero. In summary, the SSIF portfolio's exposure to the Market, SMB, and HML factors are nearly identical to those of its benchmark index over the 3-year period ending June 30, 2013.

Exhibit 6.16 Multifactor Model Analysis of SSIF Portfolio Returns

	Portfolio	Beta Estimates				R-squared	P-Values			
		Alpha	Market	SMB	HML		Alpha	Market	SMB	HML
3-Year	SSIF	0.0019	1.04	0.38	-0.03	0.95	0.35	<0.01	<0.01	0.80
	S&P Midcap 400 Index	0.0001	1.02	0.41	-0.01	0.97	0.96	<0.01	<0.01	0.94
	SSIF (Relative Returns)	0.0018	0.02	-0.04	-0.02	0.01	0.19	0.61	0.65	0.78
10-Year	SSIF	0.0022	1.05	0.34	-0.04	0.89	0.18	<0.01	<0.01	0.57
	S&P Midcap 400 Index	0.0011	1.04	0.41	-0.01	0.96	0.24	<0.01	<0.01	0.81
	SSIF (Relative Returns)	0.0011	0.00	-0.07	-0.03	0.02	0.40	0.95	0.26	0.59
Since Inception	SSIF	0.0014	1.04	0.17	0.13	0.85	0.42	<0.01	0.01	0.02
	S&P Midcap 400 Index	0.0016	1.03	0.28	0.23	0.93	0.18	<0.01	<0.01	<0.01
	SSIF (Relative Returns)	-0.0001	0.02	-0.11	-0.10	0.06	0.93	0.62	0.03	0.02

Factor	3-Year	10-Year	Since Inception
Market	0.75%	0.61%	0.25%
SMB	0.39%	0.27%	0.44%
HML	0.02%	0.22%	0.50%

Portfolio	3-Year	10-Year	Since Inception
SSIF	1.80%	0.94%	0.55%
S&P Midcap 400 Index	1.60%	0.85%	0.66%
SSIF (Relative Returns)	0.20%	0.09%	-0.11%

By examining the estimated multifactor model coefficients for the SSIF portfolio's relative returns, a similar story emerges. Specifically, the Market beta for the SSIF relative returns is small at 0.02 and statistically insignificant. Similarly, the coefficients on SMB and HML are close to and statistically indistinguishable from zero for the 3-year period. Again, this indicates that the SSIF portfolio's relative returns do not vary with the factor returns and the average returns are not significantly attributed to the average returns from these factors. Indeed, the relative returns appear to have an alpha of approximately 18 basis points per month (or 216 basis points per year, after multiplying the monthly average by 12), which is close to the 2.89% annualized relative return (in Exhibit 6.4) of the SSIF portfolio compared to the benchmark.[9] Likewise, similar observations can be made about the factor exposures for the 10-year period. Again, the alpha of the SSIF portfolio relative returns is 11 basis points per month (or 132 basis

---

[9] Care should be exercised in comparing the monthly average returns in the regression analysis and the annualized returns that are part of a performance report. Recall that performance reports use geometric averages in compounding returns, whereas linear regressions are inherently arithmetic.

points per year), which is close to the annualized relative return of 1.06% for the 10-year period. Note that the R-squared of the SSIF portfolio increased from 0.89 over the 10-year period to 0.95 over the most recent 3-year period. This apparent increase in diversification is consistent with decrease in tracking error that is reported in Exhibit 6.4 for the same 3-year and 10-year periods.

In summary, at the 3- and 10-year horizons, the analysis suggests that the SSIF portfolio has risk exposures that are similar to its benchmark index, which may be a desirable characteristic of the portfolio for the SSIF's client. Specifically, if a client expects its investment manager to remain "style pure" to its mandate, it may judge the investment manager based on whether its relative returns appear to be correlated with style-specific factors, such as those in the Fama-French model. If a client has hired other managers to occupy other areas within the style box in Exhibit 6.12, then its portfolio could be exposed to unwanted risks if managers stray into other quadrants.

The analysis of the monthly returns since inception of the SSIF portfolio reveals that the portfolio has not always been so consistent with its benchmark. Specifically, the SMB beta of 0.17 is significantly below the benchmark's SMB beta of 0.28. Moreover, its HML beta is 0.13 compared to the benchmark's beta of 0.23, for a statistically significant difference of -0.10 (after rounding). In words, the SSIF portfolio has held larger stocks than the S&P 400 benchmark and has not been as tilted toward value stocks as the benchmark over the since inception period. Furthermore, notice that the alpha of the monthly relative returns is -1 basis point. Unlike the 3- and 10-year horizon alphas that approximated the portfolio's annualized relative return, the since inception alpha is not at all close to the annualized relative return of -1.51%. So, while the alpha largely explains the annualized relative return at the 3- and 10-year horizons, it does not appear to do so at the since inception horizon.

Notice that the annualized relative return is explained by the other factors. Specifically, we can multiply the SMB and HML relative return betas by the average monthly relative returns for those factors during the since inception period to estimate their contributions. We find that the exposure to SMB contributes -5 basis points per month $(-0.05\% = -0.11 \times 0.44\%)$ and HML contributes another -5 basis points per month $(-0.05\% = -0.10 \times 0.50\%)$. Multiplying each by 12 months, contributions total about -120 basis points per year, which is approximately the same as the annualized relative return over the same period.

In summary, the SSIF portfolio's negative relative performance over its since inception period is largely explained by (1) its relative underexposure to smaller stocks at a time that small stocks had relatively good performance and (2) its relative underexposure to value-oriented stocks (i.e., an overexposure growth-oriented stocks) at a time when value outperformed growth. Since the exposure to size (SMB) and value/growth style (HML) is under the investment manager's control, it does not take the SSIF "off the hook" for the negative relative performance. Rather, it indicates what areas are primarily responsible for the negative relative performance, which could be helpful to the SSIF in considering enhancements to its investment process and internal methods.

Beyond the Fama-French 3-Factor Model

While the Fama-French model is a popular performance analysis tool, there are many variations on the theme. In some cases, other specifications of the size and growth/value-style factors are employed. For example, rather than using the Fama-French SMB factor, a size factor can be created by subtracting the return of a large cap index (e.g., the S&P 500 or S&P 100) from the return of a small cap index (e.g., the S&P 600 or Russell 2000). Likewise, growth and value index returns can be used to create a growth/value-style factor akin to HML. Some methods utilize other factors. Among them, a popular equity factor, known as Momentum, is calculated by subtracting the return to a portfolio of recent "losers" (i.e., underperforming stocks) from the return of recent "winners" (i.e., outperforming stocks).[10]

Our use of equity portfolios as examples should not be taken as a suggestion that multifactor analysis is restricted to such portfolios. Indeed, multifactor models are common in the analysis of fixed income portfolios, typically including factors relating to the level of interest rates, the credit spread, and the term spread. The latter two factors are typically calculated in the utilizing an approach similar to that of the Fama-French factors in which the return to a portfolio of low-risk bonds (e.g., Treasury bonds) is subtracted from the return to a portfolio of high-risk bonds (e.g., corporate or high yield bonds) and a return on a short portfolio of is subtracted from the return on a long duration portfolio. Inflation and other economic measures, such as GDP, energy prices, and unemployment round out the list of other commonly used factors.

Risk-Adjusted Return and Reward-to-Risk Measures

Alpha is the most common risk-adjusted measure of portfolio performance. Indeed, the word *alpha* is often used in conversations about investment strategies to mean "outperformance," as if there is only one way to measure it. In practice, alpha can be defined as (1) the average portfolio return minus the average return on the benchmark; (2) the average portfolio return minus the average return according to the single factor model; and (3) the average portfolio return minus the average return according to a multifactor model; among other less common definitions of alpha. Since we have used all three different definitions of "alpha" in this book, we have tried to make clear which

---

[10] See Carhart, M. M., 1996, On persistence in mutual fund performance, *Journal of Finance* 52, pp. 57−82.

specification of alpha is meant by the context in which it is used. Fortunately, all of these definitions of alpha are qualitatively similar, though not mathematically the same. In all cases, alpha uses the return to a portfolio with similar risk exposures to adjust the return of the portfolio, though "Jensen's Alpha" specifically means using the single factor model (using the market index).[11] A student-managed investment fund should adopt the definition of alpha that best fits its portfolio mandate and is consistent with its investment philosophy and process.

Chapter 4 discussed other risk-adjusted measures of portfolio performance. Specifically, another popular measure of a portfolio's overall performance is the Sharpe Ratio, which measures the excess return per unit of total portfolio risk. The Sharpe Ratio is less often applied to portfolios that have a specific mandate in a particular asset class, since return per unit of total risk is not necessarily the objective of such portfolios. In such circumstances, the Information Ratio may be more appropriate.

As discussed in Chapter 4, the Information Ratio is typically defined as the average relative return of the portfolio divided by the tracking error of the portfolio. The interpretation of the ratio is akin to that of the Sharpe Ratio, except that it measures the average relative return (i.e., alpha!) per unit of benchmark-relative risk. If we consider that single factor and multifactor models create implicit benchmarks via the factors and factor exposures, then the Information Ratio can also be calculated using these models' measures of alpha and residual risk (i.e., σ_e from equations 6.25 and 6.29). Regardless of the exact specification used, the Information Ratio measures the reward to active management per unit of active risk. It is useful to consider this as the signal-to-noise ratio of active management. The higher the signal or the lower the noise, the more clearly the investment manager's signal becomes. This signal-to-noise ratio helps distinguish skill from luck. For example, if an investment manager holds a relatively concentrated portfolio in which only one or two holdings have significant outperformance, then the alpha might be positive, but the tracking error and residual risk are likely to be high. Indeed, the noise here raises the question as to whether the manager is just lucky with the one or two "hits" in the portfolio. Conversely, if a manager has the same alpha, but a low tracking error or residual risk, then it is likely that the abnormal return is due to multiple "hits" and less likely that the manager is a "one hit wonder." The higher the Information Ratio, the more confident we can be about the alpha truly being "signal" rather than "noise."

Finally, the casting of the Information Ratio as a signal-to-noise ratio is beyond just an intuitive notion. The Information Ratio is mathematically related to the statistical significance of the alpha, which is determined by the alpha's t-statistic. The t-statistic for a regression alpha is calculated by dividing the alpha by its standard error. The standard error

---

[11] Jensen, M. C., 1969, Risk, the pricing of capital assets, and evaluation of investment portfolios, *Journal of Business* 42, pp. 167–247.

of the alpha from a linear regression is approximately equal to the standard deviation of the residual divided by the square root of the number of observations. Therefore, the t-statistic is approximately equal to the Information Ratio multiplied by the standard deviation of time. A higher t-statistic implies a lower p-value and a higher degree of statistical confidence. Therefore, a higher degree of statistical confidence comes with a higher information ratio and/or a longer time with the same information ratio. That is, a higher positive signal-to-noise ratio or a longer time with the same (positive) signal-to-noise ratio allows increased confidence in the signal. In sum, it is difficult to distinguish skill from luck if the Information Ratio is low.

Transactions Cost Analysis

While we have focused on the investment decisions as sources of portfolio performance, the execution of those decisions through trading can also have an impact through direct and indirect transaction costs. In short, the impact from transaction costs is the difference in performance between a theoretical (paper) portfolio and a real portfolio. The direct costs of trading are those that are measurable and include brokerage commissions, exchange fees, and transaction taxes. Indirect costs are those that are not easily measured, but have the potential to have an even larger impact on returns. The Appendix to this chapter reprints an article by Rob Kissell that discusses practical methods for measuring the impact of transaction costs on performance. The overarching goal with transaction cost analysis, as with performance analysis, is to determine the sources of impact to portfolio returns so as to understand where opportunities exist to reduce costs, enhance returns, or mitigate risk.

Transaction costs are generally accepted to be proportional (though not necessarily linearly so) to the size of an order. Transaction costs are potentially larger for larger orders. Of course, "larger" is relative here, since an order to purchase $50,000 worth of an actively traded name, such as a constituent of the S&P 500, is perhaps a small order compared to an order to purchase $25,000 in a stock whose capitalization is below $500 million and only trades less than 1,000 shares per day. Furthermore, transaction costs are incurred only when trading. Therefore, they also generally scale with the level of turnover in a portfolio. For a student-managed investment fund with a $500,000 portfolio that primarily holds U.S. large cap equities and has a turnover of less than 100% per year, the impact of transaction costs may be measurable, but it may be difficult to significantly affect those costs. That is, resources spent on analysis of trading beyond identifying those costs and attributing a portion of the portfolio's performance to those costs may not be as valuable as deploying those resources to other aspects of the investment process. For funds in which the portfolio holds less liquid securities or for which active trading is a significant source of expected alpha, transaction cost analysis may be among the highest priorities for research and analysis.

Summary of Key Points

- Performance reporting is an accounting exercise that reports the percentage change in the value of the portfolio, usually over various horizons.
- Compound returns, using geometric sums and averages, should be used in reporting performance over multiple periods.
- Performance evaluation and analysis are economic exercises that aim to provide insights into the sources of portfolio returns and risks.
- Performance attribution utilizes portfolio weights to attribute portfolio performance to sector allocation and security selection components.
- Returns-based performance analysis utilizes the time-series of portfolio returns to associate the sources of a portfolio's average return and risks with economically meaningful factors.
- Among the most popular returns-based performance analysis methods, the 3-Factor model attributes average returns and risks to the market, size, and growth/value style factors.
- Performance attribution and performance analysis can be used to analyze a portfolio's returns and a portfolio's relative returns against a specific benchmark.
- Transaction costs can have a meaningful impact on portfolio returns. Transaction costs generally increase as the liquidity of the underlying portfolio holdings decrease and the portfolio size and trading activity increase.

Exercises

1. Use the example in Exhibit 6.3 to answer the following questions.
   a. Verify that the portfolio's security weights are approximately the same on November 7, 2012, pre-flow and post-flow. That is, verify that the cash flow was converted to equities using approximately the same portfolio weights.
   b. Verify that the return on the portfolio would have been approximately the same for the entire month of November 2012 if there had been no cash flow. Hint: Use the security holdings at the end of October and the security prices at the end of November to calculate a portfolio market value for the end of the month. Also, use a cash amount of $7956.00 on November 30, 2012, which is approximately what the cash would have been if there had been no cash flow.
2. Using the monthly returns below from the first quarter of 2008, calculate the compound return for the entire quarter for the strategy and the benchmark. Also, calculate the relative returns for each month and for the entire quarter. Finally, compound the monthly relative returns to show that they are not equal to the quarterly relative return.

Month	Portfolio Return	Benchmark Return
Jan 2008	17.35%	14.87%
Feb 2008	8.57%	5.85%
Mar 2008	−26.01%	−26.12%

3. Using the annual returns below, calculate the annualized average return for strategy and the benchmark over the 3-year period. Also, calculate the annualized average 3-year

(Continued)

Exercises (Continued)

relative return. Note that the annualized average 3-year relative return is negative, despite the fact that the portfolio beat the benchmark by more than 2% in the first two years and only lagged the benchmark by 2% in the third year. Explain why this happens.

Year	Portfolio Return	Benchmark Return	Relative Return
1	26.97%	24.95%	2.02%
2	16.04%	14.03%	2.01%
3	−41.98%	−39.98%	−2.00%

4. The sector contribution to the relative return in Equation 6.19 can also be calculated using the relative return sector allocation in Equation 6.14. In general, the individual sector contributions will be different when using Equation 6.13 versus Equation 6.14. Prove algebraically that both approaches sum to the same total portfolio relative return. Hint: Simply sum each the two versions of Equation 6.19 across all sectors.
5. Using the Fama-French 3-Factor Model regression results from monthly portfolio returns in the table below, describe the strategies that each fund appears to follow. That is, describe what types of stocks the fund is likely to hold and the types of risks to which it is exposed.

Fund	Alpha	Market	SMB	HML	R-Sq.
A	−0.0012	0.71	−0.14	0.20	0.78
B	0.0008	1.02	0.10	−0.02	0.93
C	0.0019	1.11	0.34	−0.22	0.73
D	−0.0017	1.59	−0.10	−0.18	0.82
E	0.0012	1.07	0.30	−0.23	0.98

6. Consider the funds in question 5. Funds C and E appear quite similar. Which investment manager outperforms by more? Which manager would you be most confident has skill in generating value? Why?
7. Suppose that the Large Cap 500 Index Fund is the benchmark for the Growth Fund in Exhibit 6.14. Using the information in Exhibit 6.14, attribute the Growth Fund's average relative return of −0.69% per month to the components of the Fama-French 3-Factor Model. Specifically, determine the sources of the average relative return in terms of the alpha and Market, SMB, and HML factors.
8. Suppose that the Total Market Index Fund is the benchmark for the Value Fund in Exhibit 6.14. Using the information in Exhibit 6.14, attribute the Value Fund's average relative return of +0.43% per month to the components of the Fama-French 3-Factor Model. Specifically, determine the sources of the average relative return in terms of the alpha and Market, SMB, and HML factors.

Tools

Chapter Outline

Just as photographers need cameras and lenses, investment managers need tools that are appropriate to their trade. This chapter summarizes commonly used tools and resources in the investment management profession. Some of the most widely used tools in the profession are licensed, such as those from Bloomberg, S&P CapitalIQ, FactSet, and Thomson Reuters. Recognizing the resource constraints of colleges and universities, we also try to highlight tools that are currently freely available, even if they are not as commonly employed in the most prestigious investment firms. In some cases, we simply list a tool and describe some features that are relevant to a student-managed investment fund. In other cases, we provide examples of uses of the tool. Our purpose in providing more detail about some and not others is not intended to favor or endorse one tool over another. Furthermore, we do not suggest that this chapter provides a comprehensive list of available tools. Rather, we aim to provide examples of how tools might be employed in a student-managed investment fund and leave it to each organization to determine which tools meet their needs and offer the best value for their limited resources.

Throughout this text, we have already utilized the most ubiquitous business and investment management tool: Microsoft Excel. We hope that its exclusion from any list in this chapter emphasizes its importance. Without Excel, the other tools discussed below are of little or no value, as Excel is the primary means of analysis for investment professionals. Indeed, most of the tools listed in this chapter have explicit Excel links, either in the standard of exporting data in an Excel format or in the ability to interface directly with Excel. From building valuation models, to analyzing macroeconomic trends, to performing portfolio attribution and analysis, Excel's largest asset is its flexibility and adaptability to all of the

Trading and Money Management in a Student-Managed Portfolio.
DOI: http://dx.doi.org/10.1016/B978-0-12-374755-6.00007-8

various tasks. With this flexibility comes the ability and responsibility of the Excel user to create specialized or customized tools that fit the particular needs of an investment process. Every member of a student-managed investment fund must become not only familiar with Excel but also proficient in using it.

As with every other aspect of investing, the choice of tool is determined within the context of an organization's investment philosophy and process. A tool that might be essential to one investment manager might be superfluous to another if the investment processes are very different. For example, a bottom–up investment process might heavily rely on tools that provide detailed firm-specific information, while an investment process more focused on asset allocation might find little use for such a resource. Finally, we caution that the quality and the quantity of tools are not the primary determinants of the quality of the investment decisions. There is a saying in the practice of photography that the most important piece of equipment is the person behind the lens. This sentiment is especially true in investing, since every tool mentioned in this chapter is available to anyone or anyone who pays to access that tool. What differentiates one investor from another is the investment ideas that result from their investment philosophy and process. It is our hope that the tools described in this chapter will help facilitate the discovery and expression of such ideas in student-managed investment funds.

Primary Data Sources

Vendor	Website
Companies	Various company websites
Federal Reserve Economic Data (FRED)	research.stlouisfed.org/fred2
International Monetary Fund	www.imf.org
U.S. Securities and Exchange Commission EDGAR	www.sec.gov
	www.sec.gov/edgar/searchedgar/companysearch.html
World Bank	data.worldbank.org

We begin our list of data sources with the ultimate sources from which nearly all hard data on companies begin: the companies themselves. Nearly all companies in the United States maintain an investor relations website on which the company's financial statements and other disclosures are available. For example, the investor relations site for Apple is investor .apple.com and Microsoft's investor relations site is www.microsoft.com/investor. Such sites often also have archived recordings or transcripts of quarterly earnings calls and links to the company's SEC filings. In addition, most company websites contain valuable background information about the history of the firm, identification about subsidiaries, divisions or offices, biographies of key executives, and details about its products and services.

The U.S. Securities and Exchange Commission's EDGAR Online provides access to filings made by companies whose securities are publicly traded in the United States. These filings are made available through a search interface as shown in Exhibit 7.1. As shown in the exhibit, when placing Apple's ticker symbol, "AAPL," on the search page, the site's user has access to the list of the company's SEC filings results. Exhibit 7.2 shows an 8-K filing by Apple, while Exhibit 7.3 shows an example of a 10-Q filing. Some filings can be viewed in interactive mode, allowing quick access to items in a menu on the left side of the page, as shown in Exhibit 7.4. Finally, Exhibit 7.5 shows an EDGAR page of Apple's insider holdings and recent changes to those holdings as reported on Form 4.

We discuss many different data vendors below, but stress that the filings that are freely available on the EDGAR are the primary source of financial statement information from nearly all vendors. Members of student-managed investment funds might find it useful to verify the accuracy of data from other vendors by consulting this primary source. Since all publicly traded companies in the United States must file these documents, students and investors who do not have access to other vendor's resources should be confident in

Exhibit 7.1 U.S. Securities and Exchange Commission EDGAR

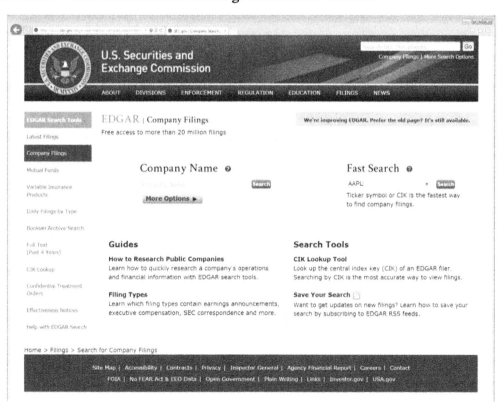

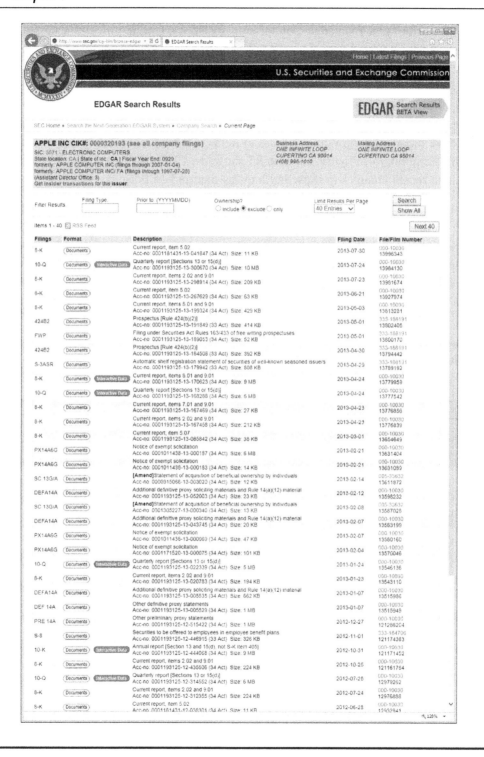

knowing that they have the highest quality financial statement information available by accessing it on EDGAR.

The Federal Reserve Bank of St. Louis maintains the Federal Reserve Economic Data site, known as FRED. As shown in Exhibit 7.6, the site has a wealth of data on macroeconomic variables, such as interest rates, employment, and GDP. Exhibit 7.7 shows bond yield and spread data that might be especially helpful for student-managed investment funds that focus on fixed income portfolios. Furthermore, note that most series on FRED can be downloaded individually to Excel spreadsheets, or even in bulk .zip files. The download screen and resulting Excel file are shown in Exhibit 7.7.

The International Monetary Fund (IMF) and World Bank compile global macroeconomic data. Exhibit 7.8 shows the homepage of each organization. Unfortunately, the IMF and World Bank do not make all of their data freely available via their websites. However, some data are available for free and others by subscription. Some universities and colleges may already subscribe to these databases (e.g., through the library), so members of student-managed investment funds should determine if these sources are available at their institutions. Some IMF and World Bank data series are also available through other vendors, such as Bloomberg.

Exhibit 7.2 Apple's 8-K on EDGAR

8-K 1 d571814d8k.htm FORM 8-K

UNITED STATES
SECURITIES AND EXCHANGE COMMISSION
Washington, D.C. 20549

FORM 8-K

CURRENT REPORT
Pursuant to Section 13 or 15(d) of
The Securities Exchange Act of 1934

July 23, 2013
Date of Report (date of earliest event reported)

APPLE INC.
(Exact name of Registrant as specified in its charter)

California	000-10030	94-2404110
(State or other jurisdiction of incorporation)	(Commission File Number)	(I.R.S. Employer Identification Number)

1 Infinite Loop
Cupertino, California 95014
(Address of principal executive offices) (Zip Code)

(408) 996-1010
(Registrant's telephone number, including area code)

(Former name or former address, if changed since last report)

Check the appropriate box below if the Form 8-K filing is intended to simultaneously satisfy the filing obligation of the registrant under any of the following provisions:

☐   Written communications pursuant to Rule 425 under the Securities Act (17 CFR 230.425)

☐   Soliciting material pursuant to Rule 14a-12 under the Exchange Act (17 CFR 240.14a-12)

☐   Pre-commencement communications pursuant to Rule 14d-2(b) under the Exchange Act (17 CFR 240.14d-2(b))

☐   Pre-commencement communications pursuant to Rule 13e-4(c) under the Exchange Act (17 CFR 240.13e-4(c))

Item 2.02   Results of Operations and Financial Condition.

On July 23, 2013, Apple Inc. ("Apple") issued a press release regarding Apple's financial results for its third fiscal quarter ended June 29, 2013 and a related data sheet. A copy of Apple's press release is attached hereto as Exhibit 99.1 and a copy of the related data sheet is attached hereto as Exhibit 99.2.

The information contained in this Current Report shall not be deemed "filed" for purposes of Section 18 of the Securities Exchange Act of 1934, as amended (the "Exchange Act"), or incorporated by reference in any filing under the Securities Act of 1933, as amended, or the Exchange Act, except as shall be expressly set forth by specific reference in such a filing.

Item 9.01   Financial Statements and Exhibits.

(d)   Exhibits.

The following exhibits are furnished herewith:

Exhibit Number	Description
99.1	Text of press release issued by Apple Inc. on July 23, 2013
99.2	Data sheet issued by Apple Inc. on July 23, 2013

SIGNATURE

Pursuant to the requirements of the Securities Exchange Act of 1934, the registrant has duly caused this report to be signed on its behalf by the undersigned hereunto duly authorized.

APPLE INC.

Date: July 23, 2013

By: /s/ Peter Oppenheimer
Peter Oppenheimer
Senior Vice President,
Chief Financial Officer

EXHIBIT INDEX

Exhibit Number	Description
99.1	Text of press release issued by Apple Inc. on July 23, 2013
99.2	Data sheet issued by Apple Inc. on July 23, 2013

EX-99.1 2 d571814dex991.htm EX-99.1

Exhibit 99.1

Apple Reports Third Quarter Results

Sales of 31 Million iPhones Set New June Quarter Record

CUPERTINO, California—July 23, 2013—Apple today announced financial results for its fiscal 2013 third quarter ended June 29, 2013. The Company posted quarterly revenue of $35.3 billion and quarterly net profit of $6.9 billion, or $7.47 per diluted share. These results compare to revenue of $35 billion and net profit of $8.8 billion, or $9.32 per diluted share, in the year-ago quarter. Gross margin was 36.9 percent compared to 42.8 percent in the year-ago quarter. International sales accounted for 57 percent of the quarter's revenue.

The Company sold 31.2 million iPhones, a record for the June quarter, compared to 26 million in the year-ago quarter. Apple also sold 14.6 million iPads during the quarter, compared to 17 million in the year-ago quarter. The Company sold 3.8 million Macs, compared to 4 million in the year-ago quarter.

Apple's Board of Directors has declared a cash dividend of $3.05 per share of the Company's common stock. The dividend is payable on August 15, 2013, to shareholders of record as of the close of business on August 12, 2013.

"We are especially proud of our record June quarter iPhone sales of over 31 million and the strong growth in revenue from iTunes, Software and Services," said Tim Cook, Apple's CEO. "We are really excited about the upcoming releases of iOS 7 and OS X Mavericks, and we are laser-focused and working hard on some amazing new products that we will introduce in the fall and across 2014."

"We generated $7.8 billion in cash flow from operations during the quarter and are pleased to have returned $18.8 billion in cash to shareholders through dividends and share repurchases," said Peter Oppenheimer, Apple's CFO.

Apple is providing the following guidance for its fiscal 2013 fourth quarter:

- revenue between $34 billion and $37 billion
- gross margin between 36 percent and 37 percent
- operating expenses between $3.9 billion and $3.95 billion
- other income/(expense) of $200 million
- tax rate of 26.5%

Apple will provide live streaming of its Q3 2013 financial results conference call beginning at 2:00 p.m. PDT on July 23, 2013 at www.apple.com/quicktime.qtv/earningsq313. This webcast will also be available for replay for approximately two weeks thereafter.

This press release contains forward-looking statements including without limitation those about the Company's estimated revenue, gross margin, operating expenses, other income (expense), and tax rate. These statements involve risks and uncertainties, and actual results may differ. Risks and uncertainties include without limitation the effect of competitive and economic factors, and the Company's reaction to those factors, on consumer and business buying decisions with respect to the Company's products; continued competitive pressures in the marketplace; the ability of the Company to deliver to the marketplace and stimulate customer demand for new programs, products, and technological innovations on a timely basis; the effect that product introductions and transitions, changes in product pricing or mix, and/or increases in component costs could have on the Company's gross margin; the inventory risk associated with the Company's need to order or commit to order product components in advance of customer orders; the continued availability on acceptable terms, or at all, of certain components and services essential to the Company's business currently obtained by the Company from sole or limited sources; the effect that the Company's dependency on manufacturing and logistics services provided by third parties may have on the quality, quantity or cost of products manufactured or services rendered; risks associated with the Company's international operations; the Company's reliance on third-party intellectual property and digital content; the potential impact of a finding that the Company has infringed on the intellectual property rights of others; the Company's dependency on the performance of distributors, carriers and other resellers of the Company's products; the effect that product and service quality problems could have on the Company's sales and operating profits; the continued service and availability of key executives and employees; war, terrorism, public health issues, natural disasters, and other circumstances that could disrupt supply, delivery, or demand of products; and unfavorable results of other legal proceedings. More information on potential factors that could affect the Company's financial results is included from time to time in the "Risk Factors" and "Management's Discussion and Analysis of Financial Condition and Results of Operations" sections of the Company's public reports filed with the SEC, including the Company's Form 10-K for the fiscal year ended September 29, 2012, its Form 10-Q for the quarter ended December 29, 2012, its Form 10-Q for the quarter ended March 30, 2013, and its Form 10-Q for the quarter ended June 29, 2013 to be filed with the SEC. The Company assumes no obligation to update any forward-looking statements or information, which speak as of their respective dates.

Apple designs Macs, the best personal computers in the world, along with OS X, iLife, iWork and professional software. Apple leads the digital music revolution with its iPods and iTunes online store. Apple has reinvented the mobile phone with its revolutionary iPhone and App Store, and is defining the future of mobile media and computing devices with iPad.

Press Contact:
Steve Dowling
Apple
dowling@apple.com
(408) 974-1896

Investor Relations Contacts:
Nancy Paxton
Apple
paxton1@apple.com
(408) 974-5420

Joan Hoover
Apple
hoover1@apple.com
(408) 974-4570

NOTE TO EDITORS: For additional information visit Apple's PR website (www.apple.com/pr), or call Apple's Media Helpline at (408) 974-2042.

Apple Inc.
UNAUDITED CONDENSED CONSOLIDATED STATEMENTS OF OPERATIONS
(In millions, except number of shares which are reflected in thousands and per share amounts)

	Three Months Ended		Nine Months Ended	
	June 29, 2013	June 30, 2012	June 29, 2013	June 30, 2012
Net sales	$ 35,323	$ 35,023	$ 133,438	$ 120,542
Cost of sales (1)	22,299	20,029	83,005	66,281

EX-99.2 3 d571814dex992.htm EX-99.2

Exhibit 99.2

Apple Inc.
Q3 2013 Unaudited Summary Data
(Units in thousands, Revenue in millions)

	Q3'13		Q2'13		Q3'12		Sequential Change		Year/Year Change	
		Revenue		Revenue		Revenue		Revenue		Revenue
Operating Segments										
Americas		$ 14,405		$ 14,052		$ 12,806		3%		12%
Europe		7,614		9,800		8,237		-22%		-8%
Greater China (a)		4,641		8,213		5,389		-43%		-14%
Japan		2,543		3,135		2,009		-19%		27%
Rest of Asia Pacific		2,046		3,162		2,498		-35%		-18%
Retail		4,074		5,241		4,084		-22%		0%
Total Apple		$ 35,323		$ 43,603		$ 35,023		-19%		1%

	Q3'13		Q2'13		Q3'12		Sequential Change		Year/Year Change	
	Units	Revenue	Units	Revenue	Units	Revenue	Units	Revenue	Units	Revenue
Product Summary										
iPhone (b)	31,241	$ 18,154	37,430	$ 22,955	26,028	$ 15,821	-17%	-21%	20%	15%
iPad (b)	14,617	6,374	19,477	8,746	17,042	8,779	-25%	-27%	-14%	-27%
Mac (b)	3,754	4,893	3,952	5,447	4,020	4,933	-5%	-10%	-7%	-1%
iPod (b)	4,569	733	5,633	962	6,751	1,060	-19%	-24%	-32%	-31%
iTunes/Software/Services (c)		3,990		4,114		3,203		-3%		25%
Accessories (d)		1,179		1,379		1,227		-15%		-4%
Total Apple		$ 35,323		$ 43,603		$ 35,023		-19%		1%

(a) Greater China includes China, Hong Kong and Taiwan
(b) Includes deferrals and amortization of related non-software services and software upgrade rights.
(c) Includes revenue from sales on the iTunes Store, the App Store, the Mac App Store, and the iBookstore, and revenue from sales of AppleCare, licensing and other services.
(d) Includes sales of hardware peripherals and Apple-branded and third-party accessories for iPhone, iPad, Mac and iPod.

Other Information and Data Sources

Vendor	Website
Industry Associations	Various association websites
World Health Organization	www.who.int

Exhibit 7.9 shows homepages for various organizations that may have useful information for an investment manager. Many industry associations exist for the purpose of promoting or lobbying on behalf of the entire industry. As such, the information provided on these websites is as varied as the sites themselves. However, these organizations can provide valuable information for both company-specific and industry- or sector-specific research. For example, an industry trade association might produce white papers on new applications, markets, products, or services within its industry. Some associations might also track and report trends affecting their industry. Finally, some organizations might provide both soft (e.g., commentary or viewpoints) and hard (e.g., objective data) information on issues of interest or related to their specific areas. Again, this information can help shape an investment analyst's understanding of issues affecting the companies for which they are

Exhibit 7.3 Apple's 10-Q on EDGAR

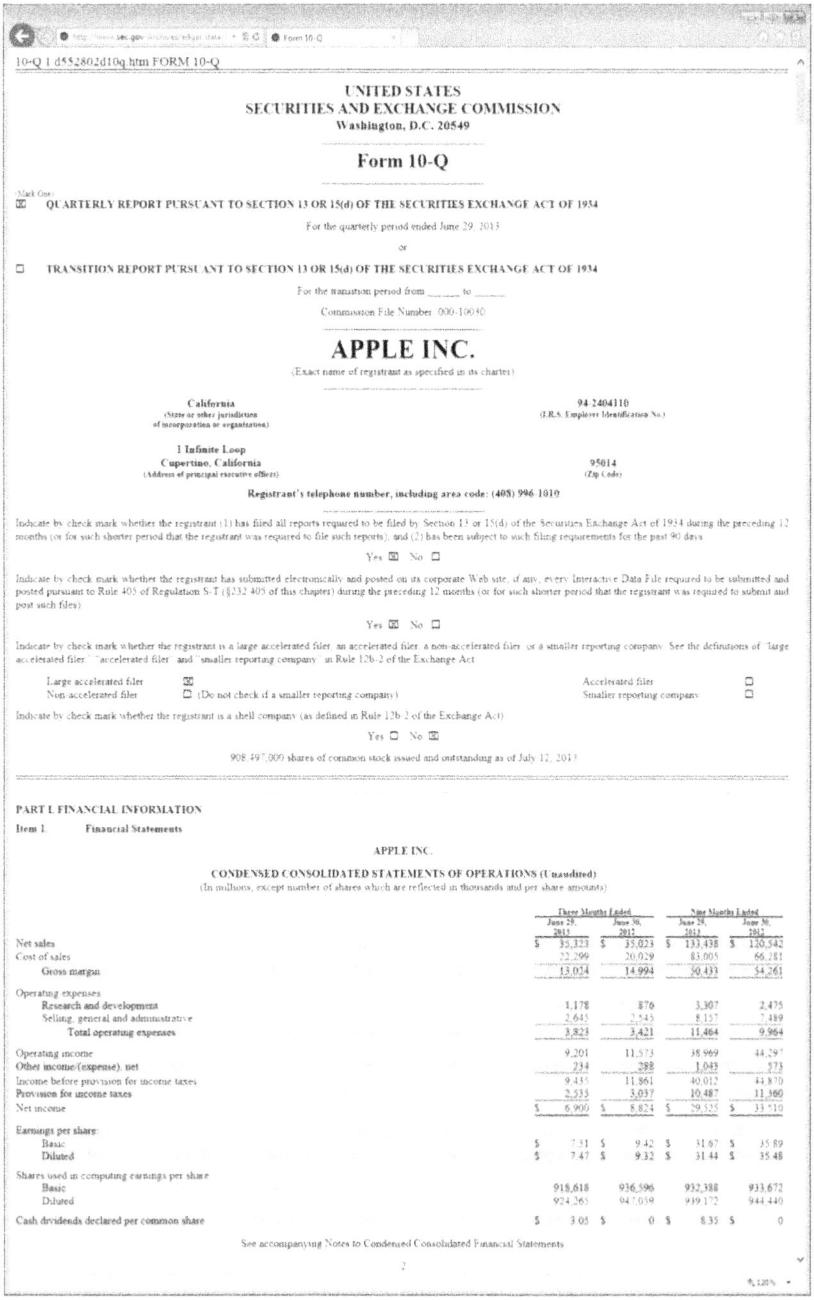

10-Q 1 d552802d10q.htm FORM 10-Q

UNITED STATES
SECURITIES AND EXCHANGE COMMISSION
Washington, D.C. 20549

Form 10-Q

(Mark One)

☒ **QUARTERLY REPORT PURSUANT TO SECTION 13 OR 15(d) OF THE SECURITIES EXCHANGE ACT OF 1934**

For the quarterly period ended June 29, 2013

or

☐ **TRANSITION REPORT PURSUANT TO SECTION 13 OR 15(d) OF THE SECURITIES EXCHANGE ACT OF 1934**

For the transition period from ______ to ______

Commission File Number: 000-10030

APPLE INC.

(Exact name of registrant as specified in its charter)

California (State or other jurisdiction of incorporation or organization)	**94-2404110** (I.R.S. Employer Identification No.)
1 Infinite Loop **Cupertino, California** (Address of principal executive offices)	**95014** (Zip Code)

Registrant's telephone number, including area code: (408) 996-1010

Indicate by check mark whether the registrant (1) has filed all reports required to be filed by Section 13 or 15(d) of the Securities Exchange Act of 1934 during the preceding 12 months (or for such shorter period that the registrant was required to file such reports), and (2) has been subject to such filing requirements for the past 90 days.

Yes ☒ No ☐

Indicate by check mark whether the registrant has submitted electronically and posted on its corporate Web site, if any, every Interactive Data File required to be submitted and posted pursuant to Rule 405 of Regulation S-T (§232.405 of this chapter) during the preceding 12 months (or for such shorter period that the registrant was required to submit and post such files).

Yes ☒ No ☐

Indicate by check mark whether the registrant is a large accelerated filer, an accelerated filer, a non-accelerated filer, or a smaller reporting company. See the definitions of "large accelerated filer," "accelerated filer" and "smaller reporting company" in Rule 12b-2 of the Exchange Act.

Large accelerated filer	☒	Accelerated filer	☐
Non-accelerated filer	☐ (Do not check if a smaller reporting company)	Smaller reporting company	☐

Indicate by check mark whether the registrant is a shell company (as defined in Rule 12b-2 of the Exchange Act).

Yes ☐ No ☒

908,497,000 shares of common stock issued and outstanding as of July 12, 2013

PART I. FINANCIAL INFORMATION

Item 1. Financial Statements

APPLE INC.

CONDENSED CONSOLIDATED STATEMENTS OF OPERATIONS (Unaudited)
(In millions, except number of shares which are reflected in thousands and per share amounts)

	Three Months Ended		Nine Months Ended	
	June 29, 2013	June 30, 2012	June 29, 2013	June 30, 2012
Net sales	$ 35,323	$ 35,023	$ 133,438	$ 120,542
Cost of sales	22,299	20,029	83,005	66,281
Gross margin	13,024	14,994	50,433	54,261
Operating expenses				
Research and development	1,178	876	3,307	2,475
Selling, general and administrative	2,645	2,545	8,157	7,489
Total operating expenses	3,823	3,421	11,464	9,964
Operating income	9,201	11,573	38,969	44,297
Other income/(expense), net	234	288	1,043	573
Income before provision for income taxes	9,435	11,861	40,012	44,870
Provision for income taxes	2,535	3,037	10,487	11,360
Net income	$ 6,900	$ 8,824	$ 29,525	$ 33,510
Earnings per share:				
Basic	$ 7.51	$ 9.42	$ 31.67	$ 35.89
Diluted	$ 7.47	$ 9.32	$ 31.44	$ 35.48
Shares used in computing earnings per share				
Basic	918,618	936,596	932,388	933,672
Diluted	924,265	947,059	939,172	944,440
Cash dividends declared per common share	$ 3.05	$ 0	$ 8.35	$ 0

See accompanying Notes to Condensed Consolidated Financial Statements

2

APPLE INC.

CONDENSED CONSOLIDATED BALANCE SHEETS (Unaudited)
(In millions, except number of shares which are reflected in thousands)

	June 29, 2013	September 29, 2012
ASSETS		
Current assets		
Cash and cash equivalents	$ 11,248	$ 10,746
Short-term marketable securities	31,358	18,383
Accounts receivable, less allowances of $104 and $98, respectively	8,839	10,930
Inventories	1,697	791
Deferred tax assets	3,193	2,583
Vendor non-trade receivables	4,614	7,762
Other current assets	7,270	6,458
Total current assets	68,219	57,653
Long-term marketable securities	104,914	92,122
Property, plant and equipment, net	16,327	15,452
Goodwill	1,522	1,135
Acquired intangible assets, net	4,353	4,224
Other assets	5,421	5,478
Total assets	$ 199,856	$ 176,064
LIABILITIES AND SHAREHOLDERS' EQUITY:		
Current liabilities		
Accounts payable	$ 15,516	$ 21,175
Accrued expenses	13,470	11,414
Deferred revenue	7,333	5,953
Total current liabilities	36,319	38,542
Deferred revenue – non-current	2,672	2,648
Long-term debt	16,958	0
Other non-current liabilities	20,553	16,664
Total liabilities	76,502	57,854
Commitments and contingencies		
Shareholders' equity		
Common stock, no par value; 1,800,000 shares authorized; 908,442 and 939,208 shares issued and outstanding, respectively	19,024	16,422
Retained earnings	104,564	101,289
Accumulated other comprehensive (loss) income	(234)	499
Total shareholders' equity	123,354	118,210
Total liabilities and shareholders' equity	$ 199,856	$ 176,064

See accompanying Notes to Condensed Consolidated Financial Statements

4

APPLE INC.

CONDENSED CONSOLIDATED STATEMENTS OF CASH FLOWS (Unaudited)
(In millions)

	Nine Months Ended	
	June 29, 2013	June 30, 2012
Cash and cash equivalents, beginning of the period	$ 10,746	$ 9,815
Operating activities:		
Net income	29,525	33,310
Adjustments to reconcile net income to cash generated by operating activities:		
Depreciation and amortization	4,974	2,296
Share-based compensation expense	1,698	1,292
Deferred income tax expense	2,524	4,066
Changes in operating assets and liabilities:		
Accounts receivable, net	2,091	(2,278)
Inventories	(906)	(346)
Vendor non-trade receivables	3,148	(293)
Other current and non-current assets	484	(3,238)
Accounts payable	(4,740)	2,450
Deferred revenue	1,404	2,575
Other current and non-current liabilities	3,556	1,686
Cash generated by operating activities	43,758	41,720
Investing activities:		
Purchases of marketable securities	(122,681)	(121,091)
Proceeds from maturities of marketable securities	13,963	10,344
Proceeds from sales of marketable securities	81,734	73,140
Payments made in connection with business acquisitions, net	(443)	(350)
Payments for acquisition of property, plant and equipment	(6,210)	(4,834)
Payments for acquisition of intangible assets	(560)	(1,067)
Other	(188)	(56)
Cash used in investing activities	(34,385)	(43,914)
Financing activities:		
Proceeds from issuance of common stock	335	433
Excess tax benefits from equity awards	644	1,036
Taxes paid related to net share settlement of equity awards	(1,001)	(1,145)
Dividends and dividend equivalent rights paid	(7,795)	0
Repurchase of common stock	(17,950)	0
Proceeds from issuance of long-term debt, net	16,896	0
Cash (used in) generated by financing activities	(8,871)	324
Increase (decrease) in cash and cash equivalents	502	(1,870)
Cash and cash equivalents, end of the period	$ 11,248	$ 7,945

Supplemental cash flow disclosure:

Exhibit 7.4 EDGAR Interactive Mode

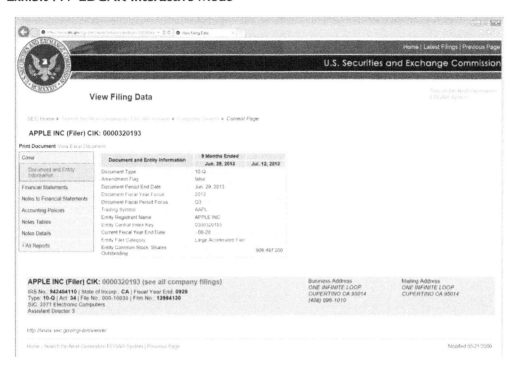

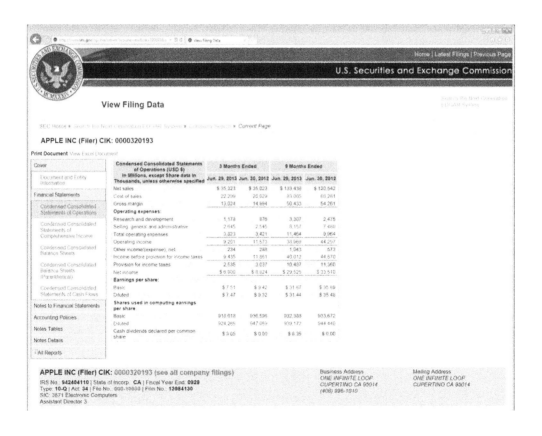

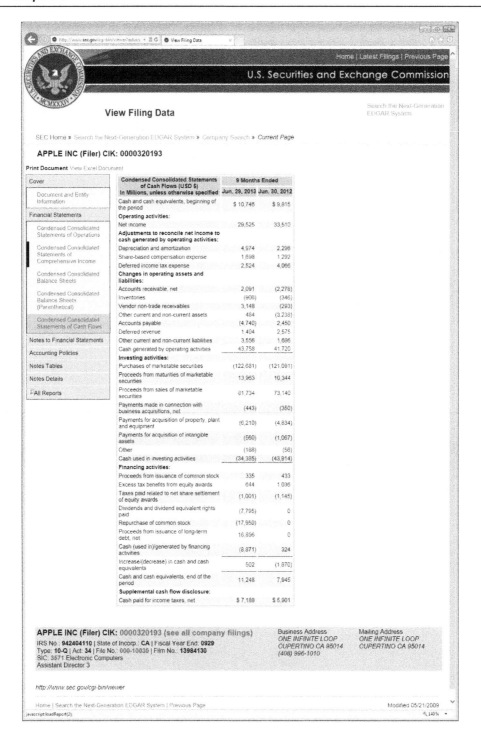

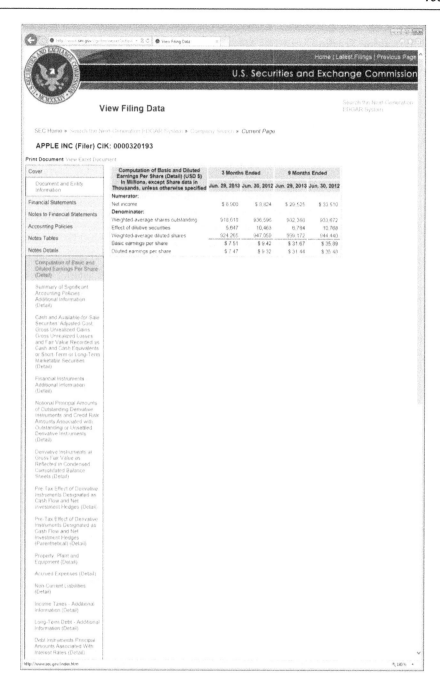

Exhibit 7.5 Insider Trading on EDGAR

Exhibit 7.6 Federal Reserve Economic Data (FRED)

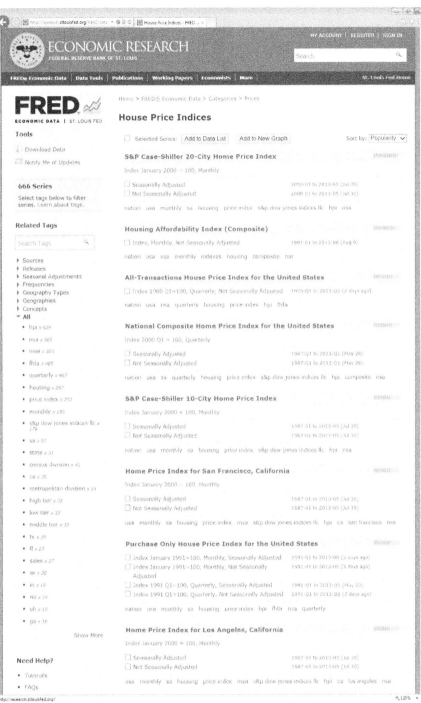

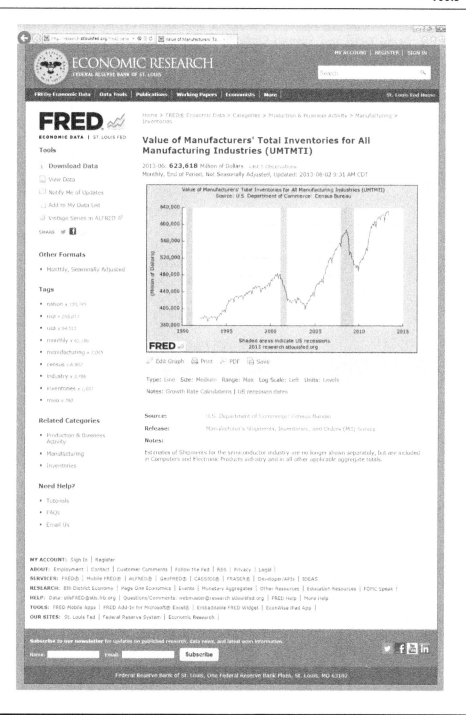

Exhibit 7.7 Bond Yield and Spread Data on FRED

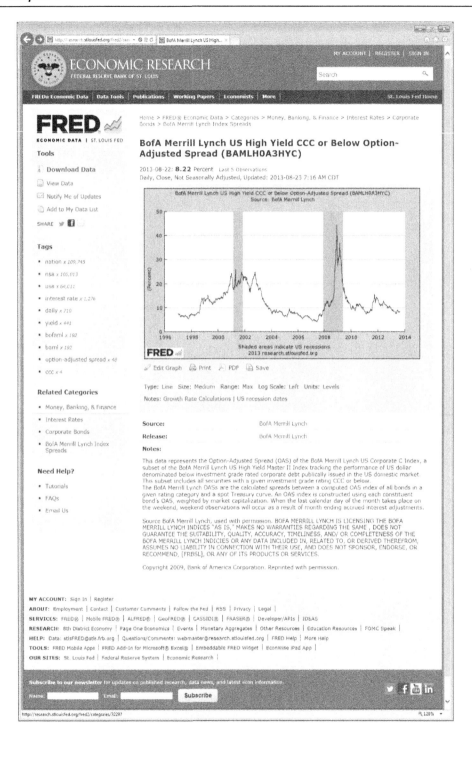

responsible. For example, data from the World Health Organization (WHO) might be used by an analyst who is trying to forecast the revenues for a biotech or pharmaceutical firm's new drug to treat a specific disease. The WHO might have data on the global incidence of the disease, as well as information about what other therapies are available. The WHO might even have estimates of the cost of competing treatments.

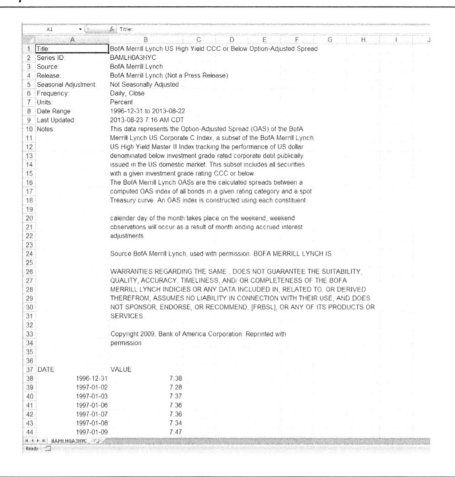

Web Portals, Search Engines, and Business News

Vendor	Website
CBS Market Watch	www.cbsmarketwatch.com
CNBC	www.cnbc.com
CNNMoney	money.cnn.com
Financial Times	www.ft.com
Google Finance	www.google.com/finance
Wall Street Journal	online.wsj.com
Yahoo! Finance	finance.yahoo.com

Exhibit 7.8 IMF and World Bank

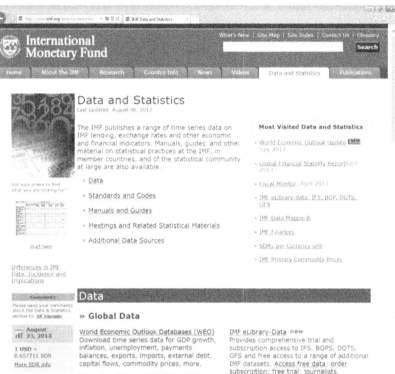

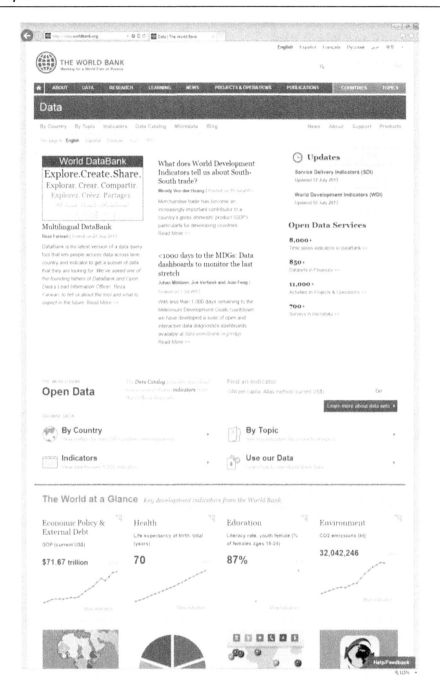

Exhibit 7.9 Alternative Information Sources

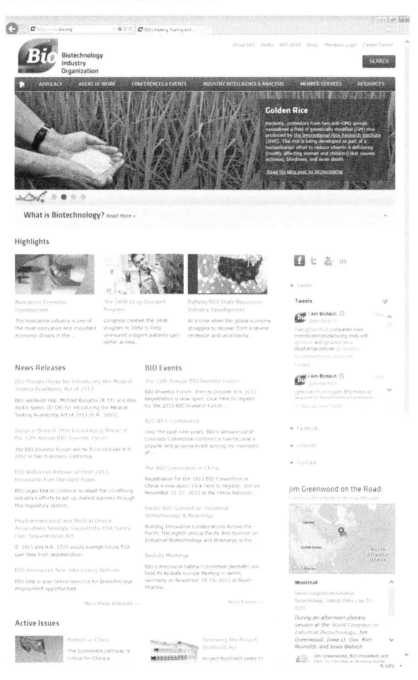

Web portals, such as Google and Yahoo! Finance, can be convenient sources of investment data for individual investors and student-managed investment funds. In some sense, these sites offer free "one-stop shopping" for information that might be useful for company analysis and security selection. For example, a user of Yahoo! Finance can enter a stock name or ticker and have access to a profile of the company, recent company or industry news, financial statements, competitor information, and market statistics. Similar information can be found on Google. In addition, portfolios can be set up in each site and tracked, with performance updated throughout the day (though perhaps not in real time).

World Health Organization

Health topics | Data and statistics | Media centre | Publications | Countries | Programmes and projects | About WHO

Data and statistics

Health systems

Achieving health targets depends on equitable access to a health system that delivers high quality services. The exact configuration of services will depend on country context, but will require
- adequate financing with pooling of risk
- a well trained and remunerated workforce
- information for policy and management decisions
- logistics for medicines, technologies and vaccines
- well-maintained facilities within a referral network
- clear leadership and governance with support

More data on health systems

Global Health Observatory

WHO's portal providing access to data and analyses for monitoring the global health situation

Data repository
World health statistics report
Statistical reports
Country statistics
Map gallery
WHO indicator registry

Health workforce

57 countries

have a health workforce crisis

Health workforce

Health financing

62 US$

is the average per capita expenditure required to reach the MDGs in the world's poorest countries

Health financing

Official Development Assistance

50%

of Official Development Assistance (ODA) for health does not flow through governments

Official Development Assistance

Mortality and global health estimates
Data   Analysis

Health systems
Essential health technologies
Data   Analysis

Essential medicines
Data   Analysis

Governance and aid effectiveness
Data   Analysis

Health financing
Data   Analysis

Health workforce
Data   Analysis

Service delivery
Data   Analysis

Health equity monitor
Data   Analysis

Women and health
Data   Analysis

Urban health
Data   Analysis

Noncommunicable diseases
Mortality/morbidity
Data   Analysis

Risk factors
Data   Analysis

Health systems response
Data   Analysis

Infectious diseases
Cholera
Data   Analysis

Global influenza virological surveillance
Data   Analysis

Meningococcal meningitis
Data   Analysis

Sexually transmitted infections (STIs)
Data   Analysis

Road safety
Data   Analysis

Substance use
Alcohol
Data   Analysis

Tobacco
Data   Analysis

Substance use disorders

Millennium Development Goals (MDGs)
MDG 1: child underweight
Data   Analysis

MDG 4: child health
Data   Analysis

MDG 4: immunization
Data   Analysis

MDG 5: maternal and reproductive health
Data   Analysis

MDG 6: HIV/AIDS
Data   Analysis

MDG 6: malaria
Data   Analysis

MDG 6: neglected tropical diseases
Data   Analysis

MDG 6: tuberculosis
Data   Analysis

MDG 7: water and sanitation
Data   Analysis

MDG 8: essential medicines
Data   Analysis

Other sites, such as those listed above, also have news or security-specific information and, in some cases, portfolio tracking features. A potentially nice feature of some of these sites, such as Yahoo! Finance, is that they can be set to provide alerts when there is news in tracked securities.

We caution that the quality control on some sites is unclear and suggest that any information obtained on such sites be confirmed with other trusted sources. For example, at this writing, Google appears to offer a "Stock Screener" feature — a tool that could be useful in narrowing the list of securities for more in-depth analysis as discussed in Chapter 3. However, when trying Google's Stock Screener, we found the results to be inconsistent with other professional-level tools. As with any tool, the user should understand the tool's purpose and limitations when trying to apply it. This is especially true of freely available tools from third parties. While the convenience of financial statement data from one of these sites might be useful in the initial analysis of a security, we recommend verifying the data against the company's EDGAR filings prior to final investment decisions that rely on such data.

Brokers and Financial Service Providers

Vendor	Website
Fidelity	www.fidelity.com
Morningstar	www.morningstar.com

Brokerage firms often provide investment tools to their clients and, in some cases, the public. Members of a student-managed investment fund might have access to these tools via their fund's account or their own personal accounts. The tools available include stock screeners, sector information, index constituent information, analysts' ratings and reports, and risk analysis. We list Fidelity and Morningstar because these two vendors currently have a number of tools available freely, in addition to "premium" tools that are available to their clients or by subscription. Fidelity offers much of the same stock-level information as found on Yahoo! Finance, in addition to a number of other tools that might be useful to student-managed investment funds. Specifically, the publicly available stock screener in Fidelity appears to have a number of options that are typically found on other professional-level screeners, such as Bloomberg. The results of a stock screen can then be downloaded and opened in Excel. Though Morningstar's free screener might seem basic by comparison, it can be useful in quickly narrowing down a list of securities. In addition, Morningstar offers free portfolio tracking, allowing customized views of portfolio holdings.

Index Providers

Vendor	Website
Barclays Index Products	indices.barcap.com
FTSE Indices	www.ftse.com/indices
MSCI Global Equity Indices	www.msci.com/products/indices
Russell Indexes	www.russell.com/indexes
S&P Dow Jones Indices	www.spdji.com

Index providers can be an excellent source for information about the composition of benchmark portfolios for specific asset classes. Since the composition of an index is proprietary to the index provider, very few offer free access to real-time constituents and weights. Indeed, most index providers charge fees to investment managers for index data. In some cases, educational institutions might be able to negotiate an agreement with an index provider at a reduced fee (or perhaps even for free). In addition, most sites have index returns, descriptive statistics, and methodology information freely available. In some cases, sector or industry weightings are also available, which can be useful to a student-managed investment fund's portfolio construction and performance analysis.

Licensed Services

Vendor	Website
Bloomberg Professional	www.bloomberg.com
Center for Research in Security Prices (CRSP)	www.crsp.com
FactSet	www.factset.com
S&P CapitalIQ	www.capitaliq.com
Compustat	
Research Insight	
Thomson Reuters	www.thomsonreuters.com
Thomson One Analytics	
Worldscope	
Value Line	www.valueline.com

Students who participate in student-managed investment funds are generally doing the same work and are faced with making the same decisions as analysts, strategists, and portfolio managers at real investment firms. This experience is what makes student-managed investment funds such valuable opportunities. The experience is further enhanced to the extent that members can utilize the same tools that professionals use in conducting the business of an investment firm. Such experience is an added asset to SMIF members as they begin their careers. Some of the most widely used professional tools are listed above. Since the development of and maintenance of these tools represents a significant source of revenue for these vendors, these tools can be expensive to academic institutions that do not use such tools to generate investment management revenues. In many cases, colleges and universities may negotiate academic licenses at reduced fees compared to what professional investment firms pay. Since many of the vendors above offer comparable tools, student-managed investment fund programs that are resource-constrained might further economize by choosing only one or two. Indeed, many investment firms choose one vendor's platform over another rather than spending money on redundant resources.

At a basic level, most of these professional tools provide raw data that can be found in other tools described in this chapter, some of which are freely available. However, these tools generally provide true "one-stop shopping" for most of the raw data and organize it in readily accessible format. For example, we illustrate some of the capabilities of Bloomberg Professional below. In many cases, the data are derived primarily from company annual reports, SEC filings, and market data that are available from free sources. However, it would likely take an analyst days to collect the information for a single stock and additional time to organize the data prior to conducting analysis. On professional platforms, such as Bloomberg, CapitalIQ, FactSet, and Thomson Reuters, these data are available to an analyst with only a few keystrokes or clicks of a mouse. Moreover, these vendors have an interest in maintaining the quality and consistency of the data that are provided on their platforms, reducing the likelihood of errors. In short, publicly and freely available tools do not begin to approach the quantity and quality of the functions that organize and analyze data that are found in these professional-level tools.

Using Bloomberg, we provide several examples of data and analysis tools that might be useful to a student-managed investment fund. Note that these examples only scratch the surface of the scale and scope of what is possible with these tools. Moreover, we show the use of Bloomberg Professional using Bloomberg workstation screens. In addition to accessing Bloomberg interactively as shown in the exhibits, many Bloomberg data items are available via functions in Microsoft Excel when running Excel and a Bloomberg add-in on a Bloomberg workstation. This allows student-managed investment funds to customize data templates or fully functioning models to run in real time on Excel.

We begin by showing the Equity Analysis function results in Exhibit 7.10. The equity analysis is accessed in Bloomberg by typing the ticker symbol and hitting the $<$Equity$>$ key on the Bloomberg keyboard (or $<$F8$>$ on standard keyboards), followed by the $<$Go$>$ key (or $<$Enter$>$). The first four screens are chosen by keyboard using the number references shown or by clicking the items on the screen. The security financial analysis functions are accessed with the "FA" code, as shown in the exhibit. These functions provide access to both the current and historical financial statements. Tabs provide access to the income statement and balance sheet, as well as tables with information about cash flows and the financial information from the company's segments (e.g., by product line and/or geography). The items are available in a standardized format and can be displayed in summary and detailed form, as well as graphically. Data can be copied from the screen to documents outside of Bloomberg, such as reports or spreadsheets.

There are numerous functions that would be useful in conducting the security analysis in Chapter 3 of this text. Specifically, Exhibit 7.11 shows a supply chain analysis of Apple. In this case, Bloomberg identifies and attributes costs and revenues to the firm's major suppliers and customers, respectively. The supply chain analysis also shows the firm's competitors or "peers," providing a starting point for conducting competitive analysis of the firm. Exhibit 7.12 shows screens with information about a company's current and past earnings, as well as estimates of future earnings from professional analysts. Access to analyst reports and research are also available. Holdings of a security by institutions, large shareholders, and a firm's insiders are easily accessed, as shown in Exhibit 7.13.

Exhibit 7.10 Bloomberg Security Description and Financial Statements*

Security Description: Profile ("AAPL <Equity> DES <GO>") or "AAPL <F8> DES <Enter>")

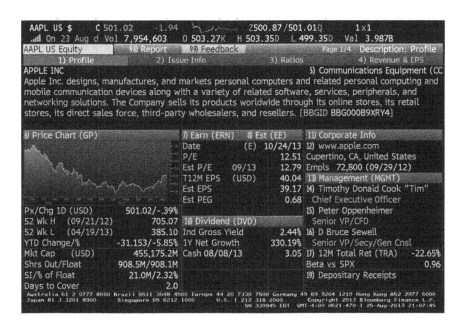

Security Description: Issue Info

Security Description: Ratios

Company Description: Revenue & EPS

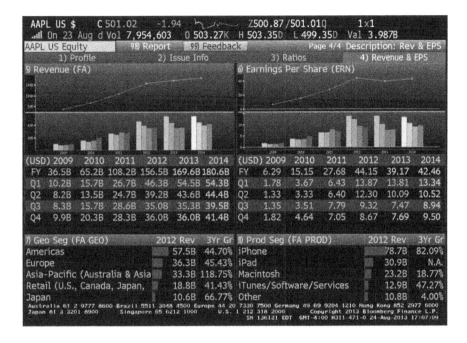

Security Financial Analysis: Key Stats ("AAPL <Equity> FA <GO>" or "AAPL <F8> FA <Enter>")

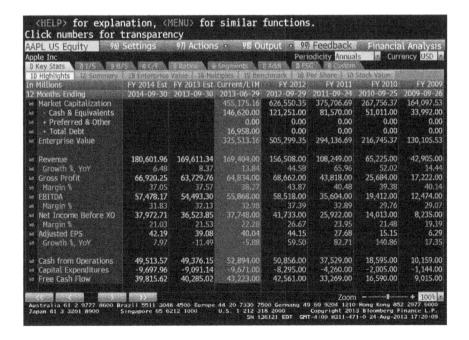

Security Financial Analysis: Key Stats

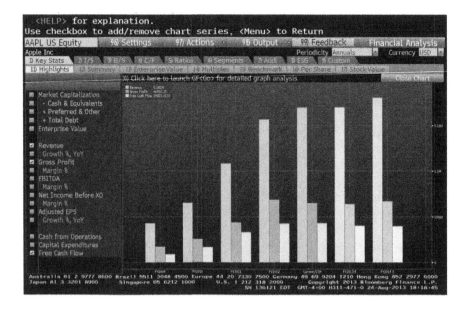

Income Statement ("AAPL <Equity> FA <GO> 2 <GO>" or "AAPL <F8> <Enter> 2 <Enter>")

In Millions (except Per Share)	FY 2014 Est	FY 2013 Est	Last 12M	FY 2012	FY 2011	FY 2010
12 Months Ending	2014-09-30	2013-09-30	2013-06-29	2012-09-29	2011-09-24	2010-09-25
Revenue	180,601.96	169,611.34	169,404.00	156,508.00	108,249.00	65,225.00
- Cost of Revenue			104,570.00	87,846.00	64,431.00	39,541.00
Gross Profit	66,920.25	63,729.76	64,834.00	68,662.00	43,818.00	25,684.00
- Operating Expenses			14,921.00	13,421.00	10,028.00	7,299.00
Operating Income	50,229.95	48,288.91	49,913.00	55,241.00	33,790.00	18,385.00
- Interest Expense			53.00	0.00	0.00	0.00
- Foreign Exchange Losses (Gains)			0.00	0.00	0.00	0.00
- Net Non-Operating Losses (Gains			-1,045.00	-522.00	-415.00	-155.00
Pretax Income	51,198.16	49,481.38	50,905.00	55,763.00	34,205.00	18,540.00
- Income Tax Expense			13,157.00	14,030.00	8,283.00	4,527.00
Income Before XO Items	37,972.71	36,523.85	37,748.00	41,733.00	25,922.00	14,013.00
- Extraordinary Loss Net of Tax			0.00	0.00	0.00	0.00
- Minority Interests			0.00	0.00	0.00	0.00
Net Income	38,124.72	36,590.60	37,748.00	41,733.00	25,922.00	14,013.00
- Total Cash Preferred Dividends			0.00	0.00	0.00	0.00
- Other Adjustments			0.00	0.00	0.00	0.00
Net Inc Avail to Common Shareholde			37,748.00	41,733.00	25,922.00	14,013.00
Abnormal Losses (Gains)			0.00	0.00	0.00	0.00
Tax Effect on Abnormal Items			0.00	0.00	0.00	0.00
Normalized Income			37,748.00	41,733.00	25,922.00	14,013.00

Income Statement ("AAPL <Equity> FA <GO> 3 <GO>" or "AAPL <F8> <Enter> 3 <Enter>")

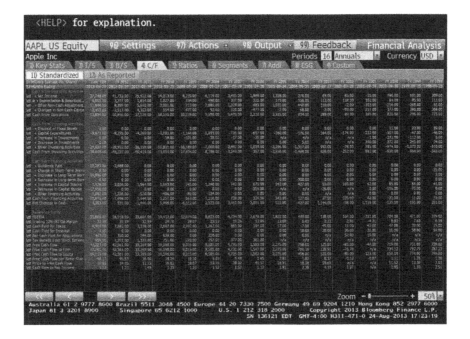

<HELP> for explanation.						
AAPL US Equity	90) Settings	97) Actions	98) Output	99) Feedback	Financial Analysis	
Apple Inc				Periods 10 Annuals	Currency USD	
1) Key Stats	2) I/S	3) B/S	4) C/F	5) Ratios	6) Segments	7) Addl	8) ESG	9) Custom
10) Standardized	11) As Reported	12) Common Size	13) Fair Value Analysis	14) Statement Chart		
In Millions (except Per Share)	FY 2012	FY 2011	FY 2010	FY 2009	FY 2008	FY 2007
12 Months Ending	2012-09-29	2011-09-24	2010-09-25	2009-09-26	2008-09-27	2007-09-29

Assets						
+ Cash & Near Cash Items	10,746.00	9,815.00	11,261.00	5,263.00	11,875.00	9,352.00
+ Short-Term Investments	18,383.00	16,137.00	14,359.00	18,201.00	10,236.00	6,034.00
+ Accounts & Notes Receivable	10,930.00	5,369.00	5,510.00	3,361.00	2,422.00	1,637.00
+ Inventories	791.00	776.00	1,051.00	455.00	509.00	346.00
+ Other Current Assets	16,803.00	12,891.00	9,497.00	4,275.00	4,964.00	4,332.00
Total Current Assets	57,653.00	44,988.00	41,678.00	31,555.00	30,006.00	21,701.00
+ LT Investments & LT Receivables	92,122.00	55,618.00	25,391.00	10,528.00	2,379.00	0.00
+ Net Fixed Assets	15,452.00	7,777.00	4,768.00	2,954.00	2,455.00	1,832.00
+ Gross Fixed Assets	21,887.00	11,768.00	7,234.00	4,667.00	3,747.00	2,841.00
- Accumulated Depreciation	6,435.00	3,991.00	2,466.00	1,713.00	1,292.00	1,009.00
+ Other Long-Term Assets	10,837.00	7,988.00	3,346.00	2,464.00	1,331.00	1,345.00
⊞ Total Long-Term Assets	118,411.00	71,383.00	33,505.00	15,946.00	6,165.00	3,177.00
⊞ Total Assets	176,064.00	116,371.00	75,183.00	47,501.00	36,171.00	24,878.00

Liabilities & Shareholders' Equity						
+ Accounts Payable	21,175.00	14,632.00	12,015.00	5,601.00	5,520.00	4,970.00
+ Short-Term Borrowings	0.00	0.00	0.00	0.00	0.00	0.00
+ Other Short-Term Liabilities	17,367.00	13,338.00	8,707.00	5,905.00	5,841.00	4,136.00
Total Current Liabilities	38,542.00	27,970.00	20,722.00	11,506.00	11,361.00	9,106.00
+ Long-Term Borrowings	0.00	0.00	0.00	0.00	0.00	0.00

Zoom — ∎ — + 100%

Australia 61 2 9777 8600 Brazil 5511 3048 4500 Europe 44 20 7330 7500 Germany 49 69 9204 1210 Hong Kong 852 2977 6000
Japan 81 3 3201 8900   Singapore 65 6212 1000   U.S. 1 212 318 2000   Copyright 2013 Bloomberg Finance L.P.
SN 136121 EDT   GMT-4:00 H311-471-0 24-Aug-2013 17:22:05

Cash Flow ("AAPL <Equity> FA <GO> 4 <GO>" or "AAPL <F8> <Enter> 4 <Enter>")

Ratios ("AAPL <Equity> FA <GO> 5 <GO>" or "AAPL <F8> <Enter> 5 <Enter>")

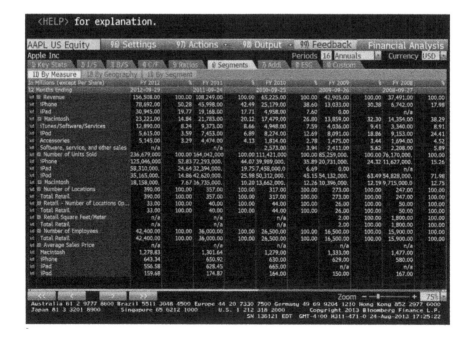

Segments ("AAPL <Equity> FA <GO> 5 <GO>" or "AAPL <F8> <Enter> 5 <Enter>")

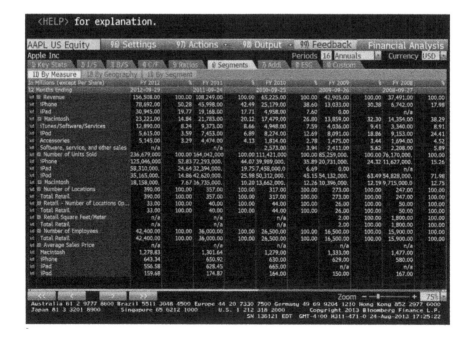

Segments

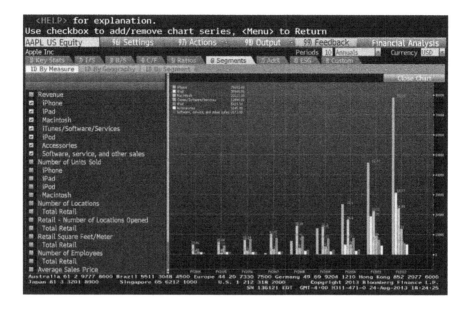

Segments

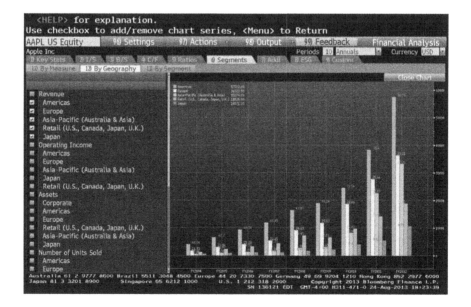

Additional Information

*Used with permission of Bloomberg L.P. Copyright © 2013. All rights reserved.

Exhibit 7.14 shows other valuation tools that would be helpful in selecting securities, including the relative valuation of a firm compared to other firms in its sector or industry. The exhibit also shows that Bloomberg can be used to calculate a stock's beta. The beta calculation is an example of how such functions can be customized. In the case of beta, the user can select the time period, frequency (e.g., daily, weekly, monthly, or yearly), and the index or portfolio with which beta is measured. Finally, Exhibit 7.15 shows several equity analysis menu screens that provide a glimpse at even more security analysis functions that are available in Bloomberg.

Chapter 3 also discusses the importance of screening and ranking stocks as an early step in the security selection process. Professional tools provide powerful stock screeners, as illustrated in Exhibit 7.16. The screening criteria shown on the Bloomberg screens include exchange, sector, index, and countries. However, nearly any item that is reported in the earlier equity analysis exhibits is available as a screening variable. Users can design and save screening criteria and then organize the output of such screens to further rank securities. Again, the results of such analysis are easily downloaded or copied for use in a spreadsheet.

Exhibit 7.11 Bloomberg Supply Chain Analysis*

Supply Chain ("AAPL <Equity> SPLC <GO>" or "AAPL <F8> SPLC <Enter>")

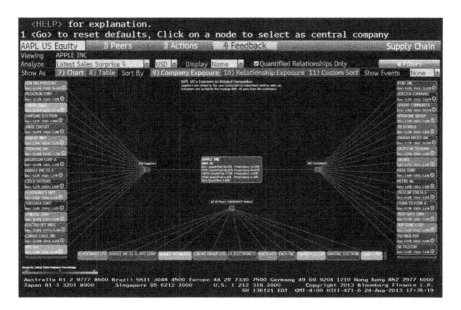

Supply Chain: Suppliers

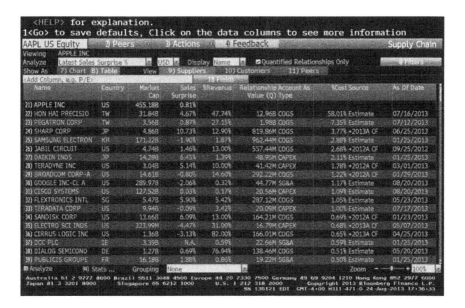

Supply Chain: Customers

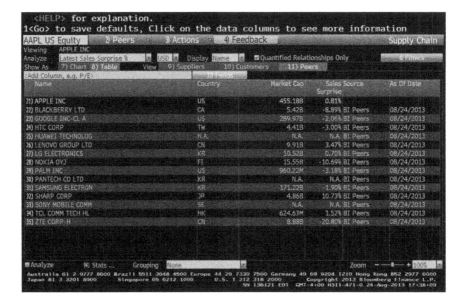

Supply Chain: Peers or Competitors

Exhibit 7.12 Bloomberg Company Earnings Information*

Earnings & Estimates ("AAPL <Equity> EE <GO>" or "AAPL <F8> EE <Enter>")

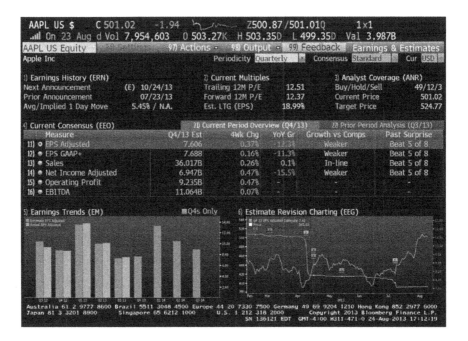

Earnings History ("AAPL <Equity> ERN <GO>" or "AAPL <F8> ERN <Enter>")

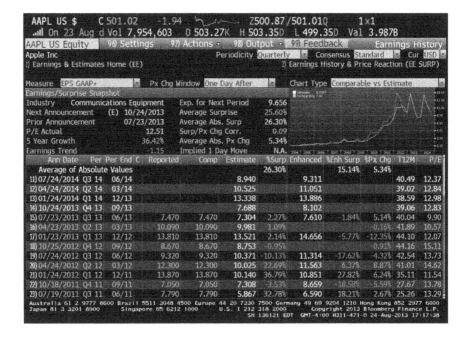

Research ("AAPL <Equity> BRC <GO>" or "AAPL <F8> BRC <Enter>")

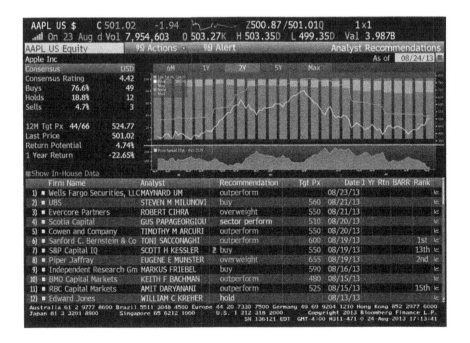

Analyst Recommendations ("AAPL <Equity> ANR <GO>" or "AAPL <F8> ANR <Enter>")

Exhibit 7.13 Bloomberg Holdings Information*

Holdings from All Sources ("AAPL <Equity> PHDC1 <GO>" or "AAPL <F8> PHDC1 <Enter>")

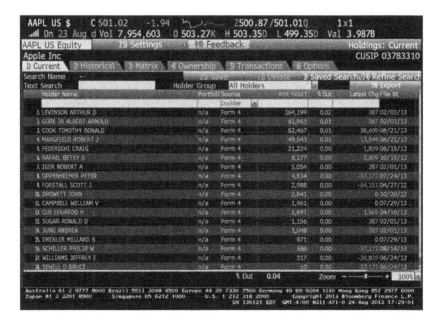

Insider Holdings ("AAPL <Equity> PHDC3 <GO>" or "AAPL <F8> PHDC3 <Enter>")

Exhibit 7.14 Bloomberg Valuation Tools*

Relative Valuation ("AAPL <Equity> RV <GO>" or "AAPL <F8> RV <Enter>")

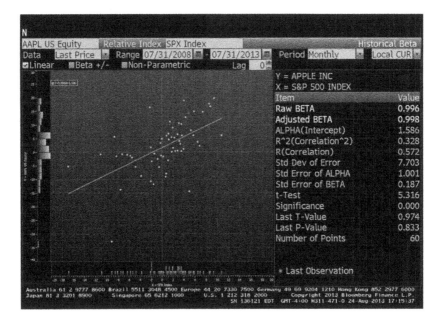

Beta ("AAPL <Equity> BETA <GO>" or "AAPL <F8> BETA <Enter>")

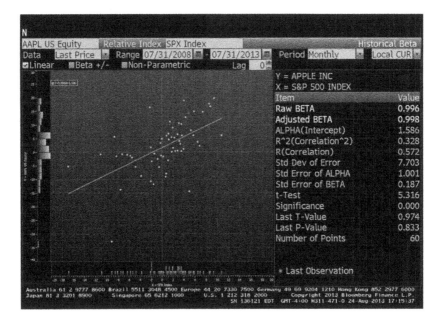

Exhibit 7.15 Bloomberg Equity Menus*

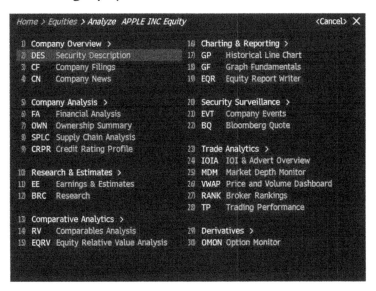

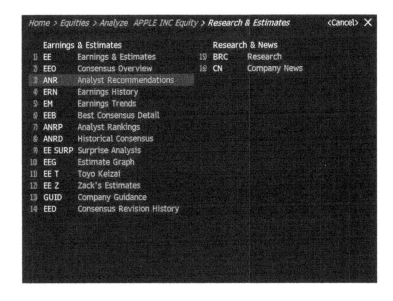

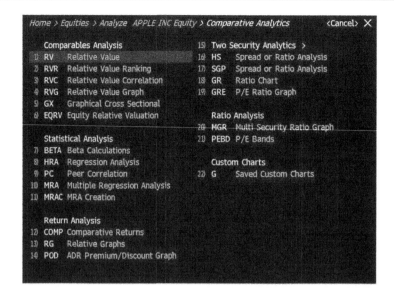

Exhibit 7.16 Bloomberg Equity Screener*

Equity Screener Biotech Example: Biotech Screen

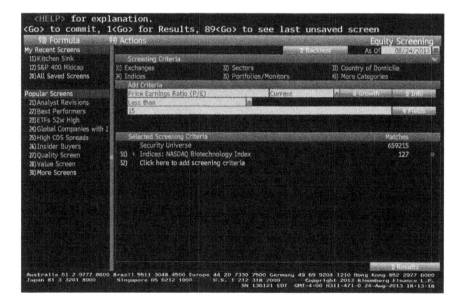

Equity Screener Biotech Example: Biotech and P/E Screen

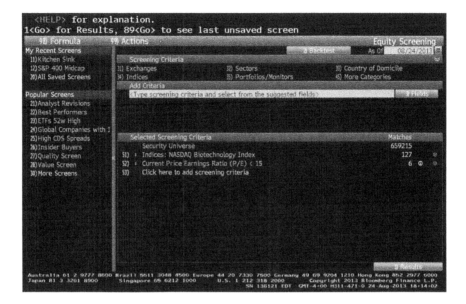

Equity Screener Biotech Example Results

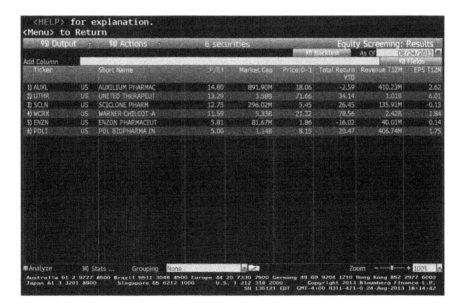

Equity Screener Consumer Goods Example

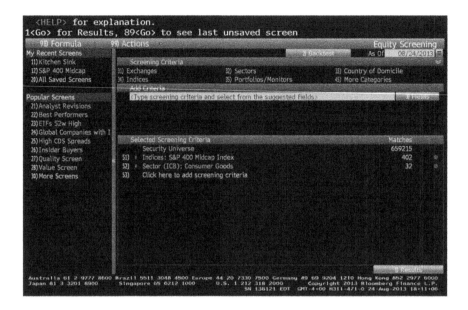

Equity Screener Consumer Goods Results

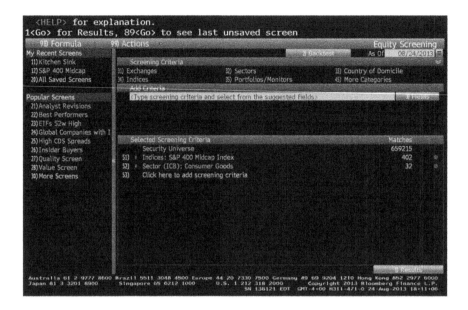

Exhibit 7.17 Bloomberg Fixed Income Tools*

Bond Yields by Sector ("CMX <GO >" or "CMX <Enter>")

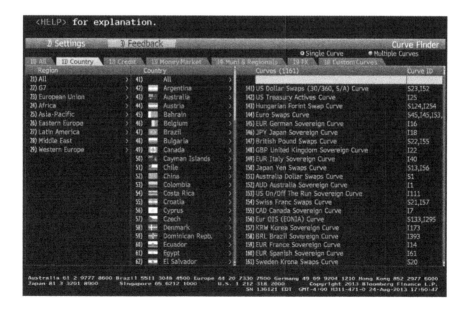

Yield Curves ("IYC1 <GO >" or "IYC1 <Enter>")

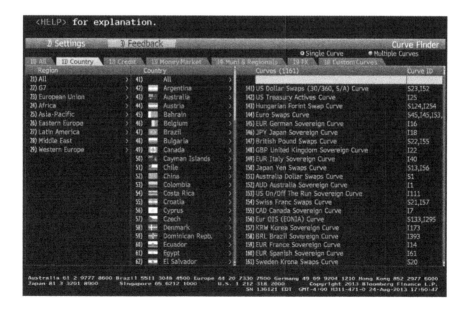

Yield Curve Example

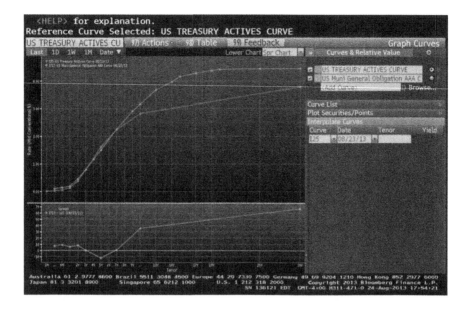

Yield Curve Example

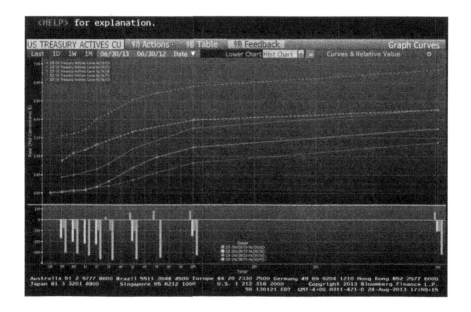

While we have used equity portfolio management in many examples throughout this text, many of the methods and tools are also generally applicable to fixed income portfolios. Indeed, professional tools such as Bloomberg are likely to be even more valuable for a student-managed investment fund that manages fixed income investments, since there are relatively few publicly and freely available resources or tools in that area. Exhibit 7.17 shows a sample of Bloomberg functions that provide detailed data about fixed income markets, including individual security and market-wide yield and spread information.

Finally, professional platforms offer numerous portfolio tracking and performance analysis tools. Exhibit 7.18 shows the performance attribution tool in Bloomberg applied to the SSIF portfolio that was used in performance attribution examples throughout Chapter 6. As discussed in Chapter 6, performance attribution utilizes portfolio and benchmark index security weights to attribute performance to sector allocation and security selection components. Since benchmark weights from the major index providers, such as Russell and S&P, are proprietary, permissions or licenses must be obtained separately for those data to be available in systems such as Bloomberg. In some cases, close proxies for such indexes can be substituted. For example, the SSIF portfolio attribution is measured against the Midcap SPDR Trust ETF, since the SSIF does not have the permissions necessary to use the S&P Midcap 400 Index. Though permissions can be an issue in the portfolio attribution function, there are relatively few functions in which such permissions cause a material effect on the usefulness of Bloomberg or other professional tools. For example, Exhibit 7.19 shows current and historical sector weights and ranked sector and constituent (e.g., member) returns for some indexes. The information from these functions is used in the performance attribution analysis in Chapter 6.

Thomson Reuters and CapitalIQ offer tools with similar scale and scope to Bloomberg, providing data and analysis functions that serve nearly every aspect of the portfolio management process. We have also included other vendors on this list that are more specialized in the product or service they offer. For example, ValueLine has a long-standing tradition of providing independent investment analysis and is available in many university libraries. On the other hand, FactSet specializes in quantitative analysis of portfolios and their underlying securities. Exhibit 7.20 provides an overview from FactSet about the ways in which it might be deployed in student-managed investment funds. Finally, CRSP (Center for Research in Security Prices) is a data vendor originating from the University of Chicago, providing one of the most comprehensive databases of U.S. securities returns. While CRSP might not have the fundamental data that would be useful in security analysis, the historical returns can be used for a student-managed investment fund to perform back-testing and simulations of quantitative investment processes. Many research universities

Exhibit 7.18 Bloomberg Portfolio Analysis*

Portfolio Performance Attribution

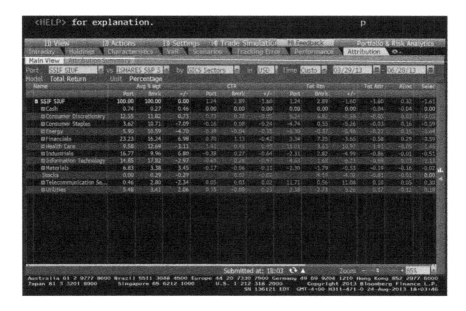

Portfolio Characteristics

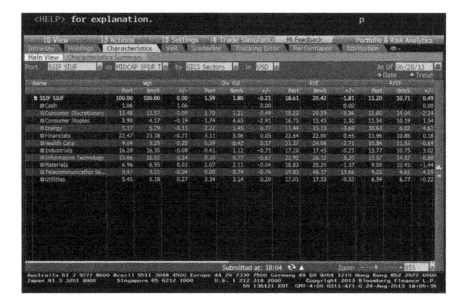

Exhibit 7.19 Bloomberg Index Analysis*

S&P 500 Sector Weights ("SPXL1 <Index> GWGT <GO>" or "SPXL1 <F10> GWGT <Enter>")

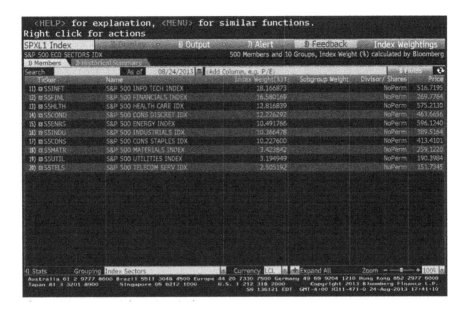

S&P 500 Sector Weights Historical Summary

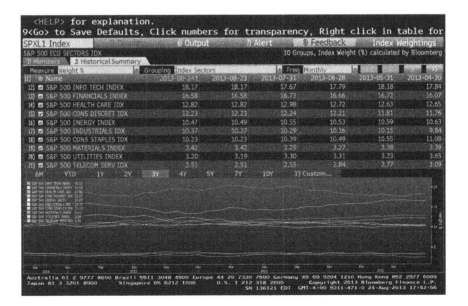

S&P 500 Sector Ranked Returns ("SPXL1 <Index> GRR <GO>" or "SPXL1 <F10> GRR <Enter>")

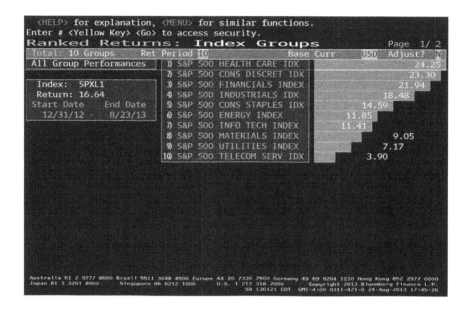

S&P 500 Index GICS Groups	10 Yr-Dt	11 Qtr 1	12 Qtr 2	13 Qtr 3	14 Qtr 4	15 Lst Yr
1) S&P 500 HEALTH CARE IDX	24.25	5.57	.50	15.22	3.33	25.05
2) S&P 500 CONS DISCRET IDX	23.30	7.07	1.57	11.76	6.43	29.35
3) S&P 500 FINANCIALS INDEX	21.94	6.44	5.32	10.92	6.78	32.78
4) S&P 500 INDUSTRIALS IDX	18.48	2.98	2.96	10.08	2.23	19.32
5) S&P 500 CONS STAPLES IDX	14.59	3.08	-2.48	13.77	-.17	14.17
6) S&P 500 ENERGY INDEX	11.85	9.52	-3.31	9.57	-.93	14.96
7) S&P 500 INFO TECH INDEX	11.41	7.04	-6.21	4.21	1.22	5.89
8) S&P 500 MATERIALS INDEX	9.05	4.46	2.04	4.17	-2.39	8.37
9) S&P 500 UTILITIES INDEX	7.17	-1.55	-3.91	11.84	-3.67	1.91
10) S&P 500 TELECOM SERV IDX	3.90	6.79	-7.06	8.20	-.07	7.31

S&P 500 Member Ranked Returns ("SPXL1 <Index> MRR <GO>" or "SPXL1 <F10> MRR <Enter>")

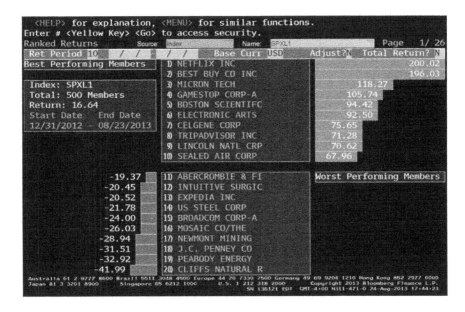

Source: S&P Down Jones Indices

Exhibit 7.20 FactSet in a Student-Managed Investment Fund

Tasks a Student Within an SMIF Might Do
1. *Portfolio Trading Scenario?*

Find New Companies
1. *Screen for new companies*
2. *Research ideas*

Analyze Companies as Potential Investments
1. *Examine financials*
2. *Examine estimates*
3. *Compare to other competitors*

Managing Portfolio
A: Equity Portfolio Analysis
1. *Track Performance in Real Time*
   Analyze performance, risk, composition, style, and characteristics for multiple portfolios and portfolio managers in real time. With the most current analytics possible, you have a more accurate picture of your portfolio and increased clarity on the impact of changes you are considering.

2. *Customize Interactive Reports and Charts*

   Interactively examine reports and charts with double-click sorting, drill down group- and security-level details, and formatting options. Spectrum functionality lets you view multiple reports and charts side-by-side, with intelligent linking that carries the portfolio, benchmark, and other details across all views. Set a standard display of reports and charts to open automatically when you launch FactSet.

3. *Access Streaming Global Data*

   Combine your proprietary holdings with FactSet content or third-party data sources, including extensive benchmark data and global exchange indices. Integrate your holdings via a nightly upload or intraday connection to your firm's OMS. FactSet seamlessly integrates intraday prices with historical data to produce any report on an up-to-the-second basis.

B: Composition and Characteristics

Gain insight into portfolio and benchmark weights using custom groupings in reports and charts.

4. *Analyze Weights*

   Customize Weights reports with multiple portfolios and benchmarks. Launch charts to see portfolio weights, benchmark weights, the difference between them, and weights over time.

5. *Examine Top-Level and Group Characteristics*

   Use Characteristics reports to view weights on a portfolio-level basis, including market capitalization, valuation measures, growth rates, profitability ratios, and other financial ratios for your portfolios and selected benchmarks. For a security-level view, examine the current valuation for individual holdings, groups, and the total portfolio using P/E, forward P/E, price to book, and dividend yield. Customize Valuation reports by adding ratios that apply to your portfolio.

C: Performance Analysis

View performance versus a benchmark between any two selected dates, or for more in-depth analysis see portfolio performance from two perspectives: attribution and contribution.

6. *Analyze Relative and Absolute Performance*

   Research the performance of a portfolio relative to a benchmark to see if your portfolio outperformed and how each group contributed to overall performance. Understand how management decisions such as group allocation, security selection, and currency tilts may have affected results. Within the Attribution report, view allocation, selection, and interaction effects at a glance. FactSet links to your proprietary holdings and benchmark index portfolios on a daily or intraday basis. Audit returns, attribution effects, weights, and characteristics data for greater transparency. You can also assess performance on an absolute basis. View how price changes and dividend payments contributed to total return and survey each company's weight, price change, market value, total return, and contribution to return.

7. *Customize Groups*

   Examine how segments of your portfolio performed by grouping by sector, industry, market cap, or your own custom groupings. Choose groupings by sector, region, or country, or create groupings of the highest and lowest securities in your portfolio based on factors like market value, P/E, or growth rate. For more flexibility, choose grouping definitions from FactSet, vendors such as S&P, or your own proprietary definitions. You can also incorporate risk-based performance attribution or fixed income attribution into your reports. Add risk factors from Barra, Axioma, APT, Northfield, and R-Squared to a report and then group by factor. For fixed income performance attribution, integrate yield change, duration, or credit quality into attribution reports to view attribution for both equity and fixed income portfolios at once.

D: Dynamic Chartings
Study performance over time or throughout the day with flexible charts.

8. *Chart Performance from Multiple Perspectives*
   Chart the performance of your portfolio management decisions over a series of months, quarters, years, or other periods, and plot this data against the overall effect. View intraday performance relative to a benchmark with Performance Heat Maps to uncover problem sectors, and then examine each sector to see which individual securities helped or hurt that sector during the day. See at-a-glance performance with reports like Top/Bottom Contributors, which shows only the best and worst performing securities in your portfolio during the report period.

9. *Customize Chart Options*
   FactSet charts are dynamic, so you can quickly customize colors, labels, and other formatting aspects or look at raw data and charts simultaneously in a split view.

E: Analysis That Fits Your Strategy
FactSet gives you the flexibility to analyze according to your unique investment style, whether it includes fixed income, alternative assets, a long/short strategy, or currency hedging.

10. *Analyze Across All Asset Classes and Strategies*
    Understand how counterparties and issuers relate to each other and what a firm's true exposure is by evaluating exposure to issuers across asset classes. To reveal the exposure of index futures, ETFs, or mutual funds to a particular security or risk factor, choose whether these composite assets should be analyzed as-is or as their underlying securities. Examine long/short and long-only portfolios by splitting the portfolio into long and short positions and creating a market neutral benchmark.

11. *Track the Impact of Ideas*
    Understand how anticipated security changes in your portfolio or portfolio changes to your composite will impact composition and characteristics. Simulate trades before they are executed, and view the implications for predicted risk, style, or fundamental characteristics and weights.

12. *Present Portfolio Results*
    Instantly create reports for client communications by combining key portfolio analytics with your proprietary portfolio information and commentary. Choose the reports and charts you want to include and publish presentation-ready documents using your firm's custom layout, colors, and design.

13. *Upload Holding Information*
    FactSet integrates portfolio holdings and transactions through automated nightly synchronization with your accounting system or custodian. View portfolio holdings more current than the previous day's positions with an intraday connection to your firm's OMS. Link to your accounting system to leverage transaction-based returns for greater accuracy.

14. *Rely on Unsurpassed Support*

    To provide the best client service in the industry, FactSet strives to be as accessible to our clients as possible. Round-the-clock client support reinforces FactSet's dedication to providing clients with superior service. Whether you have a quick question or need step-by-step guidance through a complex task, our highly trained Portfolio Analytics specialists will help you find answers and maximize the value of FactSet.

Style, Performance, and Risk Analysis

FactSet's returns-based portfolio analysis solutions provide reports and charts that help you study a portfolio relative to a benchmark, competitor fund, or peer group.

A: Style Analysis

Two portfolios with a similar benchmark and stated style can exhibit significantly different style attributes.

1. *Style Characteristics*

    When comparing your portfolios to competitors, it's important to understand style consistency or the purity of the current style. For institutional competitors, a returns-based analysis may be the only way to compare style characteristics. For competitor funds, a returns-based comparison can leverage much more frequent competitor data and complement other portfolio analysis performed in FactSet. Based on Nobel Laureate William Sharpe's concept of the "Effective Asset Mix," FactSet's style reports and charts determine how your selected portfolio and competitor returns correlate with asset class, size, and style indices.

2. *Manager Style Box*

    Plot your selected portfolios or competitor funds into a Manager Style quadrant to identify where they lie in terms of large cap, small cap, value, or growth characteristics.

3. *Rolling Manager Style Box*

    Chart your portfolio over a rolling time period to identify style consistency.

4. *Rolling Asset Allocation*

    Conceptually similar to the Rolling Manager Style Box, the Rolling Asset Allocation chart focuses on a single portfolio. This area chart emphasizes the indices that comprise your style section.

5. *Customized Style Analysis*

    FactSet lets you create custom style sets using any combination of indices or portfolios. Specify any start date, end date, data frequency, and rolling period for analysis. Control every element of a chart from colors and markers to headers and footers.

B: Risk Analysis

With the extensive historical performance data in FactSet, you can research the historical risk and risk-adjusted performance of your portfolio and competitors. Choose from more than 120 risk/return statistics, including annualized return, standard deviation, beta, tracking error and upside/downside capture.

6. *Multi-Horizon*

    Display any statistic for your selected portfolios, benchmarks, and competitors for various sub-periods within your selected time period.

7. *Multi-Statistic*

Compare risk and return statistics with the Multi-Statistic report. Customize your report by selecting from regression, semi-variance, and up-down statistics.

8. *Rolling Multi-Horizon*

   The Rolling Multi-Horizon report is similar to Multi-Horizon but uses rolling periods instead of finite sub-periods for more of a trend analysis.

9. *Cumulative Return*

   Chart the cumulative performance of portfolios, benchmarks, and competitors over any time period. You can also display the growth of your selected currency.

10. *X-Y Chart*

    Create a scatterplot of two risk/return statistics, such as standard deviation and annualized return.

C: Peer Universe Analysis

Peer Universe analysis helps you understand how your portfolios compare to a broad range of competitors. This perspective is essential to effectively position your products in the competitive marketplace.

11. *Competitor Returns*

    Choose Peer Universe reports and charts to examine portfolio returns relative to a selected peer group. Analyze portfolios against a variety of peer universes from Lipper, Morningstar, eVestment Alliance, RogersCasey, and PSN.

12. *Multi-Horizon*

    Use the Multi-Horizon report and its corresponding chart to display peer rankings for a specific statistic over various time periods. Choose from over 120 Modern Portfolio Theory statistics and any time period.

13. *Multi-Statistic*

    Compare risk and return statistics with the Multi-Statistic report. Add as many available risk/returns statistics as you want.

14. *Customize Peer Universe Analysis*

    Create your own customized peer group by combining universes, removing particular funds from a universe, or archiving a list of screened funds.

15. *Universe X-Y Chart*

    Study risk and return for your entire universe with the Universe X-Y chart. This chart illustrates two risk/return statistics for your universe, with the axes' intersection representing the median fund manager.

D: Returns-Based Research

Beyond analyzing particular portfolios, use FactSet to research the optimal allocation of a set of indices or products. When you don't know the products, use fund screening to identify all portfolios that meet your exact criteria.

16. *Efficient Frontier Analysis*

    Returns-based Efficient Frontier analysis focuses on creating optimal portfolios from an initial set of assets (indices and products) and asset constraints, such as asset returns (historical or expected), risk, and weight. Using these inputs, create and compare a variety of optimal portfolios at different risk/return levels. Once a preferred allocation of products is decided, save that combination as a composite for additional analysis of its style, risk, or peer ranking.

17. *Fund Screening*

The fund screening utility lets you screen for all funds, separate accounts, or hedge funds passing any criteria you wish.

   i. Freely combine style, performance, and risk in your screening parameters
   ii. Include multiple data sets in the same screen
   iii. Mix time periods
   iv. Include other quantitative and qualitative characteristics in your screen, such as whether the separate account is open to new assets, the number of holdings in the fund, or the tenure of the manager
   v. Apply complex logical, statistical, and mathematical criteria
   vi. You can save the results of your screen to use as a custom peer group or as a list to be considered individually in FactSet reports.

already subscribe to CRSP as an academic research resource, so it may already be available to many student-managed investment funds. Since CRSP is primary a data vendor, analysis of the data must be done on another platform, such as FactSet or Excel.

Summary of Key Points

- The quality of an investment decision is due more to the care, skill, knowledge, and insights of the analyst than the tools that the analyst uses.
- Data, information, and financial analysis functions are tools that are helpful in the practice of investment management.
- Many tools and data are freely available. Company and government websites provide access to high-quality economic and financial statement data.
- Access to one or more professional tools provides the opportunity for members of student-managed investment funds to gain practical experience with industry-standard data, functions, and platforms.
- Professional-level tools provide efficient access to a wealth of high-quality information and analysis methods.
- When students become actively engaged in utilizing these tools, the potential exists to more effectively manage the underlying student-managed portfolios.
- Professional level tools further facilitate students' active learning by immersing them in the professional environment they are studying.

Exercises

1. Suppose a biotech company is working on a drug that promises to be an effective treatment or therapy for hepatitis-C. This would be the primary source of revenues for the company. Assuming the drug is approved for use in the United States, estimate the firm's revenues from the drug over the next 5 years in the United States? What about worldwide revenues? In your answer, please address the following issues. What percentage of the U.S. (or world) population has hepatitis-C? Estimate how many people have hepatitis-C. How many new cases of hepatitis-C are reported each year? What current therapies exist for the treatment of hepatitis-C? How much do they cost per year for an individual with hepatitis-C? Assuming this new treatment is at least as effective as existing therapies and that it is priced similarly, how much market share do you estimate it can gain?

2. Choose two publicly traded companies in two different sectors. Locate their last two years' financial statements from as many sources as possible, including the company's own website, EDGAR, professional-level services, and freely available sites (e.g., Morningstar, Google, and/or Yahoo!). Are the financial statements identical regardless of the source? In cases where there are discrepancies, which sources are correct? Do some sources provide more/different details than others?

3. Using the tools in this chapter, try to separate the revenue in a company's latest income statement by geographic region (e.g., continent). Some companies that you might try are Microsoft, Caterpillar, and Tupperware.

4. Use a "stock screener" from at least two different vendors. For example, try Fidelity, Morningstar, and Google. If you have access to professional-level tools, also use their screener. Compare the results of the various screeners. Which screeners appear to have the most options? Which screeners appear to have the best quality of results? Some suggestions for screens follow. When specific indexes are not available in a screening tool, you might try to "mimic" the index by using market capitalization criteria.

   a. Build a list of S&P 500 Index stocks from the healthcare sector with a P/E ratio below 20.

   b. Build a list of stocks between a market capitalization of $100 m and $1 b in the energy sector.

   c. Build a list of the 50 stocks with the highest book-to-market ratios within the Russell 2000 Index.

   d. Build a list of S&P 500 Index stocks with the best (or worst) 6-month (or 12-month) stock price performance.

   e. Build a list of the 100 stocks with the highest dividend yield within the Russell 1000 Index.

   f. Build a list of stocks with a beta between 0.50 and 0.80.

   g. Build a list of corporate bonds rated lower than investment grade.

(Continued)

Exercises (Continued)

5. How would you estimate the before-tax and after-tax cost of debt for a firm? Specifically, what tools would you use and how would you use them?

6. Choose three companies: one large cap stock (e.g., from the S&P 500), one mid cap stock (e.g., from the S&P 400) and one small cap stock (e.g., from the Russell 2000). Estimate each stock's beta that you would use to estimate the firm's cost of equity capital according
to the CAPM. What data sources do you use? What methods do you use (e.g., frequency of data, horizon, index, etc.)? Compare the beta that you estimate with the beta available from sources such as Yahoo!, Google, Fidelity, and Morningstar. What method does each employ to estimate beta?

CHAPTER 8

Forums, Symposiums, and Competitions

Chapter Outline

The investment and classroom activities of a student-managed investment fund allow students to experience and learn the portfolio management aspect of what professional investment managers must do. However, professional investment managers must, at some point in their careers, also present their investment philosophy and process to clients and prospective clients, such as pension plans, endowment funds, foundations, consultants, family offices, financial advisors, and high-net-worth individuals. In some cases, such presentations might be made to larger audiences at investment conferences. As discussed in Chapter 5, these activities often support the business development (i.e., sales and marketing) efforts of the investment firm, which is also critical to the firm – after all, without clients, there are no assets to manage! Student-managed investment fund forums, symposiums, and competitions can provide meaningful practical experience in making such

Trading and Money Management in a Student-Managed Portfolio.
DOI: http://dx.doi.org/10.1016/B978-0-12-374755-6.00008-X

presentations. Furthermore, these activities facilitate the exchanging of ideas among student-managed investment funds from different colleges and universities, as well as among professional participants.

This chapter discusses student investment forums, symposiums, and competitions that have been offered in various regions around the United States. As with the previous chapter's discussion of tools, our purpose in using a particular example in this chapter is not intended to endorse that activity as the only or best example. Rather, we provide these examples to show the diversity in opportunities available. Features of the examples discussed in this chapter are available in other such programs that currently exist and, undoubtedly, others that will come along. In areas where no such opportunities exist, we encourage student-managed investment funds to create such events. Indeed, we begin our chapter with an example of how universities in Texas did just that in creating the Texas Investment Portfolio Symposium. We also discuss other examples of regional symposiums and competitions, such as the Tennessee Valley Authority and Cornell-Fidelity MBA Stock Pitch Competition and national and international forums, such as the R.I.S.E. forum at the University of Dayton.[1]

Texas Investment Portfolio Symposium (TIPS)

Overview

The Texas Investment Portfolio Symposium (TIPS) conference, in its 7th year in 2010, is a forum for students, faculty, and investment professionals from Texas and the Southwest. TIPS provides participants with a wonderful opportunity to learn from and interact with senior industry professionals through keynote presentations and panel discussions with senior personnel from Texas investment management firms and several networking events.

TIPS is also home to two student competitions (described in further detail below): (1) the CFA Institute's Investment Research Challenge — Texas in which finalist schools, based on a research report, present their stock research to a panel of judges; and (2) the Portfolio Manager's Finalist Competition in which student teams "pitch" their investment process to a panel of judges. In addition to providing a terrific hands-on learning experience for the finalist schools, all TIPS

---

[1] We thank Jill Foote of Rice University for her valuable contributions regarding the TIPS competition, Sharon Criswell, Leah Bennett, Brian Stype and Amanda Quinn of the CFA Institute for their contributions about the CFA activities, Eric Davis for the information about the TVA program, and Lakshmi Bhojraj of Cornell University for the review of the Cornell-Fidelity MBA Stock Pitch competition.

attendees learn by watching these well-done presentations. TIPS is hosted by Texas universities and is generously sponsored by Texas investment firms and the CFA Societies of Texas.

History

TIPS was inaugurated in 2004 by the combined efforts of Professor Brian Bruce of Baylor University and Southern Methodist University, who created the vision for TIPS, and Professor Jill Foote of Rice University, who endeavored to host the first conference. Initially, the large Texas universities, working collaboratively, thought the best hosting format would be an alternating two-year cycle as there is a significant organizational start-up effort that must be expended in the first year. However, after 5 years, TIPS had grown to such a size and prestige level that it was deemed best to host the conference in either Dallas or Houston. As such, the current plan is for Rice University and SMU to alternate years of hosting. The list of host schools and participating colleges and universities is shown in Exhibit 8.1.

Exhibit 8.1 Texas Investment Portfolio Symposium (TIPS)

Universities Represented
More than 25 universities have sent representatives to TIPS, with most years of the conference boasting 150–200 attendees.

Texas
   Baylor University
   Houston Baptist University
   Lamar University
   Prairie View A&M University
   Rice University
   Southern Methodist University
   Southwestern University
   Texas A&M University
   Texas A&M–Kingsville
   Texas Christian University
   Texas Southern University
   Texas Tech University
   Texas Wesleyan University
   Trinity University
   University of Houston
   University of North Texas
   University of St. Thomas
   University of Texas
   University of Texas at Dallas
   University of Texas at El Paso University of Texas at San Antonio

Louisiana
   Louisiana State University
   Tulane University

Mexico

Instituto Panamericano de Alta Direccion de Empresa (IPADE)

Monterey Technical Institute

Oklahoma

Oklahoma State University

University of Oklahoma

TIPS Host Universities

2004	Rice
2005	Rice
2006	Baylor
2007	Baylor
2008	A&M
2009	Rice
2010	UT Dallas
2013	Rice
2014	SMU

Note: Started as Texas region, but is now called Southwest US and includes TX, LA, and OK. In 2013, CFA IRC–SW was the second largest region in the world after India.

Winner Universities in the CFA Institute Research Challenge — Southwest US

2007	Rice
2008	U of H*
2009	A&M
2010	U of H
2011	Rice
2012	UT San Antonio
2013	Texas State University

*University of Houston won the North American finals and competed in the global finals in 2008.

As of 2013, the CFA IRC–Central America and Caribbean regional competition also takes place at TIPS. The winner in 2013 was BARNA Business School from the Dominican Republic.

Winning Universities in the Portfolio Managers Finals Competition

2006	SMU
2007	Baylor
2008	Baylor
2009	Rice
2010	U of H
2011	Baylor
2012	Rice
2013	University of Oklahoma

A few years ago, Sharon Criswell, President of the CFA Society of Dallas/Fort Worth, and Leah Bennett, President of CFA Society of Houston, teamed up to launch an exciting new initiative, the Investment Research Challenge – Texas (IRC-TX or Texas Challenge or Challenge). The finals competition for IRC-TX has, since its inception in 2006, been held at the TIPS competition.

The Investment Research Challenge was originated and trademarked by the New York Society of Security Analysts (NYSSA). As the NYSSA website reads, "The purposes of the Challenge include teaching best practices in research to the new generation of analysts, offer experience in a real-world setting and provide experienced investment professionals and society members the opportunity to contribute." The CFA Institute now sponsors the Investment Research Challenge and takes a strong role in supporting local CFA societies that decide to roll out a Challenge.

The Texas Challenge, along with other regional IRC competitions, follows the same format as the New York Society. In the Challenge, university teams of 3–5 MBA/BBA students compete with each other on analyzing and writing a research report recommending a "Buy," "Sell," or "Hold" position on a publicly traded company. Finalist teams compete before an oral panel made up of senior investment professionals at TIPS.

The basic components of the Challenge include:

- Training: Students receive training by video seminars provided by the societies on Research Tools for Analysts, Research Report Analysis and Writing (both buy-side and sell-side), and Ethics.
- Analysis of a Public Company: Teams are assigned to research the same public company, selected by the CFA-DFW and Houston Societies and located in Texas, including a question and answer session with senior company management. Teams are given a template to follow in completing their written analysis/report.
- Mentoring by a Professional Research Analyst: Each team is mentored by a professional research analyst, who reviews and critiques the team's report.
- Assessment of Written Research Reports: Written research reports are evaluated by a panel of senior investment professionals who choose finalist teams to present at TIPS.
- Finals Presentation: The finalist teams present their research to a high-profile panel of respected investment professionals. The IRC-TX winning team is selected based on the combined scores for the written report and the presentation.

The winner of IRC-TX goes on to compete against other Challenge winners in the Americas Regional IRC (Canada, United States, and Latin America) held in New York City. The winner of the Americas Regional then goes on to compete against the winners from around the world in the Global Challenge, which is held in locations around the globe. In the Texas and Southwest region, the sponsoring societies of the challenge pay 100% of

Level I enrollment for the winning team and 50% of Level I enrollment for the second place team. Exhibit 8.1 also shows the winners of the IRC-TX in recent years.

Each year IRC-TX has grown, and in 2010 was expanded beyond Texas to include a total of 10 teams: Rice, LSU, SMU, TCU, Texas A&M, Texas Tech, Tulane, U of H, UT, UTD, and UTSA. All four Texas societies — Austin, Dallas-Fort Worth, Houston, and San Antonio — provide mentors for the teams, judges, or graders. Truly this Texas Challenge has become a wonderful educational and collaborative effort between the CFA Texas societies, the involved universities, and TIPS.

Portfolio Managers Finals Competition

The Portfolio Managers Finals Competition (PM Competition or Finals Competition or Competition) is similar to a "finals presentation" that all investment firms make in order to compete to win an institutional client's business. Begun in 2006 and run annually by creator Professor Brian Bruce, the PM Competition allows student teams to truly get a real-world feel for the portfolio management pitch process through two stages of competition.

> *Preliminary Application* — First, universities that wish to be considered for the Finals Competition must submit a preliminary application (four pages maximum) providing:
> * A description of the school's investment philosophy, decision-making process, investment style, and universe from which securities are selected.
> * Presentation of long-term (minimum three years) investment results, including the results versus benchmark.
> * Other material may be included such as a discussion of risk controls or why the investment process adds value.
> *Finals Presentation* — Then finalist teams (consisting of 3—5 students), selected based on excellence in the preliminaries, make a ten-minute presentation followed by a question-and-answer period at the TIPS conference. A typical presentation consists of an introduction of team members, a description of the team's investment philosophy, decision-making process, investment style, and a review of the long-term investment results. Basically, each team has 10 minutes to convince the judges that they should be hired to manage this hypothetical account.

These PM Finals presentations are judged by a panel of practicing institutional investment professionals based on the same criteria used to judge a professional money manager: The judges will select a winner based on their perceptions about which team's investment process will most likely produce the best results over time. Awards are presented to the winning teams at the Symposium, including a take home award for the top three teams and a Winner's Cup, which is passed each year to the new winning school. Recent winners of the Finals Competition are shown in Exhibit 8.1. The University of Houston's winning presentation from 2010 is shown in Exhibit 8.2.

Exhibit 8.2 University of Houston's Winning Presentation in the 2010 Portfolio Managers Finals Competition

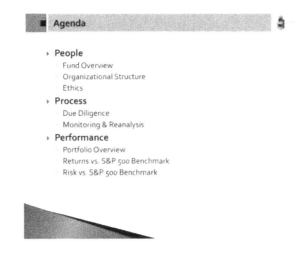

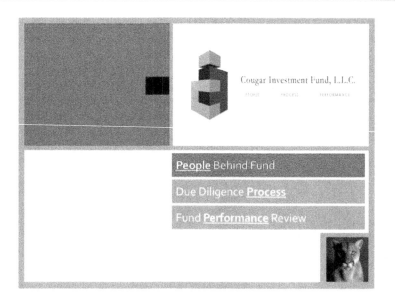

What is the Cougar Investment Fund, LLC?

- Private Investment Fund
- Financed by outside investors
- Unique: 1 of only 4 nationwide

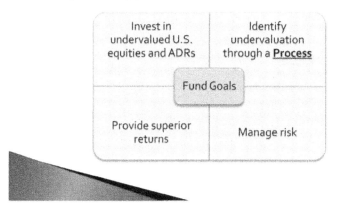

Organizational Structure

Board of Managers

LMV	LMG
SMV	SMG

ADVISORY COMMITTEE

INVESTMENT COUNSELORS

Fund Accounting

Investors' Portfolio

Custodian

Brokerage

External Audit

Ethics

› Independence and objectivity
› Integrity of capital markets
› Due diligence
› Duty to our investors

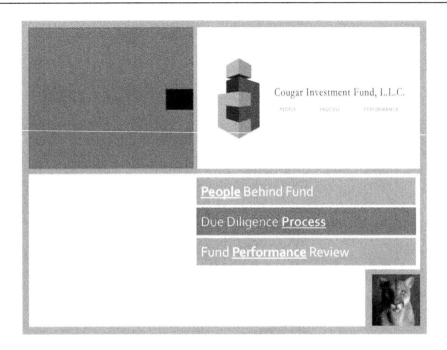

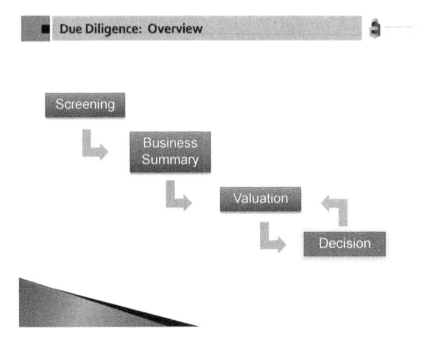

■ Due Diligence: Step 1 - Screening

▸ **Screening parameters include:**
  ◦ Market capitalization
  ◦ Sector
  ◦ Risk metrics
  ◦ AFG View® DCF model
▸ **Selection of individual stocks for analysis**

■ Due Diligence: Step 2 - Business Summary

▸ **Firm Summary**
▸ **Security Performance**
  ◦ Historical financial performance
  ◦ Wall Street projections
▸ **Security Market Valuation**
  ◦ Firm characteristics
  ◦ Quantitative metrics
  ◦ Competitor analysis

Due Diligence: Step 3 – Valuation (Bottom-Up)

▸ **Analyst's Projections**
  ○ Firm specific variables ~ Revenue, EBITDA, CAPEX, etc.
  ○ Extrinsic Variables ~ Beta, Market Premium, etc.
▸ **Projected Pro-Forma Cash Flows**
▸ **Intrinsic Value (IV)**
▸ **Projected Return**

Due Diligence: Step 4 – Investment Decision

▸ **Recommendation Factors**
  ○ Explanation of projections / valuation
  ○ Market risk (beta) and discount rate
▸ **Final Decision**
  ○ Valuation / Team recommendation
  ○ Fund risk impact
  ○ Sector balance impact

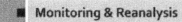 **Monitoring & Reanalysis**

> **Monitoring / Reanalysis**
>> ◦ Material events
>> ◦ Intrinsic value vs. market value
>> ◦ Sell decisions

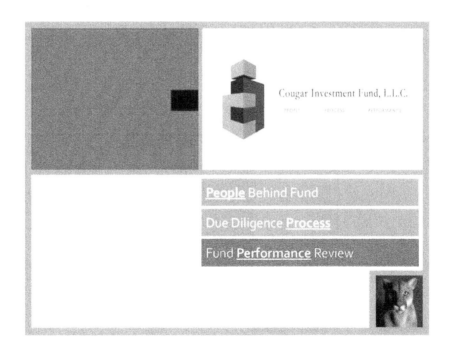

Cougar Investment Fund, L.L.C.

People Behind Fund

Due Diligence **Process**

Fund **Performance** Review

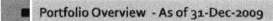

Portfolio Overview - As of 31-Dec-2009

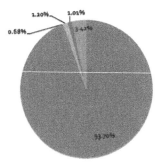

- 31 Stocks
- Materials ETF (XLB)
- Consumer Discretionary ETF (XLY)
- Cash
- Industrial ETF (XLI)

▸ **Assets under management**
  ◦ $6,868,387
▸ **Expense Ratio**
  ◦ 0.96%[1]
▸ **Dividend Yield**
  ◦ 1.79%[1]
▸ **Turnover Ratio**
  ◦ ~ 20% - 40%
▸ **Beta with respect to S&P 500**
  ◦ 0.99
▸ **$10,000 Investment[2]**
  ◦ Cougar Fund - $13,529
  ◦ S&P 500 - $12,042

1. Percentage of average asset value evaluated on a weekly basis since inception.
2. $10,000 invested since inception to 31-Dec-2009 gives the following net returns

Sector Weightings vs. S&P 500 - As of 31-Dec-2009

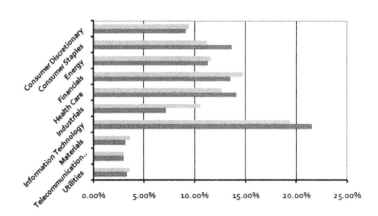

S&P 500   Cougar Fund

1 - As of 31-Dec-2009

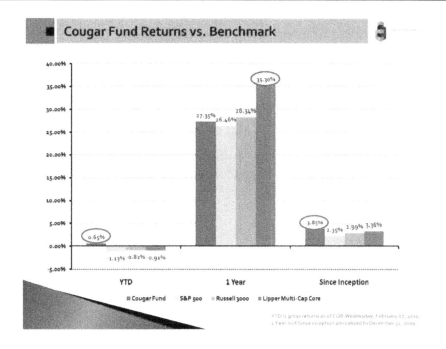

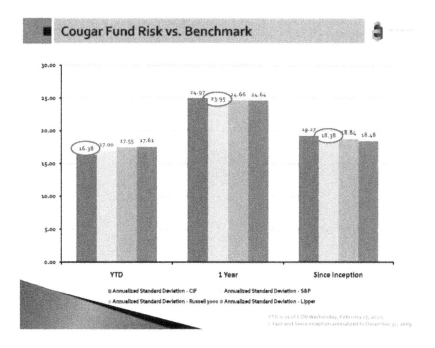

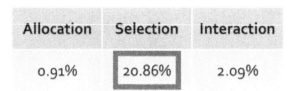

Attribution Analysis Compared to S&P 500

Allocation	Selection	Interaction
0.91%	20.86%	2.09%

1 Attribution analysis from 31-Dec-2002 to 31-Dec-2009 before expenses

Summary

People	• Combined effort of talented individuals • Investors – only 4 such funds in US
Process	• Rigorous process • Proven over time
Performance	• Out performance after expenses • Comparable in risk to the S&P 500

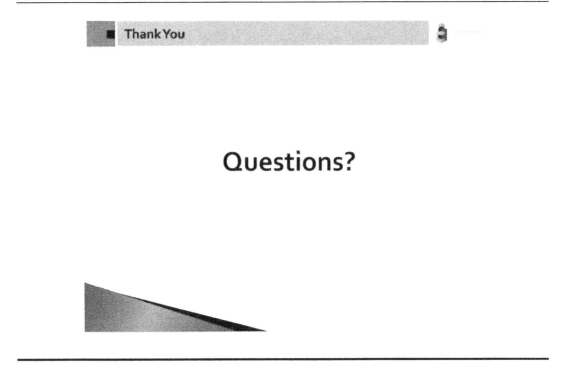

Thank You

Questions?

The CFA Institute Global Investment Research Challenge

History and Growth of the CFA Institute Global Investment Research Challenge

The Global Investment Research Challenge was introduced by NYSSA (New York Society of Security Analysts) in the 2002–2003 academic year as a means to promote best practices in equity research among the next generation of analysts. The challenge was an eight-month initiative in which top industry professionals taught business and finance students how to research and report on a publicly traded company. By the 2006–2007 academic year, a number of other local CFA societies had started their own challenges, including the Hong Kong Society of Financial Analysts, the Boston Security Analysts Society (for New England universities), and the CFA Society of Dallas-Fort Worth and CFA Society of Houston (for Texas universities). CFA Institute was an initial sponsor for these early Challenges and, in 2006–2007, became the primary manager and support, in conjunction with local societies, for the new Global Investment Research Challenge.

From working with the five local societies, New York, Boston, Dallas-Fort Worth, Houston, and Hong Kong and around 150 students from 30 plus universities in 2007, CFA Institute's Global Investment Research Challenge has expanded to involve over 100 member societies hosting local competitions and almost 2500 students from over 500 universities participating globally. Winners of the local competitions go on to compete regionally in three major competitions, the Americas region; the Europe, Middle East, and Africa region; and the Asia Pacific region. The winners of these regional competitions, along with the winner of the New York region, square off at a global competition, from which the final winner is selected. The global winning team's university is then awarded US$10,000 for its students' achievement in the Global Investment Research Challenge.

It is difficult to overemphasize the impact this Challenge has come to have. Administered by the CFA Institute and strongly supported by almost 75% of the local member societies across the globe, all student participants have the opportunity to get real-world experience in equity analysis, learn best practices and ethical decision making from investment professionals, interact with top management of public companies, and gain industry exposure for themselves and sometimes regional and/or global exposure for their universities. The Global Investment Research Challenge teaches a discipline of effective research, sell-side research report writing, and strong presentation capabilities. From the initial educational sessions on report writing, research techniques, and ethics in the investment management industry, to interviewing public company management, to working on the actual analysis and research report, and then finally presenting the results to top industry professionals, this discipline encompasses many of the key skills and tools that students will later utilize as they complete their schooling and begin their careers.

More information on the CFA Institute Global Investment Research Challenge can be found on the CFA Institute's website at www.cfainstitute.org.

Investment Research Challenge — Texas (2010–2011)

In 2006, the CFA Society of Dallas/Fort Worth and the CFA Society of Houston teamed up to launch an exciting new initiative, Investment Research Challenge — Texas. In the initial year of the Challenge, student teams from Rice, A&M, TCU, and SMU competed with each other on analyzing, writing, and presenting a report recommending a "Buy," "Sell," or "Hold" position on a publicly traded company. The societies assisted in providing education tools; the goal being to provide a value-added real-world application for these students. The teams were then assigned the company to analyze with access to the CEO. Teams were given a template to follow in completing their written analysis/report. All four Texas societies provided mentors for the teams, judges, or graders. Finalist teams competed before an oral panel made up of leaders in our investment community at TIPS. The winning team went on to compete regionally against other winners hosted by the CFA Institute in New York City.

Each year the local challenge has grown. This year a total of 13 teams (and maybe 14) are competing: LSU, Northwest Louisiana, Rice, SMU, TCU, Texas A&M, Texas Tech, Tulane, U of H, UNT, UT, UTD, UTSA, and possibly OSU. The Texas company for 2011 has yet to be selected. The competition will kick off late in November and four finalist teams will compete at TIPS, which will be held on 19 February 2011 this year at Rice University. The Investment Research Challenge – Texas is managed and supported now by all four CFA societies in Texas (Austin, Dallas-Fort Worth, Houston, and San Antonio) as well as the CFA Society of Louisiana. Once again, the winning team will get to compete in the "America's Challenge" held on 7 April 2011. This competition will include all local challenge winners across Canada, Latin America, and the United States. The winner of the Americas will then go on to compete against the winner in Europe, the Middle East and Africa, and Asia Pacific. From the beginning of the Challenge 8 years ago, it has grown from four local regions (NYC, Northeast US, Hong Kong, and Texas) to nearly 100 member societies hosting local competitions with almost 2000 students from over 425 universities globally in 2010.

Benefits of the Global Investment Research Challenge:

- Students receive real-world training in equity analysis.
- Investment professionals make an impact on the profession.
- Public companies promote education and analyst independence.
- Universities gain global exposure.
- Corporate sponsors reach universities, students, and finance professionals.

R.I.S.E.: Redefining Investment Strategy Education

The R.I.S.E. Forum, a student investment conference hosted annually at the University of Dayton in Dayton, Ohio, is sponsored by the University of Dayton, and coordinated by its School of Business Administration's Davis Center for Portfolio Management. The United Nations Global Compact has served as co-sponsor of the event since 2007, and strategic partners that have lent their name in support of the program over the years have included such notable organizations as the CFA Institute, *The Wall Street Journal*, CNBC, the New York Stock Exchange, NASDAQ, GARP, Beta Alpha Psi, Morningstar, Inc., TIAA-CREF,

Bank of America, Merrill Lynch, BlackRock, Hanley Group Capital, Moody's Investors Services, CME Group, and PNC Financial Services Group.

Response to the inaugural R.I.S.E. Forum in 2001 surpassed expectations as registration swelled to include representation by 43 universities from 27 states and Canada. This enthusiastic reception by the academic community solidified the resolve to annualize the event and encouraged the University to broaden its scope. Today, the University of Dayton's R.I.S.E. Forum is acknowledged by many as the world's largest student investment conference, drawing attendance over the years from colleges in all 50 states and a number of countries around the world. Typical annual attendance figures now number 1300 students and faculty and 350 professionals, in addition to as many as 1000 virtual participants across the globe who connect through video streaming. A Roman numeral is affixed to the title of each subsequent edition of the Forum to distinguish one year from another (e.g., R.I.S.E. I, R.I.S.E. II, R.I.S.E. III).

The first conference featured keynote addresses by five high-profile investment strategists and focused on a student-managed portfolio competition. Winning teams from U.D., Rice University, and Stetson University − in the growth, value, and blend style categories, respectively − were rewarded with the privilege of opening the NASDAQ MarketSite in Times Square on April 30, 2001.

While the R.I.S.E. Forum continues to feature an optional student-managed investment portfolio competition based on 12-month risk-adjusted performance, programming has expanded dramatically. The Forum has evolved into a two and one-half−day conference (Thursday to Saturday), utilizing a variety of formats that include panel discussions, keynote addresses, concurrent breakout sessions, career strategy forums, networking opportunities, and a faculty-only discussion of best practices.

The first day of the R.I.S.E. Forum is held on Thursday at the University of Dayton Arena, the capacity of which allows the inclusion of business professionals in addition to students and faculty. The day's format − modeled after the World Economic Forum − is generally composed of four 90-minute keynote panels focusing on such topics as the Markets, the Economy, Corporate Governance, Public Policy, and Risk Management; a Federal Reserve Perspective keynote address; and/or a Leadership Perspective keynote address.

Panelists number as many as twenty each year, spread across the four keynote panels. They are leaders from the areas of business, government, politics, labor, academics, and the media. In addition to interacting among themselves, keynote panelists interact with the audience as well through an interview-style discussion format. Following five-minute introductory remarks by each panelist regarding their thoughts on what they believe to be the issue of the day with regard to the topic at hand, the floor is opened to questions posed by students and directed to the panel. Spirited dialogue and debate ensue. The aim is to make the panel sessions dynamic and interactive as opposed to canned or scripted.

The R.I.S.E. Forum has been fortunate to attract such luminaries as Peter Coors of Molson Coors Brewing, H. Lee Scott of Wal-Mart, John Surma of U.S. Steel, Sam Zell of Equity Group Investments, Knight Kiplinger of *Kiplinger's Personal Finance*, Jeffrey Diermeier of the CFA Institute, Roger Ibbotson of Zebra Capital Management, and Georg Kell of the United Nations Global Compact. Keynote panelists have also included Nobel Laureates Myron Scholes and Finn Kydland; former and current SEC Commissioners Cynthia Glassman, Paul Atkins, and Roel Campos; and former Secretary of Commerce Donald Evans. Federal Reserve Perspectives have been offered throughout the years by Ben Bernanke, Michael Moskow, William Poole, Gary Stern, Sandra Pianalto, and Richard Fisher. Needless to say, while the first day of the conference piques the interest of the academic audience, the high-profile lineup holds equal appeal for the businessmen and -women in attendance, many of whom qualify for continuing education credit toward a variety of professional designations, including the CFA.

Friday and Saturday programming, held in classrooms and auditoriums on the University of Dayton's main campus for attendance by students and faculty only, consists of a series of six concurrent breakout sessions: two on Friday morning, two on Friday afternoon, and two on Saturday morning.

Friday sessions focus on investment-related topics such as portfolio management, investment products, venture capital, equity analysis, hedge funds, derivatives trading, socially responsible investing, asset allocation, and so forth. Friday breakout sessions take the form of panel discussions among industry professionals, presentations by investment strategists, and workshops offering more technical content. Panelists and presenters represent major firms from across the country. Friday programming terminates with a networking reception followed by an optional dinner.

Saturday morning is dedicated to an exploration of career options within the financial services industry. Attendees may choose from among a variety of career forums presented by young investment professionals who are able to provide relevant insight into the realities of the working world and to whom students easily relate. Additionally, the CFA Institute traditionally offers a presentation on the requirements and benefits of the CFA designation. Meanwhile, faculty are invited to attend a session on investment education best practices.

A good number of the attending schools opt to participate in the R.I.S.E. Forum's student-managed portfolio competition as well. First place performance is acknowledged in each of five categories in each of two divisions. The categories are based on portfolio style (growth, value, blend, hybrid, or fixed income), and the division is defined by the program level of the preponderance of the fund's student managers (undergraduate vs. graduate). Winning portfolio teams are determined by comparison of the twelve-month, risk-adjusted performances of the competing funds in each divisional category, and announced at the Friday evening dinner. Required materials are submitted by schools weeks before the conference so that competition involvement does not detract from Forum participation.

Competing schools are welcome to exhibit poster board displays describing their portfolios at the Friday afternoon networking reception, and a limited number of competing teams are invited to offer a 20-minute presentation to a panel of national investment professionals for discussion and feedback.

Exhibit 8.3 NASDAQ Remote Closing Bell Ceremony R.I.S.E. VIII Forum

The prestige and popularity of the R.I.S.E. Forum have grown significantly throughout the years, and its prominence earned the conference the distinction of hosting NASDAQ's first remote closing bell ceremony ever held on a college campus in 2008. Several hundred attending students shared the stage for the 4:00 p.m. formalities — broadcast live via satellite on the five-story Times Square NASDAQ screen in New York City — as the R.I.S.E. keynote speaker rang the closing bell for the NASDAQ.

It is estimated that the R.I.S.E. Forum has attracted nearly 13,000 participants over its first ten years, and the University of Dayton is committed to continuing this unique tradition of **R**edefining **I**nvestment **S**trategy **E**ducation.

Information regarding the R.I.S.E. conference may be found on the Forum's website at udrise.udayton.edu.

TVA Investment Challenge

Overview

The Tennessee Valley Authority (TVA) Investment Challenge program is an innovative and unique partnership between TVA and 24 universities in its service territory that provides a real-world learning experience in portfolio management. The program gives students hands-on experience managing stock portfolios. TVA's Investment Challenge program is one of the largest student-managed investment funds in the United States.

Students actively manage TVA funds by designing long-term investment strategies, placing trades, and providing performance reports to TVA — all under the guidance of a faculty member. Students learn the requirements that come along with managing real money and are held to similar guidelines as TVA's professional money managers.

To support the program, TVA makes its most experienced financial managers and analysts available to help students as they learn to apply financial management concepts to real-world situations. TVA representatives visit campuses to discuss the students' portfolio management strategies and offer constructive feedback.

TVA is the largest public power provider in the United States, and is dedicated to partnering in education with colleges and universities to invest in communities and future leaders. TVA's Investment Challenge is a creative use of TVA's resources that offers opportunities for learning and training to the region's next generation of financial leaders.

The Investment Challenge is part of TVA's Nuclear Decommissioning Trust Fund equity allocation. The Nuclear Decommissioning Trust Fund was created to meet the financial obligations for decommissioning TVA's nuclear units.

History

In 1998, TVA created the Investment Challenge by designating $1.9 million to 19 universities to be managed on behalf of TVA in actual investment portfolios.

In 2003, TVA added six new universities to the program, bringing the total to 25. TVA also increased the total Investment Challenge portfolio allocation to $10 million after the success of the program demonstrated that student-managed portfolios performed competitively against performance benchmarks.

The assets of the program were rebalanced in 2007, and one university withdrew from the Investment Challenge in 2008 for administrative reasons.

Exhibit 8.4 Universities Participating in the TVA Investment Challenge

Alabama A&M University
Austin Peay State University
Belmont University
Christian Brothers University
East Tennessee State University
Lipscomb University
Middle Tennessee State University
Mississippi State University
Mississippi University for Women
Murray State University
Tennessee State University
Tennessee Technological University
Trevecca Nazarene University
Union University
University of Alabama – Huntsville
University of Kentucky
University of Memphis
University of Mississippi
University of North Alabama
University of Tennessee – Chattanooga
University of Tennessee – Martin
Vanderbilt University
Western Carolina University
Western Kentucky University

Today, each of the participating 24 universities manages funds of about $300,000, on average, which is invested in the stock market on behalf of TVA. Exhibit 8.4 shows a list of participating universities.

Structure

Consistent with what is required of professional investment managers, participating universities must sign an investment management agreement with TVA. The investment management agreement specifies the investment guidelines that must be followed. Each university has a separate account with a trustee, where investment positions are held. Universities have access to a trustee website application to monitor account positions.

The majority of participating universities have structured the learning experience in the form of a for-credit course focused on management of the portfolio. The universities generally use an application process for acceptance into the class. The portfolio management process typically involves a practical application of theory provided through academic instruction.

Investment Guidelines

Each university agrees to abide by the investment guidelines described below. University portfolios are monitored for guideline compliance by TVA using a trustee software tool.

University Investment Manager Guidelines

Goal

The investment goal of the portfolio is to provide TVA with a strategic allocation to the domestic equity market. Manager has been selected by TVA as the portfolio manager of this strategic allocation. Manager's assignment is to construct and actively manage the portfolio in a manner consistent with this investment goal and to add value relative to return opportunities that could be achieved from a passive exposure to this market segment. The assets of the portfolio are tax-exempt.

Objective

The investment objective of the portfolio is to achieve long-term capital growth by investing in marketable U.S. common stocks with a risk profile that is similar to the risk profile of the market benchmark. Specific investment objectives are intended to define quantifiable measures by which the results of the portfolio will be measured and evaluated on an ongoing basis. The performance results and investment characteristics of the portfolio will be measured and evaluated relative to (1) an overall measure of the large segment of the domestic equity market; (2) a style-oriented benchmark (if applicable) which will measure the portfolio relative to the style segment of the large domestic equity universe; (3) a universe of professionally managed large core-oriented equity managers; and (4) a universe of other universities managing TVA decommissioning funds (together with Manager, hereafter "University Managers"). The relative domestic equity market benchmark is defined as the S&P 500 Index. Prior to each calendar year, Manager will select the S&P 500 Index, the S&P Citigroup Growth Index, or the S&P Citigroup Value Index as the relative domestic style-oriented benchmark. This annual selection will be communicated in writing to TVA's Investment Challenge Program Manager.

In light of the above, the portfolio should strive to meet or exceed the following performance objectives:

- The portfolio is expected to outperform the S&P 500 Index over a one-year horizon. Over a three- to five-year horizon, the portfolio is expected to generate a total return of at least 100 basis points over the S&P 500 Index.

- The portfolio is expected to generate a total return that ranks in the top 50% of a large core equity manager universe as may be selected by TVA from time to time.
- The portfolio is expected to generate a total return that ranks in the top 15% of the University Manager Universe over a one- to three-year horizon.
- The portfolio is expected to outperform the S&P Citigroup Growth Index or the S&P Citigroup Value Index when selected as the style benchmark over a one-year horizon. Over a three- to five-year horizon, the portfolio is expected to generate a total return of at least 100 basis points over the selected style benchmark.

Guidelines

The following points highlight the investment guidelines that have been established for the portfolio. Manager is expected to follow these guidelines carefully while implementing and executing its portfolio strategy. If Manager is in non-compliance with these guidelines, Manager will have 30 days to rebalance the portfolio to meet these guidelines.

- **Asset Allocation.** The portfolio is expected to be invested exclusively in U.S.-listed equity securities. Any cash equivalent investment should represent "frictional" or operational amounts and not strategic allocations. Therefore, cash equivalents should not exceed 5% of the portfolio at any time. Should market conditions suggest a hostile environment where this guideline may be detrimental to the financial well-being of TVA, Manager should communicate suggested tactical adjustments to this guideline with authorized representatives of TVA. Cash equivalent balances are expected to be invested in a short-term investment fund managed by the assigned custodian bank.
- **Diversification.** Portfolio performance is expected to achieve value added results through active management decisions. However, the portfolio is expected to be diversified with respect to the exposures to economic sectors, industries, and individual stocks. The following diversification guidelines apply to the construction of the portfolio:
  - The maximum allocation to any economic sector (sectors will be defined by Standard & Poor's) may not exceed the sector weight of the selected style-oriented benchmark index plus 10%. For example, if Manager selects the S&P 500 Citigroup Value Index as the style-oriented benchmark and the Energy sector comprises 10% of that index, the maximum allocation to the Energy sector must not exceed 20% of portfolio assets.
  - The maximum allocation to any one economic sector may not exceed 40% of portfolio assets, unless the sector weight of the selected style-oriented benchmark exceeds 40% in which case the maximum weight to the sector would be 110% of the sector weight. For example, if Manager selects the S&P 500 Citigroup Value Index as the style-oriented benchmark and the Technology sector comprises 41% of

that index, the maximum allocation to the Technology sector must not exceed 45.1% of portfolio assets.

- At time of purchase, no single issue should exceed 5% (at market value) of the portfolio for portfolios in excess of $150,000 and 8% (at market value) of the portfolio for portfolios equal to or less than $150,000. Positions may be allowed to drift up to 8% (at market value) of the portfolio for portfolios in excess of $150,000 and 10% (at market value) of the portfolio for portfolios equal to or less than $150,000.
- The portfolio is expected to be constructed with a minimum of 20 individual stocks for portfolios in excess of $150,000 (at market value) and 15 individual stocks for portfolios equal to or less than $150,000 (at market value).
- Investments in Real Estate Investment Trusts ("REITs") should not exceed 5% of the portfolio at any time.

- **Market Capitalization.** The majority of the portfolio is expected primarily to be invested in well-established, large market capitalization companies. Therefore, the weighted average market cap of the portfolio is expected to be above $10 billion.

  The portfolio may also invest in less established, small capitalization companies. However, based on the strategic role of this portfolio in the context of the overall investment program, no more than 35% of the portfolio may be invested in small capitalization companies. For this purpose, small capitalization is defined as companies with a market capitalization of less than $1 billion. Companies with a market capitalization below $250 million at the time of purchase are prohibited. Positions that drift below $250 million in market capitalization after purchase shall be reported to TVA and monitored carefully. The portfolio shall not have more than 5% of the portfolio invested in securities whose market capitalizations have declined below $250 million.

- **Other Transactions and Policies**
  - *American Depositary Receipts* ("ADRs") may be used to construct the portfolio. However, because of the strategic role of the portfolio, positions in stocks traded as ADRs are limited to no more than 15% of the portfolio market value. The 15% limitation includes foreign securities traded on U.S. Exchanges that are not ADRs.
  - *Exchange Traded Funds* ("ETFs") may comprise up to a maximum of 5% of the portfolio. The ETFs that can be purchased are limited to the following:
    - S&P 500 Depository Receipts (SPY)
    - iShares S&P 500 Growth Index (IVW)
    - iShares S&P 500 Value Index (IVE)
  - *Prohibited Transactions* — The portfolio is prohibited from investing in any of the following investment vehicles, or engaging in any of the following activities, unless approved by an authorized representative of TVA:

- Any securities or other obligations issued by any owner or operator of any nuclear power reactor or their affiliates, subsidiaries, successors, or assigns
- Fixed-income securities
- Non-marketable securities (including private debt securities and/or direct placements)
- Non-dollar-denominated securities
- Commingled funds (including mutual funds and ETFs except for the three ETFs identified above in the Guidelines – Other Transactions and Policies – Exchange Traded Funds section)
- Convertible or preferred securities
- Warrants
- Commodities
- Real estate investments (excluding REITs)
- Short sales
- Margin purchases
- Swaps (including, but not limited to, index or rate of return swaps)
- Securities lending
- *Derivatives Policy* – Manager is prohibited from using any derivative securities (including, but not limited to, options and futures).
- **Communications.** TVA must be informed within 24 hours if any of the following events occurs:
  - A change in Manager's investment philosophy that represents a deviation from this policy statement.
  - A change in Manager's investment style that represents a deviation from this policy statement.
  - Any development in the ability of Manager to manage the portfolio either in accordance with the standards of a prudent investment manager or within the context of this statement of investment policy.
  - Any situation that has the potential to impact the professionalism, financial position, or integrity of either TVA or Manager.

Trading Process

Each university provides TVA with a list of individuals authorized to make trades on behalf of the university. This list is shared with the trustee and broker. When the university calls the broker to place a trade, the name is checked against this authorized list. After placing a trade with the broker, the university is required to fax a trade ticket authorization form to the trustee. The trustee matches this ticket with the broker trade information.

Performance

The combined portfolio of the Investment Challenge program has performed well versus its S&P 500 benchmark since the inception of the program. In fact, the composite university portfolio has exceeded the performance of the S&P 500 Index in 8 of the 11 years through 2009, as shown in Exhibit 8.5.

Performance Awards

Each university that exceeds the performance of the S&P 500 Index over one full calendar year receives a performance-based award. The award amount is 20% of the alpha generated by the university, up to a cap of 2% of total assets managed. Alpha is defined as real excess returns, after adjusting for risk. The performance structure is similar to what is used with professional investment managers.

Future

The program has provided many benefits to TVA and the participating students and universities. Many of the faculty members and leaders of the participating universities value the program as a tool for integrating real-world learning opportunities into the curriculum. Student participants cite their experience in the Investment Challenge program as beneficial to their careers, and many believe the program improved their initial marketability for professional employment. TVA continues to benefit from the program as a way to invest in

Exhibit 8.5 Composite Annual Performance of University Portfolios in the TVA Investment Challenge

Year	Avg. University Returns	S&P 500
2009	31.9%	26.5%
2008	−39.2%	−37.0%
2007	9.8%	5.5%
2006	12.9%	15.8%
2005	6.5%	4.9%
2004	16.0%	10.9%
2003	29.7%	28.7%
2002	−20.4%	−22.1%
2001	−7.5%	−11.9%
2000	−18.6%	−9.1%
1999	36.1%	21.0%

the communities it serves and enhance its relationship with those areas, and as a potential recruiting pipeline.

See investmentchallenge.tva.com more information about the TVA Investment Challenge.

The Cornell-Fidelity MBA Stock Pitch Competition

The Cornell-Fidelity MBA Stock Pitch Competition (SPC) is organized and hosted by the Johnson School at Cornell University with lead sponsorship from Fidelity Investments. Initiated by the Johnson School, the annual MBA Stock Pitch Competition provides a forum for top MBA students to compete and showcase their stock-picking skills in front of a panel of distinguished judges. The event challenges teams of finance students from twelve top MBA programs to prepare and present buy/hold/sell recommendations and vigorously defend them. Judged by a panel of investment industry experts, the intense competition is designed to replicate the fast-paced, demanding experience of sell-side and buy-side analysts and asset managers.

In addition to gaining valuable experience and competing before judges, MBA students have a chance to shine before prospective employers. Recruiters from sponsoring firms come to shop for top talent. As one judge commented, "There's no one I wouldn't hire."

The names of the winning schools are inscribed on the Jack M. Ferraro Trophy, which honors the lead individual sponsor, a Johnson School alumnus. The SPC is generously supported by sponsors from the investment industry. Fidelity Investments is the lead corporate sponsor of the competition.

What Happens at the MBA Stock Pitch Competition?

Wednesday – Arrival: The event begins with an opportunity for student teams to meet each other at an informal dinner.

Thursday – Preparation: Students undergo a morning training session on software such as Capital IQ and FactSet at the Johnson School's Parker Center for Investment Research. After lunch, the judges assign two industries and a common stock, and give each team a list of the eligible universe of stocks. For the common stock, teams must decide whether to present it as a long (buy), neutral (hold), or a short (sell) recommendation. For each of the two assigned industries, they must select either a long or short candidate. Additional restrictions may be imposed on each selection (e.g., market capitalization, trading volume, investment style, etc.). Students have until midnight to prepare for the three presentations.

Friday – Competition/Recruiting: In the morning preliminary round, each team pitches one common stock and one industry-specific stock. For each stock pitch, a single presenter from each team makes a ten-minute presentation, followed by judges' questioning of all three team members for five minutes. For each stock pitch, teams feature a different team member as presenter. The event is held before a live audience, but other competing teams are not permitted to watch one another's presentations. The two highest scoring teams from each group in the preliminary round advance to the final afternoon round. After brief private practice sessions, the finalists make their final presentations and undergo the judges' rapid-fire questioning.

Late in the afternoon, awards are presented at a reception, and judges and recruiters have an opportunity to mingle with participants. The event has met with consistent praise over the years from judges, recruiters, and participants. Many sponsoring firms have stated that they often use the forum as an opportunity to identify strong potential hires.

Summary of Key Points

- Student-managed investment fund forums and symposiums are helpful in bringing students together to share their diverse approaches to portfolio management and to student members to hear from investment professionals on the diversity of approaches in the investments industry.
- Competitions among student-managed investment funds force fund members to articulate and defend their investment philosophies and processes, just as professional investment managers have to do in making finals presentations to prospective clients.
- Numerous competitions, forums, and symposiums take place around the world, providing student-managed investment fund members opportunities to learn and practice their aspects of portfolio management beyond what they do in their own funds or classrooms.

CHAPTER 9

The Present and Future of Student-Managed Portfolios

Chapter Outline

The guiding principle throughout this text has been to provide student-managed investment funds a professional perspective on investment management toward the goal of helping further professionalize their approaches. As such, we have focused on many of the common practical methods of issues facing professional, not personal, investors. Our goal has been to help create an education environment that will allow graduates of student-managed investment funds the training and experience needed to find employment in the money management industry. The purpose of this final chapter is to review where student-managed investing is today and where it is going in the future. Rather than offer more of our own thoughts on these issues, we find that we cannot provide any more insightful perspectives

Trading and Money Management in a Student-Managed Portfolio.
DOI: http://dx.doi.org/10.1016/B978-0-12-374755-6.00009-1

than those of leading student-managed investment fund professors Ronald Singer and Edward Lawrence.

Given the importance of trading rooms to student-managed investment funds, Ron discusses their role, not only in funds, but in the overall business. Many of the tools discussed in Chapter 7 are featured as elements of the trading room, as he points out in discussing the resources available in Bentley's trading room. As is clear from his discussion, trading rooms are not simply another tool for student-managed investment funds to use. Rather, they are integral features of both the funds and the institutions to which they belong. Using survey data, Ed provides a comprehensive review of the state of student-managed investment funds from around the world. We thank both Professor Singer and Professor Lawrence for generously agreeing to share their work herein.

The Role of Security Trading Rooms in Business Schools

By Ronald F. Singer

In the past two decades there has been an explosion of security trading rooms in business colleges throughout the United States. These rooms have generated student, faculty, and professional interest in the applied investment area. This paper provides a summary of the benefits and challenges of trading rooms. In the first section, the paper discusses the essential benefits associated with these rooms in terms of the improved learning experience, the benefits to faculty teaching and research and the benefits in terms of college interactions with outside professionals. In the second section, the paper describes the process by which trading rooms are developed and the constituent participants in the development of these rooms. In the third section, the paper describes the critical equipment and data that are incorporated into these rooms. The paper then describes the impact the room has on the college and the students. Finally, the paper ends with a summary and conclusion.

Why a Trading Room?

In the past decade we have seen an explosion of trading rooms constructed in universities. Some have been in conjunction with a student-run investment fund, but others have been installed in colleges that lacked such a fund. The question is why do we have such an explosion, and what is the point?

The argument for a trading room is compelling. The room makes a significant contribution to the various stakeholders within the college and the university. First, in terms of student learning, the room typifies the idea that learning occurs best when knowledge learned in the classroom can be applied to real world problems. The trading room typifies this concept. These rooms are generally designed to look and feel like a typical trading room found in the real world. Work stations typically consist of high power desktop computers, multiple screens, and high technology telecommunications systems. They contain sophisticated financial economic modeling and information analysis software that students learn to read and to use. By introducing students to these rooms, they become familiar with their workings and are able to transfer the knowledge gained in these rooms to a working environment.

By their very nature, the rooms induce interdisciplinary intercourse. A typical room will house data sources that can be used by finance, economics and accounting professionals. In addition, these rooms provide a working laboratory for management of information systems professionals. In fact, at the Bauer College of Business, the marketing department has installed software and hardware to enable students to learn about telemarketing techniques and technology in these rooms.

The second stakeholder that is affected by trading rooms is alumni, industry professionals, and donors. The very process of developing these rooms engages alumni and industry constituents. The trading rooms provide a very visible means of donor participation by providing a brick and mortar way of donors to provide funding and naming opportunities. In addition, the trading room engages industry professionals by providing a means by which they can provide expertise and advice in the development of the room.

The trading rooms typically become destination points for visitors to the university and the college. Most rooms contain streaming information outputs generated by the security exchanges, and video outputs displaying current news and financial data. In general, this leads to an impressive visible effect that can be designed to impress visitors to the college. As a visual focal point the college and the university can use the rooms to generate interest in the college from potential students as well as donors and recruiters.

The trading room can also provide opportunities for research by faculty and students. Its data feeds, real time and historical, can be captured to be used by researchers to generate important scholarly papers. Behavioral finance and economics faculty and students can test hypotheses using real world data, or use the rooms to identify interactions among various constituent groups. Essentially these rooms can serve as excellent behavioral laboratories for various experiments and research agendas.

How to Develop These Rooms

In order to develop a trading room it is desirable to utilize the expertise and commitment of a number of stakeholders. Typically, the stakeholders will consist of the faculty, the Dean's office, and outside professionals. Of course, the essential stakeholder is the faculty. The faculty must be committed to contribute toward the room's development, and to develop programs and curriculum which will assure that the room is utilized on a regular basis. It is not sufficient to have a "if you build it, they will come" mentality. The faculty must be committed to develop curricula which will make the trading room a critical element within the college and the university. Faculty must be committed to utilize the room in courses and curriculum development. Integrating these rooms into the curriculum is not a trivial task. It will only occur if the faculty is willing to bear the cost of developing programs that utilize the room in an efficient and productive manner. The student-managed fund can be a significant catalyst in assuring the room is well utilized. Although not essential to the success of these rooms, the student-managed fund can go a long way towards its success. First, the trading room typically becomes the "home" of the student-managed fund. As a result the room becomes a hub of activity that makes the room's environment vital and exciting. As the home of the fund, and a source of information and data for the students in the fund, the room is assured to be utilized by both faculty and students.

Essential to the success of the room is the college and university administration. It is essential that the administration understand that the room involves a commitment not only in terms of the initial investment in the room, but also in terms of ongoing support over the years. In addition to faculty support, the room will require continual support of data feeds, technology updating, and information technology specialists. To this end, the college or university administration must be willing to commit resources to encourage constituent involvement. This could include faculty released time and summer support for application and course development. It could include special training of faculty in the use of the information sources and the technology contained in the room. In addition to faculty support, the room will require continual support of data feeds, technology updating, and information technology specialists.

With the ongoing financial commitment required, many colleges have developed innovative and creative means of satisfying these commitments. The rooms have been used by outside professional organizations for personnel training and seminars. In addition, the rooms have been used for meetings of various organizations, receptions for constituents, and even for IPO parties of outside organizations. It would be particularly desirable if a room could be used as a crisis recovery center or backup for a main trading room. In order to be successful as a backup room, the sponsoring organization would have to equip the room with the same state of the art facilities utilized by the main trading room with the outside organization.

Equipment and Data

The whole idea of a trading room is to provide students with an experience that mimics as close as possible the experience that they will confront in the real world. Typically, the room will contain 20–30 work stations. Each work station will be equipped with state of the art computers, multiple flat screen technology, and communication facilities of some sort. The room will be a receptacle of the standard data streams that is critical to effective trading. Finally, the work stations should include some trading programs and simulations that would allow students to experiment with various trading strategies. For example, a typical room could include Financial Trading Systems (FTS), a web-based program that facilitates interactive trading. In addition, a room could include financial and optimization software such as Crystal Ball. Typically, a room will be set up so that the NYSE and NASDAQ data streams are captured in some sort of streaming video along the walls or windows of the room. The room will be equipped with flat screen monitors that can be used to access and continuously display standard financial news services such as Reuters, and include information terminals such as Bloomberg. The information available should also include information from the standard historical databases such as Compustat and CRSP to provide fundamental firm specific financial data, and historical price data, respectively. Ideally, the room will include historical as well as real time data to allow for research as well as ongoing trading.

The Impact of Trading Rooms on the Stakeholders

The existence of a trading room on the college can have a significant impact on the students, faculty, and outside professionals. From the students' perspective, the students have an opportunity to apply theoretical concepts and textbook knowledge in a real world setting. Although no actual trading is performed in these rooms, the environment and technology provide as close to a real world setting as you can get. As mentioned above, simulation and trading software can provide students with an experience that closely mimics the real world. To go one step further, some colleges have provided students with the opportunity to manage part of the university or college endowment. Also, some student-run funds have been created as a "real" hedge fund with actual investors who maintain ownership in the fund itself. These hedge funds require a significant increase in the complexity of managing the environment. Typically the fund will be organized as a limited liability company with limitations on the size of the funds and the number of investors. Nevertheless the existence of real investors, requiring real returns, provides an additional level of tension in the operations of the fund that furthers the whole educational experience. Students become acutely aware of the need to provide analysis and research that will not only satisfy their professors and the university administrators, they must also provide returns which are consistent with investor expectations.

Not only do the students experience a superior education as a result of the room, but the room itself improves the quality of the student body. The popularity of these funds, and the trading rooms, serves to attract first rate students who might be attracted to a specific set of colleges for the trading experience afforded them. Thus student recruiting improves, which improves the quality of the students entering the college's programs.

The existence of trading rooms can also be of particular interest to some faculty who are interested in these rooms for the teaching and research potential. This then will improve faculty recruiting, enhancing the quality of the faculty which will also improve student quality and therefore further interest by high quality faculty. Furthermore, the experiential teaching experience can be attractive to many faculty members who consider this a superior teaching experience for both the faculty and the students. As mentioned earlier, this can also enhance faculty-student interactions and research opportunities that would not exist without the trading room. Also, the faculty can improve the service component of their activity by utilizing the room for outreach to professionals and for potential students.

Finally, the student experiences can significantly improve the recruiting effectiveness of outside professionals. They can hire students who have already faced the challenges offered by a trading room, thereby reducing the need for internal training courses. Firms can also use the room as a filtering tool, to see how students will in fact do in a real world environment rather than a textbook environment.

Summary and Conclusions

In summary, trading rooms have become an integral part of the curriculum of many business schools over the past two decades. These rooms provide significant enrichment to the students' learning experience. They provide opportunities for students to understand the process by which theory and traditional academic knowledge can be applied in real world situations. Faculty involved in these rooms can develop programs which go far beyond the traditional teaching environment. They can develop research programs which utilize the unique facilities to obtain data and perform experiments and modeling which can be a significant teaching and research tool. Finally, the rooms provide an attractive tool to generate outside professional and donor interest in the college.

In many respects these rooms have revolutionized finance education, providing a unique opportunity for faculty, students, and outside professionals to wed academic learning with real world experiences.

Exhibit 9.1 Bentley University's Trading Room: The Hughey Center for Financial Services (CFS)

Environment: Three of the principal developments of financial markets in recent years are the introduction of new and increasingly complex financial instruments, unprecedented financial market volatility, and the integration of worldwide financial markets. Consequently, the management of foreign exchange risk, interest rate risk, and price risk has become a key issue for firms competing in the global economy. An unprecedented rise in capital market volatility and market crashes only reaffirms the need for improved understanding of how business decisions are made in this complex financial world.

The new challenge facing Bentley is to modify business, finance, and technology courses to properly train tomorrow's business decision makers as they compete in the global marketplace. That is why Bentley invested a significant amount of resources to create a lab environment so that students, using real time data, can apply theory to learn financial risk management. An on-site trading room provides a practical vehicle for presenting these important and applied concepts to students and the corporate community.

Historical Development

The trading room at Bentley is the showpiece of the Hughey Center for Financial Services (CFS). The first trading room and was inaugurated on May 20, 1997, by Peter S. Lynch, the legendary portfolio manager of the Magellan Fund, and currently Vice Chairman, Fidelity Management & Research. In 1999, the Center and the trading room moved to its current location at the Smith Center. The Center's mission is to further the educational objectives of Bentley University while enhancing Bentley's visibility within the local, national, and international financial services industry. Its primary objective is to bridge the gap between the academic and professional communities in the area of information technology and its application in the financial services industry. To this end, the CFS utilizes a state-of-the-art Trading Room to offer customized training sessions on the art-and-science of trading and risk management to capital markets participants.

Infrastructure: The Bentley trading room has 15 trading desks in the main floor with four additional desks in the overflow suite. Each trading desk has three computers (dual monitors) connected to online real-time datafeeds. Interactive group exercises allow a team of three students to deal, design trading and risk management strategies and conduct valuation exercises. Thus, an exposure to the trading room environment enhances the financial education of students and the corporate community.

Method of Integrating the Trading Room

A state-of-the-art trading room facility reinforces Bentley University's position as a serious player in the increasingly challenging world of business education. With an on-site trading room, Bentley continues to serve the needs of a variety of individuals. The principal method of integrating the trading room across finance and non-finance courses includes the following activities:

a. Overview sessions on capital markets concepts to finance and non-finance majors.
b. Valuation of stocks and bonds through simulated trading and real-time data.
c. Pricing and trading of derivative securities in advanced corporate, fixed income, derivatives, and international finance courses.
d. Introduction of investment and portfolio management concepts in advanced undergraduate and graduate investment and international finance courses.
e. Introducing trading simulation to study behavioral finance in advanced finance courses.

Currently, a number of finance courses have adopted trading room-based valuation modules that combine lecture, trading sessions, and exercises to deliver cutting-edge finance education to our students. A partial list would include the following graduate and undergraduate courses:

a. Capital Markets and Instruments/Money and Banking.
b. International Financial Management.
c. Investment and Portfolio Management.
d. Commercial Banking.
e. Options, Futures, and Derivatives.
f. Treasury Management/Working Capital Management.
g. M&A.
h. Market Microstructure.
i. Real Estate and Mortgages.
j. Compulsory undergraduate course on Introductory Business (all majors).
k. Financial Planning.

A trading room continues to encourage the faculty to reexamine and update course content in light of a growing infusion of technology in the classroom. It is important to note that the trading room is not a substitute for qualified instruction. Rather, a trading room absent qualified instruction is a waste of resources.

Faculty Research
Bentley's trading room continues to foster a number of research projects on various topics including the testing price discovery, rational expectations, inflation indexed bond trading, ethics and insider trading, and behavioral finance. Currently, five faculty members are studying the entire incoming freshman class every year to examine whether an exposure to ethical training affects insider trading. Combined with DIT (defined issues test) and trading sessions, the study examines if business education contributes to delinquent behavior of our students in their professional career.

Wall Street 1010 (Finance Camp for High School Students): In 1998, Professor Jahangir Sultan, Founding Director of the Trading Room, received NASDAQ sponsorship to design a week-long camp for high school students on financial markets topics. Currently, the program, in its 11th year, continues to attract top quality students from the United States and abroad to spend a week at Bentley to learn about stocks, bonds, currencies, derivatives, portfolio management, and economic analysis. The program has been featured in the local and international media prominently, including Financial Times and CNBC. The program has been instrumental in attracting top quality students to Bentley.

Executive Training
The trading room has delivered custom tailored business education to a number of corporations. A partial list would include the following corporations:

State Street Bank
Fidelity
Block Data
Thomson
IDC
Bank of NY Mellon
Volvo
Fuel Cell

Software and Data Feeds
 FACTSET
 Bloomberg
 Thomson One Analytics
 DataStream
 Morningstar Direct
 Capital IQ
 Mergent Horizon
 Oracle Crystal Ball
 OS Systems Financial Trading System
 ARGUS Valuation
 William O'Neil Direct Access
 Sponsors of the Bentley Trading Room

While Professor Jahangir Sultan was the brainchild of setting up a trading room at Bentley, the actual implementation of the concept would not have been possible without the active participation and assistance of many dedicated faculty and staff at Bentley University and many alums, friends, and supporters from the capital markets in London, NY, Melbourne, San Francisco, and Boston. Some of the major corporate sponsors include:

 American Power Conversion
 BARRA
 BNY Mellon
 BT plc
 Cabletron
 CBOT/CME
 Datastream
 Dataware
 Dow Jones
 Factset
 Fidelity Foundation
 First Call Corporation
 Fuji Securities
 INSSINC
 Leading Market Technologies
 Mathworks
 Morgan Stanley Dean Witter
 NASDAQ, NYSE, and major equity and futures exchanges
 OPRA
 Reuters plc
 Reuters-Thomson
 Rise
 State Street
 The AutEx Group
 Trans-Lux
 Woodtronics
 ZeroBase

Student-Managed Investment Funds: An International Perspective

By Edward C. Lawrence[1]

The most comprehensive survey ever conducted on student-managed investment funds shows there are now 314 universities worldwide that offer students the chance to learn about portfolio management by investing real money. In aggregate, students are directly managing more than $407 million in assets in 2007. Most of these programs supplement the more traditional investment courses, which are offered by every institution with a business college. Over the past two decades, student-managed investment funds have grown in both size and complexity as universities have tried to mirror real world experiences. The career success of students coming out of these programs demonstrates the benefits of providing students with as much hands-on experience as possible. This paper should be of interest to faculty, students, employers, and practitioners in the financial community who desire basic knowledge about state-of-the-art teaching investments and portfolio management.

In the early 1970s, there was a strong movement in Western countries for universities to start providing students with both academic knowledge and the ability to apply new skills on the job. Employers were often critical of new graduates who had difficulty stepping into employment without first receiving extensive on-the-job training. To overcome this obstacle, many business colleges began partnerships with major companies to offer students co-op and internship programs while the students were still pursuing their degrees. Deans also started encouraging their faculty to invite more guest speakers from government and industry to address classes on issues of the day. It also became common for professors to take classes on field trips to local employers to gain greater insights as to what it was like to work in a particular field. Finally, with the development of computers, interactive software became more prevalent, allowing students to simulate starting a new company, managing a bank, or investing in the stock market with play money.[2] Although all of these approaches were a significant improvement over what educational institutions had done

---

[1] Edward Lawrence is Professor of Finance and Department Chair, University of Missouri – St. Louis, St. Louis, Missouri. This article is reprinted with permission from *Journal of Applied Finance*, Fall/Winter 2008, Vol. 18, Issue 2, pp. 67–83. The author would like to acknowledge the assistance of Kerry Sallee, Ken Locke, Karen Wagster, Anthony Lerro, Brian Bruce, Larry Belcher, and all of the university faculty participants who generously gave their time to complete this survey.

[2] Most basic investment courses today use simulations or play money to allow students some practice with security analysis, stock selection, portfolio composition, and market timing. However, it is well recognized that play money often leads to excessive risk taking as students try to outperform the market without realistic penalties.

historically, there was still a need to offer students even greater realism and more practical experience.[3]

In the field of finance, student-managed investment funds (SMIFs) were created to take investment education to the next level. These funds allow students to invest real money in the stock and bond markets. The vast majority of SMIFs have close faculty involvement to provide oversight and structure to student activities. Nevertheless, students are generally responsible for making all investment decisions and managing the portfolio. Some funds have outside professionals who serve in an advisory capacity to enrich the experience for students and showcase their programs. While SMIFs were first started in the United States and have been around since 1950, only 12 colleges had them by 1969. Unfortunately, those programs were not widely known outside of those campuses. Today, there are 314 funds worldwide ranging in size from $2000 to $62 million. In aggregate, students are directly managing $407 million in assets. The purpose of this paper is to discuss the evolution of SMIFs and the impact they are having on teaching investments around the globe. Surprisingly, there has not been a single paper presenting data on funds from outside the United States.

There is much to be gained within academia and the investment community through the sharing of ideas and information on financial education in a variety of cultures and environments. Not only do new and existing SMIFs learn from the innovations of other successful programs, faculty and administrators benefit from considering a broader array of approaches to solving specific constraints faced by a particular school. Students desiring to embark on investment careers will be able to more fully evaluate the different programs being offered and select the one that most closely fits their learning style. Finally, employers and practitioners also need to become more knowledgeable of the various types of SMIFs. Besides the opportunity to hire highly trained students coming out of these programs, professionals should become educational partners by providing guest speakers, serving on boards, providing funding, sharing technical resources, etc.

Previous Studies

One of the primary reasons student investment funds were slow to be established in the 1970s was the lack of organizational information and data on the benefits and costs of these programs. Until 1990, there was not even a list of universities in the United States that had such funds. In fact, many of the faculty who were closely involved in SMIFs prior to this time had limited knowledge of other programs and almost no communication with their colleagues. As a result, it was very difficult for finance faculty to start new funds given the lack of operational data and instructional inexperience with such programs. Recognizing

---

[3] Even now, Pfeffer (2007) argues that business schools are still not doing enough to ensure students can "translate business knowledge into applicable business skills" in real-world situations. However, he does not specifically address the effectiveness of many of the initiatives mentioned above.

this problem, Lawrence (1990) conducted the first survey to profile and discuss the characteristics of almost two dozen established programs. Until then, it was common for paper authors to only describe a single fund.[4] While these efforts were insightful, it was impossible to fully understand the scope of this movement in investment education without a broader database. Furthermore, many senior university officials were still reluctant to commit their scarce resources in such funds without convincing hard data showing the clear benefits and costs of such programs. By the early 1990s, with so many leading business schools embracing the basic concept, it became an "easy sell" for finance faculty and alumni in North America. This led to an explosion of programs, which have spread to other continents including Asia and Europe.

In 1994, Lawrence expanded his study to include 34 programs in order to better describe their operations and funding sources. Johnson, Alexander, and Allen (1996) investigated alternative decision-making environments in student-managed funds. By 2003, Neely and Cooley (2004) reported 134 funds had been established in the United States alone. Ammermann and Runyon (2003) investigated risk aversion and group dynamics among students making portfolio decisions at California State University in Long Beach. All of these papers served as a major catalyst for the rapid growth in the number and size of SMIFs worldwide, especially in North America.

The Survey

From June 2007 to April 2008, a written survey was electronically sent to all universities in the United States and abroad with both known and possible SMIFs.[5] For US participants, survey participants were also asked to share their knowledge of other programs in their states. In the case of foreign countries, participants were solicited for information on existing and potential funds in their own country or neighboring countries. It was assumed that faculty involved with current programs would most likely know of other SMIFs from their professional contacts at conferences. Since locating foreign programs would be more challenging, the meeting roster of attendees at the 2007 Financial Management Association meeting in Florida was used to contact a large number of faculty from South America, Europe, Australia, and Asia. This database was supplemented by the author who attended major academic conferences in both Europe and Asia during this time period in order to make personal contact with other finance faculty who may have had knowledge of foreign funds. Finally, a significant number of contacts were made with finance department chairs

---

[4] Some of the earliest case studies included Belt (1975), Hirt (1977), Bear and Boyd (1984), Markese (1984), Kester (1986), Tatar (1987), Block and French (1991), Bhattacharya and McClung (1994), and Kahl (1997).

[5] Anthony Lerro of the Association of Student-Managed Investment Funds (ASMIF) graciously provided an initial list of American universities that were members of the association. While the list provided a good starting point for the United States, it also contained a fair number of schools that did not yet have a program and was missing a large number of other universities that did.

Exhibit 9.2 Growth in New Funds, by Decade from 1950 Through 2008

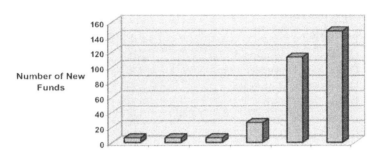

and deans at major business schools (not included in any of the previously mentioned screens) in Europe and Asia to make sure there was as much international exposure as possible, given the obvious language barriers.

This protocol resulted in locating 314 SMIFs from around the world. Each program was contacted up to seven times by email and/or phone to encourage its participation in the survey. With faculty advisors frequently rotating in and out of the programs it was sometimes difficult to find the appropriate person with sufficient knowledge to complete the 48-question survey. In addition, a small number of funds operate more like investment clubs with little or no faculty involvement. Yet, these funds give the students much of the same experience of investing real money, but as an extracurricular activity. Of the 314 funds, 224 programs returned the completed survey for a 71% participation rate. For the remaining 90 SMIFs who declined to participate, summary information about their programs was obtained from external sources including the university's website and media sources.

The Growth and Size of Programs

After 40 years of very slow growth, the number of SMIFs in the United States exploded in the 1990s and 2000s as real money funds began to supplement the more traditional methods of teaching investments. As reported in Exhibit 9.2, the 1990s was the turning point. To remain competitive in the marketplace, most business schools had to offer students the opportunity to invest in the stock market with real money.[6] The current decade has experienced the highest number of new programs created despite the data only including seven years. With 1680 business schools in the United States according to the AACSB, the country may be a long

---

[6] A university having a student investment fund has become the gold standard for investment programs at all levels. As one faculty member stated, "One cannot have a top 10 MBA program today without it."

Exhibit 9.3 Largest Student-Managed Investment Funds

Panel A. US Universities (2007)

Rank		Institution	Country	Total Assets
1		University of Wisconsin	US	$62.0 Million
2		Ohio State University	US	$25.8 Million
3		University of Minnesota	US	$25.0 Million
4		University of Utah	US	$18.2 Million
5		University of Texas	US	$17.0 Million
6		Cornell University	US	$13.5 Million
7		University of Arkansas	US	$12.0 Million
8		University of Houston	US	$9.2 Million
9 & 10	Tie	Baylor University Southern Methodist	US	$6.5 Million/$6.5 Million

Panel B. Non-US Universities

Rank	Institution	Country	Total Assets
1	Simon Fraser University	Canada	$10.0 Million
2	HEC Montreal	Canada	$3.8 Million
3	Univ. of British Columbia	Canada	$3.5 Million
4	Queens University	Canada	$3.0 Million
5	Univ. of New Brunswick	Canada	$2.2 Million
6	Concordia University	Canada	$1.4 Million
7	University of Alberta	Canada	$1.3 Million

way from reaching a saturation point. However, with the exception of Canada, SMIFs are just in the early stages of development in the rest of the world. The first non-US fund was established at the University of British Columbia in 1987. Canada actually has a higher concentration of funds within institutions of higher learning than in the United States. In other parts of the word, it could easily take another 20 years to catch up to North America.

The size of SMIFs today has expanded beyond what many people would have thought possible only a decade ago. There are 78 universities worldwide with more than $1 million under management by students. As reported in Exhibit 9.3, the largest fund is at the University of Wisconsin — Madison, which has $62 million being invested in some form by students.[7] There are eight SMIFs with more than $10 million including two funds, Ohio

---

[7] The University of Wisconsin — Madison actually has five distinct funds. Only one portfolio is invested in equity securities. The other four portfolios are fixed income portfolios, which provide a different set of learning experiences depending on the objectives of the fund. The largest portion of the fund is private money managed for clients based on set investment criteria.

State and the University of Minnesota, with $25 million each in assets.[8] The largest non-US fund is Canada's Simon Fraser University with $10 million. However, few faculty members would argue that a multi-million-dollar portfolio is necessary to have a successful program. The incredible expansion in fund size is even more impressive when one considers that most of the funds started with only $100,000 or $200,000 in initial seed capital. Of course, almost all of the SMIFs continued to receive additional investment capital from various sources as they demonstrated an ability to manage the money successfully.

One of the more interesting growth patterns for SMIFs is how widely they are being used in a broad range of educational environments. While 99% of all current SMIFs are housed within business schools, there are a few exceptions. For example, Tufts University, without a business college, has a $1 million student fund that focuses on investing in biomedical companies. Besides the traditional university undergraduate and graduate business students, there are several high schools that broke new ground by adapting the same learning principles with students less prepared in finance and business.[9] This is part of a broader trend where subjects that used to be taught only at the college level are now being introduced in high schools. According to McInerny (2003), some of the stimulus is being provided by Paul O'Neill, a former US Treasury Secretary. O'Neill has been aggressively promoting greater financial skills at the primary and secondary education level. It seems clear to faculty participating in these programs that real money portfolios have dramatically increased student interest in majoring in finance or business in college.

A surprising finding of this survey is that at least six institutions in the United States have allowed their SMIFs to become inactive over the past few years.[10] Given how difficult it is for many schools to establish SMIFs and their popularity with students and employers, this was unexpected. In personal discussions with faculty and administrators at these schools, the most common reason the program became inactive was the loss of the key faculty member (often due to retirement) who advised the students. Other finance faculty were unwilling to take over the fund, partially due to the greater amount of time it takes to stay abreast of the financial markets on a daily basis. With many schools emphasizing research productivity for promotion and raises, it is most onerous for tenure track faculty to lead the fund activities for more than a few years. Of course, many schools have dealt with this issue by hiring non-tenure track faculty or adjuncts to run the SMIFs.

---

[8] The average size for US funds was $1.4 million and $1.2 million for non-US programs.

[9] It has been reported that the following American schools at one time had active funds: Dominican High (WI), Groton High (MA), Wisconsin Lutheran (WI), Jenks High (OK), Ariel Community Academy (IL), West Allis Central (WI), Gaithersburg High (MD), and Burnsville High (MN). These scaled-down programs closely mirror those established at the university level in the way they are structured and operate.

[10] These universities include the University of Central Florida, Southern Illinois University – Edwardsville, the University of Florida, the University of Missouri – Kansas City, Winthrop University, and the University of Louisiana.

SMIFs Versus Professionally Managed Funds

The central goal of SMIFs is to create a realistic learning environment for training the next generation of portfolio managers. Unlike professionally managed funds, which are solely focused on generating the highest risk-adjusted rates of return possible, SMIF returns are secondary in nature to the educational mission.[11] Faculty advisors generally recognize that some of the best learning experiences come from failures, not successes per se. As any experienced investor knows, there is always an element of luck and incomplete data behind any decision. Thus, a very carefully analyzed opportunity with great potential can fail for an almost unlimited number of reasons that could not have been accurately forecasted a year or more in advance. However, unlike practitioners in real life, students lack a strong incentive system of monetary rewards for beating benchmarks or penalties for poor performance (being fired).

Student portfolios often have constraints that most professionals do not have. For example, most SMIFs are structured to rely on group or committee decisions rather than those of a single portfolio manager. Sometimes there are more than 30 students involved with various levels of skill and knowledge. All have an equal vote in the ultimate decision. Depending on the quality of the student research and group presentation skills, decisions are not always based entirely on objective analysis. In addition, the majority of funds offers a one- or two-semester class that may encourage students to use short-term planning horizons since they may not be around to witness the final outcome of any particular investment. Obviously, it takes several economic cycles to really evaluate the success of any investment strategy. The fund at the University of Missouri – St. Louis is one of the exceptions with a credit program structured to allow students to participate for several years (see Exhibit 9.4 for a summary).

Professional managers can react almost instantaneously to rapidly changing market conditions without the need to assemble the group for a vote. This factor alone should favor practitioner performance, provided they are not trading on unfounded rumors and there really are fundamental market changes taking place. Professionals can also trade on margin or use derivatives to enhance returns which are not widely available techniques for the majority of SMIFs. Offsetting some of these advantages, professionally managed funds must absorb all of their own operating expenses, whereas most SMIFs get subsidized resources (e.g., facilities, computers, faculty salary) from the universities and rarely pay all expenses related to the fund.

---

[11] Although there has been no systematic data collected on SMIF performance, the limited anecdotal evidence suggests students generally do as well as and sometimes better than investment professionals or the market as a whole. For example, the Tennessee Valley Authority reported that over a three-year period, the 19 universities participating in its program in 2002 outperformed the S&P 500 benchmark by 5.3% (Mansfield, 2002).

Exhibit 9.4 Profile of the University of Missouri — St. Louis Fund

Panel A. Fund Characteristics

Date established	1988
Size in 2007	$125,000
Annual student participation	45
Fund structure	Part of endowment
Funding source	Small private donations
Faculty member	Full-time regular
Credit hours per semester	1 credit hour per semester
Max credit hours	3 hours (may continue without credit)
Student level	Undergraduate
Application	None
Decision process	Majority vote of students
Investment style	Growth and value
Investment types allowed	Equities, fixed income, and options
Equity strategy	Bottom-up approach
Diversification required?	Yes
Income distributions	Scholarships

Panel B. Actual 5-Year Historical Annual Returns (Including Dividends)

Year	Annual Fund Performance	S&P 500
2003	36.78%	26.68%
2004	17.67%	10.88%
2005	5.76%	4.91%
2006	6.93%	15.80%
2007	12.25%	5.49%

Funding Sources and Organizational Structure

The majority of older SMIFs received earmarked money from alumni and other private donors to establish the funds. Twenty-eight percent of the funds got all of the money from the university's own endowment. Another 23% of schools had only a single large donor. The balance of programs was a combination of capital sources, including many small donors and corporate donations. For universities wishing to establish a new fund, the average program in the United States during the 2000s was started with approximately $414,000 in initial capital.

The most common form of organizational structure is having the SMIF be part of the university endowment. About 62% of all funds are structured this way. Another 14% are set up as a separate entity, like a nonprofit foundation or trust to provide more autonomy from the university. It is also becoming more popular for programs to establish profit-making companies (e.g., LLCs or partnerships) where students are managing the portfolio for private companies or other investors. At least ten of the largest funds, including the University of Wisconsin, University of Minnesota, Pennsylvania State University, University of Houston, and University of Texas, are all managing some private investor money.[12] It should be noted that this is a more complex structure in the United States, which requires government reporting (e.g., partnership tax returns with K-1 forms) due to the taxable nature of the investments.

Several innovative companies in the United States have long provided money to support financial education at institutions in the markets they serve. The largest is the Tennessee Valley Authority (TVA), a large electric utility company, which sponsors 25 universities in its service area. Two brokerage firms followed the TVA's lead with D. A. Davidson & Company sponsoring 20 schools and Stern Agee Group, Inc. supporting five universities. The basic model at these programs is for the company to provide all funding ($400,000 each for the TVA) with the company and universities sharing the profits. In case of a falling stock market, the company absorbs all losses and fully replenishes the money the following year. About 58% of universities have an advisory board associated with their programs. All of these boards have outside investment professionals and alumni serving as a valuable resource in a counseling capacity. This allows students to interact with professionals and showcases the program to the local community. In many cases, students make formal presentations to the boards to sharpen their presentation and analytical skills.

Student Participation

Just over 5000 students participate in SMIFs in the United States each year, with another 500 students being trained at foreign universities. Approximately 71% of the programs in the United States (45% of foreign programs) are structured as part of a formal class.[13] The number of credit hours a student can earn ranges from 1 to 12. Of those providing credit, 44% allow students to earn 6 or more semester credit hours over two or more semesters. Another 39% of schools limit students to a maximum of three credit hours. Only 22% of programs limit the student learning experience to a single semester. The SMIFs that are not part of a formal class allow students to participate as an extracurricular activity. This less structured format permits greater inclusion since almost any student enrolled in the university, regardless of major field or prior course work, can join the group. In contrast,

---

[12] At the time of this survey, Penn State had 68 private investors and was planning to expand the number to 99. The faculty advisor also reports the additional burden from accounting and tax costs for the LLC run between $25,000 and $50,000 per year.

[13] In France, universities have legal barriers for incorporating SMIFs into the curriculum. Thus, only a few informal clubs not sponsored by the school exist, which are advised by outside professionals.

formal classes often restrict the quality of students usually through an application process (59% of schools have a formal application process to screen students).

Unlike many other university programs, most SMIFs carefully control the level of student participation. Although a few schools allowed more than 100 students to manage the portfolios each year, the average fund in the United States had only 29 student managers per year (23 students for foreign funds). For approximately 90% of SMIFs, students were responsible for making all investment decisions. In the other 10% of programs, advisory boards or a faculty member also shared in the decision making. At the London Business School, students performed all of the usual research on securities but they had to make formal presentations to a professional board, which actually made the final investment selections. While the major goal of these programs is to strengthen student decision making through actual investment experience, 64% of the funds have guidelines that allow a faculty member or an advisory board to veto student recommendations if an investment is deemed inappropriate for the portfolio. However, this is a power that is rarely used. In the previous five years for those programs with a veto power, the higher authority vetoed less than 4% of all student decisions. This result indicates that students take their fiduciary roles as portfolio managers seriously and act prudently.

To facilitate investment decisions, 65% of the programs assign students to groups to manage the portfolios. Depending on the specific portfolio and its goals, these groups are often based on types of securities being traded, industries, etc. For 70% of the SMIFs, investment decisions are determined by a simple majority vote by the students. Individual portfolio managers make the decisions 6% of the time with the remaining funds using a combination of students, faculty advisors, and/or boards to reach a consensus. Of the classes, 42% of programs allow only undergraduate students, 10% permit only graduate students, and 48% allow both levels of students.

Faculty and Professional Involvement

With a small number of exceptions, faculty are closely involved with SMIFs at all levels.[14] Because so many of the programs are relatively new, many of the faculty involved today with SMIFs worked hard to obtain the original funding. Of the universities requiring students to participate through a formal class, 58% of these professors believe these classes take substantially more faculty time than a regular course. The average assessment was that the instructional load was 50% higher than a traditional class, or the equivalent to teaching

---

[14] A number of universities have real money funds that operate more as an extracurricular activity with no direct faculty involvement. In some cases, the students invest their own money. Schools that operate this way include the University of Edinburgh, Harvard University, Auburn University, the California Institute of Technology, Princeton University, Dartmouth University, Vanderbilt University, and the Georgia Institute of Technology.

a 4.5 credit hour course rather than a 3 hour course. Another 33% of faculty felt they spent about the same amount of time as they do with any other course. Only 9% of faculty thought it actually took less time than their normal instructional duties.

Despite a majority of participating faculty believing SMIF courses take significantly more time, 63% of the schools paid the same level of compensation as for a regular course. The balance of the universities provided additional compensation in the form of research funding, supplemental pay, or a reduced service load. This may partially explain why some programs have become inactive because key faculty members feel the compensation levels are not commensurate with the time involved. This would suggest college deans need to take a closer look at the cost/benefit ratio of SMIFs and make a conscious effort to adequately reward faculty involvement in these high profile programs. It would be a shame if much of the progress in financial education of past three decades would be allowed to erode based on short-term economic savings. One possible solution would be to allow the fund itself to provide additional compensation to the participating faculty members. This could be in the form of added salary, research grants, a course release, a graduate assistant, etc.

Given the nature of SMIFs, many of the programs have local investment professionals closely involved. The most direct role for outside professionals is to serve as an adjunct faculty member and run the actual program. A small but growing number of schools take this approach, drawing on the general finance community to provide the course instructor. In most cases, the adjunct faculty member is retired and thus has time available to staff day sections of the class. It works less effectively for active professionals who may have difficulty finding the free time during normal work hours when the financial markets are open. Even when the program is being taught by a full-time faculty member, it is commonplace to have professionals serve on advisory boards and be guest speakers. There is no question that professional involvement enriches the experience of students, faculty, and professionals. Frequent contact between the various parties ensures that current practice is quickly incorporated into the classroom and students leave better prepared to apply their knowledge and skills.

Investment Activity

It is interesting that 28% of schools with an SMIF have more than one fund. Many of these funds have different investment objectives and are specifically designed to give students a broader investment experience than a single fund could provide. For schools with more than one fund, the most common number was to have three distinct portfolios. It also makes sense to have more than one SMIF where there are multiple bodies of students including undergraduate/graduate, day/evening classes, etc.

With the growing size of the average portfolio, it is not surprising to find 92% of universities have formal written investment guidelines. Diversification is a principle widely emphasized by most SMIFs. Counting a mutual fund as a single holding, the average portfolio contained about 30 individual securities with three SMIFs exceeding 75 different issues. Approximately 80% of the programs have clear guidelines that specifically require the funds be diversified. It is interesting that 19% of US SMIFs are not prohibited from becoming hedge funds to increase returns by taking on more risk. Only 10% of non-US SMIFs had this same freedom. In the first reported case of an actual hedge fund on a university campus, Cornell University changed its SMIF's investment strategy from an indexed-styled fund to a "market-neutral" hedge fund in 2002.[15] The stated goal was to produce positive returns regardless of which direction the market was moving. The $3 million fund uses investors' money (alumni and friends) which allow students to manage the money for the experience without any fees.

As to types of security investments, some schools, such as the University of Toledo, are very restrictive and require that all investments must be in domestic markets. On the other extreme, Roger Williams University limits domestic investments to a maximum of 20% of the portfolio with the other 80% being comprised of international securities. Most SMIFs focused on traditional securities with common stock dominating portfolios, regardless of where the companies were domiciled. Corporate and Treasury bonds were also widely used to balance the portfolios. For alternative investments, real estate investment trusts (REITs) were the most popular, followed at a distance by limited partnerships.

For actual trading activities, full service brokerage firms were most often used by SMIFs, followed closely by discount brokerage firms. Bank trust companies were used only about half as much as either type of brokerage firm. The funds are large enough to negotiate some very favorable rates with full service brokerage firms. In addition, since the majority of the programs are charitable and tax-free by design, some of the brokerage firms are donating their services to the universities.

For SMIFs operating a single fund, only 10% of the programs characterized their investment style as focusing on growth stocks. Another 23% considered themselves to be more value investors. But the vast majority of the funds characterized their investment style to be more of a blend. The most employed equity strategy was the bottom-up approach with 37% of SMIFs primarily using this method. A close second was the top-down approach used by 27% of funds, followed at a distance by the buy-and-hold strategy reported by 11% of respondents. The balance of the SMIFs used a combination of these strategies and others (e.g., price momentum and contrarian) in making stock selections. Twice as many programs thought asset allocation was a very important consideration compared to those who deemed it not very important (38% vs. 18%). Individual security selection was rated very important

---

[15] Myers (2004).

by 58% of SMIFs. In contrast, 65% of funds believed market timing was not important, most likely reflecting their long-term investment horizons.

Comparisons of US and Foreign Funds

With the widely divergent political and economic climates abroad, it was not unexpected to find that SMIFs outside of North America evolved more slowly and in a somewhat different direction from those in the United States. For the most part, Canadian and American universities share a similar educational environment. Thus the Canadians adopted SMIF organizational structures and operating procedures modeled after those already successfully employed in the United States for several decades. Outside of North America, however, European and Asian schools were far more likely (by a ratio of 2 to 1) to have extra-curricular programs rather than formal classes. One result of a less formal structure is that fewer foreign universities (55%) have anyone with veto power over student investment decisions compared to US schools (64%). Of course, the funds outside of North America are much younger and smaller, averaging only $142,000. With maturity and more money at risk, stricter university controls may eventually develop. Unlike the United States, none of the European or Asian programs had a taxable structure similar to an LLC or partnership.

When it comes to investing, most American SMIFs focus on investing in common stock with an average portfolio in 2007 containing 82% of their money invested in these securities. Foreign programs generally leaned more toward balanced portfolios with greater allocations of fixed income securities. Canadian SMIFs averaged 70% of their money invested in common stock, while European and Asian funds were much lower at 59%. On the lower end of the scale, Hebrew University had the most balance with 25% in common stock, 20% in preferred stock, 15% in corporate bonds, 25% in Treasury bonds, and the remainder in other securities. In terms of investment policies, almost the same percentage of foreign SMIFs required diversification in their written policies as in the United States (79% vs. 81%). As to investment styles, only 10% of American funds with a single fund considered themselves "growth" investors in 2007 compared to 20% of the foreign funds. Regardless of where the fund was domiciled, the predominant investment style was a "blend" rather than a single focus. The equity strategy most used in the United States and abroad was a bottom-up approach, closely followed by the top-down approach, or a combination of the two.

Benefits to the University Community

It has long been recognized that students learn more by hands-on experience than simply reading about a topic in a textbook. Besides learning the intricacies of portfolio management and trading, students also benefit in many programs by going on field trips to Wall Street and other financial markets. Schools like Virginia Tech and Gannon University have a long tradition of taking students annually to Wall Street to view the financial markets first hand.

Roger Williams University has taken it to the next level by taking students abroad to the London and Frankfurt stock exchanges, which would not have been possible without an SMIF to generate the student interest and fund the activity.

Eighty-one percent of all program directors cited better trained students as a major benefit of having an SMIF. Almost a third of faculty believed having a real money fund provided synergy and significantly improved the quality of the overall finance program. Conversations with faculty also indicated greater job opportunities for students participating in SMIFs. Many employers, including private equity and hedge funds, bank trust companies, and mutual funds, have been aggressively recruiting students who have these experiences to draw on. These are highly competitive jobs that can be difficult for a new college graduate to obtain without sufficient experience.

As anyone involved in an SMIF can attest, having a real money portfolio generates a substantial amount of media attention. This activity not only showcases the students and the finance discipline but also the business school and the university. Alumni in particular are highly supportive of SMIFs, which creates new opportunities for guest speakers, field trips, internships, student recruitment, etc. Finally, the programs provide badly needed financial support for student scholarships, visits to financial markets, operating trading rooms, and other university programs.

For 2006, sixty-six of the American funds made cash distributions totaling more than $1.9 million to support academic programs, or an average of $29,381 per school. However, an even larger number of SMIFs reported making no cash distributions in the previous year. Many of these were still relatively new and therefore were still in the capital building years. Nevertheless, it was not all that unusual for the larger SMIFs to spin off several hundred thousand dollars in cash flow while providing students with a valuable learning experience. Very few university programs have such a high benefit/cost ratio, especially since almost all universities have endowment funds that must be managed by someone. Historically, the limited evidence shows that SMIFs have performed as well and sometimes better than funds managed by professional investment advisors (Mansfield, 2002). Of course, since SMIFs do not normally charge management fees, this saving alone favors SMIFs even without the educational benefits.

Recent Developments

Trading Rooms

A growing contingent of programs are operating trading rooms to add even more realism to student learning. Many of the universities with SMIFs have invested up to $1 million to fully furnish and equip trading rooms. The expanded programs include Pennsylvania State University, Iowa State University, Rice University, Michigan State University, Stetson

University, Texas Christian University, University of Michigan, and the University of Missouri — Columbia. These schools believe this development has raised the bar in attracting top students and community financial support. Of course, there are other universities with trading rooms that do not have SMIFs and simply simulate trading activities.

Social Responsibility Funds

Social responsibility funds are becoming more popular in academia and with investors in general. Bluffton University in Ohio has had an investment policy since 1956 of avoiding "sin stocks," which include tobacco, alcohol, and defense companies. Villanova University follows a similar investment guideline with two of its funds. The University of California at Berkeley started a new social responsibility fund in February of 2008 with $1.2 million as part of its MBA program. Students will hold long positions in firms that are socially responsible and take short positions in firms with poor social records. The director of its program maintains one does not have to sacrifice financial returns for a good record of social responsibility (Alsop, 2007). Establishing socially responsible funds can be highly controversial in academia. Some opponents argue that it is pushing a political agenda. In 1997, Stanford University rejected a student proposal for such a fund, noting their endowment already had substantial stock investments in socially responsible companies and industries and thus it was not needed.

Using Investors' Money

Several of the largest funds (including the universities of Texas, Minnesota, Houston, Wisconsin, and Pennsylvania State) manage investor money in one or more of their funds. The University of Texas was the first large for-profit fund when it raised $1.6 million of private investor money in December 1994 for their MBA students to manage. By 2007, they had three distinct funds with different investment objectives totaling $17 million from 60 investors. These funds are usually structured as a Limited Liability Company (LLC) where the income is taxable to investors similar to a partnership distribution. This structure limits the number of investors, so they must make large contributions. In exchange for managing the money, the students and university sometimes get a management fee of between 0.5% and 1.5% of the assets.

Venture Capital Funds

One of the most exciting developments over the past decade has been the emergence of venture capital funds managed by students. Given the success of SMIFs, it is only natural that the programs would evolve in new directions. The University of Michigan created the first student-managed venture capital fund in the United States in 1997 with about $3 million in capital. Yale University, the University of North Dakota, the University of Utah, Cornell University, the University of Wyoming, and Miami University of Ohio followed in

Michigan's footsteps with venture capital funds of their own dedicated to investing in emerging companies.[16] The University of Utah sponsored the largest venture capital fund with $18 million, which also permits students from more than 15 other universities to participate in the activities. Although not a student-managed fund, the University of Maryland in 2003 worked with investors to establish the New Markets Growth Fund with $20 million in capital run by professional managers but assisted by students and faculty. Others, including the University of Queensland and the University of Melbourne (both in Australia), have similar funds run by professionals.

Many of these programs are designed to provide seed capital for businesses started by students, recent graduates, faculty, or the general community at large. Doing so may speed technology transfer from universities and fulfill one mission of higher education. All of these innovative programs expand the practical training offered to finance students by conventional SMIFs in new dimensions. They encourage students to take a more entrepreneurial approach to raising capital in the private equity market (often with partner or investor money). Students benefit by evaluating business plans and performing due diligence before actually making the investment decision on companies with little or no financial performance This focus provides a nice complement to a regular SMIF where the focus is on established, publicly traded investment opportunities.[17] Finally, the venture capital funds offer an excellent vehicle for the College of Business to provide value added support to other units within the university community. For example, the Colleges of Medicine, Science, and Engineering produce a continuing stream of innovative research and technology but have great difficulty proving the commercial viability of their inventions and patents. Along with business schools, law schools can assist new startups with legal issues to further reach another segment of the community. A student-managed venture capital fund offers the best opportunity in years to capitalize and profit from the research strengths of universities while enhancing the teaching mission.

Microfinance Funds

There is an amazing amount of creativity surrounding SMIFs in the way the programs are being re-engineered to accomplish more than simply teaching students the basics of investing. Several universities, including Columbia University, are starting microfinance funds to make small entrepreneurial investments in third world countries. An organization called PlaNet Finance (a microfinance organization based in Paris) is working with

---

[16] For further information, see Rombel (2007), Yale Bulletin (2001), Daily Herald (2006) and the Business Wire (2006).

[17] The 2008 state budget for the Commonwealth of Massachusetts contained an amendment for establishing a student investment fund to encourage student entrepreneurship. There were to be three students on the governing board and it was specifically designed to fund new student businesses created within the Commonwealth. (See Section XX, Chapter 23A, of the budget.)

Columbia and several European universities to sponsor these programs. If Columbia's program is a success, it will provide another venue for students to learn about business while benefiting social welfare initiatives around the world.

Conclusion

Over the past 50 years, SMIFs have revolutionized the way in which investment education is taught in universities. These programs have expanded to 314 worldwide today from only a few funds in the 1950s. In the process, SMIFs are evolving in exciting new directions. These include managing money for private clients, establishing hedge funds or venture capital funds, and microlending initiatives. While it is much too early to evaluate the success of these new programs, it does seem clear that business schools are becoming even more relevant by addressing important issues in both the financial markets and society.

The benefits of providing students with greater practical experience and technical skills in finance are widely recognized in the job market. Students graduating today from universities with SMIFs already have at least one or two semesters of actual trading and research experience. Although the university experience is not as intense as in a professional job, it still provides a solid foundation for the knowledge needed in portfolio management. The skills and techniques learned here can be further refined in the workplace over a much shorter period of time than what would have been possible in the 1960s or 1970s.

Summary of Key Points

- Trading rooms are an integral part of many student-managed investment funds and typically house the fund's set of tools and data.
- Trading rooms facilitate collaborative and hands-on learning.
- Student-managed investment funds have grown dramatically in the past two decades to become the centerpiece of investment education in many colleges and universities.
- As in the professional investment community, the organizational form, structure, and investment approach of student-managed investment funds is as varied as the number of funds themselves. However, the common element among them all is the valuable educational and professional development that enhances the practice of investment management.

References

2001, Yale SOM Launches Student-Managed Venture Capital Fund, Yale Bulletin 29, 1 (February 16).
2006, Local News, Daily Herald (April 12).
2006, Record $18 million closing for largest student-run venture capital fund, Business Wire (June 19), 1.
Alsop, R., 2007. Talking b-School: Haas takes new tack on investing. Wall St. J. (September 18, 2007), B8.

Ammermann, P.A., Runyon, L.R., 2003. Risk aversion and group dynamics in the management of student-managed investment fund. J. Acad. Bus. Econ. 1 (1).

Bear, T., Boyd, G.M., 1984. An applied course in investment analysis and portfolio management. J. Financ. Educ. 13 (Fall), 68–71.

Belt, B., 1975. A securities portfolio managed by graduate students. J. Financ. Educ. 4 (Fall), 77–81.

Bhattacharya, T.K., McClung, J.J., 1994. Cameron University's unique student-managed investment portfolios. Financ. Pract. Educ. 4 (1), 55–59.

Block, S.B., French, D.W., 1991. The student-managed investment fund: a special opportunity in learning. Financ. Pract. Educ. 1 (1), 55–60.

Hirt, G.A., 1977. Real dollar portfolios managed by students – an evaluation. J. Financ. Educ. 6 (Fall), 57–61.

Johnson, D.W., Alexander, J.F., Allen, G.H., 1996. Student-managed investment funds: a comparison of alternative decision-making environments. Financ. Pract. Educ. 6 (1), 97–101.

Kahl, D.R., 1997. The challenges and opportunities of student-managed investment funds at metropolitan universities. Financ. Serv. Rev. 6 (3), 197–200.

Kester, G.W., 1986. Extending investments beyond the classroom through investment clubs. Financ. Manag. Collect. 1 (3), 9–10.

Lawrence, E.C., 1990. Learning portfolio management by experience: university student investment funds. Financ. Rev. 25 (1), 165–173.

Lawrence, E.C., 1994. Financial innovation: the case of student investment funds at United States universities. Financ. Pract. Educ. 4 (1), 47–53.

Mansfield, D., 2002. TVA's student investors outperform market, TVA managers. Florida Times Union. (April 5).

Markese, J.D., 1984. Applied security analysis and portfolio management. J. Financ. Educ. 13 (Fall), 65–67.

McInerny, P.M., 2003. The student-managed investment fund at the high school level. Clearing House. 76 (5), 252–254.

Myers, L., 2004. CU student-managed investment fund thrives after change in strategy. Cornell Chron. 35 (24), 5.

Neely, W.P., Cooley, P.L., 2004. A survey of student-managed funds. Adv. Financ. Educ. 2 (Spring), 1–9.

Pfeffer, J., 2007. What's right and still wrong with business schools. Biz Ed. 6 (1), 42–48.

Rombel, A., 2007. Student-run venture capital firm at Cornell invests in local tech firm. Bus. J. Central N.Y. 21 (12), 8.

Tatar, D.D., 1987. Teaching securities analysis with real funds. J. Financ. Educ. 16 (Fall), 40–45.

Index

Note: Page numbers followed by "*b*" refer to boxes.

Lightning Source UK Ltd.
Milton Keynes UK
UKOW07n0452300917

310153UK00015B/454/P